Lecture Notes in Artificial Intelligence 3476

Edited by J. G. Carbonell and J. Siekmann

Subseries of Lecture Notes in Computer Science

João Leite   Andrea Omicini
Paolo Torroni   Pınar Yolum (Eds.)

Declarative Agent Languages and Technologies II

Second International Workshop, DALT 2004
New York, NY, USA, July 19, 2004
Revised Selected Papers

 Springer

Series Editors

Jaime G. Carbonell, Carnegie Mellon University, Pittsburgh, PA, USA
Jörg Siekmann, University of Saarland, Saarbrücken, Germany

Volume Editors

João Leite
Universidade Nova de Lisboa
Departamento de Informática, Faculdade de Ciências e Tecnologia
Quinta da Torre, 2829-516 Caparica, Portugal
E-mail: jleite@di.fct.unl.pt

Andrea Omicini
Università di Bologna
Dipartimento di Elettronica, Informatica e Sistemistica
Via Venezia 52, 47023 Cesena, Italy
E-mail: andrea.omicini@unibo.it

Paolo Torroni
Università di Bologna
Dipartimento di Elettronica, Informatica e Sistemistica
Viale Risorgimento 2, 40136 Bologna, Italy
E-mail: paolo.torroni@unibo.it

Pınar Yolum
Bogazici University, Department of Computer Engineering
TR-34342 Bebek, Istanbul, Turkey
Email: pinar.yolum@boun.edu.tr

Library of Congress Control Number: 2005927863

CR Subject Classification (1998): I.2.11, C.2.4, D.2.4, D.2, D.3, F.3.1

ISSN   0302-9743
ISBN-10   3-540-26172-9 Springer Berlin Heidelberg New York
ISBN-13   978-3-540-26172-8 Springer Berlin Heidelberg New York

Springer is a part of Springer Science+Business Media

springeronline.com

© Springer-Verlag Berlin Heidelberg 2005
Printed in Germany

Typesetting: Camera-ready by author, data conversion by Scientific Publishing Services, Chennai, India
Printed on acid-free paper   SPIN: 11493402   06/3142   5 4 3 2 1 0

Preface

The second edition of the workshop on Declarative Agent Languages and Technologies (DALT 2004) was held July 2004 in New York City, and was a great success. We saw a significant increase in both the number of submitted papers and workshop attendees from the first meeting, held July 2003 in Melbourne.

Nearly 40 research groups worldwide were motivated to contribute to this event by submitting their most recent research achievements, covering a wide variety of the topics listed in the call for papers.

More than 30 top researchers agreed to join the Program Committee, which then collectively faced the hard task of selecting the one-day event program.

The fact that research in multi-agent systems is no longer only a novel and promising research horizon at dawn is, in our opinion, the main reason behind DALT's (still short) success story. On the one hand, agent theories and applications are mature enough to model complex domains and scenarios, and to successfully address a wide range of multifaceted problems, thus creating the urge to make the best use of this expressive and versatile paradigm, and also profit from all the important results achieved so far. On the other hand, building multi-agent systems still calls for models and technologies that could ensure system predictability, accommodate flexibility, heterogeneity and openness, and enable system verification.

Declarative approaches promise to satisfy precisely these challenges posed by large-scale multi-agent systems, not least because of their strong theoretical foundation grounded in classical and recent advances in the area of computational logic. Equipped with such foundations, declarative approaches can, in principle, enable agents to reason about their interactions and their environment, hence not only establish the required tasks but also handle exceptions and unexpected situations that arise in many systems, all in a formal, verifiable way.

The workshop aimed at bringing together (1) researchers working on formal methods for agent and multi-agent systems design, (2) engineers interested in exploiting the potentials of declarative approaches for specification of agent-based systems, and (3) practitioners exploring the technology issues arising from a declarative representation of systems. The main purpose of DALT was then to foster a discussion forum to export declarative paradigms and techniques into the broader community of agent researchers and practitioners, as well as to bring in the issues from real-world, complex and possibly large-scale agent-system design from the perspective of declarative programming and technologies.

Beside the five technical sessions consisting of paper presentations, attendees enjoyed a stimulating discussion on declarative agent communication, in the form of a lively panel organized and moderated by Mike Huhns from the University of South Carolina, whom we take the opportunity to thank deeply.

This book contains selected and extended versions of the papers presented at the 2004 event.

Several active research areas such as software engineering and multi-agent prototyping, agent reasoning, BDI logics and extensions, and social aspects of multi-agent systems made their presence felt in both the 2003 and the 2004 editions, showing how declarative technologies can give an answer to problems such as engineering, specification and deployment of agent systems in the small and in the large. When compared with the previous edition (also published by Springer, as LNAI 2990) this year's edition witnessed an increasing popularity in the topic of agent verification.

This book is composed of five parts: (i) Reasoning, (ii) Modelling and Engineering, (iii) Verification, (iv) Norms and Protocols, and (v) Interaction and Communication. There follows a brief overview.

Part I – Reasoning

The first part of the book contains three papers on reasoning in multi-agent systems.

M. Birna van Riemsdijk, Mehdi Dastani, Frank Dignum, and John-Jules Ch. Meyer present *Dynamics of Declarative Goals in Agent Programming*, in which they explore interesting relations between goal dropping and goal adoption in multi-agent systems. These relations are further formalized in an agent programming framework.

In *Theories of Intentions in the Framework of Situation Calculus*, Pilar Pozos Parra and Abhaya Nayak extend the action theories used in multiagent systems to intention theories using situation calculus. The proposed intention theories can be processed using a regression-based mechanism, which decreases the computational complexity of the generally applied theorem proving.

Peep Küngas and Mihhail Matskin, in their paper *Partial Deduction for Linear Logic — The Symbolic Negotiation Perspective*, show how symbolic negotiation can be formalized as partial deduction in linear logic. Their approach is particularly interesting since they prove both the soundness and completeness of their formalization.

Part II – Modelling and Engineering

The second part of the book contains four papers on modelling and engineering aspects of multiagent systems.

In *On Modelling Declaratively Multi-agent Systems*, Andrea Bracciali, Paolo Mancarella, Kostas Stathis, and Francesca Toni present a parametric framework that is based on agents' observations and their actions. This framework is then used identify important properties of multi-agent systems, such as their success, robustness, and so on.

In *The Semantics of MALLET — An Agent Teamwork Encoding Language*, Xiaocong Fan, John Yen, Michael S. Miller, and Richard A. Volz give an operational semantics to the team-oriented agent programming language MALLET. The operational semantics is based on a transition system and can be used in developing MALLET interpreters as well as in studying various properties of MALLET itself.

Yu Pan, Phan Huy Tu, Enrico Pontelli, and Tran Cao Son discuss an interesting application area for agent-based research: evolutionary biology. Their paper, *Construction of an Agent-Based Framework for Evolutionary Biology: A Progress Report* explains an agent-based system used to specify and execute phylogenetic inferences and discusses how the components of such a system can be implemented.

In *Reasoning About Agents' Interaction Protocols Inside DCaseLP*, Matteo Baldoni, Cristina Baroglio, Ivana Gungui, Alberto Martelli, Maurizio Martelli, Viviana Mascardi, Viviana Patti, and Claudio Schifanella integrate a MAS development environment with an agent programming language to help ease agent protocol development. The integration benefits from compiling AUML sequence diagrams into agent skeletons semi-automatically.

Part III – Verification

The third part of the book presents three papers on verification.

In *Model Checking Agent Dialogues* Christopher Walton defines a lightweight, yet expressive language and uses model checking to verify the correctness of this language. This paper shows that the proposed language is useful in detecting certain failures in agent dialogues, which is an important step in ensuring correct agent protocols.

L. Robert Pokorny and C.R. Ramakrishnan study how agent systems that provide services over the Web can be constructed declaratively. In *Modeling and Verification of Distributed Autonomous Agents Using Logic Programming*, they develop an approach where individual services of agents are defined using temporal logic formulas. This enables verifications of service composition of several agents that interact to carry out a service together.

In *Norm Verification and Analysis of Electronic Institutions*, Wamberto Vasconcelos proposes a formal definition of norms and shows how they apply in the context of electronic institutions. He further discusses how parts of an electronic institution can be derived when certain norm constraints are given.

Part IV – Norms and Protocols

The fourth part of the book focuses on norms and protocols, consisting of three papers. David Robertson presents *A Lightweight Coordination Calculus for Agent Social Norms*, in which he presents a declarative language for specifying social norms. The major benefit of this language is that social norms defined within it can be analyzed and deployed easily.

In *Enhancing Commitment Machines*, Michael Winikoff, Wei Liu, and James Harland study flexible interactions for agents by building on top of the commitment machine abstraction. They show that the reasoning mechanism of commitment machines can be improved when the specification of commitments and some of their operators are enhanced.

In *A Protocol for Resource Sharing in Norm-Governed Ad Hoc Networks*, Alexander Artikis, Lloyd Kamara, Jeremy Pitt, and Marek Sergot study normative relations and their application in ad hoc networks, where participating nodes may not comply with the system rules. To cope with the uncertainty in ad hoc networks, they formulate a protocol that regulates the access control of nodes in the network. This protocol is specified in event calculus and can be executed directly.

Part V – Interaction and Communication

Finally, the last part of the book contains three papers on interaction and communication in multiagent systems.

Vasu S. Alagar, Joey Paquet, and Kaiyu Wan present *Intensional Programming for Agent Communication* in which they represent the conversation contexts explicitly. They provide a calculus of contexts as well as a logic of contexts as an extension to an intensional programming language. These additions enable reasoning on contexts in agent communication languages.

In *The Logic of Communication Graphs*, Eric Pacuit and Rohit Parikh show that agents with private information can have individual communications with other agents and gather information that is private to other parties. The introduced logic is decidable and can handle a variety of cases.

In *Representational Content and the Reciprocal Interplay of Agent and Environment*, Tibor Bosse, Catholijn M. Jonker, and Jan Treur advocate the temporal-interactivist approach to denote representational content of an internal state. Using this approach, a realistic example of interactions between an agent and an environment is depicted.

DALT is now looking forward to its third meeting, which will take place in July 2005 in Utrecht, The Netherlands, again as an AAMAS workshop, and will be chaired by Matteo Baldoni, Ulle Endriss, Andrea Omicini and Paolo Torroni. We expect that DALT will once again attract a large number of submissions, each reporting on new and exciting results about agents and declarative technologies, and that the meeting will feature motivating presentations and lively discussions.

As a final word, we would like to thank the authors who presented their work at the workshop and submitted improved versions of their papers, our PC members who willingly spent their valuable time on two rounds of reviewing and selection, all the additional reviewers who helped the PC members in this task, and Gregory Wheeler for his help.

March 2005

João Leite
Andrea Omicini
Paolo Torroni
Pınar Yolum
Co-organizers
DALT 2004

Workshop Organization

Workshop Organizers

João Leite   Universidade Nova de Lisboa, Portugal
Andrea Omicini   Università di Bologna a Cesena, Italy
Paolo Torroni   Università di Bologna, Italy
Pınar Yolum   Bogazici University, Turkey

Program Committee

Rafael Bordini   The University of Liverpool, UK
Brahim Chaib-draa   Université Laval, Canada
Alessandro Cimatti   IRST, Trento, Italy
Keith Clark   Imperial College London, UK
Marco Colombetti   Politecnico di Milano, Italy
Stefania Costantini   Università degli Studi di L'Aquila, Italy
Mehdi Dastani   Universiteit Utrecht, The Netherlands
Jürgen Dix   Technical University of Clausthal, Germany
Michael Fisher   The University of Liverpool, UK
Mike Huhns   University of South Carolina, USA
Catholijn Jonker   Vrije Universiteit Amsterdam, The Netherlands
Alessio Lomuscio   King's College, London, UK
Viviana Mascardi   DISI, Università di Genova, Italy
John Jules Ch. Meyer   Universiteit Utrecht, The Netherlands
Charles L. Ortiz   SRI International, Menlo Park, CA, USA
Sascha Ossowski   Universidad Rey Juan Carlos, Madrid, Spain
Julian Padget   University of Bath, UK
Lin Padgham   RMIT University, Australia
Wojciech Penczek   Polish Academy of Sciences, Poland
Luís Moniz Pereira   Universidade Nova de Lisboa, Portugal
Jeremy Pitt   Imperial College London, UK
Juan Rodriguez-Aguilar   Spanish Research Council, Spain
Fariba Sadri   Imperial College London, UK
Marek Sergot   Imperial College London, UK
Onn Shehory   IBM Research Lab in Haifa, Israel
Munindar Singh   North Carolina State University, USA
Francesca Toni   Università di Pisa, Italy
Wiebe van der Hoek   The University of Liverpool, UK
Wamberto Vasconcelos   University of Aberdeen, UK
Michael Winikoff   RMIT University, Australia
Franco Zambonelli   Università di Modena e Reggio Emilia, Italy

Additional Reviewers

João Alcântara
Holger Billhardt
Andrea Bracciali
Amit Chopra
Marina De Vos
Ulle Endriss
Álvaro Freitas Moreira

Dorian Gaertner
Mark Hoogendoorn
Magdalena Kacprzak
John Knottenbelt
Ashok Mallya
Ken Satoh
Kostas Stathis

Arnon Sturm
Peter-Paul van Maanen
M. Birna van Riemsdijk
Bozena Wozna
Yingqian Zhang

Table of Contents – Part I

Reasoning

Modelling and Engineering

Verification

Norms and Protocols

Interaction and Communication

Dynamics of Declarative Goals in Agent Programming

M. Birna van Riemsdijk, Mehdi Dastani, Frank Dignum,
and John-Jules Ch. Meyer

Institute of Information and Computing Sciences,
Utrecht University,
The Netherlands
{birna, mehdi, dignum, jj}@cs.uu.nl

Abstract. In this paper, the notion of declarative goals as used in agent programming is central. Declarative goals describe desirable states and are updated during the execution of an agent. These goal dynamics are analyzed by distinguishing and formalizing various notions of goal dropping and goal adoption. Furthermore, possible motivations for an agent to drop or adopt goals are identified. Based on these motivations, we define specific mechanisms for implementing dropping and adoption. We show how these mechanisms are related to the general definitions of dropping and adoption.

1 Introduction

An important concept in agent theory, agent logics and agent programming is the concept of a *goal*. In agent theory, goals are introduced to explain and specify an agent's (proactive) behavior. In this view, agents are assumed to have their own objectives, for the achievement of which they initiate behavior [1,2,3,4]. Various logics have been introduced to formalize the concept of goals and reasoning about goals [5,6]. In these logics, a goal is formalized as a set of states and thus has a declarative interpretation.

Many agent programming languages have been proposed to *implement* (represent and process) an agent's goals [7,8,4,9,10]. The way in which goals are dealt with, varies from language to language. In some programming languages goals are interpreted in a procedural way as processes that need to be executed, while in other programming languages goals are interpreted in a declarative way as states to be reached. In this paper, we are interested in this *declarative* interpretation of goals.

Declarative goals have a number of advantages in agent programming. They for example provide for the possibility to decouple plan execution and goal achievement [11]. If a plan fails, the goal that was to be achieved by the plan remains in the goal base of the agent. The agent can then for example select a different plan or wait for the circumstances to change for the better. Furthermore, agents can be implemented such that they can communicate about their

J. Leite et al. (Eds.): DALT 2004, LNAI 3476, pp. 1–18, 2005.

goals [12]. Also, a representation of goals in agents enables reasoning about goal interaction [13] and declarative goals can be used in team-oriented programming [14].

During the execution of an agent, the agent's goals evolve. Goals might for example be dropped if they are believed to be achieved and goals might be adopted on certain grounds. This paper aims to analyze these *dynamics* of declarative goals in the context of agent programming. We will do this by distinguishing and formalizing various notions of goal dropping (section 3) and goal adoption (section 4). In these sections, also possible motivations for an agent to drop or adopt goals are identified. Based on these motivations, we define specific mechanisms for capturing dropping and adoption in agent programming languages. Furthermore, we show how these mechanisms are related to the general definitions of dropping and adoption.

The motivations we identify for goal dropping and goal adoption are based on ideas that have been presented in the literature. Our contribution is that we formalize these ideas within a single agent programming framework, by providing language constructs and semantics. Given the informal meaning we have in mind for these language constructs, we identify two general ways in which the formal semantics can be defined. This is reflected in the two general definitions that we provide for the notion of goal dropping as well as for the notion of goal adoption. Different semantics give rise to different agent behavior regarding the dynamics of goals. The aim of this paper is to provide a basis for a more systematic analysis of the kinds of semantics one could consider and of the properties of these semantics. A better understanding of the different possible semantics and their properties will help to identify which semantics have the more desirable characteristics, in general or for certain kinds of applications.

2   Preliminaries

In order to facilitate discussion, we give a number of definitions. In the sequel, a language defined by inclusion shall be the smallest language containing the specified elements.

First, we define the notion of an agent configuration. An agent configuration consists of a belief base, a goal base, a plan and a set of rules as defined below.

Definition 1. *(agent configuration)* Let $\mathcal{L}$ with typical element ϕ be a propositional language with negation and conjunction, let Plan be a language of plans and let R be a set of rules[1]. An agent configuration, typically denoted by c, then is a tuple $\langle \sigma, \gamma, \pi, R \rangle$ where $\sigma \subseteq \mathcal{L}$ is the belief base, $\gamma \subseteq \mathcal{L}$ is the goal base, $\pi \in$ Plan is the plan[2] of the agent and R is a set of rules.

---

[1] Agents will in general have multiple sets of rules of various types, such as rules to select or revise plans and rules to specify goal dynamics. In this paper, we will however consider only one type of rule at the time, which is why it suffices to have only one set of rules in the agent configuration.

In the sequel, we will use σ_c, γ_c, π_c and R_c to denote respectively the belief base, the goal base, the plan and the set of rules of an agent configuration c.

This paper is based on the idea that an agent consists of data structures representing the agent's mental attitudes such as beliefs, goals and rules. Agents from the 3APL language family [15, 7, 8] are for example defined based on this view, but the ideas that are presented in this paper apply to any type of cognitive agent with similar mental attitudes.

During the execution of an agent, the mental attitudes of the agent can change through for example plan execution and rule application. It will often be the case that e.g. multiple rules are applicable in a certain configuration. The decision of which rule to apply, can then be made by the agent interpreter or so called deliberation cycle [16], for example based on a certain ordering of the rules.

Given an agent configuration, we are interested in the question whether the agent has certain beliefs and goals. For this reason, we introduce a belief and a goal language.

Definition 2. *(belief and goal formulas)* The belief formulas $\mathcal{L}_B$ with typical element β and the goal formulas $\mathcal{L}_G$ with typical element κ are defined as follows.

- if $\phi \in \mathcal{L}$, then $\mathbf{B}\phi \in \mathcal{L}_B$ and $\mathbf{G}\phi \in \mathcal{L}_G$,
- if $\beta, \beta' \in \mathcal{L}_B$ and $\kappa, \kappa' \in \mathcal{L}_G$, then $\neg\beta, \beta \wedge \beta' \in \mathcal{L}_B$ and $\neg\kappa, \kappa \wedge \kappa' \in \mathcal{L}_G$.

Note that the $\mathbf{B}$ and $\mathbf{G}$ operators cannot be nested, i.e., a formula of the form $\mathbf{BG}\phi$ is not part of the language. Below, we define a semantics for the belief and goal formulas, that we call the "initial" semantics. In the sequel, we will introduce various other semantics.

Definition 3. *(initial semantics of belief and goal formulas)*   Let $\models_\mathcal{L}$ be an entailment relation defined for $\mathcal{L}$ as usual, let $\phi \in \mathcal{L}$ and let $\langle \sigma, \gamma, \pi, R \rangle$ be an agent configuration. Let $\varphi \in \mathcal{L}_B \cup \mathcal{L}_G$. The initial semantics $\models_0$ of the belief and goal formulas is then as defined below.

$$
\begin{aligned}
\langle \sigma, \gamma, \pi, R \rangle \models_0 \mathbf{B}\phi \quad &\Leftrightarrow \sigma \models_\mathcal{L} \phi \\
\langle \sigma, \gamma, \pi, R \rangle \models_0 \mathbf{G}\phi \quad &\Leftrightarrow \gamma \models_\mathcal{L} \phi \\
\langle \sigma, \gamma, \pi, R \rangle \models_0 \neg\varphi \quad &\Leftrightarrow \langle \sigma, \gamma, \pi, R \rangle \not\models_0 \varphi \\
\langle \sigma, \gamma, \pi, R \rangle \models_0 \varphi_1 \wedge \varphi_2 &\Leftrightarrow \langle \sigma, \gamma, \pi, R \rangle \models_0 \varphi_1 \text{ and } \langle \sigma, \gamma, \pi, R \rangle \models_0 \varphi_2
\end{aligned}
$$

This definition of the semantics of beliefs could be considered as being related to the so-called sentential approach to beliefs [17], in the sense that belief is defined as a relation between an agent and a sentence, rather than by means of a Kripke style possible worlds semantics. Contrary to sentential approaches however, the beliefs as defined above are closed under logical consequence.

---

[2] For the purpose of this paper, an agent configuration could be defined without a plan component, as it will not be used in the definitions. We however include it for ease of possible extensions of the paper.

Further, note that this definition specifies that an agent has logical conse-quences of its goal base as goals[3]. An agent cannot derive goals, based on certain beliefs. If an agent for example believes that being at the dentist implies feeling pain and if it has the goal to be at the dentist, it cannot derive that it has the goal to feel pain, based on these premises. If the agent would however also have the *goal* that going to the dentist implies feeling pain, it *would* be able to derive the goal of feeling pain.

In this paper, we assume the semantics of agent programming languages are defined in terms of a transition system [18]. A transition system is a set of derivation rules for deriving transitions. A transition is a transformation of one agent configuration into another and it corresponds to a single computation step. In the sequel, we use $c \to c'$ to indicate a transition from agent configuration c to c'. It will sometimes be useful to add a label, denoting the kind of transition, e.g. $c \to_l c'$.

The following definitions will be used in the sequel and are introduced for notational convenience. The first definition below specifies what we mean by an expansion or contraction of the beliefs of an agent with a certain formula. We make a distinction between expanding or contracting with formulas $\phi \in \mathcal{L}$ and formulas $\beta \in \mathcal{L}_B$, as this will turn out to be useful in the sequel. The first kind of formulas are propositional formulas without the $\mathbf{B}$ operator, although the definitions of contraction and expansion with these formulas are defined using the $\mathbf{B}$ operator[4]. The second kind of formulas are conjunctions and/or negations of formulas of the form $\mathbf{B}\phi$. The second definition specifies two notions of a formula ϕ being a goal in a goal base γ, the first defined as membership of a set (modulo equivalence) and the second as entailment.

Definition 4. *(expansion and contraction of beliefs)* Let c, c' be agent config-urations. Let $\phi \in \mathcal{L}$ and $\beta \in \mathcal{L}_B$. Then, we define respectively the notion of expanding the beliefs with ϕ or β, and contraction of the beliefs with ϕ or β over the transition $c \to c'$ as follows.

$$expansion_{\mathbf{B}}(\phi, c \to c') \Leftrightarrow c \not\models \mathbf{B}\phi \text{ and } c' \models \mathbf{B}\phi$$
$$expansion_{\mathbf{B}}(\beta, c \to c') \Leftrightarrow c \not\models \beta \quad \text{and } c' \models \beta$$
$$contraction_{\mathbf{B}}(\phi, c \to c') \Leftrightarrow c \models \mathbf{B}\phi \text{ and } c' \not\models \mathbf{B}\phi$$
$$contraction_{\mathbf{B}}(\beta, c \to c') \Leftrightarrow c \models \beta \quad \text{and } c' \not\models \beta$$

Definition 5. *(ϕ is a goal in γ)* Let γ be a goal base and let $\phi \in \mathcal{L}$. We then define the following notions specifying when ϕ is a goal in γ.

$$goal_{set}(\phi, \gamma) \Leftrightarrow \exists \phi' \in \gamma : \phi' \equiv \phi$$
$$goal_{ent}(\phi, \gamma) \Leftrightarrow \gamma \models_{\mathcal{L}} \phi$$

Note that $goal_{set}(\phi, \gamma)$ implies $goal_{ent}(\phi, \gamma)$.

---

[3] By the phrase "having a goal ϕ" in some configuration, we mean here that a formula $\mathbf{G}\phi$ is true in this configuration.

[4] An equivalent definition could be given without using the $\mathbf{B}$ operator, by referring directly to the belief bases of the configurations c and c'.

3   Goal Dropping

In this section, we consider possible reasons or motivations for an agent to drop a goal. The notion of goal dropping can be related to the level of commitment an agent has towards a goal. If the agent is not committed at all, it might for example drop its goals right after they are adopted. If the agent is very committed or even fanatic, it will not at all be inclined to abandon its goals. These various levels of commitment or the way in which a certain agent deals with goal abandonment, is often referred to as a *commitment strategy* for that agent [5]. Although in principle one could consider any level of commitment for agents, the common commitment strategies require some level of *persistency* of goals [11]. In sections 3.1, 3.2 and 3.3, we will describe two widely used strategies in some detail and discuss a few more possibilities (together with associated problems). Before we can go into a discussion on various commitment strategies however, we will first define the notion of goal dropping in general.

As we explained in section 2, the execution or semantics of an agent can be described in terms of transitions. The phenomenon of dropping a goal naturally involves a configuration change of some sort and goal dropping can thus be defined as a property of these transitions. Informally, a goal ϕ is dropped over a transition $c \rightarrow c'$, if ϕ is a goal in c, but not in c'. In order to be more precise about what we mean when we say that a goal is dropped, we first need to specify what it means that "ϕ is a goal in a configuration".

We distinguish two different notions of what we can consider to be a goal in an agent configuration. Firstly, a formula ϕ can be viewed as a goal in a configuration c if ϕ is in the goal base, i.e., $\phi \in \gamma_c$[5]. Secondly, a formula ϕ can be considered as a goal in c if the formula $\mathbf{G}\phi$ holds, i.e., $c \models \mathbf{G}\phi$ where $\models$ is an entailment relation defined for $\mathcal{L}_G$. If $\mathbf{G}\phi$ is defined such that it holds if and only if $\phi \in \gamma_c$, these notions coincide. As we will however see in the sequel, this is usually not the case. Based on these two views on the goals of an agent, we now distinguish two perspectives on dropping, i.e., a so called *deletion perspective* and a *satisfaction perspective*. The first is based on the deletion of a goal from the goal base, whereas the second is based on the satisfaction of a formula $\mathbf{G}\phi$.

Definition 6. *(dropping, deletion perspective)* Let c, c' be agent configurations and let $c \rightarrow c'$ be a transition. Let $\phi \in \mathcal{L}$. Then, we define the notion of the goal ϕ being dropped over the transition $c \rightarrow c'$, denoted by $dropped_{del}(\phi, c \rightarrow c')$, as follows:

$$dropped_{del}(\phi, c \rightarrow c') \Leftrightarrow goal_{set}(\phi, \gamma_c) \text{ and } \neg goal_{set}(\phi, \gamma_{c'}) .$$

Definition 7. *(dropping, satisfaction perspective)* Let c, c' be agent configurations and let $c \rightarrow c'$ be a transition. Let $\models$ be an entailment relation defined for $\mathcal{L}_G$ and let $\phi \in \mathcal{L}$. Then, we define the notion of the goal ϕ being dropped over the transition $c \rightarrow c'$, denoted by $dropped_{sat}(\phi, c \rightarrow c')$, as follows:

$$dropped_{sat}(\phi, c \rightarrow c') \Leftrightarrow c \models \mathbf{G}\phi \text{ and } c' \not\models \mathbf{G}\phi .$$

---

[5] Possibly modulo equivalence: ϕ is a goal in γ_c iff $goal_{set}(\phi, \gamma_c)$, i.e., $\exists \phi' \in \gamma_c : \phi' \equiv \phi$.

In the definition of dropping from a satisfaction perspective above, we assume an entailment relation $\models$, defined for $\mathcal{L}_G$. One such entailment relation is specified in definition 3 and in the sequel we will also define other entailment relations. However, in the definition of dropping from a satisfaction perspective, we want to abstract from these specific entailment relations and assume a relation $\models$.

3.1   Blind Commitment

An often mentioned and very intuitive reason for dropping a goal is, that the agent *believes to have achieved* the goal [5, 19]. In [5], an agent that only drops its goals if believed to have achieved them, is called a blindly committed agent. An agent that also drops its goals if believed to be unachievable, is called a single minded agent.

A blindly committed agent should drop a goal ϕ if it comes to believe ϕ. An implementation of a blindly committed agent should thus be such that it drops a goal ϕ as soon as it comes to believe ϕ. This dropping can be approached from the two perspectives discussed above, i.e., we can specify the dropping of ϕ as deletion or as satisfaction. The dropping from a deletion perspective can be defined as a general constraint on the transition systems that can be specified for blindly committed agents.

Definition 8. *(blind commitment, deletion perspective)* Let c, c' be agent configurations and let $\phi \in \mathcal{L}$. An agent is then blindly committed iff

$$\forall c \rightarrow c' : [(\exists \phi : expansion_{\mathbf{B}}(\phi, c \rightarrow c')) \Rightarrow (\gamma_{c'} = \gamma_c \setminus \{\phi \mid \sigma_c \models_{\mathcal{L}} \phi\})]$$

where $c \rightarrow c'$ is a transition that can be derived in the transition system for the agent.

The following proposition relates the definition of a blindly committed agent above, to the general definition of dropping from a deletion perspective.

Proposition 1. *(Goals are dropped from a deletion perspective once the agent believes they are achieved.)* If, for a blindly committed agent as specified in definition 8, an expansion with ϕ takes place over a transition $c \rightarrow c'$ and ϕ is a goal in γ_c, then ϕ is dropped over this transition from a deletion perspective, i.e.:

if $expansion_{\mathbf{B}}(\phi, c \rightarrow c')$ and $goal_{set}(\phi, \gamma_c)$ then $dropped_{del}(\phi, c \rightarrow c')$.

Besides taking the deletion perspective on blind commitment, we can also approach this issue from a satisfaction perspective. In order to do this, we extend the semantics for belief and goal formulas of definition 3, specifying that $\mathbf{G}\phi$ holds if and only if ϕ follows from the goal base *and* ϕ does not follow from the belief base.

Definition 9. *(blind commitment, satisfaction perspective)* Let $\phi \in \mathcal{L}$ and let $\langle \sigma, \gamma, \pi, R \rangle$ be an agent configuration. The semantics $\models_s$ of the belief and goal formulas for a blindly committed agent is then as defined below[6].

---

[6] The clauses for belief formulas, negation and conjunction are as in definition 3, but we do not repeat them here or in definitions in the sequel, for reasons of space.

$$\langle \sigma, \gamma, \pi, R \rangle \models_s \mathbf{G}\phi \Leftrightarrow \gamma \models_{\mathcal{L}} \phi \text{ and } \sigma \not\models_{\mathcal{L}} \phi$$

From the definition above, we can derive that $\models_s \mathbf{B}\phi \rightarrow \neg\mathbf{G}\phi$ is a validity, i.e., $\mathbf{G}\phi$ cannot hold if ϕ is believed. This implies, that if an agent comes to believe ϕ over a transition, a goal ϕ is dropped from a satisfaction perspective (assuming that ϕ was a goal before the transition). This is formulated in the following proposition.

Proposition 2. *(Goals are dropped from a satisfaction perspective once the agent believes they are achieved.)* If the semantics of belief and goal formulas of an agent is as specified in definition 9 and an expansion with ϕ takes place over a transition $c \rightarrow c'$ and ϕ is a goal in γ_c, then ϕ is dropped over this transition from a satisfaction perspective, i.e.:

$$\text{if } expansion_{\mathbf{B}}(\phi, c \rightarrow c') \text{ and } goal_{ent}(\phi, \gamma_c) \text{ then } dropped_{sat}(\phi, c \rightarrow c') .$$

Note that a consequence of defining blind commitment as in definition 9, is the following: if a goal ϕ remains in the goal base over a series of consecutive transitions, it can be the case that $\mathbf{G}\phi$ holds in one configuration, but not in the next and again in the following configuration, depending on the beliefs of the agent. If goals are not deleted from the goal base, this definition of the semantics of goals will thus implement a kind of maintenance goals. It will depend on the type of application whether this is desired behavior.

We can conclude that blindly committed agents can relatively easily be specified in terms of goals and beliefs of the agents. However, the strategy seems very limited and not very realistic. In the literature often agent commitment strategies are discussed that are a bit looser on the commitment, which means that an agent could also drop its goal if it *believes that it is unachievable* [5, 19]. We will discuss this strategy at the end of this section.

We conclude this section with a remark concerning the relation between goals and plans. Given the semantics of definition 9, there can in principle be many ϕ such that $\mathbf{G}\phi$ holds in some configuration. Goals of an agent are motivational attitudes and meant to guide the adoption of plans, i.e., an agent should adopt plans to achieve its goals. Given that an agent can have many goals, an important issue is how to generate plans, based on these goals. In this paper, we focus on defining an agents goals and we do not consider how plans are selected for the goals that an agent has.

The ideas presented in this paper could however for example be combined with the plan selection rules as presented in [7]. These rules are conditionalized by beliefs and goals, i.e., a rule can specify that if the agent has certain beliefs and goals, a certain plan can be selected. In this way, an agent does not have to compute all its goals (or all formulas ϕ such that $\mathbf{G}\phi$ is true in some configuration), but these rules can be taken as a basis and it can be checked whether the antecedent of a rule holds in a configuration. Combining the ideas presented in this paper with an approach of planning from first principles would be more difficult. It would probably call for the definition of for example a sensible preference relation among goals, such that the agent does not have to compute all its goals before selecting one to plan for.

3.2   Failure Condition

The conditions for dropping a goal can be seen as a kind of *failure condition* on the goal achievement. For blindly committed agents, the failure condition is that the agent already believes the goal is true. In [11], Winikoff et al. also consider the specification of more specific failure conditions for goals. The idea is, that this condition specifies an explicit reason for the agent to drop the goal, i.e., if the failure condition becomes true, the agent drops its goal. This failure condition is thus specific to a certain goal.

The authors do not elaborate on the intuitions behind this failure condition, but one could imagine specifying a condition which, once true, will never become false again and which falsehood is necessary for the agent to be able to achieve the goal. Suppose for example that agent A has a goal to have a certain egg sunny side up and suppose A comes to believe that the egg is scrambled, then this would be reason for A to drop its goal, as a scrambled egg can never be prepared sunny side up. The failure condition for a goal should thus correspond to a situation from which the agent will never be able to achieve the goal. This situation is however specified by the designer of the agent. The designer for example knows that a scrambled egg cannot be transformed into one that is prepared sunny side up. The reasoning is thus done at design time by the agent developer instead of leaving it up to the agent itself.

In order to implement this idea of specifying a failure condition for a goal, we propose a so called failure rule. This is a rule with a condition on beliefs as the head and a goal (being a propositional formula) as the body. The informal reading is, that the goal in the body can be dropped if the condition in the head holds.

Definition 10. *(failure rule)* The set of failure rules $\mathcal{R}_f$ is defined as follows: $\mathcal{R}_f = \{\beta \Rightarrow_{\mathbf{G}}^{-} \phi \mid \beta \in \mathcal{L}_B, \phi \in \mathcal{L}\}$.

The interpretation of failure rules can be approached from the two perspectives on goal dropping we identified. We first define the semantics of this rule from a deletion perspective, resulting in the deletion of a goal from the goal base if the rule is applied[7].

Definition 11. *(failure rule semantics, deletion perspective)* Let $\mathcal{R}_f$ be the set of failure rules of definition 10 and let $R_f \subseteq \mathcal{R}_f$. Let $f = (\beta \Rightarrow_{\mathbf{G}}^{-} \phi) \in R_f$ and let $\models$ be an entailment relation defined for $\mathcal{L}_B$. The semantics of applying this rule is then as follows, where $\gamma' = \gamma \setminus \{\phi' \mid \phi' \equiv \phi\}$.

$$\frac{\langle \sigma, \gamma, \pi, R_f \rangle \models \beta \text{ and } goal_{set}(\phi, \gamma)}{\langle \sigma, \gamma, \pi, R_f \rangle \rightarrow_{apply(f)} \langle \sigma, \gamma', \pi, R_f \rangle}$$

The following proposition relates the semantics of failure rule application above, to the general definition of dropping from a deletion perspective.

---

[7] Note that a blindly committed agent could be specified in terms of failure rules of the form $\mathbf{B}\phi \Rightarrow_{\mathbf{G}}^{-} \phi$.

Proposition 3. *(Applying a failure rule results in dropping from a deletion per-spective.)* If $c \rightarrow_{apply(f)} c'$ where $f = (\beta \Rightarrow_{\mathbf{G}}^{-} \phi)$ is a transition derived using the transition rule of definition 11, then $dropped_{del}(\phi, c \rightarrow_{apply(f)} c')$ holds.

The semantics of failure rule application that is defined above, takes an operational view on failure rules. Another option is using these rules to define, in a declarative way, the goals of an agent as the satisfaction of a formula $\mathbf{G}\phi$ in a configuration. This is done in the following definition that extends definition 9, specifying that $\mathbf{G}\phi$ holds if and only if ϕ follows from the goal base, ϕ is not believed *and* there cannot be a rule which head holds and which body is equivalent to ϕ.

Definition 12. *(failure rule semantics, satisfaction perspective)* Let $\mathcal{R}_f$ be the set of failure rules of definition 10 and let $R_f \subseteq \mathcal{R}_f$. Let $\phi \in \mathcal{L}$ and let $\langle \sigma, \gamma, \pi, R_f \rangle$ be an agent configuration. The semantics $\models_f$ of the belief and goal formulas in the presence of failure rules is then as defined below.

$$\langle \sigma, \gamma, \pi, R_f \rangle \models_f \mathbf{G}\phi \Leftrightarrow \gamma \models_{\mathcal{L}} \phi \text{ and } \sigma \not\models_{\mathcal{L}} \phi \text{ and}$$
$$\neg \exists f \in R_f : (f = (\beta \Rightarrow_{\mathbf{G}}^{-} \phi') \text{ and } \langle \sigma, \gamma, \pi, R_f \rangle \models_f \beta$$
$$\text{and } \phi' \equiv \phi)$$

From the definition above, we can conclude that $\mathbf{G}\phi$ cannot hold in a configuration if there is a rule $\beta \Rightarrow_{\mathbf{G}}^{-} \phi'$ in this configuration such that $\phi' \equiv \phi$ and such that β holds. This implies, that if an agent comes to believe β over a transition, i.e., if the rule is "activated" over this transition, the goal ϕ is dropped from a satisfaction perspective (assuming that ϕ was a goal before the transition). When stating that a rule is activated over a transition, we thus mean that the antecedent of the rule does not follow from the configuration *before* the transition, but *does* follow from the configuration *after* the transition. By means of the definition of rule activation as stated below, we can thus specify that a goal is dropped from a satisfaction perspective if a failure rule with this goal as its consequent becomes active (proposition 4).

Definition 13. *(rule activation)* Let $f = (\beta \Rightarrow_{\mathbf{G}}^{-} \phi) \in R_f$ be a failure rule, let c, c' be configurations with rule set R_f and let $c \rightarrow c'$ be a transition. The rule f is activated over the transition, denoted by $activated(f, c \rightarrow c')$, iff $expansion_{\mathbf{B}}(\beta, c \rightarrow c')$, i.e., if the rule's head is false in c and true in c'.

Proposition 4. *(If a failure rule is activated over a transition, the goal associated with that rule is dropped from a satisfaction perspective.)* If the semantics of belief and goal formulas of an agent is as specified in definition 12 and a failure rule $f = (\beta \Rightarrow_{\mathbf{G}}^{-} \phi)$ is activated over a transition $c \rightarrow c'$ and ϕ is a goal in γ_c, then ϕ is dropped from a satisfaction perspective over this transition, i.e.:

$$\text{if } activated(f, c \rightarrow c') \text{ and } goal_{set}(\phi, \gamma_c) \text{ then } dropped_{sat}(\phi, c \rightarrow c') .$$

3.3   Other Strategies

In the previous two sections we discussed two widely used strategies for dropping goals. Both strategies can be implemented in a rather straightforward way. Theoretically, one can of course have far more commitment strategies. We already mentioned the single minded commitment strategy. However, implementing a single minded agent is much more difficult. The condition stating that the agent does not believe a goal ϕ to be achievable, could be specified using CTL temporal logic [20] by the following formula: $\mathbf{B}(\neg\mathsf{EF}\ \phi)$, i.e., the agent believes that there is no possible course of future events in which ϕ is eventually true. In order to evaluate this formula however, the agent would have to reason about its possible future execution traces. In general it is very difficult to check this formula, but one could approximate it in several ways, e.g. by only considering future traces up to a certain length, or by considering only traces generated by possible plans of the agent. In whichever way the strategy is approximated though, the agent needs a mechanism to reason with temporal aspects, thus complicating the implementation considerably.

A last commitment strategy to be mentioned here is the open minded strategy. This strategy states that a goal is dropped whenever the motivation for having that goal has gone. This is directly related to the issue of goal adoption. To implement this strategy, we should keep track of why a goal is adopted, i.e., which are the conditions for adopting a goal. Whenever these conditions are no longer true, the goal will be dropped, e.g. if a goal is adopted to go to New York in order to attend an AAMAS workshop and the workshop is cancelled, we can drop the goal to go to New York (even though we might still believe it is possible to go there and we are not there yet). We will briefly get back to this in section 4.1.

4   Goal Adoption

The issue of goal adoption can be subdivided into the questions of *when* to start considering to adopt goals and *which* goals are to be adopted. Regarding the first question, a possible motivation for an agent to start adopting goals could for example be the lack of goals or the lack of appropriate plans for the goals it has. If we assume that agents generate behavior because they have goals, situations like these would call for goal adoption to prevent an agent from being idle. The decision of when to start adopting goals could be specified in the interpreter or deliberation cycle of the agent (see section 2). In this paper, we will focus on the second question.

As for goal dropping, we also distinguish two perspectives on goal adoption, i.e., an *addition perspective* and a *satisfaction perspective*. The first is based on the addition of a goal to the goal base, whereas the second is again based on the satisfaction of a formula $\mathbf{G}\phi$.

Definition 14. *(adoption, addition perspective)* Let c, c' be agent configurations and let $c \rightarrow c'$ be a transition. Let $\phi \in \mathcal{L}$. Then, we define the notion of the goal

ϕ being adopted over the transition $c \rightarrow c'$, denoted by $adopted_{add}(\phi, c \rightarrow c')$, as follows:

$$adopted_{add}(\phi, c \rightarrow c') \Leftrightarrow \neg goal_{set}(\phi, \gamma_c) \text{ and } goal_{set}(\phi, \gamma_{c'}) .$$

Definition 15. *(adoption, satisfaction perspective)* Let c, c' be agent configurations and let $c \rightarrow c'$ be a transition. Let $\models$ be an entailment relation defined for $\mathcal{L}_G$ and let $\phi \in \mathcal{L}$. Then, we define the notion of the goal ϕ being adopted over the transition $c \rightarrow c'$, denoted by $adopted_{sat}(\phi, c \rightarrow c')$, as follows:

$$adopted_{sat}(\phi, c \rightarrow c') \Leftrightarrow c \not\models \mathbf{G}\phi \text{ and } c' \models \mathbf{G}\phi .$$

In this section, we discuss important motivations for goal adoption that have been identified in the literature. We distinguish reasons for adoption based on *motivational attitudes* such as desires and norms (section 4.1), and reasons based on the notion of *subgoals* (section 4.2). Based on this analysis, we sketch mechanisms for dealing with goal adoption, such as explicit goal adoption rules. We believe it is important to analyze possible motivations for goal adoption, as different motivations may lead to different kinds of rules or other goal adoption mechanisms.

Goal adoption rules have been proposed before in for example research on 3APL [8] and BOID [4]. However, in each of these languages the focus is on one type of interpretation of the rules. 3APL for example interprets rules from an addition perspective, whereas BOID takes the satisfaction point of view. We believe that the observation that there are different interpretations of rules is important, in order to be able to identify conditions under which these perspectives are equivalent or differ. Although we do not provide this kind of analysis of similarities and differences in this paper, we take a first step towards this by identifying and defining the different perspectives.

4.1   Internal and External Motivations for Goal Adoption

In this section, we distinguish important internal and external motivations for goal adoption. As internal motivations, we will discuss so called abstract goals and desires, and as external motivations we will discuss obligations, norms and communication. After a general discussion on these motivations, we will propose a goal adoption rule to implement these ideas.

Motivations. In [21], Dignum and Conte discuss the *generation of concrete goals from built-in abstract goals* as an internal motivation for adopting goals. As Dignum and Conte put it, these abstract goals are often not really achievable but can be approximated through concrete goals. An abstract goal could for example be to be social or to be a law abiding agent. The concrete goal of not driving above the speed limit, would then for example contribute to being a law abiding agent.

Other important sources that may cause the generation of new goals for an agent are *desires, norms and obligations* of the agent. In general, desires are considered as agents' internal motivational attitude while norms and obligations are classified as external motivational attitudes. An agent's desires represent its preferences, wants and urges. They may be produced by emotional or affective processes or even by biological survival mechanisms. For example, if an agent is without food for some period, this might produce an acute desire for food. Desire may also be long-term preferences or wants such as being rich. Such long term preferences can be triggered by an observation, belief, or communication through which they are turned into goals, i.e., desires can be viewed as goals that are conditionalized by beliefs, etc. This is in contrast with the idea of abstract goals, which are not conditionalized and might be disjoint from the (concrete) goals of the agent.

The norms and obligations represent the social nature of agents or what agents have to adhere to. One might have very dutiful agents that generate a goal for any obligation they incur. In general, the norms that an agent wants to adhere to are rules of conduct that pertain in the society in which the agent operates. These could be represented through abstract goals that state that the agent tries to satisfy an obligation or adhere to a norm.

Agents usually operate in a multi-agent environment and have the ability to *communicate* with other agents. They do not only communicate knowledge or belief about the world, but they can also communicate requests for achieving goals. If an agent decides to comply with a request to achieve a goal, the request triggers the generation of a goal.

Formalization. In order to implement these reasons for goal adoption, we propose a goal adoption rule. This is a rule with a condition on abstract goals, beliefs and/or communicated formulas as the head, and a goal (being a propositional formula) as the body. The informal reading is, that the goal in the body can be adopted if the condition in the head holds. In order to define the semantics of these rules, we need to extend agent configurations, adding an abstract goal set and a set of communicated formulas.

Definition 16. *(extended agent configuration)* Let $\mathcal{A}$ be a set of abstract goals consisting of abstract goal names and let $\mathcal{L}_C$ be a set of communication formulas. Let $\langle \sigma, \gamma_{concr}, \pi, R \rangle$ be an agent configuration. An extended agent configuration is then a tuple $\langle \sigma, \gamma, \pi, R \rangle$ where γ is a tuple $\langle \alpha, \gamma_{concr}, \gamma_{comm} \rangle$ with $\alpha \subseteq \mathcal{A}$ is the abstract goal base and $\gamma_{comm} \subseteq \mathcal{L}_C$ are the communicated formulas.

Definition 17. *(goal adoption rules)* We assume a set of abstract goals $\mathcal{A}$ consisting of abstract goal names and we assume a set of communication formulas $\mathcal{L}_C$. The set of goal adoption rules $\mathcal{R}_a$ is then defined as follows:

$$\mathcal{R}_a = \{h \Rightarrow^+_{\mathbf{G}} \phi \mid h = h_1, \dots, h_n \text{ with } h_i \in (\mathcal{A} \cup \mathcal{L}_B \cup \mathcal{L}_C)\} \ .$$

Definition 18. *(semantics of goal adoption rule head)* Let $e = \langle \sigma, \gamma, \pi, R \rangle$ be an extended agent configuration with $\gamma = \langle \alpha, \gamma_{concr}, \gamma_{comm} \rangle$ and let $a \in \mathcal{A}$. We then define an entailment relation for abstract goals as follows: $e \models_{\mathcal{A}} a \Leftrightarrow$

$a \in \alpha$. We furthermore assume an entailment relation $\models_{\mathcal{L}_C}$ for the language of communication formulas. The entailment relation for the set of formulas $\mathcal{A} \cup \mathcal{L}_B \cup \mathcal{L}_C$ is then denoted as $\models_{\mathcal{A}\mathcal{L}_B\mathcal{L}_C}$. Let $h_1, \ldots, h_n$ be the head of a goal adoption rule. The entailment relation $\models_H$ for rule heads is then as follows.

$$\langle \sigma, \gamma, \pi, R \rangle \models_H h_1, \ldots, h_n \Leftrightarrow \quad \langle \sigma, \gamma, \pi, R \rangle \models_{\mathcal{A}\mathcal{L}_B\mathcal{L}_C} h_1 \text{ and}$$
$$\vdots$$
$$\text{and } \langle \sigma, \gamma, \pi, R \rangle \models_{\mathcal{A}\mathcal{L}_B\mathcal{L}_C} h_n$$

As for failure rules, we define an operational as well as a declarative semantics of the goal adoption rule. This results in semantics from an addition and a satisfaction perspective as also indicated by the propositions below.

Definition 19. *(goal adoption rule semantics, addition perspective)* Let $R_a \subseteq \mathcal{R}_a$ be a set of goal adoption rules. Let $a = (h \Rightarrow_{\mathbf{G}}^+ \phi) \in R_a$. The semantics of applying this rule is then as follows, where $\gamma' = \gamma \cup \{\phi\}$.

$$\frac{\langle \sigma, \gamma, \pi, R_a \rangle \models_H h}{\langle \sigma, \gamma, \pi, R_a \rangle \rightarrow_{apply(a)} \langle \sigma, \gamma', \pi, R_a \rangle}$$

Proposition 5. *(Applying a goal adoption rule results in adoption from an addition perspective.)* If $c \rightarrow_{apply(a)} c'$ where $a = (h \Rightarrow_{\mathbf{G}}^+ \phi)$ is a transition derived using the transition rule of definition 19 and ϕ is not a goal in γ_c, i.e., $\neg goal_{set}(\phi, \gamma_c)$, then $adopted_{add}(\phi, c \rightarrow_{apply(a)} c')$ holds.

Definition 20. *(goal adoption rule semantics, satisfaction perspective)* Let $\mathcal{R}_a$ be the set of goal adoption rules and let $R_a \subseteq \mathcal{R}_a$. The semantics $\models_a$ for belief and goal formulas in the presence of goal adoption rules is then as follows.

$$\langle \sigma, \gamma, \pi, R_a \rangle \models_a \mathbf{G}\phi \Leftrightarrow (\gamma \models_{\mathcal{L}} \phi \text{ or } \exists a \in R_a : (a = (h \Rightarrow_{\mathbf{G}}^+ \phi') \text{ and}$$
$$\langle \sigma, \gamma, \pi, R_a \rangle \models_H h \text{ and } \phi' \equiv \phi)) \text{ and } \sigma \not\models_{\mathcal{L}} \phi$$

Proposition 6. *(If a goal adoption rule is activated over a transition, the goal associated with that rule is adopted from a satisfaction perspective.)* If the semantics of belief and goal formulas of an agent is as specified in definition 20 and a goal adoption rule $a = (h \Rightarrow_{\mathbf{G}}^+ \phi)$ is activated over a transition $c \rightarrow c'$ and ϕ is not a goal in c, then ϕ is adopted from a satisfaction perspective over this transition, i.e.:

$$\text{if } activated(a, c \rightarrow c') \text{ and } c \not\models_a \mathbf{G}\phi \text{ then } adopted_{sat}(\phi, c \rightarrow c') .$$

Note that if a goal adoption rule is deactivated over a transition, the goal in the consequent *could* be dropped over this transition due to this deactivation, provided that no other adoption rule has this goal as its consequent. This phenomenon could thus be considered an implementation of the open minded commitment strategy (section 3.3).

4.2   Subgoal Adoption

A goal can be viewed as a *subgoal* if its achievement brings the agent "closer" to its topgoal. This notion of "closeness" to a topgoal is rather vague. One could argue that the achievement of a concrete goal contributing to an abstract goal, brings the agent closer to this abstract goal. A concrete goal can thus be viewed as a subgoal of an abstract goal. In this section, we distinguish two other views on subgoals, i.e., subgoals as being the "parts" of which a topgoal is composed and subgoals as landmarks or states that should be achieved on the road to achieving a topgoal. As we see it, these different kinds of subgoals can lead to different goal adoption mechanisms.

Goal Decomposition. A decomposition of a goal into subgoals should be such, that the achievement of all subgoals at the same time implies achievement of the topgoal. The goal $p \wedge q$ could for example be decomposed into the subgoals p and q. Achievement of both p and q at the same time, now implies achievement of $p \wedge q$.

Goal decomposition is most naturally reached through defining the semantics of goal formulas like was done in definition 9, i.e., such that $\mathbf{G}\phi$ holds if ϕ is a logical consequence of the goal base. In this way, if for example $p \wedge q$ is a goal in the goal base, $\mathbf{G}p$ will hold and $\mathbf{G}q$ will hold (assuming both p and q are not believed). We define the notion of a goal being a subgoal of another goal as follows: a goal ϕ' is a subgoal of ϕ, iff $\phi \models_{\mathcal{L}} \phi'$ but $\phi' \not\models_{\mathcal{L}} \phi$, which we will denote by $subgoal(\phi', \phi)$. Note that this definition of subgoals does not record any order in which the subgoals are to be achieved.

In the following proposition, we state that under the semantics of belief and goal formulas of definition 9, we can get subgoal adoption over a transition if the subgoal was achieved before the transition, but not anymore after the transition (assuming that the topgoal remains in the goal base).

Proposition 7. *(Subgoals are adopted from a satisfaction perspective once the agent believes they are not achieved anymore.)* If the semantics of belief and goal formulas of an agent is as specified in definition 9 and ϕ' is a subgoal of ϕ and contraction with ϕ' takes place over a transition $c \rightarrow c'$ and ϕ is a goal in γ_c as well as in $\gamma_{c'}$, then the subgoal ϕ' is adopted from a satisfaction perspective over this transition, i.e.:

$$\text{if } subgoal(\phi', \phi) \text{ and } contraction_{\mathbf{B}}(\phi', c \rightarrow c') \text{ and } goal_{set}(\phi, \gamma_c) \text{ and}$$
$$goal_{set}(\phi, \gamma_{c'}) \text{ then } adopted_{sat}(\phi', c \rightarrow c') .$$

Sketch of proof: $adopted_{sat}(\phi', c \rightarrow c')$ is defined as $c \not\models_s \mathbf{G}\phi'$ and $c' \models_s \mathbf{G}\phi'$ (definition 15). $c \not\models_s \mathbf{G}\phi'$ follows from the assumption that $c \models_s \mathbf{B}\phi'$ (definition

4 of $contraction_\mathbf{B}(\phi', c \to c')$). $c' \models \mathbf{G}\phi'$ follows from the assumption that $c' \not\models_s \mathbf{B}\phi'$ (definition of $contraction_\mathbf{B}(\phi', c \to c')$), $\phi \in \gamma_{c'}$ and $\phi \models_\mathcal{L} \phi'$ (using definition 9)[8]. $\square$

Landmarks. The second view on subgoals we discuss in this section, is as landmarks. If an agent for example believes that it is in Utrecht and has the topgoal to be in New York (and has a ticket for a flight to New York etc.), then a subgoal would be to be at Schiphol airport. This subgoal does not contribute to the topgoal in the sense that concrete goals contribute to abstract goals. Achievement of the subgoal neither implies in some way achievement of the topgoal (together with achievement of other subgoals for example) and it is thus different from subgoals generated through decomposition.

It is important for an agent to be able to adopt landmark goals, because it can be the case that the agent only has plans to get from landmark to landmark. It can for example be the case that the agent has a plan in its library to get from Utrecht to Schiphol and that it has another plan to get from Schiphol to New York, i.e., the second plan is only applicable if the agent is at Schiphol. If the agent now believes that it is in Utrecht and it has the goal to be in New York, it does not have an applicable plan to execute. If however the agent can adopt the goal to be at Schiphol from the goal to be in New York and the knowledge that it has a plan to get to New York from Schiphol and possibly the belief to be in Utrecht, it *can* execute an applicable plan.

The adoption of landmark subgoals could be implemented in various ways. One possibility is the introduction of a goal adoption rule as below, through which a goal can be adopted on the basis of beliefs and other goals. The semantics can be defined analogously to that of the adoption rule of definition 17.

Definition 21. *(landmark adoption rule)* The set of landmark adoption rules $\mathcal{R}_l$ is defined as follows: $\mathcal{R}_l = \{\beta, \kappa \Rightarrow_\mathbf{G}^+ \phi \mid \beta \in \mathcal{L}_B, \kappa \in \mathcal{L}_G, \phi \in \mathcal{L}\}$.

Note that this formalization does not record any structure or order among the landmarks that are adopted.

We will mention two other ways to adopt landmark goals. Due to space limitations however, we cannot elaborate on these. A first possibility could be to use plan specifications, indicating the preconditions under which the plan could be executed and the desired or expected postconditions. If the agent then has the postcondition of a plan as a goal and does not believe the precondition to be the case, it could adopt the precondition as a goal. If it then achieves this goal or precondition, it can execute the plan and reach its initial goal.

Secondly, one could consider the definition of a goal adoption statement in an agent's plans, similar to achievement goals in AgentSpeak(L) [9]. The goal in the goal adoption statement can be viewed as a subgoal of the plan at hand and the

---

[8] Strictly speaking, we do not need the assumption $goal_{set}(\phi, \gamma_c)$ to derive the desired result. The phenomenon we want to investigate is however, that a formula ϕ remains in the goal base, while subgoals of ϕ might be adopted (or dropped again) due to a belief change.

goal can be adopted if the statement is executed. Another possible interpretation of such a goal achievement statement could be, that this goal state should be achieved before proceeding with the rest of the plan. A plan will have to be selected for the specified goal. Plans with these kinds of statements could thus be viewed as partial plans, the goal achievement statements of which will need to be refined into plans.

5   Conclusion and Future Research

In agent programming languages, goals are often considered in a procedural way. In most agent specification logics on the other hand, goals are employed in a declarative way. We maintain that declarative goals are interesting and useful not only in agent specification, but also in agent programming. In this paper we have particularly explored the issue of the dynamics of declarative goals in the context of agent programming. That is to say, we have analyzed several motivations and mechanisms for dropping and adopting declarative goals in a fairly general setting. We believe this distinction between dropping and adoption and also the distinction between the different perspectives on these phenomena are important in order to get a better understanding of declarative goal dynamics. We have thus provided a basis for analyzing this phenomenon, but many issues were not addressed and remain for future research.

Most importantly, we did not discuss the relation between the two perspectives on dropping and adoption we defined. It will need to be investigated under what circumstances these notions are equivalent or yield similar agent behavior with respect to goal dynamics. Under most entailment relations for goal formulas, it will for example be the case that if a goal ϕ is adopted from an addition perspective, ϕ is also adopted from a satisfaction perspective (assuming a belief expansion with ϕ does not take place and assuming that ϕ does not follow from the goal base before the adoption). Also, it is important to establish the advantages and disadvantages of both approaches and investigate whether they can or should be combined. A possible disadvantage for example concerns the interpretation of goal adoption rules from a satisfaction perspective, as this interpretation could diminish goal persistency: these rules can be activated and deactivated again over a series of transitions. This could result in the repeated adoption and dropping of a certain goal, which could be considered undesirable.

Another issue for future research has to do with the semantics of goal formulas in the presence of dropping or adoption rules. We took a rather conservative approach, defining that only formulas equivalent to the goal in the body of the rules can be dropped or adopted (definitions 12 and 20). One could also consider for example dropping logical consequences of the goal in the body of the failure rule, or combining applicable adoption rules by defining that logical consequences of the set of goals in the bodies of applicable rules can be adopted. Moreover, we did not discuss interactions between rules for dropping and adoption.

Furthermore, we did not discuss goal consistency. Goals are often assumed or required to be consistent [11] as it is argued that it is not rational for an agent to pursue conflicting objectives. This requirement has implications for goal adoption, as goals could become inconsistent through adoption. The issue could for example be dealt with like is done in BOID [4]. In this framework, the rules are interpreted as default rules from which (consistent) extensions or goal sets can be calculated. In the language GOAL [15], individual goals in the goal base are required to be consistent, rather than the entire goal base. This has implications for the definition of the semantics of goal formulas, as it will need to be defined in terms of individual goals rather than in terms of the goal base as a whole.

Finally, we mention goal revision. It seems natural that goal revision can be characterized in terms of dropping and adoption. One could however imagine that motivations for goal revision are different from those for dropping and adoption, possibly calling for a separate treatment of this issue. Also the relation with belief revision should be investigated in order to identify whether results from this field can be applied to goal revision.

Acknowledgements

We would like to thank the anonymous reviewers for their helpful comments on an earlier version of this paper.

References

1. Wooldridge, M.: An introduction to multiagent systems. John Wiley and Sons, LTD, West Sussex (2002)
2. Newell, A.: The knowledge level. Artificial Intelligence **18** (1982) 87–127
3. Broersen, J., Dastani, M., Hulstijn, J., van der Torre, L.: Goal generation in the BOID architecture. Cognitive Science Quarterly **2(3-4)** (2002) 428–447
4. Dastani, M., van der Torre, L.: Programming BOID-Plan agents: deliberating about conflicts among defeasible mental attitudes and plans. In: Proceedings of the Third Conference on Autonomous Agents and Multi-agent Systems (AAMAS'04), New York, USA (2004) 706–713
5. Rao, A.S., Georgeff, M.P.: Modeling rational agents within a BDI-architecture. In Allen, J., Fikes, R., Sandewall, E., eds.: Proceedings of the Second International Conference on Principles of Knowledge Representation and Reasoning (KR'91), Morgan Kaufmann (1991) 473–484
6. Boutilier, C.: Toward a logic for qualitative decision theory. In: Proceedings of the KR'94. (1994) 75–86
7. van Riemsdijk, M.B., van der Hoek, W., Meyer, J.J.Ch.: Agent programming in Dribble: from beliefs to goals using plans. In: Proceedings of the Second International Joint Conference on Autonomous Agents and Multiagent Systems (AAMAS'03), Melbourne (2003) 393–400
8. Dastani, M., van Riemsdijk, M.B., Dignum, F., Meyer, J.J.Ch.: A programming language for cognitive agents: goal directed 3APL. In: Programming multiagent systems, First International Workshop (ProMAS'03). LNAI 3067. Springer-Verlag, Berlin (2004) 111–130

9. Rao, A.S.: AgentSpeak(L): BDI agents speak out in a logical computable language. In van der Velde, W., Perram, J., eds.: Agents Breaking Away (LNAI 1038), Springer-Verlag (1996) 42–55
10. Bellifemine, F., Poggi, A., Rimassa, G., Turci, P.: An object oriented framework to realize agent systems. In: Proceedings of WOA 2000 Workshop, WOA (2000) 52–57
11. Winikoff, M., Padgham, L., Harland, J., Thangarajah, J.: Declarative and procedural goals in intelligent agent systems. In: Proceedings of the Eighth International Conference on Principles of Knowledge Respresentation and Reasoning (KR2002), Toulouse (2002)
12. Moreira, A.F., Vieira, R., Bordini, R.H.: Extending the operational semantics of a BDI agent-oriented programming language for introducing speech-act based communication. In: Proceedings of the First International Workshop on Declarative Agent Languages and Technologies (DALT03). (2003) 129–145
13. Thangarajah, J., Padgham, L., Winikoff, M.: Detecting and exploiting positive goal interaction in intelligent agents. In: Proceedings of the Second International Joint Conference on Autonomous Agents and Multiagent Systems (AAMAS'03), Melbourne (2003) 401–408
14. Fan, X., Yen, J., Miller, M.S., Volz, R.A.: The semantics of MALLET - an agent teamwork encoding language. In Proceedings of the Second International Workshop on Declarative Agent Languages and Technologies (DALT'04), LNCS 3476, Springer-Verlag (2005). In this volume.
15. Hindriks, K.V., de Boer, F.S., van der Hoek, W., Meyer, J.J.Ch.: Agent programming with declarative goals. In: Intelligent Agents VI - Proceedings of the 7th International Workshop on Agent Theories, Architectures, and Languages (ATAL'2000). Lecture Notes in AI. Springer, Berlin (2001)
16. Dastani, M., de Boer, F.S., Dignum, F., Meyer, J.J.Ch.: Programming agent deliberation – an approach illustrated using the 3APL language. In: Proceedings of the Second International Joint Conference on Autonomous Agents and Multiagent Systems (AAMAS'03), Melbourne (2003) 97–104
17. Konolige, K.: What awareness isn't: A sentential view of implicit and explicit belief. In Halpern, J.Y., ed.: Theoretical Aspects of Reasoning about Knowledge (TARK'86). (1986) 241–250
18. Plotkin, G.D.: A Structural Approach to Operational Semantics. Technical Report DAIMI FN-19, University of Aarhus (1981)
19. Cohen, P.R., Levesque, H.J.: Intention is choice with commitment. Artificial Intelligence **42** (1990) 213–261
20. Clarke, E.M., Emerson, E.A.: Design and synthesis of synchronization skeletons using branching-time temporal logic. In: Logic of Programs, Workshop, Springer-Verlag (1982) 52–71
21. Dignum, F., Conte, R.: Intentional agents and goal formation. In: Agent Theories, Architectures, and Languages. (1997) 231–243

Theories of Intentions in the Framework of Situation Calculus

Pilar Pozos-Parra[1], Abhaya Nayak[1], and Robert Demolombe[2]

[1] Division of ICS, Macquarie University,
NSW 2109, Australia
{pilar, abhaya}@ics.mq.edu.au
[2] ONERA-Toulouse,
2 Avenue E. Belin BP 4025, 31055 Toulouse, France
Robert.Demolombe@cert.fr

Abstract. We propose an extension of action theories to intention theories in the framework of situation calculus. Moreover the method for implementing action theories is adapted to consider the new components. The intention theories take account of the BDI (Belief-Desire-Intention) architecture. In order to avoid the computational complexity of theorem proving in modal logic, we explore an alternative approach that introduces the notions of belief, goal and intention fluents together with their associated successor state axioms. Hence, under certain conditions, reasoning about the BDI change is computationally similar to reasoning about ordinary fluent change. This approach can be implemented using declarative programming.

1 Introduction

Various authors have attempted to logically formulate the behaviour of rational agents. Most of them use modal logics to formalize cognitive concepts, such as beliefs, desires and intentions [1, 2, 3, 4, 5, 6]. A weakness of the modal approaches is that they overestimate the reasoning capabilities of agents; consequently problems such as logical omniscience arise in such frameworks. Work on implementing modal systems is still scarce, perhaps due to the high computational complexity of theorem-proving or model-checking in such systems [7, 8, 9].

A proposal [10] based on the situation calculus allows representation of the BDI notions and their evolution, and attempts to find a trade-off between the expressive power of the formalism and the design of a realistic implementation. In the current paper we employ this proposal to enhance Reiter's action theories provided in the situation calculus [11] in order to develop intention theories. In the process, the notion of *knowledge-producing actions* is generalized to *mental attitude-producing actions*, meaning actions that modify the agent's beliefs, goals and intentions. We show that the proposed framework can be implemented using the method for implementing Reiter's action theories.

The paper is organised as follows. We start with a brief review of the situation calculus and its use in the representation issues involving the evolution of the

J. Leite et al. (Eds.): DALT 2004, LNAI 3476, pp. 19–34, 2005.

world and mental states. In Section 3, we define the basic theories of intentions
and the method used to implement such theories. In Section 4, we run through a
simple example to illustrate how our approach works. Finally we conclude with
a brief discussion.

2   Situation Calculus

The situation calculus was developed to model and reason about change in an
environment brought about by actions performed [12]. It involves three types of
terms, including *situation* and *action*. In the following, s represents an arbitrary
situation, and a an action. The result $do(a, s)$ of performing a in s is taken to be
a situation. The world's properties (in general, relations) that are susceptible to
change are represented by predicates called "fluents" whose last argument is of
type *situation*. For any fluent p and situation s, the expression $p(s)$ denotes the
truth value of p in s. It is assumed that every change in the world is caused by
an action. The evolution of fluents is represented by "successor state axioms".
These axioms were introduced to solve the infamous frame problem, namely
the problem of specifying exactly what features of a scenario are affected by
an action, and what features are not. Furthermore, in order to solve the other
attendant problem dubbed the qualification problem, namely the problem of
specifying precisely the conditions under which an action is executable, "action
precondition axioms" were introduced.

There is a difference between what relations are true (or false) in a situation
and what relations are believed to be true (or false) in that situation. However,
the change in both cases is caused by an action. So performance of actions not
only results in physical changes, but also contributes toward change in beliefs
and intentions. Accordingly, apart from the traditional frame problem, there is
a BDI-counterpart of the frame problem: how do we exactly specify which beliefs, desires and intentions undergo change, and which ones don't, as a result
of a given action. Similarly, one would expect that there are BDI-counterparts
of the qualification problem. In order to address the BDI-frame problem, the
notions of "BDI-fluents" and the corresponding "successor (BDI) state axioms"
were introduced [10]. As far as the BDI-qualification problem is concerned, only
the attitude of belief has been discussed, and accordingly the "action precondition belief axioms" have been introduced. This approach has been compared
with other formalisations of BDI architecture, in particular with the Cohen and
Levesque's approach, in [10]. A comparison with Scherl and Levesque's approach
concerning only the attitude of belief has been presented in [13].

2.1   Dynamic Worlds

In certain frameworks of reasoning such as belief revision the worlds are assumed
to be static. However, when reasoning about actions is involved, a world must
be allowed to undergo change. The features of the world that undergo   change

are syntactically captured by fluents. For a fluent p, the successor state axiom $\mathbf{S_p}$ is of the form:[1]

$(\mathbf{S_p})$ $p(do(a, s)) \leftrightarrow \Upsilon_p^+(a, s) \vee (p(s) \wedge \neg\Upsilon_p^-(a, s))$

where $\Upsilon_p^+(a, s)$ captures exactly the conditions under which p turns from false to true when a is performed in s, and similarly $\Upsilon_p^-(a, s)$ captures exactly the conditions under which p turns from true to false when a is performed in s. It effectively says that p holds in $do(a, s)$ just in case **either** the action a performed in situation s brought about p as an effect, **or** p was true beforehand, and that the action a had no bearing upon p's holding true or not. It is assumed that no action can turn p to be both true and false in a situation. These axioms define the truth values of the atomic formulas in any circumstances, and indirectly the truth value of every formula. Furthermore, in order to solve the qualification problem, a special fluent $Poss(a, s)$, meaning it is possible to execute the action a in situation s, was introduced, as well as the action preconditions axioms of the form:

$(\mathbf{P_A})$ $Poss(A, s) \leftrightarrow \Pi_A(s)$

where A is an action function symbol and $\Pi_A(s)$ a formula that defines the preconditions for the executability of the action A in s. Note that Reiter's notation [11] shows explicitly all the fluent arguments $(p(x_1, \ldots, x_n, do(a, s))$, $\Upsilon_p^+(x_1, \ldots, x_n, a, s))$ and   action   arguments $(Poss(A(x_1, \ldots, x_n), s)$, $\Pi_A(x_1, \ldots, x_n, s))$. For the sake of readability we show merely the action and situation arguments.

2.2   Dynamic Beliefs

In the last section we outlined an approach that allows representation and reasoning about the effects of actions on the physical world. This approach however fails to address the problem of expressing and reasoning with the "non-physical" effects of actions, such as epistemic effects. Starting this section, we address the problems involving beliefs, goals and intentions, with the understanding that other attitudes can be dealt with in a similar fashion. Accordingly, we introduce the notions of belief fluents, goal fluents and so on.

Consider a modal operator $\bigcirc$ where $\bigcirc(s)$ for situation s means: agent i believes that the atomic fluent p holds in situation s, for contextually fixed i and p. Similarly, $\bigcirc'(s)$ could represent i's believing q, $\bigcirc''(s)$ could be j's believing $\neg p$ and so on. For readability, we will use the modal operators $B_i p$, $B_i q$, $B_j \neg p$, $\ldots$ instead, and similar notations to represent goals and intentions. We say that the "modalised" fluent $B_i p$ holds in situation s iff agent i believes that p holds in situation s and represent it as $B_i p(s)$. Similarly $B_i \neg p(s)$ represents the fact that the fluent $B_i \neg p$ holds in situation s: the agent i believes that p does not hold in situation s.

---

[1] In what follows, it is assumed that all the free variables are universally quantified.

In this case, the evolution needs to be represented by two axioms. Each axiom allows the representation of two attitudes out of i's four possibles attitudes concerning her belief about the fluent p, namely $B_ip(s)$ and $\neg B_ip(s)$, or $B_i\neg p(s)$ and $\neg B_i\neg p(s)$. The successor belief state axioms for an agent i and fluent p are of the form:

$(\mathbf{S_{B_ip}})$ $B_ip(do(a,s)) \leftrightarrow \Upsilon^+_{B_ip}(a,s) \vee (B_ip(s) \wedge \neg\Upsilon^-_{B_ip}(a,s))$

$(\mathbf{S_{B_i\neg p}})$ $B_i\neg p(do(a,s)) \leftrightarrow \Upsilon^+_{B_i\neg p}(a,s) \vee (B_i\neg p(s) \wedge \neg\Upsilon^-_{B_i\neg p}(a,s))$

where $\Upsilon^+_{B_ip}(a,s)$ are the precise conditions under which the state of i (with regards to the fact that p holds) changes from one of disbelief to belief when a is performed in s, and similarly $\Upsilon^-_{B_ip}(a,s)$ are the precise conditions under which the state of i changes from one of belief to disbelief. The conditions $\Upsilon^+_{B_i\neg p}(a,s)$ and $\Upsilon^-_{B_i\neg p}(a,s)$ have a similar interpretation. These conditions may contain belief-producing actions such as communication or sensing actions. For example, in the Υ's we may have conditions of the form: $a = sense\_p \wedge p(s)$, that causes $B_ip(do(a,s))$, and conditions of the form: $a = sense\_p \wedge \neg p(s)$, that causes $B_i\neg p(do(a,s))$.

In these axioms as well as in the goals and intentions axioms, p is restricted to be a fluent representing a property of the real world. Some constraints must be imposed to prevent the derivation of inconsistent beliefs (see Section 3.1).

To address the qualification problem in the belief context, for each agent i, a belief fluent $B_iPoss(a,s)$, which represents the belief of agent i in s about the possible execution of the action a in s, was introduced.

2.3   Dynamic Generalised Beliefs

The statements of the form $B_ip(s)$ represent i's beliefs about the present. In order to represent the agent's beliefs about the past and the future, the notation $B_ip(s',s)$ has been introduced, which means that in situation s, the agent i believes that p holds in situation s'. Depending on whether $s' = s$, $s' \sqsubset s$ or $s \sqsubset s'$, it represents belief about the present, past or future respectively.[2]

The successor belief state axioms $\mathbf{S_{B_ip}}$ and $\mathbf{S_{B_i\neg p}}$ are further generalized to successor generalised belief state axioms as follows:

$(\mathbf{S_{B_ip(s')}})$ $B_ip(s',do(a,s)) \leftrightarrow \Upsilon^+_{B_ip(s')}(a,s) \vee (B_ip(s',s) \wedge \neg\Upsilon^-_{B_ip(s')}(a,s))$

$(\mathbf{S_{B_i\neg p(s')}})$ $B_i\neg p(s',do(a,s)) \leftrightarrow \Upsilon^+_{B_i\neg p(s')}(a,s) \vee (B_i\neg p(s',s) \wedge \neg\Upsilon^-_{B_i\neg p(s')}(a,s))$

where $\Upsilon^+_{B_ip(s')}(a,s)$ captures exactly the conditions under which, when a is performed in s, i comes believing that p holds in s'. Similarly $\Upsilon^-_{B_ip(s')}(a,s)$ captures exactly the conditions under which, when a is performed in s, i stops believing that p holds in s'. The conditions $\Upsilon^+_{B_i\neg p(s')}(a,s)$ and $\Upsilon^-_{B_i\neg p(s')}(a,s)$ are similarly

---

[2] The predicate $s' \sqsubset s$ represents the fact that the situation s is obtained from s' after performance of one or more actions.

interpreted. These conditions may contain belief-producing actions such as communication or sensing actions. It may be noted that communication actions allow the agent to gain information about the world in the past, present or future. For instance, if the agent receives one of the following messages: "it was raining yesterday", "it is raining" or "it will rain tomorrow", then her beliefs about the existence of a precipitation in the past, present and future (respectively) are revised. On the other hand sensing actions cannot provide information about the future. Strictly speaking sensing action can only inform about the past because the physical process of sensing requires time, but for most applications the duration of the sensing process is not significant and it can be assumed that sensors inform about the present. For example, if the agent observes raindrops, her belief about the existence of a current precipitation is revised. However, there may be applications where signal transmission requires a significant time, like for a sensor on Mars sending information about its environment.

$B_i Poss(a, s', s)$ was introduced in order to solve the qualification problem about i's beliefs. The action precondition belief axioms are of the form:

$(\mathbf{P_{Ai}})$ $B_i Poss(A, s', s) \leftrightarrow \Pi_{Ai}(s', s)$.

where A is an action function symbol and $\Pi_{Ai}(s', s)$ a formula that defines the preconditions for i's belief in s concerning the executability of the action A in s'. Certain agents may require to know when the execution of an action is impossible, in which case we can also consider the axioms of the form: $B_i \neg Poss(A, s', s) \leftrightarrow \Pi'_{Ai}(s', s)$ where $B_i \neg Poss(A, s', s)$ means that in s the agent i believes that it is not possible to execute the action A in s'.

Notice that s' may be non-comparable with $do(a, s)$ under $\sqsubset$. However, this can be used to represent hypothetical reasoning: although situation s' is not reachable from $do(a, s)$ by a sequence of actions, yet, $B_i p(s', do(a, s))$ may mean that i, in $do(a, s)$, believes that p would have held had s' been the case. We are however mainly interested in beliefs about the future, since to make plans, the agent must project her beliefs into the future to "discover" a situation s' in which her goal p holds. In other words, in the current situation s (present) the agent must find a sequence of actions to reach s' (hypothetical future), and she expects that her goal p will hold in s'. Therefore, we adopt the notation: $Bf_i p(s', s) \stackrel{\text{def}}{=} s \sqsubset s' \wedge B_i p(s', s)$ to denote future projections. Similarly, to represent the expectations of executability of actions, we have: $Bf_i Poss(a, s', s) \stackrel{\text{def}}{=} s \sqsubset s' \wedge B_i Poss(a, s', s)$ that represents the belief of i in s about the possible execution of a in the future situation s'. Notice that the term "future situation" in the belief context is used to identify a "hypothetical future situation". The approach cannot guarantee that the beliefs of the agent are true, unless the agent knows the law of evolution of the real world and has true beliefs in the initial situation (see an example in Section 4). Since the approach allows the representation of wrong beliefs, the logical omniscience problem can be avoided in this framework.

2.4   Dynamic Goals

The goal fluent $G_i p(s)$ (respectively $G_i \neg p(s)$) means that in situation s, the agent i has the goal that p be true (respectively false). As in the case of beliefs, an agent may have four different goal attitudes concerning the fluent p. The evolution of goals is affected by goal-producing actions such as "adopt a goal" or "admit defeat of a goal". For each agent i and fluent p, we have two successor goal state axioms of the form:

$(\mathbf{S_{G_i p}})$ $G_i p(do(a, s)) \leftrightarrow \Upsilon^+_{G_i p}(a, s) \vee (G_i p(s) \wedge \neg \Upsilon^-_{G_i p}(a, s))$

$(\mathbf{S_{G_i \neg p}})$ $G_i \neg p(do(a, s)) \leftrightarrow \Upsilon^+_{G_i \neg p}(a, s) \vee (G_i \neg p(s) \wedge \neg \Upsilon^-_{G_i \neg p}(a, s))$

As in the case of beliefs, $\Upsilon^+_{G_i p}(a, s)$ represents the exact conditions under which, when the action a is performed in s, the agent i comes to have as a goal 'p holds'. The other conditions Υ's can be analogously understood. The indifferent attitude about p can be represented by $\neg G_i p(s) \wedge \neg G_i \neg p(s)$: the agent does not care about p. Some constraints must be imposed on the conditions Υ's in order to prevent the agent from having inconsistent goals such as $G_i p(s) \wedge G_i \neg p(s)$, meaning the agent wants p to both hold and not hold simultaneously (see Section 3.1).

2.5   Dynamic Intentions

Let T be the sequence of actions $[a_1, a_2, \ldots, a_n]$. The fact that an agent has the intention to perform T in the situation s to satisfy her goal p (respectively $\neg p$) is represented by the intention fluent $I_i p(T, s)$ (respectively $I_i \neg p(T, s)$). In the following, the notation $do(T, s)$ represents $do(a_n, \ldots, do(a_2, do(a_1, s)) \ldots)$ when $n > 0$ and s when $n = 0$. For each agent i and fluent p, the successor intention state axioms are of the form:

$(\mathbf{S_{I_i p}})$ $I_i p(T, do(a, s)) \leftrightarrow G_i p(do(a, s)) \wedge [$
    $(a = commit(T) \wedge B f_i Poss(do(T, s), s) \wedge B f_i p(do(T, s), s)) \vee$
    $I_i p([a|T], s) \vee$
    $\Upsilon'^+_{I_i p}(a, s) \vee$
    $(I_i p(T, s) \wedge \neg \Upsilon'^-_{I_i p}(a, s))]$

$(\mathbf{S_{I_i \neg p}})$ $I_i \neg p(T, do(a, s)) \leftrightarrow G_i \neg p(do(a, s)) \wedge [$
    $(a = commit(T) \wedge B f_i Poss(do(T, s), s) \wedge B f_i \neg p(do(T, s), s)) \vee$
    $I_i \neg p([a|T], s) \vee$
    $\Upsilon'^+_{I_i \neg p}(a, s) \vee$
    $(I_i \neg p(T, s) \wedge \neg \Upsilon'^-_{I_i \neg p}(a, s))]$

where Υ''s capture certain conditions under which i's intention attitude (concerning T and goal p) change when a is performed in s. Intuitively, $\mathbf{S_{I_i p}}$ means that in the situation $do(a, s)$, agent i intends to perform T in order to achieve goal p iff

(a) In $do(a, s)$ the agent has goal p; and
(b) either
  (1) the following three facts hold true: the agent has just committed to execute the sequence of actions T which represents a plan (the action $commit(T)$ is executed in s), the agent believes that the execution of such a plan is possible $Bf_iPoss(do(T, s), s)$, and she expects that her goal will be satisfied after the execution of the plan $Bf_ip(do(T, s), s)$); or
  (2) in the previous situation, the agent had the intention to perform the sequence $[a|T]$ and the action a has just happened; or
  (3) a condition $\Upsilon_{I_ip}^{\prime+}(a, s)$ is satisfied; or
  (4) in the previous situation s, the agent had the same intention $I_ip(T, s)$ and $\Upsilon_{I_ip}^{\prime-}(a, s)$ does not hold. $\Upsilon_{I_ip}^{\prime-}(a, s)$ represents some conditions under which, when a is performed in s, the agent i abandons her intention.

This definition of intention, as Cohen and Levesque say, allows relating goals with beliefs and commitments. The action $commit(T)$ is an example of intention-producing actions that affect the evolution of intentions. An advantage of this approach is that we can distinguish between a rational intention trigger by condition (1) after analysis of present and future situations, and an impulsive intention trigger by condition (3) after satisfaction of $\Upsilon_{I_ip}^{\prime+}(a, s)$ that may not concern any analysis process (for example, running intention after seeing a lion, the agent runs by reflex and not having reasoned about it).

We have considered a "credulous" agent who makes plan only when she commits to follow her plan: she is convinced that there are not exogenous actions. However, other kinds of agents may be considered. For instance, if the projection to the future is placed at the goal level, we can define a "prudent" agent that replans after every action that "fails" to reach her goal. Discussion of credulous and prudent agents is beyond the scope of this paper.

Intuitively, $Bf_iPoss(do(T, s), s)$ means that in s, i believes that all the actions occurring in T can be executed one after the other.

$$Bf_iPoss(do(T, s), s) \stackrel{\text{def}}{=} \bigwedge_{j=1}^{n} Bf_iPoss(a_j, do([a_1, a_2, \ldots, a_{j-1}], s), s).$$

Notice the similarity of $Bf_iPoss(do(T, s), s)$ with an executable situation defined in [11] as follows:

$$executable(do(T, S_0)) \stackrel{\text{def}}{=} \bigwedge_{i=1}^{n} Poss(a_i, do([a_1, a_2, \ldots, a_{i-1}], S_0))$$

$executable(do(T, S_0))$ means that all the actions occurring in the action sequence T can be executed one after the other. However, there are differences to consider. In $executable(do(T, S_0))$, T is executable iff the preconditions for every action in the sequence hold in the corresponding situation. On the other hand in $Bf_iPoss(do(T, s), s)$, T is believed to be executable in s iff the agent believes that the preconditions for every action in T hold in the corresponding situation. Notice that the approach cannot again guarantee true beliefs concerning action preconditions, except when B_iPoss and $Poss$ correspond for every action. So the framework avoids problems of omniscience about the preconditions for the executability of the actions.

3   Intention Theories

Now we extend the language presented in [11] with cognitive fluents and we introduce the BDI notions to the action theories to build the intention theories. We adapt regression [11] appropriately to this more general setting. The extension of results about implementation of intention theories is immediate.

Let's assume $\mathcal{L}_{sitcalc}$, a language formally defined in [11]. This language has a countable number of predicate symbols whose last argument is of type *situation*. These predicate symbols are called relational fluents and denote situation dependent relations such as $position(x, s)$, $student(Billy, S_0)$ and $Poss(advance, s)$. We extend this language to $\mathcal{L}_{sitcalc_{BDI}}$ with the following symbols: belief predicate symbols $B_i p$ and $B_i \neg p$, goal predicate symbols $G_i p$ and $G_i \neg p$, and intention predicate symbols $I_i p$ and $I_i \neg p$, for each relational fluent p and agent i. These predicate symbols are called belief, goal and intention fluents respectively and denote situation dependent mental states of agent i such as $B_{robot} position(1, S_0)$, $G_{robot} position(3, S_0)$, $I_{robot} position(3, [advance, advance], S_0)$: in the initial situation S_0, the robot believes to be in 1, wants to be in 3 and has the intention of advancing twice to fulfill this goal.

We make the unique name assumption for actions and as a matter of simplification we consider only the languages without functional fluents (see [11] for extra axioms that deal with function fluents).

Definition 1. A *basic intention theory* $\mathcal{D}$ has the following form:
$$\mathcal{D} = \Sigma \cup \mathcal{D}_{S_0} \cup \mathcal{D}_{una} \cup \mathcal{D}_{ap} \cup \mathcal{D}_{ss} \cup \mathcal{D}_{apB} \cup \mathcal{D}_{ssB} \cup \mathcal{D}_{ssD} \cup \mathcal{D}_{ssI}$$
where,

1. Σ is the set of the foundational axioms of situation.

2. $\mathcal{D}_{S_0}$ is a set of axioms that defines the initial situation.

3. $\mathcal{D}_{una}$ is the set of unique names axioms for actions.

4. $\mathcal{D}_{ap}$ is the set of action precondition axioms. For each action function symbol A, there is an axiom of the form $\mathbf{P_A}$ (See Section 2.1).

5. $\mathcal{D}_{ss}$ is the set of successor state axioms. For each relational fluent p, there is an axiom of the form $\mathbf{S_p}$ (See Section 2.1).

6. $\mathcal{D}_{apB}$ is the set of action precondition belief axioms. For each action function symbol A and agent i, there is an axiom of the form $\mathbf{P_{Ai}}$ (See Section 2.3).

7. $\mathcal{D}_{ssgB}$ is the set of successor generalised beliefs state axioms. For each relational fluent p and agent i, there are two axioms of the form $\mathbf{S_{B_i p(s')}}$ and $\mathbf{S_{B_i \neg p(s')}}$ (See Section 2.3).

8. $\mathcal{D}_{ssG}$ is the set of successor goal state axioms. For each relational fluent p and agent i, there are two axioms of the form $\mathbf{S_{G_i p}}$ and $\mathbf{S_{G_i \neg p}}$ (See Section 2.4).

9. $\mathcal{D}_{ssI}$ is the set of successor intention state axioms. For each relational fluent p and agent i, there are two axioms of the form $\mathbf{S_{I_i p}}$ and $\mathbf{S_{I_i \neg p}}$ (See Section 2.5).

The basic action theories defined in [11] consider only the first five sets of axioms. The right hand side in $\mathbf{P_A}$, $\mathbf{P_{Ai}}$ and in the different successor state axioms must be a uniform formula in s in $\mathcal{L}_{sitcalc_{BDI}}$.[3]

3.1 Consistency Properties

For maintaining consistency in the representation of real world and mental states, the theory must satisfy the following properties:[4]
If ϕ is a relational or cognitive fluent, then

- $\mathcal{D} \models \forall \neg (\Upsilon_\phi^+ \wedge \Upsilon_\phi^-)$.

If p is a relational fluent, i an agent and $\mathcal{M} \in \{B, G, I\}$, then

- $\mathcal{D} \models \forall \neg (\Upsilon_{\mathcal{M}_i p}^+ \wedge \Upsilon_{\mathcal{M}_i \neg p}^+)$
- $\mathcal{D} \models \forall (\mathcal{M}_i p(s) \wedge \Upsilon_{\mathcal{M}_i \neg p}^+ \rightarrow \Upsilon_{\mathcal{M}_i p}^-)$
- $\mathcal{D} \models \forall (\mathcal{M}_i \neg p(s) \wedge \Upsilon_{\mathcal{M}_i p}^+ \rightarrow \Upsilon_{\mathcal{M}_i \neg p}^-)$.

Other properties can be imposed in order to represent some definitions found in the literature. For example, the following properties:

- $\mathcal{D} \models \forall ((B_i p(s) \vee \forall s'(s \sqsubset s' \rightarrow Bf_i \neg p(s', s))) \leftrightarrow \Upsilon_{G_i p}^-)$
- $\mathcal{D} \models \forall ((B_i \neg p(s) \vee \forall s'(s \sqsubset s' \rightarrow Bf_i p(s', s))) \leftrightarrow \Upsilon_{G_i \neg p}^-)$

characterize the notion of *fanatical commitment*: the agent maintains her goal until she believes either the goal is achieved or it is unachievable [6]. The following properties:

- $\mathcal{D} \models \forall (\Upsilon_{G_i p}^+ \rightarrow \exists s' \, Bf_i p(s', s))$
- $\mathcal{D} \models \forall (\Upsilon_{G_i \neg p}^+ \rightarrow \exists s' \, Bf_i \neg p(s', s))$

characterize the notion of *realism*: the agent adopts a goal that she believes to be achievable [6]. A deeper analysis of the properties that must be imposed in order to represent divers types of agents will be carried out in future investigations.

3.2 Automated Reasoning

At least two different types of reasoning are recognised in the literature: reasoning in a static environment and reasoning in a dynamic environment. The former is closely associated with belief revision, while the latter is associated with belief update [14]. The received information in the former, if in conflict with the current beliefs, is taken to mean that the agent was misinformed in the fist place.

---

[3] Intuitively, a formula is uniform in s iff it does not refer to the predicates $Poss$, $B_i Poss$ or $\sqsubset$, it does not quantify over variables of sort *situation*, it does not mention equality on situations, the only term of sort *situation* in the last position of the fluents is s.

[4] Here, we use the symbol $\forall$ to denote the universal closure of all the free variables in the scope of $\forall$. Also we omit the arguments (a, s) of the Υ's to enhance readability.

In the latter case it would signal a change in the environment instead, probably due to some action or event. In the following we deal only with the latter type of reasoning. So as a matter of simplification we assume that all the changes in the beliefs are of the type "update". This assumption allows us to represent the generalised beliefs in terms of present beliefs as follows: $B_i p(s', s) \leftrightarrow B_i p(s')$.

Automated reasoning in the situation calculus is based on a regression mechanism that takes advantage of a regression operator. The operator is applied to a regressable formula.

Definition 2. A formula W is *regressable* iff

1. Each situation used as argument in the atoms of W has syntactic form $do([\alpha_1, \ldots, \alpha_n], S_0)$, where $\alpha_1, \ldots, \alpha_n$ are terms of type *action*, for some $n \geq 0$.
2. For each atom of the form $Poss(\alpha, \sigma)$ mentioned in W, α has the form $A(t_1, \ldots, t_n)$ for some n-ary action function symbol A of $\mathcal{L}_{sitcalc_{BDI}}$.
3. For each atom of the form $B_i Poss(\alpha, \sigma'\sigma)$ mentioned in W, α has the form $A(t_1, \ldots, t_n)$ for some n-ary action function symbol A of $\mathcal{L}_{sitcalc_{BDI}}$.
4. W does not quantify over situations.

The *regression operator* $\mathcal{R}$ defined in [15] allows to reduce the length of the situation terms of a regressable formula. $\mathcal{R}$ recursively replaces the atoms of a regressable formula until all the situation terms are reduced to S_0. In particular, when the operator is applied to a regressable sentence, the regression operator produces a logically equivalent sentence whose only situation term is S_0 (for lack of space we refer the reader to [15, 11] for more details). We extend $\mathcal{R}$ with the following settings.

Let W be a regressable formula.

1. When W is an atom of the form $B_i Poss(A, \sigma'\sigma)$, whose action precondition belief axiom in $\mathcal{D}_{apB}$ is (P_{Ai}),

$$\mathcal{R}[W] = \mathcal{R}[\Pi_{Ai}(\sigma)]$$

2. When W is a cognitive fluent of the form $\mathcal{M}_i p(do(\alpha, \sigma))$, where $\mathcal{M} \in \{B, G, I\}$. If $\mathcal{M}_i p(do(a, s)) \leftrightarrow \Upsilon^+_{\mathcal{M}_i p}(a, s) \vee (\mathcal{M}_i p(s) \wedge \neg \Upsilon^-_{\mathcal{M}_i p}(a, s))$ is the associated successor state axiom in $\mathcal{D}_{ssgB} \cup \mathcal{D}_{ssG} \cup \mathcal{D}_{ssI}$,

$$\mathcal{R}[W] = \mathcal{R}[\Upsilon^+_{\mathcal{M}_i p}(\alpha, \sigma) \vee (\mathcal{M}_i p(\sigma) \wedge \neg \Upsilon^-_{\mathcal{M}_i p}(\alpha, \sigma))]$$

3. When W is a cognitive fluent of the form $\mathcal{M}_i \neg p(do(\alpha, \sigma))$, where $\mathcal{M} \in \{B, G, I\}$. If $\mathcal{M}_i \neg p(do(a, s)) \leftrightarrow \Upsilon^+_{\mathcal{M}_i \neg p}(a, s) \vee (\mathcal{M}_i \neg p(s) \wedge \neg \Upsilon^-_{\mathcal{M}_i \neg p}(a, s))$ is the associated successor state axiom in $\mathcal{D}_{ssgB} \cup \mathcal{D}_{ssG} \cup \mathcal{D}_{ssI}$,

$$\mathcal{R}[W] = \mathcal{R}[\Upsilon^+_{\mathcal{M}_i \neg p}(\alpha, \sigma) \vee (\mathcal{M}_i \neg p(\sigma) \wedge \neg \Upsilon^-_{\mathcal{M}_i \neg p}(\alpha, \sigma))]$$

Intuitively, these settings eliminates atoms involving $B_i Poss$ in favour of their definitions as given by action precondition belief axioms, and replaces cognitive fluent atoms associated with $do(\alpha, \sigma)$ by logically equivalent expressions associated with σ (as given in their associated successor state axioms).

Note that $\mathbf{S_{I_ip}}$ is logically equivalent to $I_ip(T, do(a, s)) \leftrightarrow [(((a = commit(T)$ $\wedge Bf_iPoss(do(T, s), s) \wedge Bf_ip(do(T, s), s)) \vee I_ip([a|T], s) \vee \Upsilon_{I_ip}'^{+}) \wedge G_ip(do(a, s))) \vee$ $(I_ip(T, s) \wedge \neg\Upsilon_{I_ip}'^{-} \wedge G_ip(do(a, s)))]$, hence the successor intention state axioms, as well as every successor state axioms presented can be written in the standard format: $\phi(do(a, s)) \leftrightarrow \Upsilon_\phi^{+}(a, s) \vee (\phi(s) \wedge \neg\Upsilon_\phi^{-}(a, s))$.

For the purpose of proving W with background axioms $\mathcal{D}$, it is sufficient to prove $\mathcal{R}[W]$ with background axioms $\mathcal{D}_{S_0} \cup \mathcal{D}_{una}$. This result is justified by the following theorem:

Theorem 1. The Regression Theorem. *Let W be a regressable sentence of $\mathcal{L}_{sitcalc_{BDI}}$ that mentions no functional fluents, and let $\mathcal{D}$ be a basic intention theory, then*

$$\mathcal{D} \models W \quad iff \quad \mathcal{D}_{S_0} \cup \mathcal{D}_{una} \models \mathcal{R}[W].$$

The proof is straightforward from the following theorems:

Theorem 2. The Relative Satisfiability Theorem. *A basic intention theory $\mathcal{D}$ is satisfiable iff $\mathcal{D}_{S_0} \cup \mathcal{D}_{una}$ is.*

The proof considers the construction of a model $\mathbb{M}$ of $\mathcal{D}$ from a model $\mathbb{M}_0$ of $\mathcal{D}_{S_0} \cup \mathcal{D}_{una}$. The proof is similar to the proof of Theorem 1 in [15].

Theorem 3. *Let W be a regressable formula of $\mathcal{L}_{sitcalc_{BDI}}$, and let $\mathcal{D}$ be a basic intention theory. $\mathcal{R}[W]$ is a uniform formula in S_0. Moreover*

$$\mathcal{D} \models \forall(W \leftrightarrow \mathcal{R}[W]).$$

The proof is by induction based on the binary relation $\prec$ defined in [15] concerning the length of the situation terms. Since cognitive fluents can be viewed as ordinary situation calculus fluents, the proof is quite similar to the proof of Theorem 2 in [15].

The regression-based method introduced in [15] for computing whether a ground situation is executable can be employed to compute whether a ground situation is executable-believed. Moreover, the test is reduced to a theorem-proving task in the initial situation axioms together with action unique names axioms. Regression can also be used to consider the projection problem [11], i.e., answering queries of the form: Would G be true in the world resulting from the performance of a given sequence of actions T, $\mathcal{D} \models G(do(T, S_0))$? In our proposal, regression is used to consider projections of beliefs, i.e., answer queries of the form: Does i believe in s that p will hold in the world resulting from the performance of a given sequence of actions T, $\mathcal{D} \models Bf_ip(do(T, s), s)$?

As in [16], we make the assumption that the initial theory $\mathcal{D}_{S_0}$ is complete. The closed-world assumption about belief fluents characterizes the agent's lack of beliefs. For example, suppose there is only $B_rp(S_0)$ in $\mathcal{D}_{S_0}$ but we have two fluents $p(s)$ and $q(s)$, then under the closed-world assumption we have $\neg B_rq(S_0)$ and $\neg B_r\neg q(S_0)$, this fact represents the ignorance of r about q in S_0. Similarly, this assumption is used to represent the agent's lack of goals and intentions.

The notion of Knowledge-based programs [11] can be extend to BDI-based programs, i.e., Golog programs [16] that appeal to BDI notions as well as mental attitude-producing actions. The evaluation of the programs is reduced to a task of theorem proving (of sentence relative to a background intention theory). The Golog interpreter presented in [16] can be used to execute BDI-based programs since the intention theories use the fluent representation to support beliefs,[5] goals and intentions.

4   A Planning Application

In this section we show the axiomatization for a simple robot. The goal of the robot is to reach a position x. In order to reach its goal, it can advance, reverse and remove obstacles. We consider two fluents: $p(x, s)$ meaning that the robot is in the position x in the situation s, and $o(x, s)$ meaning that there is an obstacle in the position x in the situation s. The successor state axiom of p is of the form:

$$p(x, do(a, s)) \leftrightarrow [a = advance \wedge p(x - 1, s)] \vee [a = reverse \wedge p(x + 1, s)] \vee [p(x, s) \wedge \neg(a = advance \vee a = reverse)]$$

Intuitively, the position of the robot is x in the situation that results from the performance of the action a from the situation s iff the robot was in $x - 1$ and a is advance or the robot was in $x + 1$ and a is reverse or the robot was in x and a is neither advance nor reverse.

Suppose that the robot's machinery updates its beliefs after the execution of advance and reverse, i.e., we assume that the robot knows the law of evolution of p. So the successor belief state axioms are of the form:

$$B_r p(x, do(a, s)) \leftrightarrow [a = advance \wedge B_r p(x - 1, s)] \vee [a = reverse \wedge B_r p(x + 1, s)] \vee [B_r p(x, s) \wedge \neg(a = advance \vee a = reverse)]$$

$$B_r \neg p(x, do(a, s)) \leftrightarrow [(a = advance \vee a = reverse) \wedge B_r p(x, s)] \vee [B_r \neg p(x, s) \wedge \neg((a = advance \wedge B_r p(x - 1, s)) \vee (a = reverse \wedge B_r p(x + 1, s)))]$$

The similarity between the successor state axiom of p and the successor belief state axiom of $B_r p$ reflects this assumption. If initially the robot knows its position, we can show that the robot has true beliefs about its position in every situation $\forall s \forall x (B_r p(x, s) \rightarrow p(x, s))$. Evidently the measure of truth concerns solely a model of the real world and not the real world itself.

Now if in addition we assume that there are no actions allowing revision such as $communicate.p(x, s')$ which "sense" whether in s the position is/was/will be x in s', the successor generalised belief state axioms can be represented in terms of successor belief state axioms as follows:

---

[5] In Scherl and Levesque's approach [17], the notion that has been modelled is knowledge. Our interests to consider beliefs is motivated by the desire to avoid the logical omniscience problem.

$$B_r p(x, s', s) \leftrightarrow B_r p(x, s')$$

$$B_r \neg p(x, s', s) \leftrightarrow B_r \neg p(x, s')$$

To represent the evolution of robot's goals, we consider the two goal-producing actions: $adopt.p(x)$ and $adopt.not.p(x)$, whose effect is to adopt the goal of to be in the position x and to adopt the goal of not to be in the position x, respectively. Also we consider $abandon.p(x)$ and $abandon.not.p(x)$, whose effect is to give up the goal to be and not to be in the position x, respectively. Possible motivations for an agent to adopt or drop goals are identified in [18]. The successor goal state axioms are of the form:

$$G_r p(x, do(a, s)) \leftrightarrow a = adopt.p(x) \vee G_r p(x, s) \wedge \neg(a = abandon.p(x))$$

$$G_r \neg p(x, do(a, s)) \leftrightarrow a = adopt.not.p(x) \vee G_r \neg p(x, s) \wedge \neg(a = abandon.not.p(x))$$

The successor intention state axioms are of the form:

$$I_r p(x, T, do(a, s)) \leftrightarrow G_r p(x, do(a, s)) \wedge [(a = commit(T) \wedge B f_r Poss(do(T, s), s) \wedge B f_r p(x, do(T, s), s)) \vee I_r p(x, [a|T], s) \vee I_r p(x, T, s) \wedge \neg(a = giveup(T))]$$

$$I_r \neg p(x, T, do(a, s)) \leftrightarrow G_r \neg p(x, do(a, s)) \wedge [(a = commit(T) \wedge B f_r Poss(do(T, s), s) \wedge B f_r \neg p(x, do(T, s), s)) \vee I_r \neg p(x, [a|T], s) \vee I_r \neg p(x, T, s) \wedge \neg(a = giveup(T))]$$

where the effect of action $giveup(T)$ is to give up the intention of carrying out T.

The successor state axiom of o is of the form:

$$o(x, do(a, s)) \leftrightarrow a = add\_obs(x) \vee o(x, s) \wedge \neg(a = remove\_obs(x))$$

Intuitively, an obstacle is in x in the situation that results from the performance of the action a from the situation s iff a is $add\_obs(x)$ or the obstacle was in x in s and a is not $remove\_obs(x)$. We also suppose that the robot knows also the law of evolution of o.

Notice that there are four actions affecting the real world: $advance$, $reverse$, $add\_obs(x)$ and $remove\_obs(x)$. Since the robot knows how to evolve p and o, these actions also affect the robot's beliefs. However, the mental attitude-producing action: $adopt.p(x)$, $abandon.p(x)$ $adopt.not.p(x)$, $abandon.not.p(x)$, $commit(T)$ and $giveup(T)$ do not have repercussion in the real world.

For the moment we are concerned with plans that involve only physical actions since the scope of goals are confined to physical properties. So the agent does not need to include in its plans actions that modify mental states such as $adopt.p(x)$ or $commit(T)$. The plans generated by the robot consider the following action precondition belief axioms:

$$B_r Poss(advance, s) \leftrightarrow \neg(B_r p(x, s) \wedge B_r o(x + 1, s))$$

$$B_r Poss(reverse, s) \leftrightarrow \neg(B_r p(x, s) \wedge B_r o(x - 1, s))$$

$$B_r Poss(add\_obs(x), s)$$

$$B_r Poss(remove\_obs(x), s) \leftrightarrow (B_r(x - 1, s) \vee B_r(x + 1, s)) \wedge B_r o(x, s)$$

The robot believes that the execution of *advance* is possible iff it believes that there is no obstacle in front of its position. The robot believes that the execution of *reverse* is possible iff it believes that there is no obstacle behind it. The robot believes that the execution of $add\_obs(x)$ is always possible. The robot believes that $remove\_obs(x)$ can be executed iff it is just behind or in front of the obstacle x.

Let $\mathcal{D}$ be the theory composed by the above mentioned axioms. The plans generated by the robot can be obtained by answering queries of the form: What is the intention of the robot after it executes the action $commit(T)$ in order to satisfy its goal $\mathcal{D} \models I_r p(T, do(commit(T), S_0))$? For example, suppose that we have in the initial state the following information: $p(1, S_0)$, $o(3, S_0)$, $B_r p(1, S_0)$, $G_r p(4, S_0)$, i.e., the robot believes that its position is 1 and it wants to be at 4 but it ignores the obstacle in 3. A plan determined by it is $[advance, advance, advance]$.

If the robot has incorrect information about the obstacle, for example $B_r o(2, S_0)$, a plan determined by it is $[remove\_obs, advance, advance, advance]$. Finally, if the robot's beliefs corresponds to the real world, the robot can determine a correct plan $[advance, remove\_obs, advance, advance]$.[6]

5   Conclusion

We have introduced intention theories in the framework of situation calculus. Moreover we have adapted the systematic, regression-based mechanism introduced by Reiter in order to consider formulas involving BDI. In the original approach, queries about hypothetical futures are answered by regressing them to equivalent queries solely concerning the initial situation. We used the mechanism to answer queries about the beliefs of an agent about hypothetical futures by regressing them to equivalent queries solely concerning the initial situation. In the original approach, it is the designer (external observer, looking down on the world) who knows the goals. In the current proposal, it is the agent (internal element, interacting in the world) who has goals. Moreover, under certain conditions, the action sequence that represents a plan generated by the agent is obtained as a side-effect of successor intention state axioms.

The notions of mental attitude-producing actions (belief-producing actions, goal-producing actions and intention-producing actions) have been introduced just as Scherl and Levesque introduced knowledge-producing actions. The effect of mental attitude-producing actions (such as sense, adopt, abandon, commit or give up) on mental state is similar in form to the effect of ordinary actions (such as advance or reverse) on relational fluents. Therefore, reasoning about this type of cognitive change is computationally no worse than reasoning about ordinary fluent change. Even if the framework presents strong restrictions on the expressive power of the cognitive part, the approach avoids further complication of the representation and update of the world model. Diverse scenarios can be represented and implemented.

---

[6] These plans have been automatically generated using SWI-Prolog.

The notion of omniscience, where the agent's beliefs correspond to the real world in every situation, can be represented under two assumptions: the agent knows the laws of evolution of the real world, and the agent knows the initial state of the world. In realistic situations, agents may have wrong beliefs about the evolution of world or initial state. In the proposal, wrong beliefs can be represented by introducing successor belief axioms that do not correspond to successor state axioms, or by defining different initial settings between belief fluents and their corresponding fluents.

Acknowledgements

We are thankful to all the reviewers for their helpful observations. We are also grateful to Billy Duckworth, Mehmet Orgun and Robert Cambridge for their comments. The two first authors are supported by a grant from the Australian Research Council.

References

1. Singh, M.P.: Multiagent Systems. A Theoretical Framework for Intentions, Know-How, and Communications. LNAI 799, Springer-Verlag (1994)
2. Wooldridge, M.: Reasoning about Rational Agents. MIT Press (2000)
3. Singh, M.P., Rao, A., Georgeff, M.: Formal method in dai : Logic based representation and reasoning. In Weis, G., ed.: Introduction to Distributed Artificial Intelligence, New York, MIT Press (1998)
4. van Linder, B.: Modal Logics for Rational Agents. PhD thesis, University of Utrecht (1996)
5. Rao, A., Georgeff, M.: Modeling Rational Agents within a BDI Architecture. In: Proceedings of the Second International Conference on Principles of Knowledge Representation and Reasoning, Morgan Kaufmann (1991)
6. Cohen, P.R., Levesque, H.J.: Intention is choice with commitment. Artificial Intelligence **42** (1990) 213–261
7. Rao, A.: Agentspeak(l): BDI agents speak out in a logical computable language. In: Proceedings of the 7th European Workshop on Modelling autonomous agents in a multi-agent world: Agents breaking away, Springer-Verlag (1996) 42–55
8. Dixon, C., Fisher, M., Bolotov, A.: Resolution in a logic of rational agency. In: Proceedings of the 14th European Conference on Artificial Intelligence (ECAI 2000), Berlin, Germany, IOS Press (2000)
9. Hustadt, U., Dixon, C., Schmidt, R., Fisher, M., Meyer, J.J., van der Hoek, W.: Verification within the KARO agent theory. LNCS 1871, Springer-Verlag (2001)
10. Demolombe, R., Pozos Parra, P.: BDI architecture in the framework of Situation Calculus. In: Proc. of the Workshop on Cognitive Modeling of Agents and Multi-Agent Interactions at IJCAI, Acapulco, Mexico (2003)
11. Reiter, R.: Knowledge in Action: Logical Foundations for Specifying and Implementing Dynamic Systems. The MIT Press (2001)

12. Reiter, R.: The frame problem in the situation calculus: a simple solution (sometimes) and a completeness result for goal regression. In Lifschitz, V., ed.: Artificial Intelligence and Mathematical Theory of Computation: Papers in Honor of John McCarthy, Academic Press (1991) 359–380

13. Petrick, R., Levesque, H.: Knowledge equivalence in combined action theories. In: Proceedings of the 8th International Conference on Knowledge Representation and Reasoning. (2002) 613–622

14. Katsuno, H., Mendelzon, A.: On the difference between updating a Knowledge Base and Revising it. In: Proceedings of the Second International Conference on Principles of Knowledge Representation and Reasoning. (1991) 387–394

15. Pirri, F., Reiter, R.: Some contributions to the metatheory of the situation calculus. Journal of the ACM **46** (1999) 325–361

16. Levesque, H., Reiter, R., Lespérance, Y., Lin, F., Scherl, R.: GOLOG: A Logic Programming Language for Dynamic Domains. Journal of Logic Programming **31** (1997) 59–84

17. Scherl, R., Levesque, H.: The Frame Problem and Knowledge Producing Actions. In: Proc. of the National Conference of Artificial Intelligence, AAAI Press (1993)

18. van Riemsdijk, B., Dastani, M., Dignum, F., Meyer, J.J.: Dynamics of Declarative Goals in Agent Programming. In: Proceedings of the Workshop on Declarative Agent Languages and Technologies (DALT'04), LNCS 3476, Springer-Verlag (2005). In this volume.

Partial Deduction for Linear Logic—The Symbolic Negotiation Perspective

Peep Küngas[1] and Mihhail Matskin[2]

[1] Norwegian University of Science and Technology,
Department of Computer and Information Science,
Trondheim, Norway
peep@idi.ntnu.no
[2] Royal Institute of Technology,
Department of Microelectronics and Information Technology,
Kista, Sweden
misha@imit.kth.se

Abstract. Symbolic negotiation is regarded in the field of computer science as a process, where parties try to reach an agreement on the high-level means for achieving their goals by applying symbolic reasoning techniques. It has been proposed [1] that symbolic negotiation could be formalised as Partial Deduction (PD) in Linear Logic (LL). However, the paper [1] did not provided a formalisation of the PD process in LL.

In this paper we fill the gap by providing a formalisation of PD for !-Horn fragment of LL. The framework can be easily extended for other fragments of LL as well such that more comprehensive aspects of negotiation can be described. In this paper we consider also soundness and completeness of the formalism. It turns out that, given a certain PD procedure, PD for LL in !-Horn fragment is sound and complete.

We adopt the hypothesis that an essential component of symbolic negotiation is Cooperative Problem Solving (CPS). Thus a formal system for symbolic negotiation would consist of CPS rules plus negotiation-specific rules. In this paper only CPS rules are under investigation while negotiation-specific rules shall be published in another paper.

1   Introduction

Symbolic negotiation is regarded in the field of computer science as negotiation through symbolic reasoning. Therefore it could be viewed as a process, where parties try to reach an agreement on the high-level means for achieving their goals. This approach contrasts with utility-based approaches to negotiation like game-theoretic negotiation. Despite of possible contributions, symbolic reasoning could provide to negotiation, research on symbolic negotiation is still in its preliminary stages. The work presented in this article attempts to analyse some aspects of symbolic negotiation.

Partial Deduction (PD) (or partial evaluation of logic programs, which was first introduced by Komorowski [2]) is known as one of optimisation techniques in

J. Leite et al. (Eds.): DALT 2004, LNAI 3476, pp. 35–52, 2005.

logic programming. Given a logic program, PD derives a more specific program while preserving the meaning of the original program. Since the program is more specialised, it is usually more efficient than the original program.

For instance, let A, B, C and D be propositional variables and $A \rightarrow B$, $B \rightarrow C$ and $C \rightarrow D$ computability statements in a logical framework. Then possible partial deductions are $A \rightarrow C$, $B \rightarrow D$ and $A \rightarrow D$. It is easy to notice that the first corresponds to forward chaining (from facts to goals), the second to backward chaining (from goals to facts) and the third could be either forward or backward chaining or even their combination.

Although the original motivation behind PD was deduction of specialised logic programs with respect to a given goal, our motivation for PD is a bit different. Namely, it turns out that PD could be applied for finding partial solutions to problems written in logical formalisms. In our case, given the formal specification of a problem, if we fail to solve the entire problem, we apply PD to generate partial solutions.

This approach supports detection of subgoals during distributed problem solving. If a single agent fails to solve a problem, PD is applied to solve the problem partially. As a result subproblems are detected, which could be solved further by other agents. This would lead to a distributed problem solving mechanism, where different agents contribute to different phases in problem solving—each agent applies PD to solve a fragment of the problem and forwards the modified problem to others. As a result the problem becomes solved in the distributed manner. Usage of PD in such a way provides foundations for advance interactions between agents.

As a logical formalism for the application of PD we use Linear Logic [3]. LL has been advocated [4] to be a computation-oriented logic and, because of its computation-oriented nature, LL has been applied to symbolic multi-agent negotiation in [1].

Although PD has been formalised for several frameworks, including fluent calculus [5], normal logic programs [6], etc., it turns out that there is no work considering PD for LL. Our goal is to fill this gap by providing a formal foundation of PD for LL as a framework for symbolic negotiation between agents such as it was introduced in [1].

We consider symbolic negotiation as a specialisation of cooperative problem solving (CPS). Anyway, in this paper we present only a formalisation of the CPS process. An extension of this formalism, which constitutes symbolic negotiation, shall be described in another paper.

The rest of the paper is organised as follows. Section 2 gives a short introduction to LL. Section 3 gives basic definitions of PD. Section 4 focuses on proofs of soundness and completeness of PD for !-Horn fragment of LL (HLL) [4]. Section 5 demonstrates the relationship between PD and symbolic negotiation. In Section 6 we review some of the PD strategies, which could be applied for guiding PD. Section 7 reviews the related work and Section 8 concludes the paper and discusses further research directions.

2   Linear Logic

LL is a refinement of classical logic introduced by J.-Y. Girard to provide means for keeping track of "resources". In LL two assumptions of a propositional constant A are distinguished from a single assumption of A. This does not apply in classical logic, since there the truth value of a fact does not depend on the number of copies of the fact. Indeed, LL is not about truth, it is about computation.

We consider !-Horn fragment of LL (HLL) [4] consisting of multiplicative conjunction ($\otimes$), linear implication ($\multimap$) and "of course" operator (!). In terms of resource acquisition the logical expression $A \otimes B \vdash C \otimes D$ means that resources C and D are obtainable only if both A and B are obtainable. After the sequent has been applied, A and B are consumed and C and D are produced.

While implication $A \multimap B$ as a computability statement clause in HLL could be applied only once, $!(A \multimap B)$ may be used an unbounded number of times. When $A \multimap B$ is applied, then literal A becomes deleted from and B inserted to the current set of literals. If there is no literal A available, then the clause cannot be applied. In HLL ! cannot be applied to formulae other than linear implications.

In order to illustrate some other features of LL, not presented in HLL, we can consider the following LL sequent from [7]—$(D \otimes D \otimes D \otimes D \otimes D) \vdash (H \otimes C \otimes (O\&S) \otimes !F \otimes (P \oplus I))$, which encodes a fixed price menu in a fast-food restaurant: for 5 dollars (D) you can get an hamburger (H), a coke (C), either onion soup O or salad S depending, which one *you* select, all the french fries (F) you can eat plus a pie (P) or an ice cream (I) depending on availability (restaurant owner selects for you). The formula $!F$ here means that we can use or generate a resource F as much as we want—the amount of the resource is unbounded.

Since HLL could be encoded as a Petri net, then theorem proving complexity in HLL is equivalent to the complexity of Petri net reachability checking and therefore decidable [4]. Complexity of other LL fragments have been summarised by Lincoln [8].

3   Basics of Partial Deduction

In this section we present definitions of the basic concepts of partial deduction for HLL. The names of introduced concepts are largely influenced by the computation-oriented nature of our applications, where we intend to apply the framework.

3.1   Basic Definitions

Definition 1. *A program stack is a multiplicative conjunction*

$$\bigotimes_{i=1}^{n} A_i,$$

where $A_i, i = 1 \ldots n$ is a literal.

Definition 2. *Mapping from a multiplicative conjunction to a set of conjuncts is defined as follows:*

$$\left[\bigotimes_i^n A_i \right] = \{A_1, \ldots, A_n\}$$

Definition 3. *Consumption of formula A_i from a program stack S is a mapping*

$$A_1 \otimes \ldots \otimes A_{i-1} \otimes A_i \otimes A_{i+1} \otimes \ldots \otimes A_n \mapsto_{S,A_i} A_1 \otimes \ldots \otimes A_{i-1} \otimes A_{i+1} \otimes \ldots \otimes A_n,$$

where $A_j, j = 1 \ldots n$ could be any valid formula in LL.

Definition 4. *Generation of formula A_i to a program stack S is a mapping*

$$A_1 \otimes \ldots \otimes A_{i-1} \otimes A_{i+1} \otimes \ldots \otimes A_n \mapsto_{S,A_i} A_1 \otimes \ldots \otimes A_{i-1} \otimes A_i \otimes A_{i+1} \otimes \ldots \otimes A_n,$$

where $A_j, j = 1 \ldots n$ and A_i could be any valid formulae in LL.

Definition 5. *A Computation Specification Clause (CSC) is a LL sequent*

$$\vdash I \multimap_f O,$$

where I and O are multiplicative conjunctions of any valid LL formulae and f is a function, which implements the computation step. I and O are respectively consumed and generated from the current program stack S, when a particular CSC is applied.

It has to be mentioned that a CSC can be applied only, if $[I] \subseteq [S]$. Although in HLL CSCs are represented as linear implication formulae, we represent them as extralogical axioms in our problem domain. This means that an extralogical axiom $\vdash I \multimap_f O$ is basically equal to HLL formula $!(I \multimap_f O)$.

Definition 6. *A Computation Specification (CS) is a finite set of CSCs.*

Definition 7. *A Computation Specification Application (CSA) is defined as*

$$\Gamma; S \vdash G,$$

where Γ is a CS, S is the initial program stack and G the goal program stack.

Definition 8. *Resultant is a CSC*

$$\vdash I \multimap_{\lambda a_1, \ldots, a_n \cdot f} O, n \geq 0,$$

where f is a term representing a function, which generates O from I by applying potentially composite functions over $a_1, \ldots, a_n$.

CSA determines which CSCs could be applied by PD steps to derive resultant $\vdash S \multimap_{\lambda a_1,\ldots,a_n.f} G, n \geq 0$. It should be noted that resultants are derived by applying PD steps to the CSAs, which are represented in form $A \vdash B$. The CSC form is achieved from particular programs stacks by implicitly applying the following inference figure:

$$\frac{\vdash A \multimap B \quad resultant \quad \dfrac{\dfrac{A \vdash A}{A, A \multimap B \vdash B} \; Id \quad \dfrac{B \vdash B}{} \; Id}{A, A \multimap B \vdash B} \; L \multimap}{A \vdash B} \; Cut$$

While resultants encode computation, program stacks represent computation pre- and postconditions.

3.2   PD Steps

Definition 9. *Forward chaining PD step $\mathcal{R}_f(L_i)$ is defined as a rule*

$$\frac{B \otimes C \vdash G}{A \otimes C \vdash G} \; \mathcal{R}_f(L_i)$$

where L_i is a labeling of CSC $\vdash A \multimap_{L_i} B$. A, B, C and G are multiplicative conjunctions.

Definition 10. *Backward chaining PD step $\mathcal{R}_b(L_i)$ is defined as a rule*

$$\frac{S \vdash A \otimes C}{S \vdash B \otimes C} \; \mathcal{R}_b(L_i)$$

where L_i is a labeling of CSC $\vdash A \multimap_{L_i} B$. A, B, C and S are multiplicative conjunctions.

PD steps $\mathcal{R}_f(L_i)$ and $\mathcal{R}_b(L_i)$, respectively, apply CSC L_i to move the initial program stack towards the goal stack or vice versa. In the $\mathcal{R}_b(L_i)$ inference figure formulae $B \otimes C$ and $A \otimes C$ denote respectively an original goal stack G and a modified goal stack G'. Thus the inference figure encodes that, if there is an CSC $\vdash A \multimap_{L_i} B$, then we can change goal stack $B \otimes C$ to $A \otimes C$. Similarly, in the inference figure $\mathcal{R}_f(L_i)$ formulae $B \otimes C$ and $A \otimes C$ denote, respectively, an original initial stack S and its modification S'. And the inference figure encodes that, if there is a CSC $\vdash A \multimap_{L_i} B$, then we can change initial program stack $A \otimes C$ to $B \otimes C$.

In order to manage access to unbounded resources, we need PD steps $\mathcal{R}_{C_l}$, $\mathcal{R}_{L_l}$, $\mathcal{R}_{W_l}$ and $\mathcal{R}_{!_l}(n)$.

Definition 11. *PD step $\mathcal{R}_{C_l}$ is defined as a rule*

$$\frac{!A \otimes !A \otimes B \vdash C}{!A \otimes B \vdash C} \; \mathcal{R}_{C_l}$$

where A is a literal, while B and C are multiplicative conjunctions.

Definition 12. *PD step $\mathcal{R}_{L_l}$ is defined as a rule*

$$\frac{A \otimes B \vdash C}{!A \otimes B \vdash C} \; \mathcal{R}_{L_l}$$

where A is a literal, while B and C are multiplicative conjunctions.

Definition 13. *PD step $\mathcal{R}_{W_l}$ is defined as a rule*

$$\frac{B \vdash C}{!A \otimes B \vdash C} \; \mathcal{R}_{W_l}$$

where A is a literal, while B and C are multiplicative conjunctions.

Definition 14. *PD step $\mathcal{R}_{!_l}(n), n > 0$ is defined as a rule*

$$\frac{!A \otimes A^n \otimes B \vdash C}{!A \otimes B \vdash C} \; \mathcal{R}_{!_l}(n)$$

where A is a literal, while B and C are multiplicative conjunctions. $A^n = \underbrace{A \otimes \ldots \otimes A}_{n}$, for $n > 0$.

Considering the first-order HLL we have to replace PD steps $\mathcal{R}_f(L_i)$ and $\mathcal{R}_b(L_i)$ with their respective first-order variants $\mathcal{R}_f(L_i(\underline{x}))$ and $\mathcal{R}_b(L_i(\underline{x}))$. Other PD steps can remain the same. We also require that the initial and the goal program stack are ground.

Definition 15. *First-order forward chaining PD step $\mathcal{R}_f(L_i(\underline{x}))$ is defined as a rule*

$$\frac{B \otimes C \vdash G}{A \otimes C \vdash G} \; \mathcal{R}_f(L_i(\underline{x}))$$

Definition 16. *First-order backward chaining PD step $\mathcal{R}_b(L_i(\underline{x}))$ is defined as a rule*

$$\frac{S \vdash A \otimes C}{S \vdash B \otimes C} \; \mathcal{R}_b(L_i(\underline{x}))$$

In the above definitions A, B, C are LL formulae and $L_i(\underline{x})$ is defined as $\vdash \forall \underline{x}(A' \multimap_{L_i(\underline{x})} B')$. Additionally we assume that $\underline{a} \overset{def}{=} a_1, a_2, \ldots$ is an ordered set of constants, $\underline{x} \overset{def}{=} x_1, x_2, \ldots$ is an ordered set of variables, $[\underline{a}/\underline{x}]$ denotes substitution, and $X = X'[\underline{a}/\underline{x}]$. When substitution is applied, elements in $\underline{a}$ and $\underline{x}$ are mapped to each other in the order they appear in the ordered sets. These sets must have the same number of elements.

3.3   Derivation and PD

Definition 17 (Derivation of a resultant). *Let $\mathcal{R}$ be any predefined PD step. A derivation of a resultant R_0 is a finite sequence of resultants: $R_0 \Rightarrow_{\mathcal{R}} R_1 \Rightarrow_{\mathcal{R}} R_2 \Rightarrow_{\mathcal{R}} \ldots \Rightarrow_{\mathcal{R}} R_n$, where $\Rightarrow_{\mathcal{R}}$ denotes to an application of a PD step $\mathcal{R}$.*

Definition 18 (Partial deduction). *Partial deduction of a CSA $\Gamma; S \vdash G$ is a set of all resultants R_i derivable from $CSC \vdash S \multimap G$.*

It is easy to see that this definition of PD generates the set of all proof trees for CSA $\Gamma; S \vdash G$. Due to the non-monotonicity of LL we need a sort of backtracking mechanism in our formalism for preserving completeness. Therefore we need backtracking ability, which is achieved by keeping the all the proof trees encountered.

Definition 19. *A CSA $\Gamma; S \vdash G$ is executable, iff given Γ as a CS, resultant $\vdash S \multimap_{\lambda a_1,\ldots,a_n . f} G, n \geq 0$ can be derived such that derivation ends with resultant R_n, which equals to $\vdash A \multimap A$, where A is a program stack.*

4   Soundness and Completeness of PD in HLL

4.1   PD Steps as Inference Figures in HLL

In this section we prove that PD steps are inference figures in HLL.

Proposition 1. *Forward chaining PD step $\mathcal{R}_f(L_i)$ is sound with respect to LL rules.*

Proof. The proof in LL follows here:

$$
\cfrac{
  \cfrac{A \otimes C \vdash A \otimes C \;\; Id \qquad \cfrac{\vdash (A \multimap_{L_i} B)}{} \; Axiom}{A \otimes C \vdash A \otimes C \otimes (A \multimap_{L_i} B)} \; R\otimes
  \qquad
  \cfrac{
    \cfrac{C \vdash C \; Id \qquad \cfrac{\cfrac{A \vdash A \; Id \qquad B \vdash B \; Id}{A, (A \multimap_{L_i} B) \vdash B} \; L\multimap}{A \otimes (A \multimap_{L_i} B) \vdash B} \; L\otimes}{C, A \otimes (A \multimap_{L_i} B) \vdash B \otimes C} \; R\otimes
    }{A \otimes C \otimes (A \multimap_{L_i} B) \vdash B \otimes C} \; L\otimes
    \qquad B \otimes C \vdash G
  }{A \otimes C \otimes (A \multimap_{L_i} B) \vdash G} \; Cut
}{A \otimes C \vdash G} \; Cut
$$

Proposition 2. *Backward chaining PD step $\mathcal{R}_b(L_i)$ is sound with respect to LL rules.*

Proof. The proof in LL follows here:

$$
\cfrac{
  \cfrac{S \vdash A \otimes C \qquad \cfrac{\vdash (A \multimap_{L_i} B)}{} \; Axiom}{S \vdash A \otimes C \otimes (A \multimap_{L_i} B)} \; R\otimes
  \qquad
  \cfrac{
    \cfrac{C \vdash C \; Id \qquad \cfrac{\cfrac{A \vdash A \; Id \qquad B \vdash B \; Id}{A, (A \multimap_{L_i} B) \vdash B} \; L\multimap}{A \otimes (A \multimap_{L_i} B) \vdash B} \; L\otimes}{C, A \otimes (A \multimap_{L_i} B) \vdash B \otimes C} \; R\otimes
    }{A \otimes C \otimes (A \multimap_{L_i} B) \vdash B \otimes C} \; L\otimes
  }{S \vdash B \otimes C} \; Cut
}{}
$$

Proposition 3. *PD step $\mathcal{R}_{C_l}$ is sound with respect to LL rules.*

Proof. The proof in LL follows here:

$$
\cfrac{
  \cfrac{
    \cfrac{
      \cfrac{
        \cfrac{\overline{!A \vdash !A}\;{}^{Id} \quad \overline{!A \vdash !A}\;{}^{Id}}{!A,!A \vdash !A \otimes !A}{}^{R\otimes}
      }{!A \vdash !A \otimes !A}{}^{C!} \quad \cfrac{\overline{B \vdash B}\;{}^{Id}}{}
    }{
      \cfrac{!A, B \vdash !A \otimes !A \otimes B}{!A \otimes B \vdash !A \otimes !A \otimes B}{}^{L\otimes}
    }{}^{R\otimes} \quad \overline{!A \otimes !A \otimes B \vdash C}
  }{!A \otimes B \vdash C}{}^{Cut}
}{}
$$

Proposition 4. *PD step $\mathcal{R}_{L_l}$ is sound with respect to LL rules.*

Proof. The proof in LL follows here:

$$
\cfrac{
  \cfrac{
    \cfrac{
      \cfrac{\overline{A \vdash A}\;{}^{Id}}{!A \vdash A}{}^{L!} \quad \overline{B \vdash B}\;{}^{Id}
    }{
      \cfrac{!A, B \vdash A \otimes B}{!A \otimes B \vdash A \otimes B}{}^{L\otimes}
    }{}^{R\otimes} \quad \overline{A \otimes B \vdash C}
  }{!A \otimes B \vdash C}{}^{Cut}
}{}
$$

Proposition 5. *PD step $\mathcal{R}_{W_l}$ is sound with respect to LL rules.*

Proof. The proof in LL follows here:

$$
\cfrac{
  \cfrac{
    \cfrac{\overline{B \vdash B}\;{}^{Id}}{!A, B \vdash B}{}^{W!}
  }{!A \otimes B \vdash B}{}^{L\otimes} \quad \overline{B \vdash C}
}{!A \otimes B \vdash C}{}^{Cut}
$$

Proposition 6. *PD step $\mathcal{R}_{!_l}$ is sound with respect to LL rules.*

Proof. The proof in LL follows here:

$$
\cfrac{
  \cfrac{
    \cfrac{
      \begin{array}{c} !A \otimes A^n \otimes B \vdash C \\ \vdots \\ !A \otimes A \otimes B \vdash C \end{array}
    }{!A \otimes !A \otimes B \vdash C}{}^{\mathcal{R}_{L_l}}
  }{!A \otimes B \vdash C}{}^{\mathcal{R}_{C_l}}
}{}
$$

Proposition 7. *First-order forward chaining PD step $\mathcal{R}_f(L_i(\underline{x}))$ is sound with respect to first order LL rules.*

Proof.

Proposition 8. *First-order backward chaining PD step $\mathcal{R}_b(L_i(\underline{x}))$ is sound with respect to first order LL rules.*

Proof. The proof in LL is the following

$$
\cfrac{
  S \vdash A \otimes C \qquad
  \cfrac{
    \vdash \forall\underline{x}(A' \multimap_{L_i(\underline{x})} B')
  }{}
}{
  \cfrac{
    S \vdash A \otimes C \otimes (\forall\underline{x}(A' \multimap_{L_i(\underline{x})} B'))
  }{
    S \vdash B \otimes C
  }
}
$$

$$
\cfrac{
  \cfrac{
    \cfrac{
      \vdash C \quad Id
    }{}
    \quad
    \cfrac{
      \cfrac{\overline{A \vdash A}\ Id \quad \overline{B \vdash B}\ Id}{A, (A \multimap_{L_i(\underline{a})} B) \vdash B}\ L\multimap
    }{A \otimes (A \multimap_{L_i(\underline{a})} B) \vdash B}\ L\otimes
  }{C, A \otimes (A \multimap_{L_i(\underline{a})} B) \vdash B \otimes C}\ R\otimes
}{
  \cfrac{
    A \otimes C \otimes (A \multimap_{L_i(\underline{a})} B) \vdash B \otimes C
  }{A \otimes C \otimes (\forall\underline{x}(A' \multimap_{L_i(\underline{x})} B')) \vdash B \otimes C}\ L\forall
}
$$

4.2   Soundness and Completeness

Soundness and completeness are defined via executability of CSAs.

Definition 20 (Soundness of PD of a CSA). *A $CSC \vdash S' \multimap G'$ is executable, if a $CSC \vdash S \multimap G$ is executable in a CSA $\Gamma; S \vdash G$ and there is a derivation $\vdash S \multimap G \Rightarrow_{\mathcal{R}} \ldots \Rightarrow_{\mathcal{R}} \vdash S' \multimap G'$.*

Completeness is the converse:

Definition 21 (Completeness of PD of a CSA). *A $CSC \vdash S \multimap G$ is executable, if a $CSC \vdash S' \multimap G'$ is executable in a CSA $\Gamma; S' \vdash G'$ and there is a derivation $\vdash S \multimap G \Rightarrow_{\mathcal{R}} \ldots \Rightarrow_{\mathcal{R}} \vdash S' \multimap G'$.*

Our proofs of soundness and completeness are based on proving that derivation of a resultant is a derivation in a CSA using PD steps, which were defined as inference figures in HLL. However, it should be emphasised that soundness and completeness of PD as defined here have no relation with respective properties of (H)LL.

Lemma 1. *A $CSC \vdash S \multimap G$ is executable, if there is a proof of $\Gamma; S \vdash G$ in HLL.*

Proof. Since the derivation of a resultant is based on PD steps, which represent particular inference figures in HLL, then if there is a HLL proof for $\Gamma; S \vdash G$, based on inference figures in Section 4.1, then the proof can be transformed to a derivation of resultant $\vdash S \multimap G$.

Lemma 2. *Resultants in a derivation are nodes in the respective HLL proof tree and they correspond to partial proof trees, where leaves are other resultants.*

Proof. Since each resultant $\vdash A \multimap B$ in a derivation is achieved by an application of a PD step, which is defined with a respective LL inference figure, then it represents a node $A \vdash B$ in the proof tree, whereas the derivation of $\vdash A \multimap B$ represents a partial proof tree.

Theorem 1 (Soundness of propositional PD). *PD for LL in propositional HLL is sound.*

Proof. According to Lemma 1 and Lemma 2 PD for LL in propositional HLL is sound, if we apply propositional PD steps. The latter derives from the fact that, if there exists a derivation $\vdash S \multimap G \Rightarrow_{\mathcal{R}} \ldots \Rightarrow_{\mathcal{R}} \vdash S' \multimap G'$, then the derivation is constructed by PD in a formally correct manner.

Theorem 2 (Completeness of propositional PD). *PD for LL in propositional HLL is complete.*

Proof. When applying PD with propositional PD steps, we first generate all possible derivations until no derivations could be found, or all proofs have been found. If $CSC \vdash S' \multimap G'$ is executable then according to Lemma 1, Lemma 2 and Definition 19 there should be a path in the HLL proof tree starting with $CSC \vdash S \multimap G$, ending with $\vdash A \multimap A$ and containing $CSC \vdash S' \multimap G'$. There is no possibility to have a path from $CSC \vdash S' \multimap G'$ to $\vdash A \multimap A$ without having a path from $CSC \vdash S \multimap G$ to $CSC \vdash S' \multimap G'$ in the same HLL proof tree.

Then according to Lemma 1 and Lemma 2, derivation $\vdash S \multimap G \Rightarrow_{\mathcal{R}} \ldots \Rightarrow_{\mathcal{R}} \vdash S' \multimap G'$ would be either discovered or it will be detected that there is no such derivation. Therefore PD for LL in HLL fragment of LL is complete.

Theorem 3 (Soundness of PD of a first-order CSA). *PD for LL in first-order HLL is sound.*

Proof. The proof follows the pattern of the proof for Theorem 1, with the difference that instead of applying PD steps $\mathcal{R}_b(L_i)$ and $\mathcal{R}_f(L_i)$, we apply their first-order counterparts $\mathcal{R}_b(L_i(\underline{x}))$ and $\mathcal{R}_f(L_i(\underline{x}))$.

Theorem 4 (Completeness of PD of a first-order CSA). *PD for LL in first-order HLL is complete.*

Proof. The proof follows the pattern of the proof for Theorem 2, with the difference that instead of applying PD steps $\mathcal{R}_b(L_i)$ and $\mathcal{R}_f(L_i)$, we apply their first-order counterparts $\mathcal{R}_b(L_i(\underline{x}))$ and $\mathcal{R}_f(L_i(\underline{x}))$.

In the general case first-order HLL is undecidable. However, Kanovich and Vauzeilles [9] determine certain constraints, which help to reduce the complexity of theorem proving in first-order HLL. By applying those constraints, theorem proving complexity could be reduced to PSPACE. Propositional HLL is equivalent to Petri net reachability checking, which is according to Mayr [10] decidable.

5   Application of PD to Symbolic Negotiation

In this section we demonstrate the usage of PD symbolic negotiation. We consider here communication only between two agents and show only offers, which are relevant to the demonstration of our framework. However, in more practical cases possibly more agents can participate and more offers can be exchanged. In particular, if agent A cannot help agent B to solve a problem, then A might consider contacting agent C for help in order to solve B's problem. This would lead to many concurrently running negotiations.

Definition 22. *An agent is defined with a CSA* $\Gamma; S \vdash G$, *where* Γ, S *and* G *represent agent's capabilities, what the agent can provide, and what the agent requires, respectively.*

Definition 23. *An offer* $A \vdash B$ *is a CSC with* $\Gamma \equiv \emptyset$.

In our scenario we have two agents—a traveller $\mathcal{T}$ and an airline company $\mathcal{F}$. The goal of $\mathcal{T}$ is to make a booking (*Booking*). Initially $\mathcal{T}$ knows only its starting (*From*) and final (*To*) locations. Additionally the agent has two capabilities, *findSchedule* and *getPassword*, for finding a schedule (*Schedule*) for a journey and retrieving a password (*Password*) from its internal database for a particular Web site (*Site*). Goals ($G_\mathcal{T}$), resources ($S_\mathcal{T}$) and capabilities ($\Gamma_\mathcal{T}$) of the traveller $\mathcal{T}$ are described in LL with the following formulae.

$$G_\mathcal{T} = \{Booking\},$$

$$S_\mathcal{T} = \{From \otimes To\},$$

$$\Gamma_\mathcal{T} = \begin{array}{l} \vdash From \otimes To \multimap_{findSchedule} Schedule, \\ \vdash Site \multimap_{getPassword} Password. \end{array}$$

For booking a flight agent $\mathcal{T}$ should contact a travel agent or an airline company. The airline company agent $\mathcal{F}$ does not have any explicit declarative goals that is usual for companies, whose information systems are based mainly on business process models. The only fact $\mathcal{F}$ can expose, is its company Web site (*Site*). Since access to *Site* is an unbounded resource (includes !), it can be delivered to customers any number of times.

$\mathcal{F}$ has two capabilities—*bookFlight* and *login* for booking a flight and identifying customers plus creating a secure channel for information transfer. Goals, resources and capabilities of the airline company $\mathcal{F}$ are described in LL as the following formulae.

$$G_\mathcal{F} = \{1\},$$

$$S_\mathcal{F} = \{!Site\},$$

$$\Gamma_\mathcal{F} = \begin{array}{l} \vdash SecureChannel \otimes Schedule \multimap_{bookFlight} Booking, \\ \vdash Password \multimap_{login} SecureChannel. \end{array}$$

Given the specification, agent $\mathcal{T}$ derives and sends out the following offer:

$$Schedule \vdash Booking.$$

The offer was deduced by PD as follows:

$$\frac{Schedule \vdash Booking}{From \otimes To \vdash Booking} \; \mathcal{R}_f(findSchedule)$$

Since $\mathcal{F}$ cannot satisfy the proposal, it derives a new offer:

$$Schedule \vdash Password \otimes Schedule.$$

The offer was deduced by PD as follows:

$$\frac{\dfrac{Schedule \vdash Password \otimes Schedule}{Schedule \vdash SecureChannel \otimes Schedule} \; \mathcal{R}_b(login)}{Schedule \vdash Booking} \; \mathcal{R}_b(bookFlight)$$

Agent $\mathcal{T}$ deduces the offer further:

$$\frac{Schedule \vdash Site \otimes Schedule}{Schedule \vdash Password \otimes Schedule} \; \mathcal{R}_b(getPassword)$$

and sends the following offer to $\mathcal{F}$:

$$Schedule \vdash Site \otimes Schedule.$$

For further reasoning in symbolic negotiation, we need the following definitions. They determine the case where two agents can achieve their goals together, by exchanging symbolic information.

Definition 24. *An offer $A \vdash B$ is complementary to an offer $C \vdash D$, if $A \otimes D \vdash B \otimes C$ is a theorem of LL. A, B, C and D represent potentially identical formulae.*

The logical justification to merging complementary offers could be given from the global problem solving/theorem proving viewpoint. Having two complementary offers means that although two problems were locally (at a single agent) unsolvable, they have a solution globally (if the problems of several agents have been merged together).

Proposition 9. *If two derived offers are complementary to each-other, then the agents who proposed the initial offers (which led to the complementary offers) can complete their symbolic negotiation by merging their offers.*

Proof. Since the left hand side of an offer encodes what an agent can provide and the right hand side of the offer represents what the agent is looking for, then having two offers, which are complementary to each other, we have found a solution satisfying both agents, who sent out the initial offers and whose derivations led to the complementary offers.

Now agent $\mathcal{F}$ constructs a new offer:

$$\frac{Site \vdash 1}{!Site \vdash 1} \; \mathcal{R}_{L_l}$$

However, instead of forwarding it to $\mathcal{T}$, it merges the offer with the received complementary offer:

$$\frac{\overline{Site \otimes Schedule \vdash Site \otimes Schedule} \; Id \quad \overline{\vdash 1} \; Axiom}{Site \otimes Schedule \vdash Site \otimes Schedule \otimes 1} \; R\otimes$$

Thereby $\mathcal{T}$ composed (with the help of $\mathcal{F}$) a composite service, which execution achieves the goals of agents $\mathcal{T}$ and $\mathcal{F}$ (in the current example, the goal of $\mathcal{F}$ is represented as constant 1). The resulting plan (a side effect of symbolic negotiation) is graphically represented in Figure 1. The rectangles in the figure represent the agent capabilities applied, while circles denote information collection/delivery nodes. Arrows denote the flow of symbolic information.

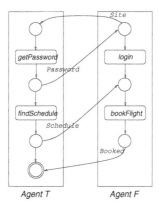

Fig. 1. The distributed plan

6   Partial Deduction Strategies

The practical value of PD is very limited without defining appropriate PD strategies. These are called tactics and refer to selection and stopping criteria. Successful tactics depend generally quite much on a specific logic application. Therefore we only list some possible tactics here. From agent negotiation point of view the strategies represent to some extent agents' policies—they determine which offers are proposed next.

Tammet [11] proposes a set of theorem proving strategies for speeding up LL theorem proving. He also presents experimental results, which indicate a good performance of the proposed strategies. Some of his strategies remind the usage of our inference figures. Thus some LL theorem proving strategies are already implicitly handled in our PD framework.

We also would like to point out that by using LL inference figures instead of basic LL rules, PD, as we defined it here, could be more efficient than pure LL theorem proving. The latter is due to the smaller search space, which emerges through the usage of inference figures.

Definition 25. *Length l of a derivation is equal to the number of the applications of PD steps $\mathcal{R}$ in the derivation.*

Definition 26. *Two derivations are computationally equivalent, regardless of the length of their derivations, if they both start and end with the same resultant.*

6.1   Selection Criteria

Selection criteria define which formulae and PD steps should be considered next for derivation of a resultant. We consider the following selection criteria.

- Mixed backward and forward chaining—a resultant is extended by interleaving backward and forward chaining.
- Different search methods—depth-first, breadth-first, iterative deepening, etc could be used. While breadth-first allows discovering shorter derivations faster, depth-first requires less computational overhead, since less memory is used for storing the current search status.
- Prefer resultants with smaller derivation length—the strategy implicitly leads to breadth-first search.
- Apply only one PD step at time.
- Combine several PD steps together. The approach is justified, if there is some domain knowledge available, which states that certain CSCs are executed in sequence.
- Priority-based selection—some literals have a higher weight, which is determined either manually by the user or calculated by the system according to predefined criteria. During PD literals/resultants having higher weights are selected first.

We would like to emphasise that the above criteria are not mutually exclusive but rather complementary to each other.

6.2   Stopping Criteria

Stopping criteria define when to stop derivation of resultants. They could be combined with the above-mentioned selection criteria. We suggest the following stopping criteria:

- The derived resultant is computationally equivalent to a previous one—since the resultants were already derived and used in other derivations, proceeding PD again with the same resultant does not yield neither new resultants nor unique derivations (which are not computationally equivalent with any previously considered one).

- A generative cycle is detected—if we derived a resultant $\vdash A \multimap B \otimes C$ from a resultant $\vdash A \multimap C$, then by repeatedly applying PD steps between the former resultants we end up with resultants $\vdash A \multimap B^n \otimes C$, where $n > 1$. Therefore we can skip the PD steps in further derivation and reason analytically how many instances of literal B we need. The approach is largely identical to Karp-Miller [12] algorithm, which is applied for state space collapsing during Petri net reachability checking. A similar method is also applied by Andreoli et al [13] for analysing LL programs.
- Maximum derivation length l is reached—given that our computational resources are limited and the time for problem solving is limited as well, we may not be able to explore the full search space anyway. Then setting a limit to derivation length helps to constrain the search space.
- A resultant is equal to the goal—since we found a solution to the problem, there is no need to proceed further, unless we are interested in other solutions as well.
- Stepwise—the user is queried before each derivation in order to determine, which derivations s/he wants to perform. This stopping criterion could be used during debugging, since it provides the user with an overview of the derivation process.
- Exhaustive—derivation stops, when no new resultants are available.

7   Related Work

Although PD was first introduced by Komorowski [2], Lloyd and Shepherdson [6] were first who formalised PD for normal logic programs. They showed PD's correctness with respect to Clark's program completion semantics. Since then several formalisations of PD for different logic formalisms have been developed. Lehmann and Leuschel [5] developed a PD method capable of solving planning problems in the fluent calculus. A Petri net reachability checking algorithm is used there for proving completeness of the PD method.

Analogically Leuschel and Lehmann [14] applied PD of logic programs for solving Petri net coverability problems while Petri nets are encoded as logic programs. De Schreye et al [15] presented experiments related to the preceding mechanisms by Lehmann and Leuschel, which support evaluation of certain PD control strategies.

Matskin and Komorowski [16] applied PD to automated software synthesis. One of their motivations was debugging of declarative software specification. The idea of using PD for debugging is quite similar to the application of PD in symbolic agent negotiation [1]. In both cases PD helps to determine computability statements, which cannot be solved by a system.

Our formalism for PD, through backward chaining PD step, relates to abduction. Given the simplification that induction is abduction together with justification, PD relates to induction as well. An overview of inductive logic programming (ILP) s given by Muggleton and de Raedt [17].

Forward and backward chaining for linear logic have been considered by Harland et al [18] in the logic programming context. In this article we define backward and forward chaining in PD context. Indeed, the main difference between our work and the work by Harland et al could be characterised with a different formalism for different purposes.

There is a similarity between the ideology behind an inductive bias in ILP and a strategy in PD. This means that we could adapt some ILP inductive biases as strategies for PD. In ILP θ-subsumption is defined to order clauses partially and to generate a lattice of clauses. For instance clause $parent(X, Y) \leftarrow mother(X, Y), mother(X, Z)$ θ-subsumes clause $parent(X, Y) \leftarrow mother(X, Y)$. The approach could be useful as a PD strategy in our formalism. However, the idea has not been evaluated yet.

8 Conclusions

In this paper we formalised PD for LL, more specifically for !-Horn fragment of LL. The main reason for choosing the particular LL fragment was that (!)Horn fragment of LL has been designed for rule-based applications. Therefore it suits well for formalising CPS and symbolic negotiation.

We proved that for both propositional and first-order HLL the PD method are sound and complete. It was also demonstrated how PD could be applied in symbolic negotiation. The theorems proposed here can be easily adapted for other fragments of LL, relevant to CPS and symbolic negotiation.

In this paper we assumed that symbolic negotiation would be built upon a CPS framework. Therefore we formalised here only CPS part of symbolic negotiation. This formalisation would be extended with negotiation-specific rules in another paper. Anyway, from computational point of view, we can regard CPS as AI planning and symbolic negotiation as plan reuse/repair. Then it has been showed [19] that from problem solving point of view neither approach in general has an advantage over another.

However, symbolic negotiation provides a more human-like way of problem solving, which can be more naturally followed by human participants. In addition, symbolic negotiation may encode a sort of search heuristics, which would make CPS computationally less demanding. Therefore we shall focus our further research for developing a set of rules, which would specialise our CPS framework to symbolic negotiation.

We have implemented an agent system, where PD is applied for symbolic negotiation. The system is based on JADE and can be download from homepage `http://www.idi.ntnu.no/~peep/symbolic`. Although in the current version of the agent software the derived offers are broadcasted, we are working on heuristics, which would allow us to limit the number of offer receivers. In the long term we would like to end up with a P2P agent software where a large number of agents would apply symbolic negotiation for concurrent problem solving.

Acknowledgements

This work was partially supported by the Norwegian Research Foundation in the framework of Information and Communication Technology (IKT-2010) program— the ADIS project. The authors would additionally like to thank anonymous referees for their comments.

References

1. Küngas, P., Matskin, M.: Linear logic, partial deduction and cooperative problem solving. In: Proceedings of the First International Workshop on Declarative Agent Languages and Technologies (DALT'2003). Volume 2990 of Lecture Notes in Artificial Intelligence., Springer-Verlag (2004)
2. Komorowski, J.: A Specification of An Abstract Prolog Machine and Its Application to Partial Evaluation. PhD thesis, Department of Computer and Information Science, Linkoping University, Linkoping, Sweden (1981)
3. Girard, J.Y.: Linear logic. Theoretical Computer Science **50** (1987) 1–102
4. Kanovich, M.I.: Linear logic as a logic of computations. Annals of Pure and Applied Logic **67** (1994) 183–212
5. Lehmann, H., Leuschel, M.: Solving planning problems by partial deduction. In: Proceedings of the 7th International Conference on Logic for Programming and Automated Reasoning, LPAR'2000, Reunion Island, France, November 11–12, 2000. Volume 1955 of Lecture Notes in Artificial Intelligence. Springer-Verlag (2000) 451–467
6. Lloyd, J.W., Shepherdson, J.C.: Partial evaluation in logic programming. Journal of Logic Programming **11** (1991) 217–242
7. Lincoln, P.: Linear logic. ACM SIGACT Notices **23** (1992) 29–37
8. Lincoln, P.: Deciding provability of linear logic formulas. In Girard, J.Y., Lafont, Y., Regnier, L., eds.: Advances in Linear Logic. Volume 222 of London Mathematical Society Lecture Note Series. Cambridge University Press (1995) 109–122
9. Kanovich, M.I., Vauzeilles, J.: The classical AI planning problems in the mirror of Horn linear logic: Semantics, expressibility, complexity. Mathematical Structures in Computer Science **11** (2001) 689–716
10. Mayr, E.: An algorithm for the general Petri net reachability problem. SIAM Journal on Computing **13** (1984) 441–460
11. Tammet, T.: Proof strategies in linear logic. Journal of Automated Reasoning **12** (1994) 273–304
12. Karp, R.M., Miller, R.E.: Parallel program schemata. Journal of Computer and Systems Sciences **3** (1969) 147–195
13. Andreoli, J.M., R.Pareschi, Castagnetti, T.: Static analysis of linear logic programming. New Generation Computing **15** (1997) 449–481
14. Leuschel, M., Lehmann, H.: Solving coverability problems of Petri nets by partial deduction. In: Proceedings of the 2nd International ACM SIGPLAN Conference on Principles and Practice of Declarative Programming, PPDP'2000, Montreal, Canada, September 20–23, 2000, ACM Press (2000) 268–279
15. de Schreye, D., Glück, R., Jørgensen, J., Leuschel, M., Martens, B., Sørensen, M.H.: Conjunctive partial deduction: Foundations, control, algorithms and experiments. Journal of Logic Programming **41** (1999) 231–277

16. Matskin, M., Komorowski, J.: Partial structural synthesis of programs. Fundamenta Informaticae **30** (1997) 23–41
17. Muggleton, S., de Raedt, L.: Inductive logic programming: Theory and methods. Journal of Logic Programming **19/20** (1994) 629–679
18. Harland, J., Pym, D., Winikoff, M.: Forward and backward chaining in linear logic. In: Proceedings of the CADE-17 Workshop on Proof-Search in Type-Theoretic Systems, Pittsburgh, June 20–21, 2000. Volume 37 of Electronic Notes in Theoretical Computer Science. Elsevier (2000)
19. Nebel, B., Koehler, J.: Plan reuse versus plan generation: A theoretical and empirical analysis. Artificial Intelligence **76** (1995) 427–454

On Modelling Multi-agent Systems Declaratively

Andrea Bracciali[1], Paolo Mancarella[1], Kostas Stathis[1,2], and Francesca Toni[1,3]

[1] Dipartimento di Informatica, Università di Pisa
{braccia, paolo}@di.unipi.it
[2] Department of Computing, City University London
kostas@soi.city.ac.uk
[3] Department of Computing, Imperial College London
ft@doc.ic.ac.uk

Abstract. We propose a declarative framework for modelling multi-agent systems and specify a number of properties of these systems and agents within them. The framework is parametric with respect to an input/output semantics for agents, whereby inputs are the agents' observations, and outputs are their actions. The observations include actions performed by other agents and events happening in the world. We define the semantics of a multi-agent system via a stability condition over the individual agents' semantics. We instantiate the framework with respect to simple abductive logic agents. We illustrate the framework and the proposed properties by means of a simple example of agent negotiation.

1 Introduction

The ever-growing use of agents and multi-agent systems in practical applications poses the problem of formally verifying their properties; the idea being that by verifying properties of the overall system we can make informed judgements about the suitability of agents and multi-agent systems in solving problems posed within application domains. For example, if a multi-agent system is to be used to negotiate on behalf of people, in order to solve problems of re-allocation and sharing of resources (e.g., as in [1]), the problem arises as to whether a specific set of agents/multi-agent system can actually solve a concrete problem of resource-reallocation.

We specify a set of generic properties, which we believe to be interesting, of individual agents, multi-agent systems and agents within multi-agent systems. Rather than proposing a specific architecture or theory for agents, we view agents as "black-boxes", whose "semantics" is expressed solely in terms of (i) their *observable behaviour*, which is public and thus visible to other agents in the same multi-agent system, and (ii) their *mental state*, which is private and thus inaccessible to other agents in the same multi-agent system. Our proposed properties can be instantiated for any concrete agent architecture/theory that can be abstracted away in terms of the aforementioned "semantics", and apply to systems consisting of architecturally heterogeneous agents, including legacy systems. Thus, our approach is not concerned with the specification or programming of agents and agents' applications, but rather it is tailored towards the specification of properties of agents, which is to serve for their verification.

J. Leite et al. (Eds.): DALT 2004, LNAI 3476, pp. 53–68, 2005.

The observable behaviour of an agent is expressed in terms of an output set of actions from a pool of actions that the agent can perform, given an input set of observations from a pool of observations that the agent can make. Actions and observation can be communicative or not. Actions of one agent may be observations of another. Observations may include also events in the world in which agents are situated. The set of visible events and actions by other agents that an agent can observe in the world constitute its environment. If all agents in a multi-agent system can observe all events happening in the world and all actions performed by the other agents, then we call the multi-agent system *fully transparent*. Otherwise, we call the system *partially transparent*. The mental state is seen as a set of beliefs by the agent. Actions, observations, events and beliefs are seen as atoms in some logical languages.

Given the "semantics" of agents as described above, we define the semantics of a multi-agent system via a definition of *stability* on the set of all actions performed by all agents in the system, possibly arising from their communication and interaction via observation: a set of actions (by the different agents) is stable if, assuming that an "oracle" could feed each of the agents with all the actions in the set performed by the other agents (and all events happening in the world), then each agent would do exactly what is in the set, namely their observable behaviour would be exactly what the set envisages.

We specify properties of individual success of agents, overall success of a multi-agent system, robustness and world-dependence of a multi-agent system, as well as a number of properties of agents within systems. We then instantiate our framework by means of simple abductive logic agents, whose mental state and observable behaviour can be computed by applying an adaptation of the T_p operator of logic programs (see e.g., [2]) starting from the observations of the agents. If a multi-agent system consists of these simple agents, we show how stable sets of actions by all the agents can be computed incrementally. We also illustrate the framework and the properties we propose in the context of multi-agent systems consisting of the simple abductive logic agents.

2   Preliminaries

A *multi-agent system* $\langle \mathcal{A}, \mathcal{W} \rangle$ consists of a set $\mathcal{A}$ of n *agents* ($n \geq 2$) that we refer to simply as $1, \ldots, n$, and a *world* $\mathcal{W}$ in which events may happen which the agents may perceive. Until section 5, we will abstract away from the details of the agents' architecture and model, and simply rely upon the existence of a *semantics* of agents, as understood below. Thus, note that our model applies to systems of architecturally heterogeneous agents. We will also abstract away from the details of the world, except for assuming that it is characterised by a (possibly empty, possibly infinite) set of *events*, which may be observed by the agents. We will refer to these events as $E(\mathcal{W})$.

Each agent i is associated with a (possibly empty, possibly infinite) set of potential *actions* that it can perform, indicated as $A(i)$, and a (possibly empty, possibly infinite) set of *observations* it can make, indicated as $O(i)$. Without loss of generality, we will assume that $A(i) \cap A(j) = \emptyset$, for $i \neq j$, namely no action can be performed by two different agents. For example, the action whereby agent 1 asks agent 2 for some resource can only be performed by agent 1, while the action whereby agent 2 asks agent

3 for some resource can only be performed by agent 2, and so on. For simplicity, we do not explicitly deal with the representation of time, but we assume that actions are distinguished by their execution time (i.e. the same action executed at different instants will be represented by different elements in $A(i)$) and executed in the "proper" order. Also, given some set Δ, we will denote by $\Delta(j)$ the set of actions in Δ pertaining to the agent j, namely $\Delta(j) = \Delta \cap A(j)$.

Actions performed by one agent may be observations of another, namely the language in which actions and observations are represented is common amongst the agents. E.g., actions may be outgoing communication and observations may be incoming communication, and the language in which they are represented may be an agent communication language. Observations by agents may also be events happening in the world, taken from $E(\mathcal{W})$. Formally,

$$\bigcup_{i \in A} O(i) \subseteq E(\mathcal{W}) \cup \bigcup_{i \in A} A(i)$$

In Section 3.1 we will first consider the case in which each agent can observe all other agents' actions as well as the whole world. In Section 3.2 we will consider the case in which each agent may have only a partial visibility both of other agents' actions and of the world. This may be due to its inability to fully observe the other agents and the world, as well as to the unwillingness of some agents to disclose all their actions to every other agent. The portion of the world and of the (actions performed by) other agents visible to an agent can be seen as the *environment* in which this agent is situated.

The semantics of agent i is indicated as

$$\mathcal{S}^i(\Delta_{in}, \Delta_0) = \langle M, \Delta_{out} \rangle,$$

where

- $\Delta_{in} \subseteq O(i)$ is a (possibly infinite) set of observations by agent i,
- $\Delta_0 \subseteq A(i)$ is a (possibly infinite) set of actions by agent i,
- M is a (possibly infinite) set of atomic sentences (from a given "private" language that the agent is equipped with), understood as the *mental state* of the agent, and
- $\Delta_{out} \subseteq A(i)$ is a (possibly infinite) set of actions performed by agent i, understood as the *observable behaviour* of the agent.

Δ_0 will typically belong to some initial plan of the agent i, allowing i to achieve its *goals* or *desires*, according to its mental state. We will refer to the goals of agent i as G_i. Syntactically, goals are sets of atoms in the internal language of the agent. In particular, the set of goals may be empty. M can be seen as the set of atomic beliefs held by the agent, and *private* to the agent itself. It may be $\bot$, indicating the inconsistency of a mental state of the agent. Δ_{out} is instead the *public* side of the agent. Given Δ_{in} and Δ_0, $\mathcal{S}^i(\Delta_{in}, \Delta_0)$ may not be unique (namely $\mathcal{S}^i$ may not be a function in general).

Although this declarative formulation of our model can deal with infinite sets, e.g., accounting for reactive agent behaviour, its operational counterparts for verification will typically revert to finite instances of agents' behaviour (as in well-known verification methodologies, like finite model checking). Section 5 proposes a possible way to construct a concrete such semantics for agents based on abductive logic programming.

3   Semantics of a Multi-agent System

We define a semantics for a multi-agent system, parametric with respect to the semantics of the individual agents. This semantics relies upon the notion of stable set of actions (by all agents in the system). Agents are assumed to start with (possibly empty) initial plans $\Delta_0^1, \ldots, \Delta_0^n$. Moreover, the world is supposed to provide a set $\Delta_E \subseteq E(\mathcal{W})$ of happened events. We provide two definitions for the notion of stable set, according to whether the agents fully or partially perceive the world and the other agents.

3.1   Fully Transparent Multi-agent Systems

In this section we assume that each agent has full perception of each other agent as well as of the world. We call such a multi-agent system *fully transparent*.

Definition 1. *A fully transparent multi-agent system* $\langle \mathcal{A}, \mathcal{W} \rangle$ *is* stable *if there exists* $\Delta \subseteq \bigcup_{i \in \mathcal{A}} A(i)$, *such that*

  i. $\bigcup_{i \in \mathcal{A}} \Delta_{out}^i = \Delta$

  ii. $\mathcal{S}^i(\Delta^{-i} \cup \Delta_E, \Delta_0^i) = \langle M^i, \Delta_{out}^i \rangle$

  iii. $\Delta \supseteq \bigcup_{i \in \mathcal{A}} \Delta_0^i$

where Δ^{-i} *is the set of all actions performed by all agents except agent* i, *namely*

$$\Delta^{-i} = \bigcup_{\substack{j \in \mathcal{A} \\ j \neq i}} \Delta(j)$$

The set Δ *is called a* stable *set for* $\langle \mathcal{A}, \mathcal{W} \rangle$.

By the previous definition, the sets $\Delta_{out}^1, \ldots, \Delta_{out}^n$, if they exist, are a solution for the set of mutually recursive equations

$$\mathcal{S}^1(\Delta^{-1} \cup \Delta_E, \Delta_0^1) = \langle M^1, \Delta_{out}^1 \rangle$$
$$\vdots$$
$$\mathcal{S}^n(\Delta^{-n} \cup \Delta_E, \Delta_0^n) = \langle M^n, \Delta_{out}^n \rangle$$

where each Δ^{-i} occurring on the left-hand side of the $i-th$ equation is defined in terms of the Δ_{out}^j sets, occurring in all the other equations. Intuitively speaking, a set of actions (by the different agents) is stable if, assuming that an "oracle" could feed each of the agents with all the actions in the set performed by the other agents (and all events happening in the world), then each agent would do exactly what is in the set, namely their observable behaviour would be exactly what the set envisages. Note that the assumption on the existence of an "oracle" is justified by the fact that we are providing a semantics for multi-agent systems, rather than relying upon their execution model.

Note that conditions *i.* and *ii.* in Definition 1 imply that $\Delta_0^i \subseteq \Delta_{out}^i$, namely that agents cannot change their initial plans. This condition could be relaxed.

3.2   Partially Transparent Multi-agent Systems

We model now multi-agent systems where each agent may have only a partial visibility of the rest of the system and of the world. We call such multi-agent systems *partially transparent*. We assume that the perception of the world by every agent i is given by $\Delta_E^i \subseteq \Delta_E$, as opposed to the whole Δ_E in Definition 1(*ii.*). Δ_E^i could be defined via a suitable projection function. Clearly, for fully transparent multi-agent systems $\Delta_E^i = \Delta_E$.

Definition 2. *A partially transparent multi-agent system $\langle \mathcal{A}, \mathcal{W} \rangle$ is stable if there exists $\Delta \subseteq \bigcup_{i \in \mathcal{A}} A(i)$ such that*

  i. $\displaystyle\bigcup_{i \in \mathcal{A}} \Delta_{out}^i = \Delta$

  ii. $\mathcal{S}^i(\Delta^{-i} \cup \Delta_E^i, \Delta_0^i) = \langle M^i, \Delta_{out}^i \rangle$

  iii. $\displaystyle\Delta \supseteq \bigcup_{i \in \mathcal{A}} \Delta_0^i$

where

$$\Delta^{-i} \subseteq \bigcup_{\substack{j \in \mathcal{A} \\ j \neq i}} \Delta(j)$$

The set Δ is called a stable *set for $\langle \mathcal{A}, \mathcal{W} \rangle$.*

Moreover, the set Δ^{-i} does not consists, in the general case, of the whole set of actions performed by other agents. Concretely, for each agent i and set $\Delta \subseteq \bigcup_{i \in \mathcal{A}} A(i)$, the set Δ^{-i} can be given by a suitable *visibility projection function* which filters out the elements of Δ that are not visible to agent i. For example

$$\Delta^{-i} = \bigcup_{\substack{j \in \mathcal{A} \\ j \neq i}} v_i^j(\Delta(j))$$

where v_i^j is the visibility projection function of agent i on agent j, expressing what agent i sees of what agent j does. Necessarily, $v_i^j(X) \subseteq X$, and, for fully transparent multi-agent systems, $v_i^j(X) = X$. Actions performed by j and not "seen" by i may be private to j, or simply not under i's jurisdiction. Note that the visible environment of i, given Δ_E and Δ, can be formally defined as

$$\mathcal{E}(i) = \Delta_E^i \cup \bigcup_{\substack{j \in \mathcal{A} \\ j \neq i}} v_i^j(\Delta(j))$$

4   Properties

In this section we define properties of individual agents, of multi-agent systems, and of agents in multi-agent systems. These properties rely upon agents having the semantics we describe in section 2 and multi-agent systems having the semantics we describe in sections 3.1 and 3.2, depending on whether they are fully or partially transparent.

4.1   Individual Agents

Definition 3. *(Successful agent)*
Assume that agent i is equipped with a set of desires G_i. We say that the agent is successful with respect to input Δ_{in} and initial plan Δ_0 (for G_i) if $\mathcal{S}^i(\Delta_{in}, \Delta_0) = \langle M, \Delta_{out} \rangle$ and $G_i \subseteq M$.

Namely, a successful agent is one that achieves its desires, in that its desires hold in the mental state of the agent. Note that our notion of success is local and subjective to the agent, namely, an agent may believe to be successful without being so in the world. Note also that, if the agent has no desires, then success amounts to its mental state being different from $\perp$. This is required also in the case of the agent being equipped with desires.

4.2   Multi-agent Systems

Definition 4. *(Overall successful system)*
$\langle \mathcal{A}, \mathcal{W} \rangle$ is overall successful wrt some Δ_E, $\Delta_0^1, \ldots, \Delta_0^n$, if there exists a stable Δ such that each i is successful, wrt Δ^{-i} and Δ_0^i.

Namely, overall success amounts to individual success for all the agents. Note that this is a rather weak notion of overall success, as it only requires for *one* successful stable set to exist. Stronger versions could also be interesting. Note also that, if agents have no desires, then overall success amounts to the existence of a stable set and to the property that no agent has $\perp$ as its mental state.

Definition 5. *(Robust system)*
An overall successful system $\langle \mathcal{A}, \mathcal{W} \rangle$ is robust if there exists no $i \in A$ such that $\langle \mathcal{A} \setminus \{i\}, \mathcal{W} \rangle$ is not.

Namely, a robust system is one that does not need any of its agents to be overall successful, or, alternatively, one in which no agent needs any of the others in order to be successful.

Definition 6. *(World-dependent system)*
$\langle \mathcal{A}, \mathcal{W} \rangle$ is world-dependent if it is not overall successful wrt $\Delta_E = \emptyset$ (and any $\Delta_0^1, \ldots, \Delta_0^n$) but it is overall successful wrt some $\Delta_E \neq \emptyset$ (and some $\Delta_0^1, \ldots, \Delta_0^n$).

Namely, a world-dependent multi-agent system is one that cannot do without the world, and events happening in it, to be successful.

4.3   Agents in Multi-agent Systems

Definition 7. *(Aware agent)*
Let $\langle \mathcal{A}, \mathcal{W} \rangle$ be a (fully or partially) transparent multi-agent system, and $i \in \mathcal{A}$. Given input Δ_{in}, initial plan Δ_0, and set of events Δ_E, let $\mathcal{S}^i(\Delta_{in}, \Delta_0) = \langle M^i, \Delta_{out}^i \rangle$. Then, we say that agent $i \in \mathcal{A}$ is

- *world aware, if $\Delta_E^i \cap \Delta_{in} \subseteq M^i$,*
- *j-aware, for some $j \in \mathcal{A}$, $j \neq i$, if $A(j) \cap \Delta_{in} \subseteq M^i$,*
- *environment aware, if it is world-aware and j-aware, for all $j \in \mathcal{A}$, $j \neq i$.*

Namely, a world-aware agent is one that holds, within its mental state, a belief of all the events that have happened in the world and that it has observed. An other-agent aware agent is one that believes in all the observations it made upon the other. An environment-aware agent is one that believes in everything it observes, including events in the world and actions by other agents it can observe.

Definition 8. *(System dependent agent)*
Let $\langle \mathcal{A}, \mathcal{W} \rangle$ be a (fully or partially) transparent multi-agent system, and $i \in \mathcal{A}$. Given Δ_E and G^i, assume that for no initial plan Δ_0, agent i is successful with respect to Δ_E and Δ_0. We say that agent i is system dependent *if there exists a stable set Δ for $\langle \mathcal{A}, \mathcal{W} \rangle$ such that agent i is successful with respect to Δ^{-i} and some initial plan Δ_0.*

Namely, a system-dependent agent is one that cannot be successful alone, but it can be successful if with other agents in a multi-agent system. Thus, this agent has a motivation to look for other agents with which to join forces.

Definition 9. *(Dispensable agent)*
Let $\langle \mathcal{A}, \mathcal{W} \rangle$ be a (fully or partially) transparent multi-agent system, and $i \in \mathcal{A}$. Agent i is dispensable within $\langle \mathcal{A}, \mathcal{W} \rangle$ if $\langle \mathcal{A} \setminus \{i\}, \mathcal{W} \rangle$ is overall successful.

Namely, a dispensable agent is one that is not needed to guarantee success of the other agents in the system. So, designers of a multi-agent systems, or individual agents having control over which agents belong to the system, could exclude any dispensable agent from it (e.g., to reduce communication costs).

Definition 10. *(Dangerous agent)*
Let $\langle \mathcal{A}, \mathcal{W} \rangle$ be a (fully or partially) transparent multi-agent system. $i \notin \mathcal{A}$ is dangerous to $\langle \mathcal{A}, \mathcal{W} \rangle$ if $\langle \mathcal{A}, \mathcal{W} \rangle$ is overall successful but $\langle \mathcal{A} \cup \{i\}, \mathcal{W} \rangle$ is not.

Namely, a dangerous agent is one that can undermine the overall success of a multi-agent system, if added to it. So, designers of a multi-agent systems, or individual agents having control over which agents belong to the system, should make sure that no dangerous agent belong to the system.

5   A Concrete Multi-agent Semantics

We illustrate our framework by means of a simple example where agents are *abductive logic agents*. Abductive logic programming has been recently used to describe agents and their interactions (see e.g., [3, 4, 5]). The semantics $\mathcal{S}$ of a single (abductive) agent is defined by means of a bottom-up construction, in the spirit of the T_p operator for logic programs [2], and adapted here for abductive logic programs. Informally, given a *"partial semantics"*, the operator returns a more defined semantics, if it exists, by adding the immediate consequences of it. The (possibly infinite) repeated application of the operator is proved to converge to a semantics which is taken as the semantics $\mathcal{S}$ of the agent. This kind of semantics is then lifted to multi-agent systems by defining a bottom-up semantics in terms of the operators of the single agents the multi-agent system is made up of. This construction of $\mathcal{S}$ is not to be interpreted as the execution model of the agent. For simplicity, we concentrate upon fully transparent multi-agent systems.

5.1   Single Agent Language and Semantics

Due to lack of space, we assume that the reader has some familiarity with abductive logic programming (ALP for short, see e.g., [6]). An agent i consists of an abductive theory $\langle P, O \cup A, IC \rangle$, where P is a logic program, $O \cup A$ is a set of *abducible atoms* partitioned in *observations* and *actions*, and IC is a set of *integrity constraints*. [1] P consists of a set of clauses of the form

$$p \leftarrow p_1, \ldots, p_n \qquad n \geq 0$$

where p is a non-abducible atom and $p_1, \ldots, p_n$ are (possibly abducible) atoms. As usual in ALP, we assume that abducibles have no definition in P. The integrity constraints IC are of the form

$$p_1, \ldots, p_n \Rightarrow false \qquad\qquad p_1, \ldots, p_n \Rightarrow a$$

where $false$ is a special symbol denoting *integrity violation*, each p_j is a (possibly abducible) atom and a is an action, namely $a \in A$. Notice that $\perp$ can occur only in the conclusion of integrity constraints. We assume that variables occurring in clauses and integrity constraints are implicitly universally quantified from the outside, with scope the entire formula in which they occur. Moreover, we assume that no variable occurs in the conclusion of an IC that does not occur in its body. As usual in logic programming, given an abductive logic agent as defined above, we will denote by $ground(P)$ (resp. $ground(IC)$) the (possibly infinite) set of all possible ground instantiations of the clauses in P (resp. of the integrity constraints in IC). Moreover, given a set of ground abducibles $\Delta \subseteq O \cup A$, we indicate with I an interpretation for $P \cup \Delta$. Roughly speaking, the semantics of an abductive theory $\langle P, O \cup A, IC \rangle$, if it exists, can be given as a pair $\langle I, \Delta \rangle$, where $\Delta \subseteq O \cup A$, I is a model of $P \cup \Delta \cup IC$ and $false \notin I$ (see e.g., [7]).

In the sequel, given an abductive logic agent, we define its input/output semantics $\mathcal{S}(\Delta_{in}, \Delta_0)$ by a suitable $\mathcal{T}$ operator, which step-wise approximates both the mental state and the observable behaviour of the agent, and which is a simple generalization of the immediate consequences operator T_P of logic programming, suitably extended in order to take integrity constraints into account.

---

[1] The sets O and A correspond to the sets $O(i)$ and $A(i)$ of Section 2, respectively.

Definition 11 ($\mathcal{T}$ **operator**). *Given an abductive logic agent* $\langle P, O \cup A, IC \rangle$, *let* $\Delta \subseteq O \cup A$ *and let* I *be an interpretation. The* $\mathcal{T}$ *operator is defined as:*

$$\mathcal{T}(I, \Delta) = \langle I', \Delta' \rangle$$

where:
$I' = \{p \mid p \leftarrow l_1, \ldots l_n \in ground(P) \land \{l_1, \ldots l_n\} \subseteq I \cup \Delta\},$
$\Delta' = \Delta \cup \{a \in A \cup \{false\} \mid l_1, \ldots l_n \Rightarrow a \in ground(IC) \land \{l_1, \ldots l_n\} \subseteq I \cup \Delta\}.$

It is not difficult to see that the $\mathcal{T}$ operator is monotonic. For simplicity, in the sequel we use $\subseteq$ to denote pairwise set inclusion.

Lemma 1 ($\mathcal{T}$ **is monotonic**). *Let be* $\langle I_1, \Delta_1 \rangle \subseteq \langle I_2, \Delta_2 \rangle$, *then:*

$$\mathcal{T}(I_1, \Delta_1) \subseteq \mathcal{T}(I_2, \Delta_2).$$

Proof. Let $\mathcal{T}(I_1, \Delta_1) = \langle I'_1, \Delta'_1 \rangle$ and $\mathcal{T}(I_2, \Delta_2) = \langle I'_2, \Delta'_2 \rangle$. We show that $I'_1 \subseteq I'_2$ (the proof of $\Delta'_1 \subseteq \Delta'_2$ is analogous). Let $p \in I'_1$. Then there exists a clause in $ground(P)$ of the form $p \leftarrow l_1, \ldots l_n$ such that $\{l_1, \ldots l_n\} \subseteq I_1 \cup \Delta_1$. Since, by hypothesis, $I_1 \cup \Delta_1 \subseteq I_2 \cup \Delta_2$, $\{l_1, \ldots l_n\} \subseteq I_2 \cup \Delta_2$ and hence $p \in I'_2$. □

The monotonicity of $\mathcal{T}$ ensures that, given a set of observations $\Delta_{in} \subseteq O$ and an initial plan $\Delta_0 \subseteq A$, we can define the semantics of an abductive logic agent i in terms of the least fix-point of the $\mathcal{T}$ operator, that we denote by $\mathcal{T}_\infty(\emptyset, \Delta_{in} \cup \Delta_0)$, starting from the initial pair $\langle \emptyset, \Delta_{in} \cup \Delta_0 \rangle$.

Definition 12. *Given an abductive logic agent* i, *an initial set of observations* Δ_{in} *and an initial plan* Δ_0, *let* $\mathcal{T}_\infty(\emptyset, \Delta_{in} \cup \Delta_0) = \langle M, \Delta \rangle$. *Then*

$$S^i(\Delta_{in}, \Delta_0) = \begin{cases} \langle M, \Delta(i) \rangle & \text{if } false \notin M \\ \langle \perp, \Delta(i) \rangle & \text{otherwise} \end{cases}$$

Example: A Concrete Agent. Consider a simple agent 1 who can achieve some goal g by asking to get a resource from a friend (we assume that resources can be shared amongst agents and be re-used as many times as required). This simplifying assumption allows us to present our model within a monotonic framework. Agent 1 believes that agent 2 is a friend. Agent 1 can observe that another agent gives something to it and can perform the actions of paying and thanking. It is forced to thank a friend or pay an enemy for a received resource.

P: $g \leftarrow friend(Y), ask(1, Y, r), getfrom(Y, r)$ O: $give(Y, 1, r)$
   $getfrom(Y, r) \leftarrow give(Y, 1, r)$ A: $thank(1, Y)$
   $friend(2)$ $pay(1, Y)$
IC: $give(Y, 1, r), friend(Y) \Rightarrow thanks(1, Y)$ $ask(1, Y, r)$
   $give(Y, 1, r), enemy(Y) \Rightarrow pay(1, Y)$

We also assume here an implicit treatment of time, so that an asking action is performed before the asked resource is obtained.

Let us imagine that the agent has the initial plan to ask for the resource from agent 2, i.e., $ask(1,2,r) \in \Delta_0$, and that agent 2 is actually giving the owned resource to 1, as confirmed by the observation $give(2,1,r) \in \Delta_{in}$. The semantics of the agent is then defined as follows (note that in this case the fix-point has been reached in few iterations):

$$\mathcal{T}_1(\emptyset, \{give(2,1,r), ask(1,2,r)\}) =$$
$$\langle \{friend(2), getfrom(2,r)\}, \{give(2,1,r), ask(1,2,r)\}\rangle$$
$$\mathcal{T}_2(\emptyset, \{give(2,1,r), ask(1,2,r)\}) =$$
$$\langle \{friend(2), getfrom(2,r), g\}, \{give(2,1,r), ask(1,2,r)\}\rangle$$
$$\mathcal{T}_3(\emptyset, \{give(2,1,r), ask(1,2,r)\}) =$$
$$\langle \{friend(2), getfrom(2,r), g\}, \{give(2,1,r), ask(1,2,r), thank(1,2)\}\rangle$$
$$\mathcal{T}_4(\emptyset, \{give(2,1,r), ask(1,2,r)\}) = \mathcal{T}_3(\emptyset, \{give(2,1,r), ask(1,2,r)\})$$

that is, the agent satisfies its goal g. In the notation of Section 3.1:

$$\mathcal{S}^1(\{give(2,1,r)\}, \{ask(1,2,r)\}) =$$
$$\langle \{friend(2), getfrom(2,r), g\}, \{ask(1,2,r), thank(1,2)\}\rangle.$$

Instead, considering the case in which agent 1 asks another agent not believed to be a friend, say agent 3 that behaves as agent 2, it still acquires the resource, but fails its goal g:

$$\mathcal{S}^1(\{give(2,1,r)\}, \{ask(1,3,r)\}) =$$
$$\langle \{friend(2), getfrom(2,r)\}, \{ask(1,3,r), thank(1,2)\}\rangle.$$

5.2   Multi-agent Semantics

A fully transparent multi-agent system, as defined in Section 3.1, can consist of agents whose concrete semantics is the one defined in Section 5.1. We first show a simple example of the resulting semantics for a multi-agent system consisting of agent 1 previously introduced, and two new agents. Then, we define an operational bottom-up semantics for the multi-agent system, by lifting the single agent semantics. Semantics hence consists of a set of mutually recursive $\mathcal{T}^j$, one for each agent participating into the system. Finally, we prove that, under specific circumstances, the operational semantics entails the one defined in Section 3.1.

Example: A Fully Transparent Multi-agent System. Let us consider a system consisting of agent 1 of Section 1, together with agents 2 and 3, as below defined:

2:
  P: $have(r) \leftarrow offer(Y,2,r)$
  A: $give(2,X,r)$
  O: $ask(X,2,r)$
      $offer(Y,2,r)$
  IC: $ask(X,2,r), have(r) \Rightarrow give(2,X,r)$

3:
  P: $friend(2)$
      $have(r)$
  A: $offer(3,X,r)$
  IC: $have(r), friend(X) \Rightarrow$
      $offer(3,X,r)$

Agent 2 has a resource if it observes that the resource has been offered by someone. In this case the agent is forced to give the resource to anybody who requires it. Agent

3 has the resource and a friend, and it must give the owned resource to the friend. Agent 1 is the only agent having a goal, g namely, while all the others have a reactive behaviour with respect to (their representation of) the world and the behaviour of the other agents. Given their knowledge bases, agents are able to cooperate and allow agent 1 to accomplish its goal, as soon as it adopts the initial plan to ask for the resource ($\Delta_0^1 = \{ask(1, 2, r)\}$).

Assuming that no other information is provided by the environment $\Delta_E = \emptyset$, and that agents 2 and 3 have empty initial plans, $\Delta_0^2 = \Delta_0^3 = \emptyset$,

$$\Delta = \{ask(1, 2, r), give(2, 1, r), thank(1, 2), offer(3, 2, r)\}$$

is a *stable set* for the multi-agent system $\langle \mathcal{A} = \{1, 2, 3\}, \mathcal{W}\rangle$ with $E(\mathcal{W}) = \emptyset$. Indeed, we have

$$\mathcal{S}^1(\Delta^{-1}, \{ask(1, 2, r)\}) = \langle\{g, friend(2), getfrom(2, r)\},$$
$$\{\mathbf{ask(1, 2, r)}, \mathbf{thank(1, 2)}\}\rangle$$
$$\mathcal{S}^2(\Delta^{-2}, \emptyset) = \langle\{have(r)\}, \{\mathbf{give(2, 1, r)}\}\rangle$$
$$\mathcal{S}^3(\Delta^{-3}, \emptyset) = \langle\{friend(2), have(r)\}, \{\mathbf{offer(3, 2, r)}\}\rangle$$

and $\bigcup_{i \in \mathcal{A}} \Delta_{out}^i = \Delta \supseteq \bigcup_{i \in \mathcal{A}} \Delta_0^i$, where Δ_{out}^i are boldface. Notice how some of the *actions* performed by an agent are interpreted as *observations* by the other agents (e.g., $ask(1, 2, r)$ for agents 1 and 2, respectively).

The multi-agent system is thus *overall successful*, but it is not *robust* (e.g., 2 is needed for the overall success of the system, and so is 3). Agent 1 is *system-dependent*, whereas agents 2, 3 are not. Finally, $\langle \mathcal{A} = \{1, 2, 3\}, \mathcal{W}\rangle$ is obviously not *world-dependent*.

5.3   Fully Transparent Multi-agent System Operational Semantics

Similarly to the case of the single agent operational semantics presented in Section 5.1, also multi-agent system can be provided with a bottom-up semantics in the case of the simple agent language taken into account. The semantics of a system builds upon the semantic operators T^i of the single agents i belonging to the system. The overall semantics is then obtained by the mutual interaction of agent semantics, where each application of the semantic operators takes into account not only the single agent so-far approximated, but also the observable semantics, namely the actions, produced up to now by the repeated application of the semantic operators of the other agents. In this way, agents "react" to the output actions by the other agents in the system as soon as they are observed.

The operational counterpart of $S^j(\Delta_{in}^j, \Delta_0^j)$ within the context of the chosen language, is defined on top of the single agent operational semantics as a class of mutually recursive operators, which step-wise approximate the semantics of the system. In the following we will use the short-hand $\langle \overline{I}, \overline{\Delta}\rangle$ for the tuple $\langle\langle I^1, \Delta^1\rangle, \ldots, \langle I^n, \Delta^n\rangle\rangle$, where $1, \ldots, n$ are the agents in $\mathcal{A}$. On the other hand, when clear from the context, $\langle I^i, \Delta^i\rangle$ will denote the i–th component of the tuple $\langle \overline{I}, \overline{\Delta}\rangle$. Finally, given two tuples $\langle \overline{I}, \overline{\Delta}\rangle$ and $\langle \overline{J}, \overline{\Gamma}\rangle$, we will write $\langle \overline{I}, \overline{\Delta}\rangle \subseteq \langle \overline{J}, \overline{\Gamma}\rangle$ as a shorthand for the conjunction $\langle I^1, \Delta^1\rangle \subseteq \langle J^1, \Gamma^1\rangle \wedge \ldots \langle I^n, \Delta^n\rangle \subseteq \langle J^n, \Gamma^n\rangle$.

For simplicity, in this section we consider multi-agent systems where the world component $\mathcal{W}$ is not present. Hence, in the sequel we refer to a multi-agent system consisting only of a set $\mathcal{A}$, where each agent i is an abductive logic agent $\langle P_i, O_i \cup A_i, IC_i \rangle$ (as introduced in Section 5.1). For each agent $i \in \mathcal{A}$ we denote by T^i its operator as defined in Definition 11.

Definition 13 ($T^{\mathcal{A}}$). *Let* $\mathcal{A} = \{1, \ldots, n\}$, I^i *and* Δ^i *be an interpretation and a subset of abducibles for each agent* i, *respectively. The* $T_{\mathcal{A}}$ *operator is defined as follows*

$$T_{\mathcal{A}}(\overline{I}, \overline{\Delta}) = \langle \overline{J}, \overline{\Gamma} \rangle$$

where for each i,

$$\langle J^i, \Gamma^i \rangle = T^i(I^i, \Delta^i \cup \Delta^{-i})$$

where $\Delta^{-i} = \bigcup_{j \in \mathcal{A}, \; j \neq i} \Delta^j(j)$.

It is not difficult to show that the operator $T_{\mathcal{A}}$ is monotonic.

Lemma 2 ($T^{\mathcal{A}}$ **is monotonic**).
Let $\langle \overline{I}, \overline{\Delta} \rangle$ *and* $\langle \overline{J}, \overline{\Gamma} \rangle$ *be such that* $\langle \overline{I}, \overline{\Delta} \rangle \subseteq \langle \overline{J}, \overline{\Gamma} \rangle$. *Then*

$$T_{\mathcal{A}}(\overline{I}, \overline{\Delta}) \subseteq T_{\mathcal{A}}(\overline{J}, \overline{\Gamma}).$$

Proof. Let:

- $\langle \overline{I_1}, \overline{\Delta_1} \rangle = T_{\mathcal{A}}(\overline{I}, \overline{\Delta})$
- $\langle \overline{J_1}, \overline{\Gamma_1} \rangle = T_{\mathcal{A}}(\overline{J}, \overline{\Gamma})$

We need to show that, for each i, $\langle I_1^i, \Delta_1^i \rangle \subseteq \langle J_1^i, \Gamma_1^i \rangle$. By definition, for all i, $\langle I_1^i, \Delta_1^i \rangle = T^i(I^i, \Delta^i \cup \Delta^{-i})$. By the hypothesis $\langle \overline{I}, \overline{\Delta} \rangle \subseteq \langle \overline{J}, \overline{\Gamma} \rangle$, it is clear that $\Delta^{-i} \subseteq \Gamma^{-i}$ and hence $\langle I_1^i, \Delta_1^i \rangle = \langle I^i, \Delta^i \cup \Delta^{-i} \rangle \subseteq \langle J^i, \Gamma^i \cup \Gamma^{-i} \rangle$. By the monotonicity of T^i it follows that $T^i(I^i, \Delta^i \cup \Delta^{-i}) \subseteq T^i(J^i, \Gamma^i \cup \Gamma^{-i}) = \langle J_1^i, \Gamma_1^i \rangle$. □

The monotonicity of $T^{\mathcal{A}}$ allows us to give a bottom-up characterisation of the semantics of a multi-agent system as a whole, similarly to what we have done in Definition 12 for a single agent. In the next definition we denote by $T_{\infty}^{\mathcal{A}}(\overline{\emptyset}, \overline{\Delta_0})$ the least fix-point of $T^{\mathcal{A}}$, obtained by repeatedly applying it starting from the initial tuple $\langle \overline{\emptyset}, \overline{\Delta_0} \rangle$, where, for each i, Δ_0^i is a (possibly empty) initial plan for the agent i.

Definition 14. *Given a multi-agent system* $\mathcal{A}$, *and and initial plan* Δ_0^i *for each* $i \in \mathcal{A}$, *let* $\langle \overline{I}, \overline{\Delta} \rangle = T_{\infty}^{\mathcal{A}}(\overline{\emptyset}, \overline{\Delta_0})$. *Then the* concrete semantics $\mathcal{S}^{\mathcal{A}}(\overline{\Delta_0})$ *of the system is defined as follows:*

$$\mathcal{S}^{\mathcal{A}}(\overline{\Delta_0}) = \langle \overline{I}, \overline{\Delta} \rangle$$

Notice that the semantics of the system as a whole is defined even if the semantics of some or all of the agents in the system is undefined. This is somewhat an arbitrary decision, that could be changed according to the needs of applications.

Example: A Fully Transparent Multi-agent System Concrete Semantics. We show how the operator $\mathcal{T}^A$ behaves in the case of the multi-agent system of Section 5.2. The process is summed up by the following table, where rows represent the iteration steps and columns represent the agents. In the example, the initial plans are empty as far as agents 2 and 3 are concerned, whereas the initial plan of agent 1 consists of asking to agent 2 for the resource. We highlight in boldface the pairs $\langle I^i, \Delta^i \rangle$ which do not change in the future iterations. Hence the operator's fix-point is obtained by the tuple composed by the boldface pairs.

1	2	3
$\langle \{friend(2)\}, \{ask(1,2,r)\} \rangle$	$\langle \emptyset, \emptyset \rangle$	$\langle \{friend(2), have(r)\},$ $\{\} \rangle$
$\langle \{friend(2)\}, \{ask(1,2,r)\} \rangle$	$\langle \emptyset, \{ask(1,2,r)\} \rangle$	$\langle \{\mathbf{friend(2)}, \mathbf{have(r)}\},$ $\{\mathbf{offer(3,2,r)}\} \rangle$
$\langle \{friend(2)\}, \{ask(1,2,r)\} \rangle$	$\langle \{have(r)\}, \{ask(1,2,r),$ $offer(3,2,r)\} \rangle$	
$\langle \{friend(2)\}, \{ask(1,2,r)\} \rangle$	$\langle \{\mathbf{have(r)}\}, \{\mathbf{ask(1,2,r)},$ $\mathbf{offer(3,2,r)}, \mathbf{give(2,1,r)}\} \rangle$	
$\langle \{friend(2), getfrom(2,r)\},$ $\{ask(1,2,r), give(2,1,r),$ $thank(1,2)\} \rangle$		
$\langle \{\mathbf{friend(2)}, \mathbf{getfrom(2,r)}, \mathbf{g}\},$ $\{\mathbf{ask(1,2,r)}, \mathbf{give(2,1,r)},$ $\mathbf{thank(1,2)}, \mathbf{g}\} \rangle$		

From the fix-point, we can extract the set

$$\Delta = \{ask(1,2,r), give(2,1,r), thank(1,2), offer(3,2,r)\}$$

of the actions performed by each agent (and hence their single semantics). It is worth noting that this set coincides with the stable set shown in Section 5.2.

Indeed, we conjecture that a stable set can be constructed from the fix-points of the operator $\mathcal{T}^A$. If this is the case, the latter can be seen as a way of incrementally building stable sets for the multi-agent system.

6   Related Work

Viroli and Omicini in [8] view a multi-agent system (MAS) as the composition of observable systems. The focus on observation is based, like in our framework, on the assumption that the hidden part of an agent manifests itself through interactions with the environment, and on how an agent makes its internal state perceivable in the outside. However, our work further distinguishes between different kinds of environment accessibility by agents through the use of visibility projection functions used by these agents. In addition, we combine observable behaviour with the mental state of the agent, so as to permit to have partial access to the mental state of an agent in order to prove properties that are useful to a MAS, e.g. by allowing MAS designers to tests the desires against the mental state of an agent, without necessarily revealing/computing the full mental state.

Wooldridge and Lomuscio in [9] define a family of multi-modal logics for reasoning about the information properties of situated computational agents. They distinguish between what is objectively true in the environment, which in our approach is defined by what holds true in the world, the information that is visible, which our approach does not provide, information that an agent perceives, as with our observations, and finally information that the agent knows of the environment, which in our framework is defined by the mental state of an agent. Apart from the fact that we do not use a modal logic semantics, we also differ in the way we understand an environment. Wooldridge and Lomuscio's work is based on a definition often found in distributed systems [10], in that an environment does not contain the other agents (a bit like our notion of world). Instead in our approach the environment of an agent contains the state of the world and the other agents, and is closer to [11].

Another related approach to our work, presented by Ashri et al. in [12], is the identification and management of relationships in MASs. A formal model of the different kinds of relationships formed between interacting agents is presented and the way such relationships impact the overall system functioning is being investigated. If relationships between agents can be seen as properties, their work is similar to ours in that it attempts to identify properties in relation to observable parts of the environment in an application neutral manner. In this context, their way of managing relationships using control mechanisms can be thought in our terms as the required mechanisms that can be used to compute the semantics. However, Ashri et al. focus more on finding dependencies and influences between agent actions in the environment and less upon our concern of proving properties using the notion of stability.

Computational Logic approaches for formally describing and understanding MASs systems have been proposed in the past, e.g. [13, 14, 15], and are being pursued currently, possibly enhanced with other techniques, like Temporal Model Checking in [16]. Closer to our work is the work on the ALIAS system [17, 13], which relies on abductive logic programming to define a MAS. One major difference between ALIAS and our work is that agents in ALIAS have all the part of their mental states public, while in our approach part of the mental state needs to be public to the designer only.

7   Conclusions

We have proposed a semantics for multi-agent systems and a catalogue of properties for individual agents, multi-agent systems, and agents in multi-agent systems that we believe to be useful to aid the designers of concrete applications. Our semantics is fully declarative and abstract, and does not rely upon any concrete agent architecture or model, except for assuming that the semantics of individual agents is given in terms of their (public) observable behaviour and (private) mental state. We have illustrated the proposed notions for concrete abductive logic agents, whose beliefs are held within an abductive logic program, and whose mental state and observable behaviour is given by adapting the T_p operator for logic programming. We have adopted a qualitative approach to the definition of success of agents, rather than assuming they are equipped with quantitative utility functions. The resulting model is not based upon game-theoretic concepts, but it would be interesting to compare/integrate our approach with that theory, e.g., comparing our notion of stable set with that of Nash equilibrium.

Other notions of individual welfare, different from the notion of individual success, would also be interesting. For example, we could consider maximising the number of achieved goals. Also, rather than having a "yes-no" kind success, we could compare multi-agent systems in terms of how close to success they are.

As future work, we plan to investigate the relationships between fix-points of the T^A operator, i.e., the concrete semantics of a multi-agent system, and stable sets of A, as described in the final example of Section 5.3. A further important problem for future studies is that of identifying means for the automatic verification of properties of multi-agent systems, in terms of properties of the individual agents composing them. This would aid the effective design of the such systems for the solution of concrete problems. Additional, less simplistic instances of our framework would also be interesting, e.g., 3APL agents [18]. In particular, we plan to adopt this framework for KGP agents, as defined in [19], and study the problem of properties verification in that context.

Acknowledgments

We would like to thank the anonymous referees for their valuable comments. This work has been supported by the SOCS project (IST-2001-32530), funded under the EU Global Computing initiative. The last two authors would also like to acknowledge support from the Italian programme "Rientro dei cervelli".

References

1. Sadri, F., Toni, F., Torroni, P.: Dialogues for negotiation: agent varieties and dialogue sequences. In: Intelligent Agents VIII: 8th International Workshop, ATAL 2001, LNAI 2333, Springer-Verlag (2002)
2. Apt, K.R.: Logic programming. In: Handbook of Theoretical Computer Science. Volume B. Elsevier Science Publishers (1990) 493–574
3. Kowalski, R.A., Sadri, F.: From logic programming towards multi-agent systems. Annals of Mathematics and Artificial Intelligence 25 (1999) 391–419
4. Sadri, F., Toni, F., Torroni, P.: An abductive logic programming architecture for negotiating agents. In Greco, S., Leone, N., eds.: Proceedings of the 8th European Conference on Logics in Artificial Intelligence (JELIA), LNCS 2424, Springer-Verlag (2002)
5. Toni, F., Stathis, K.: Access-as-you-need: a computational logic framework for flexible resource access in artificial societies. In: Proceedings of the Third International Workshop on Engineering Societies in the Agents World (ESAW'02), LNAI 2577, Springer-Verlag (2002)
6. Kakas, A., Kowalski, R.A., Toni, F.: Abductive Logic Programming. Journal of Logic and Computation 2 (1993) 719–770
7. Kakas, A., Mancarella, P.: Generalized stable models: a semantics for abduction. In: Proc. 9th European Conference on Artificial Intelligence, Pitman Pub. (1990)

8. Viroli, M., Omicini, A.: Multi-agent systems as composition of observable systems. In Omicini, A., Viroli, M., eds.: AI*IA/TABOO Workshop - Dagli oggetti agli agenti: tendenze evolutive dei sistemi software" (WOA 2001). (2001)

9. Wooldridge, M., Lomuscio, A.: A logic of visibility, perception, and knowledge: completeness and correspondence results. Journal of the IGPL **9** (2001)

10. Fagin, R., Halpern, J.Y., Moses, Y., Vardi, M.Y.: Reasoning About Knowledge. MIT Press (1995)

11. Abramsky, S.:   Semantics of Interaction.   (Technical report) Available at `http://www.dcs.ed.ac.uk/home/samson/coursenotes.ps.gz`.

12. Ashri, R., Luck, M., d'Inverno, M.: On identifying and managing relationships in multi-agent systems. In: Proc. of 18th International Joint Conference on Artificial Intelligence (IJCAI03), Acapulco, Mexico (2003)

13. Ciampolini, A., Lamma, E., Mello, P., Toni, F., Torroni, P.: Co-operation and competition in *ALIAS*: a logic framework for agents that negotiate. Computational Logic in Multi-Agent Systems. Annals of Mathematics and Artificial Intelligence **37** (2003) 65–91

14. Alferes, J., Brogi, A., Leite, J.A., Pereira, L.M.: Computing environment-aware agent behaviours with logic program updates. In Pettorossi, A., ed.: Logic Based Program Synthesis and Transformation, 11th International Workshop, (LOPSTR'01), LNCS 2372, Springer-Verlag (2002)

15. Alferes, J.J., Brogi, A., Leite, J.A., Pereira, L.M.: Evolving logic programs. In Flesca, S., Greco, S., Leone, N., Ianni, G., eds.: Proceedings of the 8th European Conference on Logics in Artificial Intelligence (JELIA'02), LNAI 2424, Springer-Verlag (2002)

16. Pokorny, L.R., Ramakrishnan, C.R.: Modeling and verification of distributed autonomous agents using logic programming. In: Proceedings of the Workshop on Declarative Agent Languages and Technologies (DALT'04), LNCS 3476, Springer-Verlag (2005). In this volume.

17. Ciampolini, A., Lamma, E., Mello, P., Torroni, P.: Rambling abductive agents in ALIAS. In: Proc. ICLP Workshop on Multi-Agent Sytems in Logic Programming (MAS'99), Las Cruces, New Mexico (1999)

18. Dastani, M., de Boer, F.S., Dignum, F., van der Hoek, W., Kroese, M., Meyer, J.C.: Programming the deliberation cycle of cognitive robots. In: Proc. of 3rd International Cognitive Robotics Workshop (CogRob) (2002)

19. Kakas, A., Mancarella, P., Sadri, F., Stathis, K., Toni, F.: The KGP model of agency. In: Proceedings of the 16th European Conference on Artificial Intelligence (ECAI), Valencia, Spain (2004)

The Semantics of MALLET–An Agent Teamwork Encoding Language

Xiaocong Fan[1], John Yen[1], Michael S. Miller[2], and Richard A. Volz[2]

[1] School of Information Sciences and Technology,
The Pennsylvania State University, University Park, PA 16802
[2] Department of Computer Science,
Texas A&M University, College Station, TX 77843
{zfan, jyen}@ist.psu.edu, {mmiller, volz}@cs.tamu.edu

Abstract. MALLET is a team-oriented agent specification and programming language. In this paper, we define an operational semantics for MALLET in terms of a transition system. The semantics can be used to guide the implementation of MALLET interpreters, and to formally study the properties of team-based agents specified in MALLET.

1 Introduction

Agent teamwork has been the focus of a great deal of research in both theories [1, 2, 3, 4] and practices [5, 6, 7, 8]. A team is a group of agents having a shared objective and a shared mental state [2]. While the notion of joint goal (joint intention) provides the glue that binds team members together, it is not sufficient to guarantee that cooperative problem solving will ensue [3]. The agreement of a common recipe among team members is essential for them to achieve their shared objective in an effective and collaborative way [4]. Languages for specifying common recipes (plans) and other teamwork related knowledge are thus highly needed both for agent designers to specify and implement cohesive teamwork behaviors, and for agents themselves to easily interpret and manipulate the mutually committed course of actions so that they could collaborate smoothly both when everything is progressing as planned and when something goes wrong unexpectedly.

The term "team-oriented programming" has been used to refer to both the idea of using a meta-language to describe team behaviors (based on mutual beliefs, joint plans and social structures) [9] and the effort of using a reusable team wrapper for supporting rapid development of agent teams from existing heterogeneous distributed agents [10, 11]. In this paper, we take the former meaning and focus on the semantics of an agent teamwork encoding language called MALLET (Multi-Agent Logic Language for Encoding Teamwork), which has been developed and used in the CAST (Collaborative Agents for Simulating Teamwork) system [8] to specify agents' individual and teamwork behaviors.

There have been several efforts in defining languages for describing team activities [12, 13, 3]. What distinguishes MALLET from the existing efforts is two-

J. Leite et al. (Eds.): DALT 2004, LNAI 3476, pp. 69–91, 2005.

fold. First, MALLET is a generic language for encoding teamwork knowledge. Teamwork knowledge may include both declarative knowledge and procedural knowledge. Declarative knowledge (knowing "that") describes objects, events, and their relationships. Procedural knowledge (knowing "how") focuses on the way needed to obtain a result, where the control information for using the knowledge is embedded in the knowledge itself. MALLET supports the specification of both declarative and procedural teamwork knowledge. For instance, MALLET has reserved keywords for specifying team structure-related knowledge (such as who are in a team, what roles an agent can play) as well as inference knowledge (in terms of horn-clauses).

Second, MALLET is a richer language for encoding teamwork process. MALLET has constructs for specifying control flows (e.g., sequential, conditional, iterative) in a team process. Tidhar also adopted such an synthesized approach [9], where the notions of social structure and plan structure respectively correspond to the team structure and team process in our term. While MALLET does not describe team structure in the command and control dimension as Tidhar did, it is more expressive than the simple OR-AND plan graphs and thus more suitable for describing complex team processes. In addition, MALLET allows the constraints for task assignments, preconditions of actions, dynamic agent selection, decision points within a process and termination conditions of a process to be explicitly specified. The recipe language used in [3] lacks the support for specifying decision points in a process, which is often desirable in dealing with uncertainty. While OR nodes of a plan graph [9] can be used for such a purpose, the language cannot specify processes with complex execution orders. Team/agent selection (i.e., the process of selecting a group of agents that have complimentary skills to achieve a given goal) is a key activity for effective collaboration [14]. No existing languages except MALLET allow the task of agent-selection to be explicitly specified in a team process. Using MALLET, a group of agents can collaboratively recruit doers for the subsequent activities based on the constraints associated with agent-selection statements.

The structure of this paper is as follows. Section 2 gives the syntax of MALLET and Section 3 gives some preparations. We give the transition semantics in Section 4, and in Section 5 introduce the CAST architecture, which has implemented a MALLET interpreter. Section 6 gives comparisons and discussions and Section 7 concludes the paper.

2   Syntax

The syntax of MALLET is given in Table 1. A MALLET specification is composed of definitions for agents, teams, membership of a team, team goals, initial team activities, agent capabilities, roles, roles each agent can play, agents playing a certain role, individual operators, team operators, plans (recipes), and inference rules.

Operators are atomic domain actions, each of which is associated with preconditions and effects. Individual operators are supposed to be carried out by

Table 1. The Abstract Syntax of MALLET

CompilationUnit ::=	(AgentDef	TeamDef	MemberOf	GoalDef	Start	
	CapabilityDef	RoleDef	PlaysRole	FulfilledBy	
	IOperDef	TOperDef	PlanDef	RuleDecl)*
AgentDef ::=	'(' ⟨AGENT⟩ AgentName ')'
TeamDef ::=	'(' ⟨TEAM⟩ TeamName ('(' (AgentName)+ ')')? ')'
MemberOf ::=	'(' ⟨MEMBEROF⟩ AgentName
	(TeamName	'(' (TeamName)+ ')') ')'
GoalDef ::=	'(' ⟨GOAL⟩ AgentOrTeamName (Cond)+ ')'
Start ::=	'(' ⟨START⟩ AgentOrTeamName Invocation ')'
CapabilityDef ::=	'(' ⟨CAPABILITY⟩ (AgentName	'(' (AgentName)+')')
	(Invocation	'(' (Invocation)+ ')') ')'
RoleDef ::=	'(' ⟨ROLE⟩ RoleName (Invocation	'('(Invocation)+')')')'
PlaysRole ::=	'(' ⟨PLAYSROLE⟩ AgentName '(' (RoleName)+ ')' ')'
FulfilledBy ::=	'(' ⟨FULFILLEDBY⟩ RoleName '(' (AgentName)+ ')' ')'
IOperDef ::=	'(' ⟨IOPER⟩ OperName '(' (⟨Variable⟩)* ')'
	(PreConditionList)* (EffectsList)? ')'
TOperDef ::=	'(' ⟨TOPER⟩ OperName '(' (⟨Variable⟩)* ')'
	(PreConditionList)* (EffectsList)? (NumSpec)? ')'
PlanDef ::=	'(' ⟨PLAN⟩ PlanName '(' (⟨Variable⟩)* ')'
	(PreConditionList | EffectsList | TermConditionList)*
	'(' ⟨PROCESS⟩ MalletProcess ')' ')'
RuleDecl ::=	'(' (Pred)+ ')'
Cond ::=	Pred	'(' ⟨NOT⟩ Cond ')'
Pred ::=	'(' ⟨IDENTIFIER⟩ (⟨IDENTIFIER⟩ | ⟨VARIABLE⟩)* ')'
Invocation ::=	'('PlanOrOperName (⟨IDENTIFIER⟩ | ⟨VARIABLE⟩)* ')'
PreConditionList ::=	'(' ⟨PRECOND⟩ (Cond)+ (':IF-FALSE' (⟨SKIP⟩	
	⟨FAIL⟩	⟨WAIT-SKIP⟩ ((⟨DIGIT⟩)+)?	
	⟨WAIT-FAIL⟩ ((⟨DIGIT⟩)+)?	
	⟨ACHIEVE-SKIP⟩	⟨ACHIEVE-FAIL⟩))? ')'
EffectsList ::=	'(' ⟨EFFECTS⟩ (Cond)+ ')'
TermConditionList ::=	'('⟨TERMCOND⟩ ((⟨SUCCESS-SKIP>⟩	
	⟨SUCCESS-FAIL>⟩	⟨FAILURE-SKIP⟩	
	⟨FAILURE-FAIL⟩)? (Cond)+')'
NumSpec ::=	'(' ⟨NUM⟩ ('='|' <'|' >'|' ≤'|' ≥') (⟨DIGIT⟩)+ ')'
PrefCondList ::=	'(' ⟨PREFCOND⟩ (Cond)+ (':IF-FALSE' (⟨FAIL⟩	
	⟨WAIT⟩ ((⟨DIGIT⟩)+)?	⟨ACHIEVE⟩))? ')'
Priority ::=	'('⟨PRIORITY⟩ (⟨DIGIT⟩)+ ')'
ByWhom ::=	AgentOrTeamName	⟨VARIABLE⟩	MixedList
MixedList ::=	'(' (⟨IDENTIFIER⟩ | ⟨VARIABLE⟩)+ ')'
Branch ::=	'('(PrefCondList)?(Priority)? '('⟨DO⟩ByWhom Invocation')'")'
MalletProcess ::=	Invocation	'('⟨DO⟩ ByWhom MalletProcess ')'
		'('⟨AGENTBIND⟩ VariableList '(' (Cond)+ ')' ')'
		'('⟨JOINTDO⟩ (⟨AND⟩	⟨OR⟩	⟨XOR⟩)?
	('(' ByWhom MalletProcess ')')+ ')'
		'('⟨SEQ⟩ (MalletProcess)+ ')'
		'('⟨PAR⟩ (MalletProcess)+ ')'
		'('⟨IF⟩'('⟨COND⟩(Cond)+')'MalletProcess(MalletProcess)?')'
		'('⟨WHILE⟩ '(' ⟨COND⟩ (Cond)+ ')' MalletProcess ')'
		'('⟨FOREACH⟩ '(' ⟨COND⟩ (Cond)+')'MalletProcess')'
		'('⟨FORALL⟩ '(' ⟨COND⟩ (Cond)+ ')'MalletProcess')'
		'('⟨CHOICE⟩ (Branch)+ ')'

only one agent independently, while team operators can only be invoked by more than one agent who play specific roles as required by the operators. Before doing a team action, all the involving agents should synchronize their activities and satisfy the corresponding preconditions.

Plans are decomposable higher-level actions, which are built upon lower-level atomic operators hierarchically. Plans play the same role as recipes in the SharedPlan theory. A plan in MALLET specifies which agents (variables), under what pre-conditions, can achieve what effects by following what a process, and optionally under what conditions the execution of the plan can be terminated.

The process component of a plan plays essential role in supporting coordinations among team members. A process can be specified using constructs such as sequential (SEQ), parallel (PAR), iterative (WHILE, FOREACH, FORALL), conditional (IF) and choice (CHOICE). An invocation statement is used to directly execute an action or invoke a plan; since there is no associated doer specification, each agent coming to such a statement will do it individually. A DO process is composed of a doer specification and an embedded process. An agent coming to a DO statement has to check if itself belongs to the doer specification. If so, the agent simply does the action and moves on; otherwise the agent waits until being informed of the ending of the action. A joint-do process (JOINTDO) specifies a share type (i.e., *AND, OR, XOR*) and a list of (*ByWhom process*) pairs. A joint-do of share type "*AND*" requires all the involved agents acting simultaneously— the joint-do succeeds only after all the pairs have be executed successfully. For an "*XOR*", exactly one must be executed to avoid potential conflicts, and for an "*OR*", at least one must be executed (with no potential conflicts). An agent-bind statement is used to dynamically select agents satisfying certain constraints (e.g., finding an agent that is capable of some role or action). An agent-bind statement becomes eligible for execution at the point when progress of the embedding plan has reached it, as opposed to being executed when the plan is entered. The scope for the binding to a variable extends to either the end of the embedding plan, or the beginning of the next agent-bind statement that also binds this variable, whichever comes first.

3   Preparation

The following notational conventions are adopted. We use i, j, k, m, n as indexes; a's [1] to denote individual agents; A's to denote sets of agents; b's to denote beliefs; g's to denote goals; h's to denote intentions; ρ's to denote plan templates; p's to denote plan preconditions; q's to denote plan effects; e's to denote plan termination-conditions; β's and α's to denote individual operators; Γ's to denote team operators; s's and l's to denote Mallet process statements; ψ's and ϕ's to denote first-order formulas; t's to denote terms; bold $\boldsymbol{t}$ and $\boldsymbol{v}$ to denote vector of terms and variables. A substitution (binding) is a set of variable-term pairs

---

[1] We use a's to refer to a and a with a subscript or superscript. The same applies to the description of other notations.

$\{[x_i/t_i]\}$, where variable x_i is associated with term t_i (x_i does not occur free in t_i). We use $\theta, \delta, \eta, \mu, \tau$ to denote substitutions. *Wffs* is the set of well-formed formulas.

Given a team specification in MALLET, let *Agent* be the set of agent names, *Ioper* be the set of individual operators, *TOper* be the set of team operators, *Plan* be the set of plans, B be the initial set of beliefs (belief base), and G be the initial set of goals (goal base).

Let $P = Plan \cup Toper \cup Ioper$. We call P the plan (template) base, which consists of all the specified operators and plans. Every invocation of a template in P is associated with a substitution: each formal parameter of the template is bound to the corresponding actual parameter. For instance, given a template (**plan** ρ ($v_1 \cdots v_j$)

(**pre-cond** $p_1 \cdots p_k$) (**effects** $q_1 \cdots q_m$) (**term-cond** $e_1 \cdots e_n$) (**process** s)). A plan call (ρ $t_1 \cdots t_j$) will instantiate the template with binding $\theta = \{v/t\}$, where the evaluation of t_i may further depend on some other (environment) binding μ. Note that such instantiation process will substitute t_i for all the occurrence of v_i in the precondition, effects, term-condition, and plan body s (for all $1 \le i \le j$). The instantiation of ρ wrt. binding η is denoted by $\rho \cdot \eta$, or $\rho\eta$ for simplicity.

We define some auxiliary functions. For any operator α, $pre(\alpha)$ and $post(\alpha)$ return the conjunction of the preconditions and effects specified for α respectively, $\lambda(\alpha)$ returns the binding if α is an instantiated operator. For team operator Γ, $|\Gamma|$ returns the minimal number of agents required for executing Γ. For any plan ρ, in addition to $pre(\rho)$, $post(\rho)$ and $\lambda(\rho)$ as defined above, $tc(\rho)$, $\chi_p(\rho)$, $\chi_t(\rho)$, and $body(\rho)$ return the conjunction of termination-conditions, the precondition type ($\in$ {**skip, fail, wait-skip, wait-fail, achieve-skip, achieve-fail,** ϵ}), the termination type ($\in$ {**success-skip, success-fail, failure-skip, failure-fail,** ϵ}), and the plan body of ρ, respectively. The precondition, effects and termination-condition components of a plan are optional. When they are not specified, $pre(\rho)$ and $post(\rho)$ return **true** and $\chi_t(\rho) = \epsilon$. For any statement s, $isPlan(s)$ returns **true** if s is of form (ρ t) or (**Do** A (ρ t)) for some A, where ρ is a plan defined in P; otherwise, it returns **false**. (**SEQ** $s_1 \cdots s_i$) is abbreviated as ($s_1; \cdots ; s_i$). ε is used to denote the empty Mallet process statement. For any statement s, $\varepsilon; s = s; \varepsilon = s$. (**wait until** ϕ) is an abbreviation of (**while** (**cond** $\neg\phi$) (**do self** skip)) [2], where *skip* is a built-in individual operator with $pre(skip) = true$ and $post(skip) = true$ (i.e., the execution of *skip* changes nothing).

Messages Control messages are needed in defining the operational semantics of MALLET. A control message is a tuple $\langle type, aid, gid, pid, \cdots \rangle$, where $aid \in Agent$, $gid \in Wffs$, $pid \in P \cup \{nil\}$, and $type \in \{sync, ctell, cask, unachievable\}$. A message of type *sync* is used by agent aid to synchronize with the recipient with respect to the committed goal gid and the activity pid; a message of type

---

[2] The keyword "*self*" can be used in specifying doers of a process. An agent always evaluate *self* as itself.

ctell is used by agent *aid* to tell the recipient about the status of *pid*; a message of type *cask* is used by agent *aid* to request the recipient to perform *pid*; a message of type *unachievable* is used by agent *aid* to inform the recipient of the unachievability of *pid*.

MALLET has a built-in domain-independent operator **send**(*receivers, msg*), which is used for inter-agent communications. $pre(send) = true$. We assume that the execution of **send** always succeeds. If $\langle type, a_1, \cdots \rangle$ is a control message, the effect of $send(a_2, \langle type, a_1, \cdots \rangle)$ is that agent a_1 will assert the fact $(typ\ a_1\ \cdots)$ into its belief base, and agent a_2 will do the same thing when it receives the message.

Goals and Intentions. A goal g is a pair $\langle \phi, A \rangle$, where $A \subseteq Agent$ is a set of agents responsible for achieving a state satisfying ϕ. When A is a singleton, g is an individual goal; otherwise, it is a team goal.

An *intention slice* is of form $(\psi, A) \leftarrow s$, where the execution of statement s by agents in A is to achieve a state satisfying ψ. An *intention* is a stack of intention slices, denoted by $[\omega_0 \backslash \cdots \backslash \omega_k]$ $(0 \le k)^3$, where ω_i $(0 \le i \le k)$ are of form $(\psi_i, A_i) \leftarrow s_i$. ω_0 and ω_k are the bottom and top slice of the intention, respectively. The ultimate goal state of intention $h = [(\psi_0, A_0) \leftarrow s_0 \backslash \cdots \backslash \omega_k]$ is ψ_0, referred to by $o(h)$. The empty intention is denoted by $\top$. For $h = [\omega_0 \backslash \cdots \backslash \omega_k]$, $[h \backslash \omega'] \triangleq [\omega_0 \backslash \cdots \backslash \omega_k \backslash \omega']$. If ω_i is of form $(true, A) \leftarrow \varepsilon$ $(0 \le i \le k)$ for some A, then $h = [\omega_0 \backslash \cdots \backslash \omega_{i-1} \backslash \omega_{i+1} \backslash \cdots \backslash \omega_k]$. Let H denote the intention set.

Definition 1 (configuration). *A Mallet configuration is a tuple $\langle B, G, H, \theta \rangle$, where B, G, H, θ are the belief base, the goal base, the intention set, and the current substitution, respectively[4]. And, (1) $B \not\models \bot$, (2) for any goal $g \in G$, $B \not\models g$, and $g \not\models \bot$ hold.*

B, G, H, θ are used in defining Mallet configurations, because beliefs, goals, and intentions of an agent are dynamically changing, and a substitution is required to store the current environment bindings for free variables. Plan base P is omitted since we assume P will not be changed at run time.

Similar to [17] we give an auxiliary function to facilitate the definition of semantics of intentions.

Definition 2. *Function agls is defined recursively as: $agls(\top) = \{\}$, and for any intention $h = [\omega_0 \backslash \cdots \backslash \omega_{k-1} \backslash (\psi_k, A_k) \leftarrow s_k]$ $(k \ge 0)$, $agls(h) = \{\psi_k\} \cup agls([\omega_0 \backslash \cdots \backslash \omega_{k-1}])$.*

Note that goals in G are top-level goals specified initially, while function *agls* returns a set of achievement goals generated at run time in pursuing some (top-level) goal in G.

---

³ The form of intentions here is similar to Rao's approach [15]. Some researchers also borrow the idea of fluents to represent intentions, see [16] for an example.

⁴ There are no global beliefs, goals, and intentions. Mallet configurations are defined with respect to individual agents. The transitions of an agent team are made up of the transitions of member agents. Here, B, G, H, θ should all be understood as the belief base, goal base, intention set, and current substitution of an individual agent. Of course, for agents in a team, their Bs, Gs and Hs may overlap.

4   Operational Semantics

Usually there are two ways of defining semantics for an agent-oriented programming language: operational semantics and temporal semantics. For instance, temporal semantics is given to MABLE [18]; while 3APL [19] and AgentSpeak(L) [15] have operational semantics, and transition semantics is defined for ConGolog based on Situation calculus [20]. Temporal semantics is better for property verification using existing tools, such as SPIN (a model checking tool which can check whether temporal formulas hold for the implemented systems), while operational semantics is better for implementing interpreters for the language.

We define an operational semantics for MALLET in terms of a transition system, aiming to guide the implementation of interpreters. Each transition corresponds to a single computation step which transforms the system from one configuration to another. A computation run of an agent is a finite or infinite sequence of configurations connected by transition relation $\rightarrow$. The meaning of an agent is a set of computation runs starting from the initial configuration. We assume a belief update function $BU(B, p)$, which revises the belief base B with a new fact p. The details of BU is out the scope of this paper. For convenience, we assume two domain-independent operators over B: **unsync**(ψ, ρ) and **untell**(ψ, s). Their effects are to remove all the predicates that can be unified with $sync(?a, \psi, \rho)$ and $ctell(?a, \psi, s, ?id)$, respectively, from B.

4.1   Semantics of Beliefs, Goals and Intentions in MALLET

We allow *explicit negation* in B, and for each $b(t) \in B$, its explicit negation is denoted by $\tilde{b}(t)$. Such treatment enables the representation of 'unknown'.

Definition 3. *Given a Mallet configuration* $M = \langle B, G, H, \theta \rangle$, *for any wff* ϕ, *any belief or goal formula* ψ, ψ', *any agent* a,

1. $M \models Bel(\phi)$ *iff* $B \models \phi$,
2. $M \models \neg Bel(\phi)$ *iff* $B \models \tilde{\phi}$,
3. $M \models Unknown(\phi)$ *iff* $B \not\models \phi$ *and* $B \not\models \tilde{\phi}$,
4. $M \models Goal(\phi)$ *iff* $\exists \langle \phi', A \rangle \in G$ *such that* $\phi' \models \phi$ *and* $B \not\models \phi$,
5. $M \models \neg Goal(\phi)$ *iff* $M \not\models Goal(\phi)$,
6. $M \models Goal_a(\phi)$ *iff* $\exists \langle \phi', A \rangle \in G$ *such that* $a \in A$, $\phi' \models \phi$ *and* $B \not\models \phi$,
7. $M \models \neg Goal(\phi)$ *iff* $M \not\models Goal(\phi)$, $M \models \neg Goal_a(\phi)$ *iff* $M \not\models Goal_a(\phi)$,
8. $M \models \psi \wedge \psi'$ *iff* $M \models \psi$ *and* $M \models \psi'$,
9. $M \models Intend(\phi)$ *iff* $\phi \in \bigcup_{h \in H} agls(h)$.

4.2   Failures in MALLET

We start with the semantics of failures in MALLET. MALLET imposes the following semantics rules on execution failures:

- There are three causes of process failures:
    - The precondition is false when an agent is ready to enter a plan or execute an operator. The execution continues or terminates depending on the type of the precondition:

skip: skip this plan/operator and execute the next one;

fail: terminate execution and propagate the failure upward;

wait-skip: check the precondition after a certain time period, if it is still false, proceed to the next plan/operator;

wait-fail: check the precondition after a certain time period, if it is still false, terminate execution and propagate the failure upward;

achieve-skip: try to bring about the precondition (e.g., triggering another plan that might make the precondition true), if failed after the attempt then skip this plan/operator and execute the next one;

achieve-fail: try to bring about the precondition, if failed after the attempt then terminate execution and propagate the failure upward;

- An agent monitors the termination condition, if any, of a plan during the execution of the plan. The execution continues or terminates depending on the type of the termination condition:

  success-skip: if the termination condition is true, then skip the rest of the plan and proceed to the next statement after the plan;

  success-fail: if the termination condition is true, then terminate execution and propagate the failure upward;

  failure-skip: if the termination condition is false, then skip the rest of the plan and proceed to the next statement after the plan;

  failure-fail: if the termination condition is false, then terminate execution and propagate the failure upward;

- When doing **agent-bind**, an agent cannot find solutions to the agent variables;

- Process failures must propagate upward until a **choice** point:

  - If any MalletProcess in a **seq** returns fail, then the entire **seq** terminates execution and fails;
  - If any branch of a **par** fails, the entire **par** terminates and fails;
  - If the body of a **while**, **foreach**, or **forall** fails, the entire iterative statement terminates execution and fails;
  - If any branch of an **if** fails, the entire **if** terminates execution and fails;
  - If any branch of a **JointDo** fails, the **JointDo** terminates and fails;
  - If the body of a plan fails, the plan invocation fails;

- Process failures are captured and processed at a **choice** point:

  - If, except for those branches the execution of which has caused process failures, the **choice** point still has other alternatives to try, then select one and the execution continues;
  - If the **choice** point has no more alternatives to try, then propagate the failure backward/upward until another **choice** point.

Note 1. Operators are considered atomic from the perspective of MALLET; they do not have termination conditions. If there is a concern that operators may not succeed, they should be embedded in a plan and the result be checked, with use of the termination condition in the case of failure.

Note 2. MALLET allows a *skip* or *fail* mode to be included with preconditions and termination conditions (supported since version V.3). One argument for allowing both modes is that continuing operations, even when some precondition is not satisfied, is what happens in real life. To the extent that we are trying to allow agent designs to respond to real-life, we need this capability. This argument is also related to the argument that we wanted to leave as much flexibility as possible in the MALLET specification so that different implementations and levels of intelligence could be experimented with.

We thus can formally define rules for failure propagation. Given the current configuration $\langle B, G, H, \theta \rangle$, a plan template $(\rho\ v)$ and an invocation $(\rho\ t)$ or $(\mathbf{Do}\ A\ (\rho\ t))$, let $\eta = \{v/t\}$.

- Assert $(failed\ \rho\ \eta)$ into B, if $\chi_p(\rho) = \mathbf{fail}$, and $\not\exists \tau \cdot B \models pre(\rho)\theta\eta\tau$;
- Assert $(failed\ \rho\ \eta)$ into B, if $\chi_p(\rho) = \mathbf{wait\text{-}fail}$, and $\not\exists \tau \cdot B \models pre(\rho)\theta\eta\tau$ for neither before nor after the specified waiting time period;
- Assert $(failed\ \rho\ \eta)$ into B, if $\chi_p(\rho) = \mathbf{achieve\text{-}fail}$, and $\not\exists \tau \cdot B \models pre(\rho)\theta\eta\tau$ for neither before nor after the 'achieve' attempt;
- Assert $(failed\ \rho\ \eta)$ into B, if $\chi_t(\rho) = \mathbf{success\text{-}fail}$, and $\exists \tau \cdot B \models tc(\rho)\theta\eta\tau$;
- Assert $(failed\ \rho\ \eta)$ into B, if $\chi_t(\rho) = \mathbf{failure\text{-}fail}$, and $\not\exists \tau \cdot B \models tc(\rho)\theta\eta\tau$;
- Assert $(failed\ s\ \eta)$ into B, where $s = (\rho\ t)$ or $s = (\mathbf{Do}\ A\ (\rho\ t))$, if $\exists \tau \cdot B \models (failed\ body(\rho)\ \tau)$;
- Assert $(failed\ s\ \theta)$ into B, where $s = (\mathbf{agent\text{-}bind}\ v\ \psi)$, if $\not\exists \tau \cdot B \models \psi\theta\tau$;
- Assert $(failed\ s\ \theta)$ into B, where $s = (l_1; \cdots l_m)$, if $\exists \theta' \cdot B \models (failed\ l_1\ \theta')$;
- Assert $(failed\ s\ \theta)$ into B, where $s = (\mathbf{par}\ l_1 \cdots l_m)$, if $B \models \bigvee_{i=1}^{m} \exists \theta' \cdot (failed\ l_i\ \theta')$;
- Assert $(failed\ s\ \theta)$ into B, where $s = (\mathbf{forall}\ (\mathbf{cond}\ \psi)\ l_1)$ or $s = (\mathbf{foreach}\ (\mathbf{cond}\ \psi)\ l_1)$, if $B \models \bigvee_{\tau \in \{\eta : B \models \psi\eta\}} \exists \theta' \cdot (failed\ l_1\tau\ \theta')$;
- Assert $(failed\ s\ \theta)$ into B, where $s = (\mathbf{while}\ (\mathbf{cond}\ \psi)\ l_1)$, if $\exists \theta' \cdot B \models (failed\ l_1\ \theta')$;
- Assert $(failed\ s\ \theta)$ into B, where $s = (\mathbf{if}\ (\mathbf{cond}\ \psi)\ l_1\ l_2)$, if $\exists \theta' \cdot B \models (failed\ l_1\ \theta') \vee (failed\ l_2\ \theta')$;
- Assert $(failed\ s\ \theta)$ into B, where $s = (\mathbf{JointDo}\ \mathbf{X}\ (A_1\ l_1) \cdots (A_m\ l_m))$ $(\mathbf{X} \in \{\mathbf{AND}, \mathbf{OR}, \mathbf{XOR}\})$, if $B \models \bigvee_{i=1}^{m} \exists \theta' \cdot (failed\ l_i\ \theta')$;
- Assert $(failed\ s\ \theta)$ into B, where $s = (\mathbf{choice}\ l_1 \cdots l_m)$, if $B \models \bigwedge_{i=1}^{m} \exists \theta' \cdot (failed\ l_i\ \theta')$.

Note that conjunction rather than disjunction is used in the rule about **choice**. This is because the semantics of choice allows re-try upon failures: a **choice** statement fails only when all the branches have failed.

The semantics of failure is defined in terms of *failed*.

Definition 4 (semantics of failure). *Let s be any Mallet statement.* $\langle B, G, H, \theta \rangle \models failed(s)$ *iff* $\exists \theta' \cdot B \models (failed\ s\ \theta')$.

4.3   Transition System

We use **SUCCEED** to denote the terminal configuration where the execution terminates successfully (i.e., all the specified goals and generated intentions are fulfilled); use **STOP** to denote the terminal configuration where the execution terminates abnormally—all the remaining goals are unachievable. In particular, we use **STOP**(h) to denote the execution of intention h terminates abnormally.

Definition 5. *Let* $h = [h' \backslash (\psi_k, A_k) \leftarrow l_1; l_2]$. *UC is defined recursively:*
$UC(\top) = \top$,
$UC(h) = h$, *if* l_1 *is of form* (**choice** $s_1 \cdots s_m$);
$UC(h) = UC(h')$, *if* l_1 *is not of form* (**choice** $s_1 \cdots s_m$).

Function $UC(h)$ returns h', where h' is h with all the top intention slices popped until the first choice point is found.

Definition 6 (Backtracking upon failure). *Let* $h = [h' \backslash (\psi_k, A_k) \leftarrow s \backslash \cdots]$,

$$\frac{\langle B, G, h, \theta \rangle \models failed(s),\ UC(h) \neq \top}{\langle B, G, h, \theta \rangle \rightarrow \langle B, G, UC(h), \theta \rangle}, \tag{F1}$$

$$\frac{\langle B, G, h, \theta \rangle \models failed(s),\ UC(h) = \top}{\langle B, G, h, \theta \rangle \rightarrow \mathbf{STOP}(h)}. \tag{F2}$$

In Definition 6, **F1** is a transition rule for backtracking upon process failure. Rule (**F2**) states that the execution of an intention stops if there is no choice point backward.

Definition 7 (Goal selection).

$$\exists g = \langle \psi, A \rangle \in G,\ \exists (\rho\ \boldsymbol{v}) \in P,\ self \in A,$$

$$\frac{\exists \tau, (\theta\tau\ has\ bindings\ for\ \boldsymbol{v}), B \models pre(\rho)\theta\tau, and\ post(\rho)\theta\tau \models \psi}{\langle B, G, \emptyset, \theta \rangle \rightarrow \langle B, G \setminus \{g\}, \{[(\psi, A) \leftarrow (\mathbf{Do}\ A\ (\rho\ \boldsymbol{v})\theta\tau)]\}, \theta\tau \rangle}, \tag{G1}$$

$$\frac{\forall g = \langle \psi, A \rangle \in G, \forall (\rho\ \boldsymbol{v}) \in P\ \ \nexists \tau \cdot post(\rho)\theta\tau \models \psi}{\langle B, G, \emptyset, \theta \rangle \rightarrow \mathbf{STOP}}, \tag{G2}$$

$$\frac{}{\langle B, \emptyset, \emptyset, \theta \rangle \rightarrow \mathbf{SUCCEED}}. \tag{G3}$$

In Definition 7, Rule **G1** states that when the intention set is empty, the agent will choose one goal from its goal set and select an appropriate plan, if there exists such a plan, to achieve that goal. Rule **G2** states that an agent will stop running if there is no plan can be used to pursue any goal in G. Rule **G3** states that an agent terminates successfully if all the goals and intentions have been achieved. **G1** is the only rule introducing new intentions. It indicates that an agent can only have one intention in focus (it cannot commit to another intention until the current one has already been achieved or dropped). **G1** can be modified to allow intention shifting (i.e., pursue multiple top-level goals simultaneously).

Definition 8 (End of intention/intention slice). *Let*
$h_1 = [\cdots \backslash \omega_{k-1} \backslash (\psi_k, A_k) \leftarrow \varepsilon]$,
$h_2 = [(\psi_0, A_0) \leftarrow s \backslash \cdots]$,

$$\frac{B \not\models \psi_k\theta,\ UC(h_1) \neq \top}{\langle B, G, h_1, \theta \rangle \rightarrow \langle B, G, UC(h_1), \theta \rangle},$$ (EI1)

$$\frac{B \not\models \psi_k\theta,\ UC(h_1) = \top}{\langle B, G, h_1, \theta \rangle \rightarrow \mathbf{STOP}(h_1)},$$ (EI2)

$$\frac{B \models \psi_k\theta}{\langle B, G, h_1, \theta \rangle \rightarrow \langle B, G, [\cdots \backslash \omega_{k-1}], \theta \rangle},$$ (EI3)

$$\frac{h_2 \in H, B \models \psi_0\theta}{\langle B, G, H, \theta \rangle \rightarrow \langle B, G, H \setminus \{h_2\}, \theta \rangle}.$$ (EI4)

In Definition 8, **EI1** and **EI2** are the counterparts of rules **F1** and **F2**, respectively. According to Rule **P3** in Definition 15, the achievement goal ψ_k comes from the effects condition of some plan. The effects condition associated with a plan represents an obligation that the plan must achieve. Normally, ψ_k can be achieved unless the execution of the plan body failed. But this is not always the case (e.g., an agent simply had made a wrong choice). It is thus useful to verify that a plan has, in fact, achieved the effects condition, although this is not a requirement of MALLET. In the definition, when the execution of the top intention slice is done (the body becomes ε), the corresponding achievement goal ψ_k will be checked. If ψ_k is false, the execution backtracks to the latest choice point (**EI1**) or stops (**EI2**). If ψ_k is true, then the top intention slice is popped and the execution proceeds (**EI3**). Rule **EI4** states that at any stage if the ultimate goal ψ_0 of an intention becomes true, then drop this already fulfilled intention.

Goals in G are declarative abstract goals while intention set H including all the intermediate subgoals. Definition 7 and Definition 8 give rules for adopting and dropping goals, respectively. Later we will give other rules that are relevant to goal adoption and termination (e.g. propagation of failure in plan execution). Birna van Riemsdijk, et al. [21] analyzed several motivations and mechanisms for dropping and adopting declarative goals. In their terminology, MALLET supports goals in both procedural and declarative ways, and employs the landmark view of subgoals.

As we have explained earlier, the **choice** construct is used to specify explicit choice points in a complex team process, and it is a language-level mechanism for handling process failures. For example, suppose a fire-fighting team is assigned to extinguish a fire caused by an explosion at a chemical plant. After collecting enough information (e.g., there are toxic materials in the plant, there are facilities endangered, etc.), the team needs to decide how to put out the fire. They have to select one plan if there exist several options. And they have to resort to another option if one is found to be unworkable.

In syntax, the **choice** construct is composed of a list of branches, each of which specifies a plan (a course of actions) and may be associated with preference condition and a priority information. The preference condition of a branch is a collection of first-order formulas; the evaluation of their conjunction determines whether the branch can be selected under that context. The priority information is considered when the preference conditions of more than one branch are satisfiable.

Given a configuration $\langle B, G, H, \theta \rangle$ and a statement $(\textbf{choice } Br_1 \ Br_2 \cdots Br_m)$ where $Br_i = (pref_i \ pro_i \ (\textbf{DO} \ A_i \ (\rho_i \ t_i)))$, let $BR = \{Br_i | 1 \leq i \leq m\}$, $BR_- \subseteq BR$ be the set of branches in BR which have already been considered but failed. We assume that B can track the changes of BR_-. Let $BR^+ = \{Br_k | \ \exists \tau \cdot B \models pref_k \cdot \theta\tau, 1 \leq k \leq m\} \setminus BR_-$, which is the set of branches that have not been considered and the associated preference conditions can be satisfied by B. In addition, let $BR^\oplus$ be the subset of BR^+ such that all the branches in $BR^\oplus$ have the maximal priority value among those in BR^+, and $ram(BR^\oplus)$ can randomly select and return one branch from $BR^\oplus$.

Definition 9 (Choice construct). *Let*
$h = [\omega_0 \setminus \cdots \setminus (\psi_k, A_k) \leftarrow (\textbf{choice } Br_1 \ Br_2 \cdots Br_m); s],$
$h_1 = [h \setminus (true, A_k) \leftarrow (\textbf{DO} \ A_i \ (\rho_i \ t_i)); \textbf{cend}],$
$h_2 = [h \setminus (true, A_k) \leftarrow \textbf{cend}],$

$$\frac{ram(BR^\oplus) = Br_i, B' = BU(B, BR_-.add(Br_i))}{\langle B, G, h, \theta \rangle \rightarrow \langle B', G, h_1, \theta \rangle}, \tag{C1}$$

$$\frac{self \in A_i, \langle B, G, h_2, \theta \rangle \not\models failed(\rho_i), B' = BU(B, post(\rho_i)\theta)}{\langle B, G, h_2, \theta \rangle \rightarrow \langle B', G, [\omega_0 \setminus \cdots \setminus (\psi_k, A_k) \leftarrow s], \theta \rangle}. \tag{C2}$$

In Definition 9, Rule **C1** applies when there exists a workable branch. The intention h is appended with a new slice ended with **cend**, which marks explicitly the scope of the choice point. An agent has to wait (e.g., until more information becomes available) if there is no workable branch. Rule **C2** states that when an agent comes to the statement **cend** and the execution of ρ_i is successful, it proceeds to the next statement following the choice point. Rule **C3** states that if $failed(\rho_i)$ is true, the execution returns to the choice point to try another branch.

Note 3. First, when a selected branch has failed, according to Rule **F1** the execution backtracks to this choice point (i.e., the intention of the current configuration becomes h again). When all the branches $Br_i(1 \leq i \leq m)$ have failed (i.e., $failed(\textbf{choice } Br_1 \ Br_2 \cdots Br_m)$ holds), again by Rule **F1** the execution backtracks to the next choice point, if there is one. Second, an implementation can enforce the agents in a group to synchronize with others when backtracking to a preceding choice point, although this is not required by MALLET, which, as a generic language, allows experimentation with different levels and forms of team intelligence. By explicitly marking the scope of choice points, synchronization can be enforced, if necessary, when agents reaching **cend**.

Definition 10 (Agent selection). *Let intention*
$h = [\omega_0 \setminus \cdots \setminus (\psi_k, A_k) \leftarrow (\textbf{agent-bind } \ v \ \phi); s],$

$$\frac{\exists \tau \cdot B \models \phi\theta\tau}{\langle B, G, h, \theta \rangle \rightarrow \langle B, G, [\omega_0 \setminus \cdots \setminus (\psi_k, A_k) \leftarrow s], \theta\tau \rangle}. \tag{B1}$$

The successful execution of an agent-bind statement is to compose the substitution obtained from evaluating the constraint ϕ with θ (Rule **B1**). The execution fails if there is no solution to the constraints. Since each agent has an individual belief base, one complication can arise here if the individual agents in A_k reach a different choice for the agents to bind to the agent variables. Consequences can involve vary from two different agents performing an operation that only one was supposed to do, to some agents successfully determining a binding while others fail to do so. Different strategies can be adopted when an interpreter of MALLET is implemented. For instance, in case there is a leader in a team, one solution is to delegate the binding task to the leader, who informs the results to other teammates once it finishes. If so, **B1** has to be adapted accordingly.

Note 4. Given any configuration $\langle B, G, H, \theta \rangle$, for any instantiated plan ρ, variables in $body(\rho)$ are all bounded either by some binding τ where $B \models pre(p)\theta\tau$, or by some preceeding agent-bind statement in $body(\rho)$.

Definition 11 (Sequential execution). *Let intention*
$h = [\omega_0 \backslash \cdots \backslash (\psi_k, A_k) \leftarrow l_1; \cdots ; l_m],$

$$\frac{\langle B, \emptyset, [(true, A_k) \leftarrow l_1], \theta \rangle \rightarrow \langle B', \emptyset, [(true, A_k) \leftarrow \varepsilon], \theta' \rangle}{\langle B, G, h, \theta \rangle \rightarrow \langle B', G, [\omega_0 \backslash \cdots \backslash (\psi_k, A_k) \leftarrow l_2; \cdots ; l_m], \theta' \rangle}. \quad \textbf{(SE)}$$

seq is a basic construct for composing complex processes. As shown in Definition 11, if the execution of l_1 can transform B and θ into B' and θ' respectively, the rest will be executed in the context settled by the execution of l_1.

Definition 12 (Individual operator execution). *Let intention*
$h = [\omega_0 \backslash \cdots \backslash (\psi_k, A_k) \leftarrow (Do\ a\ (\alpha\ t)); s],$
$h_2 = [\omega_0 \backslash \cdots \backslash (\psi_k, A_k) \leftarrow (\alpha\ t); s],$ *where* $(\alpha\ v) \in Ioper,\ \eta = \{v/t\},$

$$\frac{self = a, \exists \tau, B \models pre(\alpha)\theta\eta\tau, B' = BU(B, post(\alpha)\theta\eta\tau)}{\langle B, G, h, \theta \rangle \rightarrow \langle B', G, [\omega_0 \backslash \cdots \backslash (\psi_k, A_k) \leftarrow l; s], \theta \rangle}, \quad \textbf{(I1)}$$

$$\frac{self \neq a}{\langle B, G, h, \theta \rangle \rightarrow \langle B, G, [\omega_0 \backslash \cdots \backslash (\psi_k, A_k) \leftarrow l_2; s], \theta \rangle}, \quad \textbf{(I2)}$$

$$\frac{self = a, \not\exists \tau \cdot B \models pre(\alpha)\theta\eta\tau, \chi_p(\rho) = \mathbf{X}}{\langle B, G, h, \theta \rangle \rightarrow \langle B, G, [\omega_0 \backslash \cdots \backslash (\psi_k, A_k) \leftarrow s'; s], \theta \rangle}, \quad \textbf{(I3)}$$

$$\frac{\exists \tau, B \models pre(\alpha)\theta\eta\tau, B' = BU(B, post(\alpha)\theta\eta\tau)}{\langle B, G, h_2, \theta \rangle \rightarrow \langle B', G, [\omega_0 \backslash \cdots \backslash (\psi_k, A_k) \leftarrow s], \theta \rangle}, \quad \textbf{(I4)}$$

$$\frac{\not\exists \tau \cdot B \models pre(\alpha)\theta\eta\tau, \chi_p(\rho) = \mathbf{X}}{\langle B, G, h_2, \theta \rangle \rightarrow \langle B, G, [\omega_0 \backslash \cdots \backslash (\psi_k, A_k) \leftarrow s''; s], \theta \rangle}. \quad \textbf{(I5)}$$

where l *and* l_2 *are points for team synchronization, if needed;* s' *and* s'' *are points for responding to different precondition types when the precondition is false.*

In Definition 12, Rule **I1** states that if an agent is the assigned doer a, and the precondition of α is satisfiable wrt. the agent's belief base, then the execution of the individual operator is to update the belief base with the postcondition of the operator. Rule **I2** states that the agents other than the doer a can either synchronize or proceeds, depending on the actual implementation of MALLET interpreters. In Rule **I3**, s' can be replaced by different statements, depending on the actual precondition types. Rules **I4** and **I5** are similar to **I1** and **I3** except that the intention is of form h_2, which by default all the individual agents in A_k are the doers of α.

Note 5. The statements l, l_2, s', and s'' are left open for flexibility so that alternate interpretations of agent interaction semantics can be implemented. For instance, when l and l_2 are replaced by ε, each agent in A_k can just do their own jobs. Alternatively, if we let $l = (\textbf{Do } self \ (\textbf{send } A_k \setminus \{self\}, \langle ctell, self, \psi_0, \alpha \rangle))$, $l_2 = (\textbf{wait until } ctell(a, \psi_0, \alpha) \in B)$, then the team has to synchronize before proceeding next. Precondition failures have already been covered by Rules **F1** and **F2**. Rules **I3** and **I5** apply when the precondition is false and the precondition type is of 'skip' mode. For instance, if **X** is **skip**, then s' and s'' can be ε or statements for synchronization, depending to the agent interaction semantics as explained above. If **X** is **wait-skip**, it is feasible to let $s' = (\textbf{wait until } \exists \tau \cdot B \models pre(\alpha)\theta\eta\tau); (\textbf{Do } self \ (\alpha \ t))$, and $s'' = (\textbf{wait until } \exists \tau \cdot B \models pre(\alpha)\theta\eta\tau); (\alpha \ t)$.

To execute a team operator, all the involved agents need to synchronize. Let $Y(\psi, \Gamma) = \{a' | sync(a', \psi, \Gamma) \in B\}$, which is a set of agent names from whom, according to the current agent's beliefs, it has received a synchronization message wrt. ψ and Γ.

Definition 13 (Team operator execution). *Let intention* $h = [\omega_0 \setminus \cdots \setminus (\psi_k, A_k) \leftarrow (\textbf{Do } A \ (\Gamma \ t)); s]$, *where* $(\Gamma \ v) \in Toper$, $\eta = \{v/t\}$,

$$\frac{self \in A, \exists \tau \cdot B \models pre(\Gamma)\theta\eta\tau, sync(self, \psi_0, \Gamma) \notin B}{\langle B, G, h, \theta \rangle \rightarrow \langle B, G, [\omega_0 \setminus \cdots \setminus (\psi_k, A_k) \leftarrow s^1; s], \theta \rangle} , \quad \textbf{(T1)}$$

$$\frac{self \in A, \exists \tau \cdot B \models pre(\Gamma)\theta\eta\tau, sync(self, \psi_0, \Gamma) \in B, |Y(\psi_0, \Gamma)| < |\Gamma|}{\langle B, G, h, \theta \rangle \rightarrow \langle B, G, [\omega_0 \setminus \cdots \setminus (\psi_k, A_k) \leftarrow s^2; s], \theta \rangle} , \quad \textbf{(T2)}$$

$$\frac{\begin{array}{c} self \in A, \exists \tau, B \models pre(\Gamma)\theta\eta\tau, \\ sync(self, \psi_0, \Gamma) \in B, |Y(\psi_0, \Gamma)| \geq |\Gamma|, B' = BU(B, post(\Gamma)\theta\eta\tau) \end{array}}{\langle B, G, h, \theta \rangle \rightarrow \langle B', G, [\omega_0 \setminus \cdots \setminus (\psi_k, A_k) \leftarrow s^3; s], \theta \rangle} , \quad \textbf{(T3)}$$

$$\frac{self \notin A}{\langle B, G, h, \theta \rangle \rightarrow \langle B, G, [\omega_0 \setminus \cdots \setminus (\psi_k, A_k) \leftarrow s^4; s], \theta \rangle} , \quad \textbf{(T4)}$$

$$\frac{self \in A, \nexists \tau \cdot B \models pre(\Gamma)\theta\eta\tau, \chi_p(\Gamma) = \textbf{wait-skip}}{\langle B, G, h, \theta \rangle \rightarrow \langle B, G, [\omega_0 \setminus \cdots \setminus (\psi_k, A_k) \leftarrow s^5; s], \theta \rangle} . \quad \textbf{(T5)}$$

where $s^1 = (\textbf{Do } self \ \textbf{send}(A, \langle sync, self, \psi_0, \Gamma \rangle)); (\textbf{Do } A \ (\Gamma \ t))$, $s^2 = (\textbf{wait until } (|Y(\psi_0, \Gamma)| \geq |\Gamma|)); (\textbf{Do } A \ (\Gamma \ t))$, $s^3 = (\textbf{Do } self \ \textbf{unsync}(\psi_0, \Gamma)); (\textbf{Do } self \ \textbf{send}(A_k \setminus A, \langle ctell, self, \psi_0, \Gamma \rangle))$, $s^4 = (\textbf{wait until } \forall a \in A \cdot ctell(a, \psi_0, \Gamma) \in B)$, $s^5 = (\textbf{wait until } \exists \tau \cdot B \models pre(\Gamma)\theta\eta\tau); (\textbf{Do } A \ (\Gamma \ t))$.

In Definition 13, Rule **T1** states that if an agent itself is one of the assigned doers, the precondition of the team operator holds, and the agent has not synchronized with other agents in A, then it will first send out synchronization messages before executing Γ. Rule **T2** states that an agent has already synchronized with others, but has not received enough synchronization messages from others, then it continues waiting. Rule **T3** states that the execution of Γ will update B with the effects of the team operator, and before proceeding, the agent has to retract the sync messages regarding Γ (to ensure proper agent behavior in case that Γ needs to be re-executed later) and inform the agents not in A of the accomplishment of Γ. Rule **T4** deals with the case when an agent belongs to $A_k \setminus A$—the agent has to wait until being informed of the accomplishment of Γ. Rule **T5** applies when the preconditions of Γ does not hold. Variants of **T5** can be given when $\chi_p(\Gamma)$ is **skip** or **achieve-skip**.

Note 6. Usually in the use of transition systems (as in concurrency semantics) the aspect of 'waiting' is modeled implicitly by the fact that if the proper conditions are not met the rule cannot be applied so that the transition must wait to take place until the condition becomes true. In this paper, there are a number of places where 'waiting' is included in the transitions explicitly. It is true that in some places implicit modeling of waiting can be used (say, the rule T2), but not all the 'wait' can be removed without sacrificing the semantics (say, the rule T4). We use explicit modeling of waiting mainly for two reasons. First, agents in a team typically need to synchronize with other team members while waiting. For example, the doers of a team operator need to synchronize with each other both before and after the execution. Here, the agents are not passively waiting, but waiting for a certain number of incoming messages. Second, 'wait' in the rules provides a hook for further extensions. For instance, currently the wait semantics states that an agent has to wait until the precondition of an action to be executed is satisfied. We can ascribe a "proactive" semantics to the language such that the doer of an action will proactive bring about a state that can make the precondition true or seek help from other teammates.

The semantics of **JointDo** is a little complicated. A joint-do statement implies agent synchronization both at the beginning and at the end of its execution. Its semantics is given in terms of basic constructs.

Definition 14 (Joint-Do). *Let intentions*
$h_1 = [\omega_0 \setminus \cdots \setminus (\psi_k, A_k) \leftarrow (\textbf{JointDo AND } (A'_1 \ l_1) \cdots (A'_n \ l_n)); s],$
$h_2 = [\omega_0 \setminus \cdots \setminus (\psi_k, A_k) \leftarrow (\textbf{JointDo OR } (A'_1 \ l_1) \cdots (A'_n \ l_n)); s],$
$h_3 = [\omega_0 \setminus \cdots \setminus (\psi_k, A_k) \leftarrow (\textbf{JointDo XOR } (A'_1 \ l_1) \cdots (A'_n \ l_n)); s],$

$$\frac{\bigcap_{j=1}^{n} A'_j = \emptyset, self \in A'_i}{\langle B, G, h_1, \theta \rangle \rightarrow \langle B, G, [\omega_0 \setminus \cdots \setminus (\psi_k, A_k) \leftarrow s^1; s], \theta \rangle} \tag{J1}$$

$$\frac{\bigcap_{j=1}^{n} A'_j = \emptyset, self \in A'_i}{\langle B, G, h_2, \theta \rangle \rightarrow \langle B, G, [\omega_0 \setminus \cdots \setminus (\psi_k, A_k) \leftarrow s^0; s^{21}; s^{22}; s^0; s], \theta \rangle} \tag{J2}$$

$$\frac{self \in A'_i, isSelected(A'_i)}{\langle B,G,h_3,\theta\rangle \rightarrow \langle B,G,[\omega_0\backslash \cdots \backslash(\psi_k,A_k) \leftarrow s^1;s],\theta\rangle}, \quad \textbf{(J3)}$$

$$\frac{self \in A'_i, \neg isSelected(A'_i)}{\langle B,G,h_3,\theta\rangle \rightarrow \langle B,G,[\omega_0\backslash \cdots \backslash(\psi_k,A_k) \leftarrow s^0;s^0;s],\theta\rangle}, \quad \textbf{(J4)}$$

where $s^0 = (\textbf{Do}\ self\ (\textbf{send}\ \bigcup_{j=1}^{n} A'_j, \langle sync, self, \psi_0, nil\rangle));$
$\quad (\textbf{wait until}\ (\forall a \in \bigcup_{j=1}^{n} A'_j \cdot sync(a, \psi_0, nil) \in B)); (\textbf{Do}\ self\ (\textbf{unsync}\ \psi_0, nil));$
$s^1 = s^0; (\textbf{Do}\ A'_i\ l_i); s^0,$
$s^{21} = (\textbf{If}(\textbf{cond}\ \ \nexists l_x, a \cdot ctell(a, \psi_0, l_x, 0) \in B)$
$\quad\quad (s^3; (\textbf{Do}\ A'_i\ l_i); (\textbf{Do}\ self\ (\textbf{send}\ \bigcup_{j=1,j\neq i}^{n} A'_j, \langle ctell, self, \psi_0, l_i, 1\rangle))\ )\ ),$
$s^3 = (\textbf{If}\ (\textbf{cond}\ \ \nexists a \cdot cask(a, \psi_0, l_i) \in B)$
$\quad\quad (\ (\textbf{Do}\ self\ (\textbf{send}\ \bigcup_{j=1,j\neq i}^{n} A'_j, \langle ctell, self, \psi_0, l_i, 0\rangle));$
$\quad\quad (\textbf{Do}\ self\ (\textbf{send}\ A'_i \backslash \{self\}, \langle cask, self, \psi_0, l_i\rangle))\ )\ ),$
$s^{22} = (\textbf{while}(\textbf{cond}\ \exists \phi_x, a \cdot ctell(a, \psi_0, l_x, 0) \in B)$
$\quad\quad (\textbf{wait until}\ \forall b \in A'_x \cdot ctell(b, \psi_0, l_x, 1) \in B); (\textbf{Do}\ (\textbf{untell}\ \psi_0, l_x))\ ).$

In Definition 14, Rule **J1** defines semantics for joint-do with share type "AND". It states that before and after an agent does its task l_i, it needs to synchronize (i.e., s^0) with the other teammates wrt. l_i. A joint-do statement with share type "OR" requires that at least one sub-process has to be executed. In Rule **J2**, the joint-do statement is replaced by $s^0; s^{21}; s^{22}; s^0$. Statement s^{21} states that if an agent has not received any message regarding the start of some sub-statement l_x (i.e., this agent itself is the first ready to execute the joint-do statement), it will sequentially do (a) s^3: if among A'_i this agent is the first ready to execute l_i, then tell all other agents not in A'_i regarding the start of l_i (i.e., $\langle ctell \cdots 0\rangle$) and request other agents in A'_i to execute l_i; (b) agents in A'_i together execute l_i; (c) tell other agents not in A'_i the accomplishment of l_i (i.e., $\langle ctell \cdots 1\rangle$). Statement s^{22} states that if this agent was informed of the start of some other sub-statement l_x, it needs to wait until being informed by all the doers that l_x has been completed. The semantics of joint-do with share type "XOR" is based on a function $isSelected()$[5]: if an agent belongs to the group of selected agents, it simply synchronizes and executes the corresponding sub-statement (Rule **J3**); otherwise, only synchronization is needed (Rule **J4**).

Plan execution is a process of hierarchical expansion of (sub-)plans. In Definition 15 below, Rule **P1** states that if an agent is not involved, it simply waits until ρ is done. Before entering a plan, an agent first checks the corresponding pre-conditions. Rule **P2** applies when the precondition is false and Rule **P3** applies when the precondition is true. Rule **P2** is defined for the case where the precondition type is **skip**. Variants of **P2** can be given for other 'skip' modes. In Rule **P3**, s^1 states that on entering a plan, a new intention slice will be appended where the agent needs to synchronize with others (when everyone is ready the

---

[5] Some negotiation strategies, even social norms [22], can be employed to allow agents to know each others' commitments [23] in determining the selected agents in $isSelected$. We leave such an issue to the designers of MALLET interpreters.

synchronization messages are dropped to ensure that this plan can be properly re-entered later), then execute the plan body instantiated by the environment binding θ and local binding τ, and then tell other agents not involved in ρ about the accomplishment of ρ. Rule **P4** states that when exiting a plan (i.e., **endp** is the only statement in the body of the top intention slice), if ρ has been successfully executed, the execution proceeds to the statement after the plan call, with B being updated with the effects of ρ. Rules **P5** and **P6** complement Rules **F1** and **F2**. Rule **F1** (**F2**) applies when $failed(\mathbf{Do}\ A\ (\rho\ t))$ holds, that is, when the execution of the body of ρ fails (including the failures propagated from sub-plans of ρ). Rule **P5** (**P6**) applies when $failed(\rho)$ holds, that is, when failures emerge from the precondition or termination condition of ρ. This means, an agent needs to monitor all the termination conditions of the calling plans. The semantics of plan invocation of form $(\rho\ t)$ (i.e., no doers are explicitly specified) can be similarly defined, except that A_k will be used as the doers of ρ.

Definition 15 (Plan entering, executing and exiting). *Let*
$h_1 = [\omega_0 \backslash \cdots \backslash (\psi_k, A_k) \leftarrow (\mathbf{Do}\ A\ (\rho\ t)); s],$
$h_1' = [\omega_0 \backslash \cdots \backslash (\psi_k, A_k) \leftarrow (\mathbf{Do}\ A\ (\rho\ t))\theta\eta\tau; s\theta],$
$h_1'' = [\omega_0 \backslash \cdots \backslash (\psi_k, A_k) \leftarrow (\mathbf{Do}\ A\ (\rho\ t))\theta\eta\tau; s\theta \backslash (post(\rho)\theta\eta\tau, A) \leftarrow \mathbf{endp}],$
$h_1''' = [\omega_0 \backslash \cdots \backslash (\psi_k, A_k) \leftarrow (\mathbf{Do}\ A\ (\rho\ t)); s \backslash \cdots], \text{ where } (\rho\ v) \in Plan, \eta = \{v/t\},$

$$\frac{self \notin A}{\langle B, G, h_1, \theta \rangle \to \langle B, G, [\omega_0 \backslash \cdots \backslash (\psi_k, A_k) \leftarrow s^2; s], \theta \rangle} \quad (\textbf{P1})$$

$$\frac{self \in A,\ \not\exists\tau \cdot B \models pre(\rho)\theta\eta\tau, \chi_p(\rho) = \mathbf{skip}}{\langle B, G, h_1, \theta \rangle \to \langle B, G, [\omega_0 \backslash \cdots \backslash (\psi_k, A_k) \leftarrow s^0; s], \theta \rangle} \quad (\textbf{P2})$$

$$\frac{self \in A, \exists\tau \cdot B \models pre(\rho)\theta\eta\tau}{\langle B, G, h_1, \theta \rangle \to \langle B, G, [h_1' \backslash (post(\rho)\theta\eta\tau, A) \leftarrow s^1; \mathbf{endp}], \theta\eta\tau \rangle} \quad (\textbf{P3})$$

$$\frac{self \in A, \langle B, G, h_1'', \iota \rangle \not\models failed(\rho), B' = BU(B, post(\rho)\iota)}{\langle B, G, h_1'', \iota \rangle \to \langle B', G, [\omega_0 \backslash \cdots \backslash (\psi_k, A_k) \leftarrow s\theta], \iota \rangle}, \quad (\textbf{P4})$$

$$\frac{self \in A_k, \langle B, G, h_1''', \theta \rangle \models failed(\rho), UC(h_1''') \neq \top}{\langle B, G, h_1''', \theta \rangle \to \langle B, G, UC(h_1'''), \theta \rangle}, \quad (\textbf{P5})$$

$$\frac{self \in A_k, \langle B, G, h_1''', \theta \rangle \models failed(\rho), UC(h_1''') = \top}{\langle B, G, h_1''', \theta \rangle \to \mathbf{STOP}(h_1''')}. \quad (\textbf{P6})$$

where $s^0 = (\mathbf{Do}\ self\ (\mathbf{send}\ A_k, \langle ctell, self, \psi_0, \rho \rangle));$
$\quad (\mathbf{wait\ until}\ (\forall a \in A \cdot ctell(a, \psi_0, \rho) \in B)),$
$s^1 = (\mathbf{Do}\ self\ (\mathbf{send}\ A, \langle sync, self, \psi_0, \rho \rangle)); (\mathbf{wait\ until}\ (\forall a \in A \cdot sync(a, \psi_0, \rho) \in B));$
$\quad (\mathbf{Do}\ self\ (\mathbf{unsync}\ \psi_0, \rho)); body(\rho)\theta\eta\tau; s^0,$
$s^2 = (\mathbf{wait\ until}\ (\forall a \in A \cdot ctell(a, \psi_0, \rho) \in B)).$

Par is a construct that takes a list of processes and executes them in any order. When each process in the list has completed successfully, the entire **par** process is said to complete successfully. If at any point one of the process fails, then the entire **par** process returns failure and gives up executing any of the statements after that point.

Intuitively, a parallel statement with k branches requires the current process (transition) to split itself into k processes. These spawned processes each will be responsible for the execution of exactly one parallel branch, and they have to be merged into one process immediately after each has completed its own responsibility. To prevent the spawned processes from committing to other tasks, their initial transitions need to be established such that (1) the intention set only has one intention with one intention slice at its top; (2) the goal base is empty (so that the transition cannot proceed further after the unique intention has been completed). Because the original goal set and intention set has to be recovered after the execution of the parallel statement, we adopt an extra transition, which has the same components as the original transition except that $\#$ is pushed as the top intention slice, which indicates that this specific intention is *suspended*.

Definition 16 (Parallel construct). *Let* $h_0 = [\omega_0 \backslash \cdots \backslash (\psi_k, A_k) \leftarrow s_k; s]$,
$h = [\omega_0 \backslash \cdots \backslash (\psi_k, A_k) \leftarrow s_k; s \backslash \#]$, *where* $s_k = (\mathbf{par}\ l_1\ l_2 \cdots l_m)$,
$T_j = \langle B, \emptyset, [(true, A_k) \leftarrow l_j], \theta \rangle \rightarrow^* \langle B_j, \emptyset, [(true, A_k) \leftarrow \varepsilon], \theta_j \rangle \wedge B_j \not\models failed(l_j)$,
and
$P_B = \langle B, G, h, \theta \rangle \parallel \langle B, \emptyset, [(true, A_k) \leftarrow l_1], \theta \rangle \parallel \cdots \parallel \langle B, \emptyset, [(true, A_k) \leftarrow l_m], \theta \rangle$,

$$\frac{\langle B, G, h_0, \theta \not\models failed(s_k) \rangle}{\langle B, G, h_0, \theta \rangle \rightarrow P_B}, \tag{PA1}$$

$$\frac{\bigwedge_{j=1}^{m}(T_j), B' = BU(\bigcup_{j=1}^{m} B_j, B), \theta' = \theta_0 \theta_1 \cdots \theta_m}{\langle B, G, h, \theta \rangle \rightarrow \langle B', G, [\omega_0 \backslash \cdots \backslash (\psi_k, A_k) \leftarrow s], \theta' \rangle}. \tag{PA2}$$

In Definition 16, Rule **PA1** states that when an agent reaches a **par** statement, if the par statement is not failed, the transition is split into $k + 1$ parallel transitions. Rule **PA2** states that if all the spawned processes execute successfully, the suspended intention will be reactivated with the belief base and substitution modified.

Now, it is straightforward to define semantics for composite processes. For instance, the **forall** construct is an implied **par** over the condition bindings, whereas the **foreach** is an implied **seq** over the condition bindings. The constructs **forall** and **foreach** are fairly expressive when the number of choices is unknown before runtime.

Definition 17 (Composite plans). *Let*
$h_1 = [\omega_0 \backslash \cdots \backslash (\psi_k, A_k) \leftarrow (\mathbf{if}\ (\mathbf{cond}\ \phi)\ l_1\ l_2); s]$,
$h_2 = [\omega_0 \backslash \cdots \backslash (\psi_k, A_k) \leftarrow (\mathbf{while}\ (\mathbf{cond}\ \phi)\ l); s]$,
$h_3 = [\omega_0 \backslash \cdots \backslash (\psi_k, A_k) \leftarrow (\mathbf{foreach}\ (\mathbf{cond}\ \phi)\ l); s]$,
$h_4 = [\omega_0 \backslash \cdots \backslash (\psi_k, A_k) \leftarrow (\mathbf{forall}\ (\mathbf{cond}\ \phi)\ l); s]$,

$$\frac{B \models \phi\theta\tau}{\langle B, G, \{h_1\}, \theta \rangle \rightarrow \langle B, G, \{[\omega_0 \backslash \cdots \backslash (\psi_k, A_k) \leftarrow l_1\tau; s]\}, \theta \rangle}, \tag{S1}$$

$$\frac{\not\exists \tau \cdot B \models \phi\theta\tau}{\langle B, G, \{h_1\}, \theta\rangle \rightarrow \langle B, G, \{[\omega_0 \backslash \cdots \backslash (\psi_k, A_k) \leftarrow l_2; s]\}, \theta\rangle}, \tag{S2}$$

$$\frac{B \models \phi\theta\tau}{\langle B, G, \{h_2\}, \theta\rangle \rightarrow \langle B, G, \{[\omega_0 \backslash \cdots \backslash (\psi_k, A_k) \leftarrow l\tau; (\textbf{while } (\textbf{cond } \phi) \ l); s]\}, \theta\rangle}, \tag{S3}$$

$$\frac{\not\exists \tau \cdot B \models \phi\theta\tau}{\langle B, G, \{h_2\}, \theta\rangle \rightarrow \langle B, G, \{[\omega_0 \backslash \cdots \backslash (\psi_k, A_k) \leftarrow s], \theta\rangle}, \tag{S4}$$

$$\frac{\exists \tau_1, \cdots, \tau_k \cdot \bigwedge_{j=1}^{k} B \models \phi\theta\tau_j}{\langle B, G, \{h_3\}, \theta\rangle \rightarrow \langle B, G, \{[\omega_0 \backslash \cdots \backslash (\psi_k, A_k) \leftarrow l\tau_1; \cdots; l\tau_k; s]\}, \theta\rangle}, \tag{S5}$$

$$\frac{\not\exists \tau \cdot B \models \phi\theta\tau}{\langle B, G, \{h_3\}, \theta\rangle \rightarrow \langle B, G, \{[\omega_0 \backslash \cdots \backslash (\psi_k, A_k) \leftarrow s]\}, \theta\rangle}, \tag{S6}$$

$$\frac{\exists \tau_1, \cdots, \tau_k \cdot \bigwedge_{j=1}^{k} B \models \phi\theta\tau_j}{\langle B, G, \{h_4\}, \theta\rangle \rightarrow \langle B, G, \{[\omega_0 \backslash \cdots \backslash (\psi_k, A_k) \leftarrow (\textbf{par } l\tau_1 \cdots l\tau_k); s]\}, \theta\rangle}, \tag{S7}$$

$$\frac{\not\exists \tau \cdot B \models \phi\theta\tau}{\langle B, G, \{h_4\}, \theta\rangle \rightarrow \langle B, G, \{[\omega_0 \backslash \cdots \backslash (\psi_k, A_k) \leftarrow s]\}, \theta\rangle} \tag{S8}$$

5   CAST–An Agent Architecture Realizing MALLET

CAST (Collaborative Agents for Simulating Teamwork) is a team-oriented agent architecture that supports teamwork using a shared mental model (SMM) among teammates [8]. The CAST kernel includes an implemented interpreter of MAL-LET. At compile time, CAST translates processes specified in MALLET into PrT nets (specialized Petri-Nets), which use predicate evaluation at decision points. CAST supports predicate evaluation using a knowledge base with a Java-based backward chaining reasoning engine called JARE. The main distinguishing feature of CAST is proactive team behaviors enabled by the fact that agents within a CAST architecture share the same declarative specification of team structure and process as well as share explicit declaration of what each agent can observe. Therefore, every agent can reason about what other teammates are working on, what the preconditions of teammates' actions are, whether a team-mate can observe the information required to evaluate a precondition, and hence what information might be potentially useful to the teammate. As such, agents can figure out what information to proactively deliver to teammates, and use a decision theoretic cost/benefit analysis for doing proactive information delivery. CAST has been used in several domains including fire-fighting, simulated battle fields [24]. Examples and practices of using MALLET can be found in [25].

Figure 1 is a screen shot of CAST monitor. CAST monitor can display the PrT nets (visual representation of MALLET plans) that a team of agents are working on. Different colors are used to indicate the progress of activities, so that a human can track the running status of a team process.

It is worth noting that MALLET is designed to be a language for encoding teamwork knowledge, and CAST is just one agent architecture that realizes

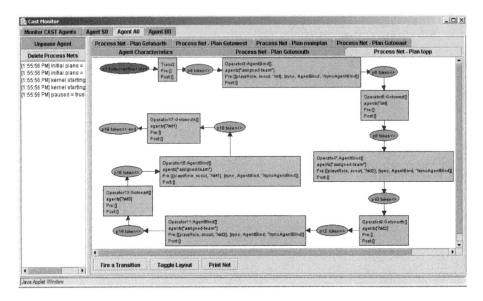

Fig. 1. The CAST Monitor

MALLET. It is not required that all agents in a team have to be homogeneous in that they are all implemented in the same way. Agents with different architectures can form a team and work together with CAST agents as long as they conform to the semantics of MALLET and the same communication protocols.

6   Comparison and Discussion

We compare MALLET with JACK Teams [26], OWL-S [27], PDDL [28], and the team-oriented programming framework [9].

JACK Teams [26], instead of providing a higher-level plan-encoding language like MALLET, extends a traditional programming language (i.e. Java) with special statements for programming team activities. In JACK Teams, a team is an individual reasoning entity characterized by the roles it performs and the roles it requires others to perform. To form a team is to set up the declared role obligation structure by identifying particular sub-teams capable of performing the roles to be filled.

JACK Teams has constructs particularly for specifying team-oriented behaviors. **Teamdata** is a concept that allows propagation of beliefs from teams to sub-teams and vice versa. In a sense, belief propagation in JACK is comparable to the maintenance of SMM in CAST. However, SMM in CAST is a much more general concept, which includes team plans, progress of team activities, results of task allocations, decision results of choice points, information needs graphs, etc. CAST Agents in a team need to proactively exchange information (beliefs) to maintain the consistency of their SMM. Statements @*team_achieve* and @*parallel* are used in JACK for team goal handling. @*team_achieve* is similar to the *DO* statement in MALLET, except that @*team_achieve* is realized by sending an event to the involved sub-team while the agents involved in a *DO* statement can start to perform the associated activity whenever they reach the statement along the team process. A @*parallel* statement can specify success condition, termination condition, how termination is notified, and whether to monitor and control the parallel execution. In semantics, @*parallel* statements can be simulated using *PAR* or *CHOICE* in MALLET. As far as failure handling is concerned, JACK Teams leverages the Java exception mechanism to throw and catch exceptions while in CAST, *CHOICE* points are used as places to catch failures and re-attempt the failed goals if needed, which is much more flexible in recovery from failure at the team plan level.

OWL-S [27] is an ontology language for describing properties and capabilities of Web services. It enables users and software agents to automatically discover, invoke, compose, and monitor Web services. Similar to MALLET, OWL-S provides constructs (such as Sequence, Split, Split+Join, Choice, Unordered, If-Then-Else, Iterate, etc.) for composing composite processes, to which preconditions and effects can be specified. There exist correspondences between OWL-S and MALLET. For instance, both 'Split' in OWL-S and *PAR* in MALLET can be used to specify concurrent activities. The main difference between these two languages lies in the fact that MALLET is designed for encoding team intelligence where the actors of each activity within a team process need to collaborate with each other in pursuing their joint goals, while OML-S, as an abstract framework for describing service workflows, does not consider collaboration issues from the perspective of teamwork.

PDDL (the Planning Domain Definition Language) [28], inspired by the well-known STRIPS formulations of planning problems, is a standard language for the encoding of planning domains. PDDL is capable of capturing a wide variety of complex behaviors using constructs such as *seq*, *parallel*, *choice*, *foreach* and *forsome*. The semantics of processes in PDDL is grounded on a branching time structure. One key difference between PDDL and MALLET is that PDDL is used for guiding planning while MALLET is used for encoding the planning results. The processes defined in PDDL serve as guides for a planner to compose actions to achieve certain goals, while the processes in MALLET serve as common recipes for a team of agents to collaborate their behaviors.

In summary, MALLET has been designed as a language for encoding teamwork knowledge, and CAST is just one agent architecture that realizes MALLET. It is not required that all agents in a team have to be homogeneous in that they are all implemented in the same way. Agents with different architectures can form a team and work together with CAST agents as long as their kernels conform to the semantics of MALLET and the same communication protocols.

MALLET does have several limitations. For instance, there is no clear semantics defined for dynamic joining or leaving a team. Also, MALLET does not specify what to do if agents do not have a plan to reach a goal. Although some of these issues can be left open to agent system designers, providing a language-level solution might be helpful in guiding the implementation of team-based agent systems. One way is to extend MALLET with certain build-in meta-plans. For instance, meta-plans, say, *resource-based-planner*, can be added so that agents could execute it to construct a plan when they need but do not have one.

7   Conclusion

MALLET is a language that organizes plans hierarchically in terms of different process constructs such as sequential, parallel, selective, iterative, or conditional. It can be used to represent teamwork knowledge in a way that is independent of the context in which the knowledge is used. In this paper, we defined an operational semantics for MALLET in terms of a transition system, which is important in further studying the formal properties of team-based agents specified in MALLET. The effectiveness of MALLET in encoding complex teamwork knowledge has already been shown in the CAST system [8], which implements an interpreter for MALLET using PrT nets as the internal representation of team process.

Acknowledgments

This research has been supported by AFOSR MURI grant No. F49620-00-1-0326.

References

1. Cohen, P.R., Levesque, H.J.: Teamwork. Nous **25**:487–512, (1991)
2. Cohen, P.R., Levesque, H.J., Smith, I.A.: On team formation. In Hintikka, J., Tuomela, R., eds.: Contemporary Action Theory. (1997)
3. Jennings, N.R.: Controlling cooperative problem solving in industrial multi-agent systems using joint intentions. Artificial Intelligence **75** (1995) 195–240
4. Grosz, B., Kraus, S.: Collaborative plans for complex group actions. Artificial Intelligence **86** (1996) 269–358
5. Tambe, M.: Towards flexible teamwork. Journal of AI Research **7** (1997) 83–124
6. Rich, C., Sidner, C.: Collagen: When agents collaborate with people. In: Proceedings of the International Conference on Autonomous Agents (Agents'97). (1997) 284–291
7. Giampapa, J., Sycara, K.: Team-oriented agent coordination in the RETSINA multi-agent system. Technical Report CMU-RI-TR-02-34, CMU (2002)
8. Yen, J., Yin, J., Ioerger, T., Miller, M., Xu, D., Volz, R.: CAST: Collaborative agents for simulating teamworks. In: Proceedings of IJCAI'2001. (2001) 1135–1142
9. Tidhar, G.: Team oriented programming: Preliminary report. In: Technical Report 41, AAII, Australia. (1993)
10. Pynadath, D.V., Tambe, M., Chauvat, N., Cavedon, L.: Toward team-oriented programming. In: Agent Theories, Architectures, and Languages. (1999) 233–247

11. Scerri, P., Pynadath, D.V., Schurr, N., Farinelli, A.: Team oriented programming and proxy agents: the next generation. In: Proc. of the 1st Inter. Workshop on Prog. MAS at AAMAS'03. (2003) 131–138

12. Rao, A.S., Georgeff, M.P., Sonenberg, E.A.: Social plans: A preliminary report. In Werner, E., Demazeau, Y., eds.: Decentralized AI 3 –Proceedings of MAAMAW-91), Elsevier Science B.V.: Amsterdam, Netherland (1992) 57–76

13. Kinny, D., Ljungberg, M., Rao, A.S., Sonenberg, E., Tidhar, G., Werner, E.: Planned team activity. In Castelfranchi, C., Werner, E., eds.: Artificial Social Systems (LNAI-830), Springer-Verlag: Heidelberg, Germany (1992) 226–256

14. Tidhar, G., Rao, A., Sonenberg, E.: Guided team selection. In: Proceedings of the 2nd International Conference on Multi-agent Systems (ICMAS-96). (1996)

15. Rao, A.: AgentSpeak(L): BDI agents speak out in a logical computable language. In: MAAMAW'96, LNAI 1038, Springer-Verlag: Heidelberg, Germany (1996) 42–55

16. Pozos-Parra, P., Nayak, A., Demolombe, R.: Theories of intentions in the framework of situation calculus. In Leite, J., Omicini, A., Torroni, P., Yolum, P., eds.: Declarative Agent Languages and Technologies (DALT 2004), LNCS 3476, Springer-Verlag (2005). In this volume.

17. Bordini, R., Fisher, M., Pardavila, C., Wooldridge, M.: Model checking agentspeak. In: Proceedings of AAMAS-2003. (2003) 409–416

18. Wooldridge, M., Fisher, M., Huget, M., Parsons, S.: Model checking multiagent systems with MABLE. In: Proceedings of AAMAS-2002. (2002) 952–959

19. Dastani, M., van Riemsdijk, B., Dignum, F., Meyer, J.J.C.: A programming language for cognitive agents: Goal directed 3APL. In: Proc. of the 1st Inter. Workshop on Prog. MAS at AAMAS'03. (2003) 111–130

20. Giacomo, G.D., Lesperance, Y., Levesque, H.J.: ConGolog, a concurrent programming language based on the situation calculus. AI **121** (2000) 109–169

21. van Riemsdijk, M.B., Dastani, M., Dignum, F., Meyer, J.J.C.: Dynamics of declarative goals in agent programming. In Leite, J., Omicini, A., Torroni, P., Yolum, P., eds.: Declarative Agent Languages and Technologies (DALT 2004), LNCS 3476, Springer-Verlag (2005). In this volume.

22. Robertson, D.: A lightweight coordination calculus for agent systems. In Leite, J., Omicini, A., Torroni, P., Yolum, P., eds.: Declarative Agent Languages and Technologies (DALT 2004), LNCS 3476, Springer-Verlag (2005). In this volume.

23. Winikoff, M., Liu, W., Harland, J.: Enhancing commitment machines. In Leite, J., Omicini, A., Torroni, P., Yolum, P., eds.: Declarative Agent Languages and Technologies (DALT 2004), LNCS 3476, Springer-Verlag (2005). In this volume.

24. Yen, J., Fan, X., Sun, S., Hanratty, T., Dumer, J.: Agents with shared mental models for enhancing team decision-makings. Decision Support Systems, Special issue on Intelligence and Security Informatics (In press) (2004)

25. Yen, J., et al: CAST manual. Technical report, IST, The Pennsylvania State University (2004)

26. JACK Teams Manual. http://www.agent-software.com/shared/demosNdocs/JACK-Teams-Manual.pdf. (2004)

27. OWL-S. http://www.daml.org/services/owl-s/1.0/owl-s.html (2003)

28. McDermott, D.: The formal semantics of processes in PDDL. In: Proc. ICAPS Workshop on PDDL. (2003)

Construction of an Agent-Based Framework for Evolutionary Biology: A Progress Report

Yu Pan, Phan Huy Tu, Enrico Pontelli, and Tran Cao Son

Department of Computer Science,
New Mexico State University,
{ypan,tphan,epontell,tson}@cs.nmsu.edu

Abstract. We report on the development of an agent-based system, called ΦLOG, for the specification and execution of phylogenetic inference applications. We detail the implementation of the main components of the system. In the process, we discuss how advanced techniques developed in different research areas such as domain-specific languages, planning, Web Services discovery and invocation, and Web Service compositions can be applied in the building of the ΦLOG system.

1 Introduction

In biological sciences data is accumulating much faster than our ability to convert it into meaningful knowledge. For example, the Human Genome Project and related activities have flooded our databases with molecular data. The size of the DNA sequence database maintained by NCBI has surpassed 15 million sequences and keeps growing at a rapid pace. Our modeling tools are woefully inadequate for the task of integrating all that information into the rest of biology, preventing scientists from using these data to draw meaningful biological inferences. Thus, one of the major challenges faced by computer scientists and biologists *together* is the enhancement of information technology suitable for modeling a diversity of biological entities, leading to a greater *understanding* from the influx of data. Instead of allowing the direct expression of high-level concepts natural to a scientific discipline, current development techniques require mastery of programming and access to low level aspects of software development.

1.1 The ΦLOG Project

The ΦLOG project at NMSU is aimed at the development of a computational workbench to allow evolutionary biologists to rapidly and independently construct computational analysis processes in phylogenetic inference. Phylogenetic inference involves the study of evolutionary change of traits (genetic or genomic sequences, morphology, physiology, behavior, etc.) in the context of biological entities (genes, genomes, individuals, species, higher taxa, etc.) related to each other by a phylogenetic tree or genealogy depicting the hierarchical relationship of common ancestors.

The overall objective of the ΦLOG framework is to allow biologists to design computational analysis processes by describing them at the same level of abstraction com-

J. Leite et al. (Eds.): DALT 2004, LNAI 3476, pp. 92–111, 2005.

monly used by biologists to think and communicate—and not in terms of complex low-level programming constructs and communication protocols. The ΦLOG framework will automatically translate these high-level descriptions into executable programs—commonly containing appropriately composed sequences of invocations to external bioinformatics tools (e.g., BLAST, DNAML).

The ΦLOG framework is characterized by two innovative aspects: the use of a *Domain Specific Language (DSL)* as interface to the biologists and the adoption of an agent-based platform for the execution of ΦLOG programs. These aspects are discussed in the next subsections.

1.2   The ΦLOG Language

The ΦLOG framework offers biologists a *Domain Specific Language (DSL)* for the description of computational analysis processes in evolutionary biology. The DSL allows biologists to computationally solve a problem by programming solutions *at the same level of abstraction they use for thinking and reasoning*. In the DSL approach, a language is developed to allow users to build software in an application domain by using programming constructs that are natural for the specific domain. A DSL results in programs that are more likely to be correct, easier to write and reason about, and easier to maintain. The DSL approach to software engineering has been advocated by many researchers [11, 14, 15, 20, 29].

The ΦLOG DSL has been extensively described in [25]. The language provides:

- high-level data types representing the classes of entities typically encountered in evolutionary biology analysis (e.g., genes, taxon, alignments). The set of types and their properties have been derived as a combination of existing data description languages (e.g., NEXUS [22]) and biological ontologies (e.g., Bio-Ontology [28]).
- high-level operations corresponding to the transformations commonly adopted in computational analyses for evolutionary biology (e.g., sequence alignment, phylogenetic tree construction, sequence similarity search). The operations are described at a high-level; the mapping from high-level operations to concrete computational tools can be either automatically realized by the ΦLOG execution model, or explicitly resolved by the programmer.
- both declarative as well as imperative control structures to describe execution flow. Declarative control relies on high-level combinators (e.g., functions, quantifiers) while imperative control relies on more traditional sequencing, conditional, and iterative control forms.

1.3   The ΦLOG Agent Infrastructure

An essential goal behind the development of ΦLOG is to provide biologists with a framework that facilitates discovery and use of the variety of bioinformatics tools and data repository publicly available. The Web has become a means for the widespread distribution of a large quantity of analysis tools and data sources, each providing different capabilities, interfaces, data formats and different modalities of operation. Biologists are left with the daunting task of locating the most appropriate tools for each specific analysis task, learning how to use them, dealing with the issues of interoperability (e.g., data format conversions), and interpreting the results. As a result of this state of things, frequently biologists make use of suboptimal tools, are forced to perform time-consuming manual tasks, and, more in general, are limited in the scope of analysis and range of hypothesis they can explore.

ΦLOG relies on an agent infrastructure, where existing bioinformatics tools and data sources are viewed as *bioinformatics services*. Services are formally described; the agent infrastructure is in charge of making use of such formal descriptions and of the content of ΦLOG programs to determine the appropriate sequence of service invocations required to accomplish the task described by the biologist. The reasoning component of the agent is employed to select services and compose them, eventually introducing additional services to guarantee interoperability. The rest of this paper describes in detail the structure of such agent infrastructure.

1.4   Related Work

Relatively limited effort has been invested in the use of agent-based technology to facilitate the creation of analysis processes and computational biology applications. TAMBIS [10] provides a knowledge base for accessing a set of data sources, and it can map queries expressed in graphical form to sequences of accesses. Some proposals have recently appeared addressing some of the aspects covered by ΦLOG , such as ontologies for computational biology (e.g., BIOML [12] and Bio-Ontology [28]), interoperability initiatives (e.g., the Bioperl Project [6], XOL project [21] and the TAMBIS project [10]), low-level infrastructure for bioinformatics services (e.g., OmniGene [8], BioMOBY [9], and the DAS [24]), and generic bioinformatics computational infrastructures (e.g., BioSoft [13, 16]). Most of the aforementioned projects concentrate on the problem of accessing and querying various biological data sources, while we emphasize on the problem of automatic composition of biological web services. Like others, we propose to use ontologies and web services as a means to overcome different obstacles in the integration and exploitation of biological services.

2   System Overview

The overall architecture of our system is illustrated in Figure 1. The execution of ΦLOG programs will be carried out by an agent infrastructure and will develop according to the flow denoted by the arrows in Figure 1. In this framework, bioinformatics tools are viewed as *Web services*; in turn, each agent treats such services as *actions*, and the execution of ΦLOG programs is treated as an instance of the *planning and execution monitoring problem* [19]. Each data source and tool has to be properly described (in terms of capabilities, inputs and outputs) so that the agent can determine when a particular data source or tool can be used to satisfy one of the steps required by the ΦLOG program. This description process is supported by a *bioinformatics ontologies* for the description of the entities involved in this process. ΦLOG programs will be processed by a compiler and translated into an *abstract plan*, that identifies the high-level actions (i.e., analysis steps) required, along with their correct execution order. The abstract plan is processed by a *configuration component*; the output of the configuration component is a situation calculus theory [26] and a ConGolog program [17]. The ConGolog program represents the underlying skeleton of the plan required to perform the computation described in the original ΦLOG program. The action theory describes the actions that can be

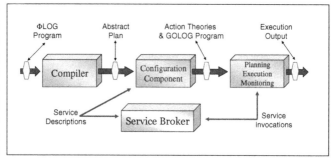

Fig. 1. Overall System Organization

used in such plan. These actions correspond to the bioinformatics services that can be employed to carry out the tasks described by the high-level actions present in the abstract plan. The descriptions of such actions are retrieved from a *service broker*, which maintains (DAML-S) descriptions of all registered bioinformatics services.

The situation calculus theory and the ConGolog program are then processed by a *planner*; the task of the planner is to develop a *concrete plan*, which indicates how to compose individual bioinformatics services to accomplish the objectives required by biologists in their ΦLOG programs. In the concrete plan, the high-level actions are replaced by invocation calls to concrete bioinformatics services; the concrete plan might also include additional steps not indicated in the original ΦLOG program, e.g., to support interoperation between services (e.g., data format conversions) and to resolve ambiguities (e.g., tests to select one of possible services). The creation of the concrete plan relies on technology for *reasoning about actions and change*. The planner is integrated with an execution monitor, in charge of executing the concrete plan, by repeatedly contacting the broker to request the execution of specific services. The execution monitor interacts with the planner to resolve situations where a plan fails and replanning is required.

3   Service Description and Management

Bioinformatics services are described in our framework using DAML-S 0.7[1], a language built on top of the DAML+OIL[2] ontology for Web Services. We adopt DAML-S over previously developed Web Service languages (e.g., WSDL[3],SOAP[4]), for its expressiveness and declarativeness. Furthermore, DAML-S is developed for the purpose of making Web Services computer-interpretable, thus allowing the development of agents for service discovery, invocation, and composition. As such, it should be a good representation language for representing bioinformatic services. We used DAML-

---

[1] www.daml.org/services/daml-s/0.7/.

[2] www.daml.org/2001/03/daml+oil-index.html.

[3] www.w3.org/TR/wsdl.

[4] ws.apache.org/soap/.

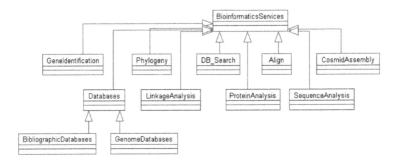

Fig. 2. Part of Service Hierarchy

S to represent the bioinformatic services necessary for our experiment. DAML-S turned out to be adequate to provide high-level descriptions of services. The main obstacle we encountered is the mismatch between the current technology and the execution of DAML-S services: for each service, we have to develop our own interface between the ΦLOG system and the bioinformatic service, being the latter still provided through HTTP-requests.

3.1   Service Description

Bioinformatic services in ΦLOG are classified into a hierarchy. This classification facilitates the matching between the high-level actions present in a ΦLOG program and the services. More details related to this topic will be discussed in Section 5. A part of the hierarchy used for services classification is shown in Figures 2. The top class in this hierarchy is called `BioinformaticsServices` and is specified by the XML-element:

```
<daml:Class rdf:ID="BiologyServices">
 <rdfs:label>Biology Service</rdfs:label>
 <rdfs:comment> ... </rdfs:comment>
 <rdfs:subClassOf rdf:resource= "www.daml.org/services/
   daml-s/0.7/ProfileHierarchy.daml#Information_Service" />
</daml:Class>
```

All the other classes are derived directly or indirectly from this class. As an example (Figure 2), `BibliographicDatabases` and `GenomeDatabases` are subclasses of the `Databases` class, which, in turn, is a subclass of `BioinformaticsServices`. Both of them are database related services which allow users to access different databases. Some of these services are GDB [3] (Human genomic information), OMIM [4] (Catalogue of human genetic disorders), EMBASE [7] (Excerpta Medica Database), etc.. Their representation is as follows.

```
<daml:Class rdf:ID="GenomeDatabases">
    <rdfs:subClassOf rdf:resource="#Databases"/>
</daml:Class>
<daml:Class rdf:ID="BiliographicDatabases">
```

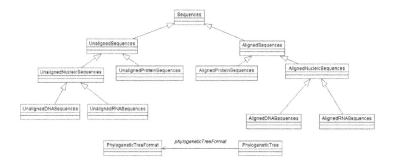

Fig. 3. Part of Bioinformatic Object Classification

```
    <rdfs:subClassOf rdf:resource="#Databases"/>
</daml:Class>
```

Information about the service classification is stored in the file *datatypes.daml* [5] In addition to the classification of services, this file also contains information about the types of biological entities that are important for the development of our system. As with services, these objects are also organized as class hierarchies to facilitate reasoning about types of objects in different components of our system. For example, to represent biological sequences, we use a corresponding class `Sequences`. Part of this classification is shown in Figure 3. The file *datatypes.daml* also includes some predefined instances of classes. E.g., the FASTA format is represented as an instance `SF_FASTA` of the class `SequenceFormat` in the *datatypes.daml*.

```
<SequenceFormat rdf:ID="SF_FASTA">
  <sequenceFormatProvider rdf:resource="#P_FASTA"/>
</SequenceFormat>
```

Let us now describe the DAML-S representation of services through an example. We will present the description of the `ClustalW` service, a multiple sequence alignment program [2]. In DAML-S, each service is characterized by a *profile* representing the capabilities and parameters of the service, a *process model* illustrating the workflow of the service and a *grounding* file specifying in details how to access the service. The DAML-S representation of the `ClustalW` service will correspondingly compose of four files[6].

The first file *clustalw-service.daml*[7] stores information about the locations of the profile, the process model, and the grounding:

```
<service:Service rdf:ID="Service_ClustalW">
  <service:presents
```

---

[5] www.cs.nmsu.edu/~tphan/philog/nondet/datatypes.daml.

[6] The complete DAML-S descriptions of this service can be found at www.cs.nmsu.edu/~tphan/philog/nondet/.

[7] www.cs.nmsu.edu/~tphan/philog/nondet/clustalw-service.daml.

```
    rdf:resource="&clw_profile;#Profile_ClustalW"/>
  <service:describedBy
    rdf:resource="&clw_process;#Process_ClustalW"/>
  <service:supports
    rdf:resource="&clw_grounding;#Grounding_ClustalW"/>
</service:Service>
```

The second file, *clustalw-profile.daml*[8] is the profile for `ClustalW` service. It defines the parameters needed for the invocation of this service and specifies the membership of this service in the service classification hierarchy. For example, `ClustalW` is an instance of the class `Align`. This is specified by the element

```
<ftypes:Align rdf:ID="Profile_ClustalW">
  . . .
</ftypes:Align>
```

This file also contains input, output, or precondition elements defining the service's inputs, outputs, and preconditions, respectively. They are the parameters of the service. The type of each parameter is specified by the `restrictedTo` property. For example, the element

```
<profile:input> <profile:ParameterDescription
rdf:ID="Sequences">
<profile:restrictedTo rdf:resource="&ftypes;#UnalignedSequences"/>
  <profile:refersTo rdf:resource="&clw_process;#sequences"/>
</profile:ParameterDescription> </profile:input>
```

encodes   an   input   parameter   named   `Sequences`   of   the   type `UnalignedSequences`.

The third file (the process model file) provides the necessary information for an agent to use the service. For example, whether it is an atomic process or a composed process, what are its inputs, outputs, and preconditions. For the `ClustalW` service[9], the element:

```
<daml:Class rdf:ID="ClustalWProcess">
  <rdfs:subClassOf rdf:resource="&process;#AtomicProcess" />
</daml:Class>
```

specifies that it is an atomic process. The element:

```
<daml:Property rdf:ID="sequences">
  <daml:subPropertyOf rdf:resource="&process;#input"/>
  <daml:domain rdf:resource="#ClustalWProcess"/>
  <daml:range rdf:resource="&ftypes;#UnalignedSequences"/>
</daml:Property>
```

specifies that it has an input of the type `UnalignedSequence`.

---

[8] `www.cs.nmsu.edu/~tphan/philog/nondet/clustalw-profile.daml`.
[9] `www.cs.nmsu.edu/~tphan/philog/nondet/clustalw-process.daml`.

The grounding model for `ClustalW` specifies the details of how to access the service—details having mainly to do with protocol and message formats, serialization, transport, and addressing. It consists of two complementary parts: a DAML-S file specifying the mapping between DAML processes/types and WSDL operations/messages, and a WSDL file designating the binding of messages to various protocols and formats.

For example, in the file *clustalw-grounding.daml* we can find the description of the mapping from the DAML type description of `ClustalW`'s input to the corresponding WSDL type:

```
<grounding:wsdlInputMessage rdf:resource="&wsdl;#clustalwInput"/>
<grounding:wsdlInputs rdf:parseType="daml:collection">
  <grounding:wsdlInputMessageMap>
  <grounding:damlsParameter rdf:resource="#sequence">
  <grounding:wsdlMessagePart>
  <xsd:uriReference rdf:value="&wsdl;#sequence">
  </grounding:wsdlMessagePart>
  </grounding:wsdlInputMessageMap>
</grounding:wsdlInputs>
```

In the companion WSDL file (*clustalw-grounding.wsdl*) we can find the binding information—protocol and message format—for the `ClustalW` operation, along with the URL of the service.

3.2   Service Management

The services, together with their classification, are registered with the service broker, which is responsible for providing service descriptions to the configuration module and fulfilling service execution requests from the execution monitoring modules. We employ the OAA system [30] in the development of the service broker. To facilitate these tasks, a *lookup agent* and several *service wrappers* have been developed. The lookup agent receives high-level action names from the compiler and will match these actions with possible available services. For example, a request for a high-level action `align` will be answered with the set of all available alignment services such as `service_clustalw` and `service_dialign`. This process will be detailed in Section 5. Service wrappers have been developed for the purpose of executing the services since most of the bioinformatic services are still offered through http-requests and not as Web services. Agents—playing the role of service wrappers—are ready for the instantiation and execution of bioinformatic services.

4   ΦLOG Compiler

The objective of the ΦLOG compiler is to process a program written in ΦLOG and produce as output a high-level sketch of the execution plan—what we call an *abstract plan*—a symbol table describing the entities involved in the computation, in terms of their names and types. The main tasks of the ΦLOG compiler include syntax analysis, type checking, and construction of the abstract plan.

4.1   Syntax Analysis

Each ΦLOG program contains a sequence of declarations and a sequence of statements. The declaration part is used to:

- describe the data items (variables) used by the program;
- allow users to select the computational components to be used during execution—e.g., associate high-level ΦLOG operations to specific bioinformatics tools;
- provide parameters affecting the behavior of the different components.

Each data item used in the program must be properly declared. Declarations are of the type `<variable> : <type> [<properties>]` and are used to explicitly describe data items, by providing a name (`<variable>`), a description of the nature of the values that are going to be stored in it (`<type>`) and eventually properties of the item. For example, `gene1 : Gene ( gi | 557882 )` declares an entity called `gene1`, of type `Gene`, and identifies the initial value for this object—the gene with accession number `557882` in the GenBank database.

Declarations are also used to identify computational components to be used during the execution—this allows the user to customize some of the operations performed. For example, a declaration of the type

```
align_sequences : Operation(CLUSTALW -- alignment = full,
    score type = percent, matrix = pam, pairgap = 4 );
```

allows the user to configure the language operation `align_sequences`—a ΦLOG operation to perform sequence alignments—by associating this operation with the alignment program (`ClustalW`), with the given values for the input parameters.

Variable assignments are expressed as:

```
        <output variable> is <operation>(<input variable>).
```

The syntax itself is self-explanatory. In this prototype, we have focused our attention on a subset of the possible classes of operations—i.e., `<searchOp>`, `<alignOp>`, `<buildTreeOp>`, and `<specificOp>`.

4.2   Type Checking

All variables used in a ΦLOG program must be declared with specific types. ΦLOG provides two classes of datatypes. The first class includes generic (non-domain specific) datatypes, while the second class includes all those datatypes that are domain-specific, like DNA Sequence, Protein, etc. These domain-specific types are defined in our type system. Part of the datatype hierarchy is shown in Fig. 3. There are two major types of type checking

- type checking against attributes of objects;
- type checking against input and output variables of operations.

Domain specific datatypes contain attributes that are specific to each type. Those attributes could be either generic or domain specific. Consider the following ΦLOG program segment

```
g1 : Gene ( gi | 557882 )
se : Sequence
se is sequence(g1)
```

It assigns to the variable g1 the Gene having accession number GI | 557882 and extracts its sequence data, which is stored in the variable se. The compiler must check the datatype hierarchy to verify that GI | 557882 is a legal value for an object of type Gene—i.e., it is a well-formed accession number—and an attribute called sequence with type Sequence exists for the type Gene. Attribute mismatches and type mismatches will cause compiling error.

Type checking is also performed for each operation in the program. Datatypes of input and output variables are defined in our services ontology (see Figure 2). The ΦLOG compiler must check the validity of such parameters; for example s2 is align(s1) performs a multi-sequence alignment operation on the data item s1, storing the result in data item s2. In order to be able to perform the action, s1 must be of type UnalignedSequences (i.e., a set of unaligned sequences) and s2 must be of type AlignedSequences (i.e., a set of aligned sequences).

4.3   Operations Identification and Abstract Plan Assembly

As described in the syntax analysis section, the current preliminary prototype focuses on a limited classes of operations (explored for feasibility purposes):

```
<operation> ::= <searchOp> | <alignOp> | <buildTreeOp> |
                <specificOp>
<searchOp> ::= <variable> : <variable> is <complexType> and
                <attribute>(<variable>) <verb> <literal>
<alignOp> ::= align
<buildTreeOp> ::= build_tree
```

Database search operations are conveniently expressed using intensional set constructions. For example, the following command defines a database search operation

```
p is { x : x is Gene and name(x) contains "fever" }
```

The operation searches a nucleotide database—automatically inferred from the type of the collected variable x—for all genes whose name contains the keyword "fever", and the resulting collection of genes is stored in the variable p.

Each syntactic occurrence of an operations leads to the generation of one high-level action in the abstract plan assembled by the compiler. The identification of the operation is accomplished by navigating the services hierarchy, with the goal of locating the most specific class of services corresponding to the specified operation. The operation provides a link to the most general class of services in the ontology corresponding to such operation (e.g., the align operation used in a ΦLOG program will link to the general class of sequence alignment services in service hierarchy); the usage of the operation—and, in particular, the type of the parameters, inputs, and outputs—will constrain the focus on appropriate subclasses of services.

The ΦLOG language allows us also to directly refer to specific services (e.g., either through a declaration, as illustrated in the previous section, or directly as an operation). For example, s is ClustalW_JP(p) identifies the ClustalW multi-sequence alignment service located at clustalw.genome.ad.jp. This operation is described in the service hierarchy, with input type UnalignedSequences and output type AlignedSequences. However, the use of a specific service is not recommended in a ΦLOG program because user then can not take advantage of the power of dynamic service plan composition of the ΦLOG framework.

As another example, the service hierarchy offers three subclasses of build_tree operation—used to construct a phylogenetic inference tree—that use different algorithms: ParsimonyAlign, DistanceMatrixAlign, and MaximumLikelyhoodAlign. These operations are differentiated by their input parameters and the ΦLOG compiler must be able to find the correct match. For example,

```
p : UnalignedSequences
m : DistanceMatrix
s is align(p, m)
```

identifies the operation DistanceMatrixAlign(p, m) because it has two inputs: a set of unaligned sequences and a distance matrix.

The output produced by the compiler is an abstract plan. The abstract plan is a ConGolog program whose actions are high-level actions. Each service is described by a three elements tuple: $\langle A, IL, OL \rangle$ where A is the operation name, IL is the list of A's input parameters and OL is the list of A's output parameters respectively. Each input or output is of the form (*name, type, value*), where *name, type*, and *value* are the name, type and value of the input/output respectively. The value of an input or output must be either a constant or a variable.

In addition to the abstract plan, the output of the compiler also contains information about all the variables used in the ΦLOG program and a list of high-level actions. Specifically, for each variable X of type T in the program, there is a corresponding fact $var(X, T)$ in the output. As an example, consider the ΦLOG program:

```
Program sample is
        p : UnalignedSequences;
        s : AlignedSequences;
        t : PhylogeneticTree;
begin
        p is  x : x is Gene and name(x) contains "fever";
        s is align(p);
        t is build_tree(s);
end
```

This simple program defines a sequence of operations—first search a database to find all the genes contains the keyword "fever", then conduct a multiple sequence alignment operation on the returned sequence set, and finally build a evolution tree based on the aligned sequence set. The output of the compiler is a list of three high-level actions db_search, align, and build_tree and the Prolog program

```
plan([(db_search, [(db,str,nucleotide),(term,str,fever)],
            [(sequence,unalignedsequences,p)]),
      (align, [(sequence,unalignedsequences,p)],
            [(sequence,alignedsequences,s)]),
      (build_tree,[(inFile,alignedsequences,s)],
            [(outputFile,phylogenetictree,t)])]).
var(t,phylogenetictree). var(s,alignedsequences).
var(p,unalignedsequences).
```

Here, the fact `plan(...)` represents the ΦLOG program and the set of facts of the form `var(.,.)` list the variables used in the program.

5   Configuration Component

The configuration component plays an important role in preparing the ΦLOG program for execution. Its input is an abstract plan from the compiler. Its output is a ConGolog program with a underlying situation calculus theory that will be used by the Planning and Execution monitoring module to execute the ΦLOG program. For the background

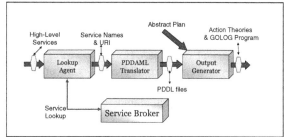

Fig. 4. Configuration Component

behind this design and its advantages, we refer the readers to our previous paper [27]. Figure 4 shows the phases of the configuration component. We next describe these phases in more detail.

5.1   DAML-PDDL Translator

The DAML-PDDL translator, in concert with the lookup agent from the broker, which is developed for the maintenance of the service registry, is responsible for collecting DAML-S service descriptions, needed for the execution of the ΦLOG program, and converting them into PDDL files. The lookup agent, after receiving the list of high-level actions from the compiler, will request the broker for the list of bioinformatic services which can be used to realize the high-level actions. The lookup agent will obtain the list of bioinformatic services' names and locations (URIs) and send them to the translator. For example, the `db_search` service is realized by the bioinformatic services `ncbi` and `blast` at `www.cs.nmsu.edu/~tphan/philog/nondet/`. For each service, the translator will download the service descriptions from the specified URIs and convert them to PDDL files[10].

---

[10] More precisely, the output is in WebPDDL format.

The DAML-PDDL translator used in this project, called PDDAML, is an automatic translator between PDDL and DAML from [5]. It is worth noticing that this step could be eliminated and replaced by a module that translates DAML-S service descriptions directly into a situation calculus theory. However, we still adopt this path for several reasons. First of all, the language DAML-S is still under development, and any changes in its specification would also mean changes to our system. Secondly, the language PDDL is well-known and accepted as the input language for many planning systems. Furthermore, the DAML-S parser and analyzer are being developed and updated by the DAML coalition. By using PDDAML, we make our system less sensitive to changes in the DAML-S specification and avoid the need of writing programs for processing DAML-S specifications.

Each DAML-S file (service, profile, process model, or grounding) — as described in Section 3 — is translated into a PDDL file, often referred to as a *PDDL domain*. Each PDDL domain consists of several sections specifying the external domains that are extended by the current domain and defining the domain's entities and their relationships such as data types, objects, predicates, axioms, etc. As an example, the PDDL domain representing the profile of the service `ClustaW` [11], named `clustalw-profile-ont`, uses the external domains `clustalw-service-ont` (representing the service) and `clustalw-process-ont` (representing the process model) and defines objects named `Profile_ClustalW`, `Sequences`, `OutputSequences`, etc.; it also contains axioms describing the input, output, and precondition of the services.

5.2   Generating the Situation Calculus Theory and the ConGolog Program

In the second phase, the configuration component takes the output from the DAML-PDDL translator (a collection of PDDL files) and from the compiler (the abstract plan) and generates the situation calculus theory and the ConGolog program for the Planning and Execution module. This is done in two steps. First, the set of PDDL domains is combined into a single Prolog file whose facts and rules represent the objects and axioms in the PDDL files. To avoid naming conflicts between entities from different domains, we associate to each domain a unique string, called *tag*, and prefix each entity of the domain with the corresponding tag. Consider, for example, the object `Sequences`, that represents the input of `ClustalW`, and is defined in the PDDL domain `clustalw-profile-ont` (originated from *clustalw-profile.daml*) with the type `UnalignedSequences`. Assume that this domain is associated with the tag `F17`. In this case, the object is translated into a predicate `unalignedSequences(F17_Sequences)` of the Prolog program.

The final step in the configuration component is to generate the situation calculus theory and to formulate the ConGolog program corresponding to the ΦLOG program. This process involves collecting all the necessary information about a particular service from the Prolog program produced in the previous step and from the abstract plan—the output of the compiler (*see* Section 4). This step is performed as follows.

---

[11] Results of the translation process are at www.cs.nmsu.edu/~tphan/philog/nondet.

Generating the Facts. Each variable X of type T in the ΦLOG program corresponds to a fact $T(X)$ in the action theory. Similarly, a constant C of type T has the corresponding fact $T(C)$. For example, for the output of the ΦLOG program described in Section 4, the destination theory contains the following facts: `phylogenetictree(p).`

```
alignedsequences(s). unalignedsequences(t).
str(nucleotide). str(fever).
```

where p, s, and t are variables, while `nucleotide` and `fever` are constants.

Generating the Fluents. For each variable X used in the ΦLOG program, there is a corresponding fluent `variable(X)` in the destination ConGolog program. In addition, there is one more fluent `has_value(X)` to indicate whether that variable has been assigned some value or not. At the beginning, no variable has been assigned a value.

```
prim_fluent(variable(p)).
prim_fluent(variable(s)).
prim_fluent(variable(t)).
prim_fluent(has_value(X)) :- prim_fluent(variable(X)).
```

Besides, it might be the case that an input of an action[12] is required to have some fixed value. For example, the abstract plan in Section 4 requires that all the `db-search` services have "nucleotide" as the value of their first argument and "fever" as the value of their second argument. To deal with this case, we use a fluent of the form $value(X, V)$ to say that the value of the input X must be V. The meaning of this kind of fluents will become more precise when we discuss the executability condition of an action in the following parts. As an example, the translator will automatically generate the following fluents for the ΦLOG program output above.

```
prim_fluent(value(f13_db,nucleotide)).
prim_fluent(value(f13_term,fever)).
prim_fluent(value(f0_db,nucleotide)).
prim_fluent(value(f0_term,fever)).
```

Furthermore, depending on the service description, the situation calculus might have some additional fluents. For example, since the precondition of ClustalW involves the format property, the theory will contain the fluent `format(X,V)` to denote that the format of some object X is V.

Generating the Actions. Each service occurring in the previous step corresponds to an action in the destination theory, whose parameters are the inputs and outputs of the service. The translator will automatically assign a unique variable name for each input and output of a service. For example, the service ClustalW corresponds to the following action in the action theory:

```
prim_action(service_clustalw(input(F17_sequences),
                             output(F17_outputsequences))):-
```

---

[12] Recall that in our system, bioinformatics services are viewed as actions.

```
unalignedsequences(F17_sequences),
alignedsequences(F17_outputsequences).
```

It says that the service ClustalW has an input F17_sequences
and output F17_outputsequences, where F17_sequences and
F17_outputsequences are of the types unalignedsequences and
alignedsequences respectively.

In several cases, some services in the local database might be used to formulate
actions in the theory. For instance, we notice that we may need to do some kind of
format conversions for our ΦLOG program. Hence, all the format conversion services
in the local database are looked up and included in the theory. In the future, the search
for related services will be done online, through the service broker.

Generating the Executability Conditions. The following is an example of the executability condition for the ClustalW service.

```
executable(service_clustalw(input(F17_sequences),
              output(F17_outputsequences)),
              and(format(F17_sequences,sf_ncbi),
                       or(value(f17_sequences,F17_sequences),
                       and(variable(F17_sequences),
                       has_value(F17_sequences))))) :-
unalignedsequences(F17_sequences),
alignedsequences(F17_outputsequences).
```

The intuition behind the above condition is that, for the service ClustalW to be executable, it requires each of its input parameters either to be a variable that is already
assigned to some value or to have some default value. In addition, it also requires that
the format of the input F17_sequences be sf_ncbi.

Generating the Effects. One type of effect of an action is that its outputs will be
assigned some value. For example, the effect of the ClustalW service in the action
theory looks like:

```
causes_val(service_clustalw(input(F17_sequences),
              output(F17_outputsequences)),
              has_value(F17_outputsequences),true,true) :-
  unalignedsequences(F17_sequences),
  alignedsequences(F17_outputsequences).
```

The other type of effect relates to effects that are explicitly described in the service
description. For example, the BLAST search service has an effect stating that the format
of its output is sf_blast. This is represented as follows.

```
causes_val(service_blast(input(F13_db,F13_term),
              output(F13_outputsequences)),
              format(F13_outputsequences,sf_blast),true,true) :-
  str(F13_db),str(F13_term),
  unalignedsequences(F13_outputsequences).
```

Generating the Initial State. As mentioned previously, for the ΦLOG program we are considering, initially no variable has been assigned any value. This is represented in ConGolog as:

```
initially(variable(p),true).
initially(variable(s),true).
initially(variable(t),true).
initially(has_value(t),false).
initially(has_value(s),false).
initially(has_value(p),false).
initially(value(f13_db,nucleotide),true).
initially(value(f13_term,nucleotide),true).
initially(value(f0_db,nucleotide),true).
initially(value(f0_term,fever),true).
```

Generating ConGolog Programs. Based on the abstract plan and the domain description, a ConGolog program representing the concrete plan can be constructed. The following is an example of such a ConGolog program for the ΦLOG program in Section 4.

```
proc(plan,
  [service_ncbi(input(F0_db,F0_term),output(F0_outputsequences))
  make_doable
  service_dialign(input(F21_sequence),output(F21_outputsequences)):
  service_clustalw(input(F17_sequence),output(F17_outputsequences))
  make_doable
  service_treeview(input(F29_inputfile),
     output(F29_outputphylogenetictree)):
  service_dnaml(input(F25_inputfile),
     output(F25_outputphylogenetictree))]).
```

Notice that any pair of consecutive plan steps has a construct make_doable in-between. This construct, introduced in [23], is a relaxation of the sequence construct of ConGolog.

6   Planning and Execution Monitoring Module

The input of the planning and execution monitoring module consists of a ConGolog program and a situation calculus theory which represents the original ΦLOG program and the bioinformatic services, respectively. The module's job is to execute the Con-Golog program. To do so, it repeatedly generates traces of the ConGolog program and executes them until at least one concrete plan succeeds, or all of them fail (Figure 5).

6.1   Planning

The main job of this component is to find a possible trace of the ConGolog program which can be successfully executed and then executes this trace. Given a

ConGolog program and the underlying situation calculus theory, this problem can be solved in different ways by employing different ConGolog interpreters [17, 19]. In this paper, we use an off-line ConGolog interpreter with the insertion constructor 'make_doable' from

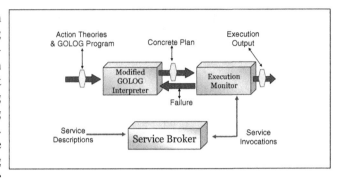

Fig. 5. Planning and Execution Monitoring Module

[23] to generate traces, which we will call hereafter *concrete plans*.

We prefer the off-line interpreter over the on-line interpreter for different reasons. First of all, the effects of the actions in our ConGolog programs do not change over time, i.e., the execution of a service with the same set of input will yield the same output regardless of its execution time. In this sense, domains in our application satisfy the IPR condition of [23], and therefore this model of planning and execution monitoring is suitable. In addition, there are some services whose runtime is large. As such, a service should be invoked only if it can lead to a successful execution of the program at hand. This property cannot be satisfied by an on-line interpreter, since it does not guarantee completeness [19].

The use of the insertion constructor allows ΦLOG 's users to write ΦLOG programs without the need of worrying about the data conversion operator in their programs. This simplifies the process of writing ΦLOG programs considerably since the number of data formats currently used by bioinformatic services is huge, and each service only works with certain formats. During the planning phase, the interpreter will automatically insert the *data format conversion* operators into the program, whenever needed. Due to the frequent use of the format conversion utility, we decided to add the situation calculus representation of the format conversion service to every situation calculus theory generated by the configuration component.

To illustrate this process, consider the ConGolog program and the corresponding situation calculus theory from the last section. A possible trace of this program is:

```
| ?- do(plan,s0,S).
S = do(service_treeview(input(s),output(t)),
    do(service_clustalw(input(p),output(s)),
    do(service_ncbi(input(nucleotide,fever),output(p)),s0)))) ?
```

Suppose that the output format of the service NCBI does not match the input format of the service ClustalW. In this case, the output of the planning process is

```
| ?- do(plan,s0,S).
S = do(service_treeview(input(s),output(t)),
    do(service_clustalw(input(p),output(s)),
    do(conversion(input(p),output(p)),
    do(service_blast(input(nucleotide,fever),output(p)),s0)))) ?
```

The action `conversion(input(p),output(p))` that converts the output format of `service_blast` into a format suitable to `service_clustalw`, is the main difference between the two traces. It ensures that the sequence of actions is executable from `s0`.

In order to deal with conditional and loop statements in ΦLOG programs we have modified the ConGolog interpreter and its output so that it can deal with conditions whose truth value can only be determined at runtime. We choose to do so instead of using one of the available modified ConGolog interpreters, such as IndiGolog [18], for the same reasons that make us favor an off-line over an on-line ConGolog interpreter. Presently, whenever the interpreter cannot evaluate a condition in a conditional/loop statement, the planning process will continue with the guess that the condition is true/false, thus leaving the job of evaluating the condition for the execution monitoring module. If the evaluation of the condition turns out to be not different than the guess, the execution monitoring module will report a failure (i.e., a backtrack occurs) and the planning process will continue with the opposite guess that the condition is false/true, respectively. To illustrate this, let us consider the ConGolog program s_1; if $v = 2$ then s_2 else s_3, which involves three services s_1, s_2, s_3 where s_1 computes the value of a parameter v, $0 \leq v \leq 3$. The off-line ConGolog interpreter will fail to find a trace of this program since it cannot evaluate the condition $v = 2$ if the service s_1 has not been executed. In our interpreter, the first output is $s_1; (v = 2)?; s_2$ (obtained by guessing that $v = 2$ is true). If a backtrack occurs, the next output is $s_1; (\neg(v = 2))?; s_3$. Notice that if a backtrack occurs, s_1 will be executed twice. This might not be a good practice when s_1 is a irreversible action (e.g., killing the turkey is an irreversible action). Because we can always restart (the execution of) a ΦLOG program, we can safely assume that actions or bioinformatic services in our application domain are always reversible. Nevertheless, we plan to address this issue in the next phase of our project.

6.2   Execution Monitoring

The result of the planning process is a concrete plan which is a sequence of bioinformatic services and test conditions. The execution monitoring component will execute the concrete plan by sequentially executing each services or test for the correctness of the condition of the plan. If the service somehow fails or the condition is not satisfied, the execution of the plan fails.

It should be noted that if the low-level services occurring in the concrete plan are web services, i.e., they are properly constructed and described using a web service markup language (DAML and WSDL in our case), the invocation of the service is just a matter of using a standard parser to parse the service grounding information and construct invocation messages accordingly. In the current prototype we have created simple agent wrappers for the services to support service invocation. Each wrapper agent must register their functionalities with the OAA broker—in this case, the functionalities provide the name of the service and the invocation parameters. For example,

```
oaa_Register(parent, 'ClustalW_JP',
    [clustalw_jp([(sequence, _Sequence)], _Resp)], [])
```

registers with OAA a service called 'ClustalW_JP' which takes one input parameter named `sequence`. The service invocation is simply a request to the OAA broker for execution of one particular service:

```
oaa_Solve(clustalw_jp([(sequence, Sequence)], Result), [])
```

The wrapper agent will handle the actual service invocation—i.e., building the connection between client and server, constructing the message using either HTTP GET or POST method, parsing the returning message, and storing the result.

In case of execution failure—e.g., a time-out or loss of connection to the remote provider—the monitor will take appropriate actions. Repair may involve either repeating the execution of the service or re-entering the configuration agent. The latter case may lead to exploring alternative ways of instantiating the partial plan, to avoid the failing service. The replanning process is developed in such a way to attempt to reuse as much as possible the part of the concrete plan executed before the failure.

7   Conclusions and Future Work

This paper reports the work that has been done so far in our ΦLOG project. It demonstrates the feasibility of applying agent technologies in phylogenetic inference applications. The main achievement in this phase is the development of the ΦLOG compiler, the configuration component, the execution monitor, and the integration of these components within the OAA system and the ConGolog interpreter. The current system can be used to work with a small class of ΦLOG programs. Much work is still needed before we can get a system that can execute ΦLOG programs as described in [25], i.e., most general ΦLOG programs. This will be our concentration in the near future. We plan to complete the compiler and the configuration component to allow control constructors in ΦLOG programs. This will also demand changes in the planning and execution monitoring module. Furthermore, we would like to improve the planning and execution monitoring module in such a way that results, that have been computed by a failed concrete plan, can be reused as much as possible in the replanning process.

References

1. Entrez, The Life Sciences Search Engine. www.ncbi.nlm.nih.gov/Entrez/.
2. European Bioinformatics Institute. www.ebi.ac.uk/clustalw/.
3. Gene Data Bank. gdbwww.gdb.org/.
4. OMIN. www.ncbi.nlm.nih.gov/omim/.
5. PDDAML – An Automatic Translator Between PDDL and DAML. www.cs.yale.edu/homes/dvm/daml/pddl_daml_translator1.html.
6. The Bioperl Project. www.bioperl.org.
7. UK Human Genome Mapping Project Resource Center. www.hgmp.mrc.ac.uk/MANUAL/.
8. OmniGene: Standardizing Biological Data Interchange Through Web Services, omnigene.sourceforge.net, 2001.
9. The BioMOBY Project. biomoby.org, 2002.

10. P.G. Baker, A. Brass, S. Bechoofer, C. Goble, N. Paton, and R. Stevens. TAMBIS – Transparent Access to Multiple Bioinformatics Information Sources. In *Proceedings of the International Conference on Intelligent Systems for Molecular Biology*, 1998.

11. T. Ball, editor. *Proc. of the 2nd Conference on Domain-specific Languages*. 2000.

12. R. Beavis. The Biopolymer Markup Language (BIOML). TR, ProteoMetrics, LLC, 1999.

13. S. Cao, L. Qin, W. Wang, Y. Zhu, and Y. Li. Application of Gene Ontology in Bio-data Warehouse. In R. Stevens and R. McEntire, eds, *6th Annual Bio-Ontologies Meeting*. 2003.

14. W. Codenie, K. De Hondt, P. Stayaert, and A. Vercammen. From custom applications to domain-specific frameworks. *Communications of the ACM*, 40(10):70–77, 1997.

15. C. Consel. Architecturing software using a methodology for language development. In *PLILP*, pages 170–194. Springer Verlag, 1998.

16. F. Corradini, L. Mariani, and E. Merelli. A Programming Environment for Global Activity-based Aplications. In *WOA*, 2003.

17. G. De Giacomo, Y. Lespérance, and H. Levesque. *ConGolog*, a concurrent programming language based on the situation calculus. *Artificial Intelligence*, 121(1-2):109–169, 2000.

18. G. De Giacomo, H. J. Levesque, and S. Sardiña. Incremental execution of guarded theories. *ACM Transactions on Computational Logic*, 2(4):495–525, 2001.

19. G. De Giacomo, R. Reiter, and M. Soutchanski. Execution monitoring of high-level robot programs. In *KRR'98*, pages 453–465. Morgan Kaufmann Publishers, 1998.

20. G. Gupta and E. Pontelli. Specification, Implementation, and Verification of Domain Specific Languages: a Logic Programming-based Approach. In *CL: from LP into the Future*. Springer, 2001.

21. A.H. Karp. Programming for Parallelism. *Computer*, 20, May 1987.

22. D. R. Maddison, D.L. Swofford, and W.P. Maddison. NEXUS: An Extensible File Format for Systematic Information. *Syst. Biol.*, 464(4):590–621, 1997.

23. S. McIlraith and T.C. Son. Adapting golog for composition of semantic web services. In *(KR'2002)*, pages 482–493. Morgan Kaufmann Publisher, 2002.

24. S. Pearson. DAS: Open Source System for Exchanging Annotations of Genomic Sequence Data. Technical report, Open Bioinformatics Foundation, 2002.

25. E. Pontelli, D. Ranjan, G. Gupta, and B. Milligan. Design and Implementation of a Domain Specific Language for Phylogenetic Inference. *J. Bio. and Comp. Bio.*, 2(1):201–230, 2003.

26. R. Reiter. *KNOWLEDGE IN ACTION: Logical Foundations for Describing and Implementing Dynamical Systems*. MIT Press, 2001.

27. T.C. Son, E. Pontelli, D. Ranjan, B. Milligan, and G. Gupta. An Agent-based Domain Specific Framework for Rapid Prototyping of Applications in Evolutionary Biology. In *Proceedings of the 1st Workshop on Declarative Agent Languages and Technologies*, 2003.

28. R. Stevens. Bio-Ontology Reference Collection, cs.man.ac.uk/~stevens/onto-publications.html.

29. M.G.J. Van Den Brand, J. Heering, P. Klint, and P.A. Olivier. Compiling Language Definitions: the ASF+SDF Compiler. *ACM Trans. on Prog. Languages and Systems*, 24(4), 2002.

30. R. Waldinger. Deductive composition of Web software agents. In *Proc. NASA Wkshp on Formal Approaches to Agent-Based Systems, LNCS*. Springer-Verlag, 2000.

Reasoning About Agents' Interaction Protocols Inside DCaseLP

M. Baldoni[1], C. Baroglio[1], I. Gungui[2], A. Martelli[1],
M. Martelli[2], V. Mascardi[2], V. Patti[1], and C. Schifanella[1]

[1] Dipartimento di Informatica,
Università degli Studi di Torino, Italy
{baldoni, baroglio, mrt, patti, schi}@di.unito.it
[2] Dipartimento di Informatica e Scienze dell'Informazione,
Università degli Studi di Genova, Italy
1995s133@educ.disi.unige.it, {martelli, mascardi}@disi.unige.it

Abstract. Engineering systems of heterogeneous agents is a difficult
task; one of the ways for achieving the successful industrial deployment
of agent technology is the development of engineering tools that support
the developer in all the steps of design and implementation. In this work
we focus on the problem of supporting the design of agent interaction
protocols by carrying out a methodological integration of the MAS prototyping environment DCaseLP with the agent programming language
DyLOG for reasoning about action and change.

1 Introduction

Multiagent Systems (MASs) involve heterogeneous components which have different ways of representing their knowledge of the world, themselves, and other
agents, and also adopt different mechanisms for reasoning. Despite heterogeneity, agents need to interact and exchange information in order to cooperate or
compete not only for the control of shared resources but also to achieve their
aims; this interaction may follow sophisticated communication protocols.

For these reasons and due to the complexity of agents' behavior, MASs are
difficult to be correctly and efficiently engineered; even developing a working
prototype may require a long time and a lot of effort. In this paper we present
an ongoing research aimed at developing a "multi-language" environment for engineering systems of heterogeneous agents. This environment will allow the prototype developer to specify, verify and implement different aspects of the MAS
and different agents inside the MAS, choosing the most appropriate language
from a given set. In particular, the discussion will be focused on the advantages of integrating an agent programming language for reasoning about actions
and change (using the language DyLOG [9, 7]) into the DCaseLP [4, 21, 29] MAS
prototyping environment.

The development of a prototype system of heterogeneous agents can be carried out in different ways. The "one-size-fits-all" solution consists of developing

J. Leite et al. (Eds.): DALT 2004, LNAI 3476, pp. 112–131, 2005.

all the agents by means of the same implementation language and to execute the obtained program. If this approach is adopted, during the specification stage it would be natural to select a language that can be directly executed or easily translated into code, and to use it to specify all the agents in the MAS. The other solution is to specify each "view" of the MAS (that includes its architecture, the interaction protocols among agents, the internal architecture and functioning of each agent), with the most suitable language in order to deal with the MAS's peculiar features, and then to verify and execute the obtained specifications inside an integrated environment. Such a multi-language environment should offer the means not only to select the proper specification language for each view of the MAS but also to check the specifications exploiting formal validation and verification methods and to produce an implementation of the prototype in a semi-automatic way. The prototype implementation should be composed of heterogeneous pieces of code created by semi-automatic translations of heterogeneous specifications. Moreover, the multi-language environment should allow these pieces of code to be seamlessly integrated and capable of interacting.

The greater complexity associated with the latter solution is proportional to the advantages it gives with respect to the former. In particular, by allowing different specification languages for modeling different aspects of the MAS, *it provides the flexibility needed to describe the MAS from different points of view*. Moreover, by allowing different specification languages for the internal architecture and functioning of each agent, *it respects the differences existing among agents*, namely the way they reason and the way they represent their knowledge, other agents, and the world. Clearly, this solution also has some drawbacks in respect to the former. The coherent integration of different languages into the same environment must be carefully designed and implemented by the environment creators, who must also take care of the environment maintenance. It must be emphasized that the developer of the MAS does not have to be an expert of *all* the supported languages: he/she will use those he/she is more familiar with, and this will lead to more reliable specifications and implementations.

DCaseLP (Distributed CaseLP, [4, 21, 29]) integrates a set of specification and implementation languages in order to model and prototype MASs. It defines a methodology which covers the engineering stages, from the requirements analysis to the prototype execution, and relies on the use of UML and AUML (Agent UML, [6]) not only during the requirements analysis, but also to describe the *interaction protocols* followed by the agents. The choice of UML and AUML, initially developed for documentation purposes, to represent interaction protocols in DCaseLP is motivated by the wide support that it is obtaining from the agent research community. Even if AUML cannot be considered a standard agent modeling language yet, it has many chances to become such, as shown by the interest that both the FIPA modeling technical committee (http://www.fipa.org/activities/modeling.html) and the OMG Agent Platform Special Interest Group (http://www.objs.com/agent/) demonstrate in it. Quoting [31]: "The successful industrial deployment of agent technology requires techniques that reduce the inherent risks in any new technology and there are two ways in which this can be done: presenting a new technology as an extension of a previous, well-established one, or providing engineering tools that support industry-accepted methods of technology deployment." We can say that by choosing a UML-based language we place DCaseLP in the line of both the proposed strategies.

In DCaseLP, UML and AUML are used to describe the *public interaction protocols*, which can be animated by creating agents whose behavior adheres to the given protocols. The idea of translating UML and AUML diagrams into a formalism and check their properties by either animating or formally verifying the resulting code is shared by many researchers working in the agent-oriented software engineering field [24, 30, 35]. We followed an animation approach to check that the interaction protocols produced during the requirement specification stage are the ones necessary to describe the system requirements and, moreover, that they are correct. The "coherence check" is done by comparing the results of the execution runs with the interaction specification [4]. Despite its usefulness, this approach does not straightforwardly allow the formal proof of properties of the resulting system *a priori*: indeed, a key issue in the design and engineering of interaction protocols, that DCaseLP does not currently address. One possible extension in the line of [25] is the integration of *formal methods* to perform validation tests, i.e., to check the coherence of the AUML description with the specifications derived from the analysis. To this aim, it is possible to rely on works that give to AUML sequence diagrams a semantics based on Petri Nets [22, 23, 12]. Validation tests, however, are just one side of the problem. In fact, another kind of a priori verification that is very important for the MAS designer is to check properties of *specific* implementations, obtained on the basis of the public protocol description.

One step in this direction is to exploit the characteristic of DCaseLP of being a multi-language development environment and to integrate a language, DyLOG [9, 7], which, being based on computational logic, can be exploited both as an implementation language and for verifying properties. DyLOG is a logic-based agent language that includes a fully integrated "communication kit", that allows the implementation of *interaction protocols* as *agent conversation policies* based on speech acts, and it supports reasoning about interaction properties. In the language reasoning about the conversations, defined by a protocol implementation, basically means to check if there is a conversation after whose execution a given set of properties holds. This characteristic can for instance be exploited to determine which protocol, from a set of available ones, satisfies a goal of interest, and also to compose many protocols for accomplishing complex tasks. In this perspective, DyLOG is particularly interesting because there is a *conformance relation* between DyLOG implementations of interaction protocols and AUML sequence diagrams: in fact it is possible to prove in a formal way if every conversation generated by a DyLOG program is correct w.r.t. a specification expressed by AUML diagrams [8]. After proving desired properties of the interaction protocols, the developer can animate them thanks to the facilities offered by DCaseLP, discussed in Section 2.

So far, the integration of DyLOG into DCaseLP is a *methodological integration*: it extends the set of languages supported by DCaseLP during the MAS engineering process and augments the verification capabilities of DCaseLP, without requiring any real integration of the DyLOG working interpreter into DCaseLP (see Section 4). Nevertheless, DyLOG can also be used to directly specify agents and execute them inside the DCaseLP environment, in order to exploit the distribution, concurrency, monitoring and debugging facilities that DCaseLP offers.

2   The DCaseLP Environment

DCaseLP is a prototyping environment where agents specified and implemented in a given set of languages can be seamlessly integrated. It provides an agent-oriented software engineering methodology to guide the developer during the analysis of the MAS requirements, its design, and the development of a working MAS prototype. The methodology is sketched in Figure 1. Solid arrows represent the information flow from one stage to the next one. Dotted arrows represent the iterative refinement of previous choices. The first release of DCaseLP did not realize all the stages of the methodology. In particular, as we have pointed in last section, the stage of properties verification was not addressed. The integration of DyLOG into DCaseLP discussed in Section 4 will allow us to address also the verification phase. The tools and languages supported by the first release of

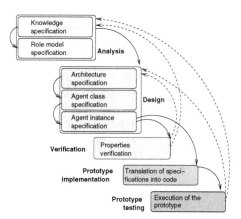

Fig. 1. DCaseLP's methodology

DCaseLP, discussed in [29, 4], included UML and AUML for the specification of the general structure of the MAS, and Jess [27] and Java for the implementation of the agents.

DCaseLP adopts an existing multi-view, use-case driven and UML-based method [5] in the phase of requirements analysis. Once the requirements of the application have been clearly identified, the developer can use UML and/or AUML to describe the interaction protocols followed by the agents, the general MAS architecture and the agent types and instances. Moreover, the developer can automatically translate the UML/AUML diagrams, describing the agents in the MAS, into Jess rule-based code. In the following we will assume that AUML is used during the requirements analysis stage, although the translation from AUML into Jess is not fully automated (while the translation from pure UML into Jess is).

The Jess code obtained from the translation of AUML diagrams must be manually completed by the developer with the behavioral knowledge which was not explicitly provided at the specification level. The developer does not need to have a deep insight into rule-based languages in order to complete the Jess code, since he/she is guided by comments included in the automatically generated code. The agents obtained by means of the manual completion of the Jess code are integrated into the JADE (Java Agent Development Framework, [26]) middle-ware. JADE complies with the FIPA specifications [16] and provides a set of graphical tools that support the execution, debugging and deployment phases. The agents can be distributed across several machines and can run concurrently. By integrating Jess into JADE, we were able to easily monitor and debug the execution of Jess agents thanks to the monitoring facilities that JADE provides.

A recent extension of DCaseLP, discussed in [21], has been the integration of tuProlog [36]. The choice of tuProlog was due to two of its features:

1. it is implemented in Java, which makes its integration into JADE easier, and
2. it is very light, which ensures a certain level of efficiency to the prototype.

By extending DCaseLP with tuProlog we have obtained the possibility to execute agents, whose behavior is completely described by a Prolog-like theory, in the JADE platform. For this purpose, we have developed a library of predicates that allow agents specified in tuProlog to access the communication primitives provided by JADE: asynchronous send, asynchronous receive, and blocking receive (with and without timeout). These predicates are mapped onto the corresponding JADE primitives. Two predicates for converting strings into terms and vice-versa are also provided, in order to allow agents to send strings as the content of their messages, and to reason over them as if they were Prolog terms.

A developer who wants to define tuProlog agents and integrate them into JADE can do it without even knowing the details of JADE's functioning. An agent whose behavior is written in tuProlog is, in fact, loaded in JADE as an ordinary agent written in Java. The developer just needs to know how to start JADE.

3   Interaction Protocols in DyLOG

Logic-based executable agent specification languages have been deeply investigated in the last years [3, 17, 13, 9, 28]. In this section we will briefly recall the main features of DyLOG, by focussing on how the communicative behavior of an agent can be specified and on the form of reasoning supported.

DyLOG is a high-level logic programming language for modeling rational agents, based on a modal theory of actions and mental attitudes where *modalities* are used for representing *actions*, while *beliefs* model the agent's internal state. We refer to a mentalistic approach, which is also adopted by the standard FIPA-ACL [16], where communicative actions affect the internal mental state of the agent. More recently, some authors have proposed a *social approach* to agent communication [34], where communicative actions affect the "social state" of the system, rather than the internal states of the agents. The social state records the social facts, like the *permissions* and the *commitments* of the agents, which are created and modified along the interaction. The dissatisfaction to the mentalistic approach is mostly due to the difficulty of verifying that an agent acts according to a commonly agreed semantics, because it is not possible to have access to the agents' private mental state [37], a problem known as *semantics verification*. The growing interest into the social approach is motivated by the fact that it overcomes this problem by exploiting a set of established commitments between the agents, that are stored as part of the MAS social state. In this framework it is possible to formally prove the correctness of public interaction protocols with respect to the specifications outcoming from the analysis phases; such proof can be obtained, for instance, by means of model checking techniques [32, 37, 19, 10] (but not only, e.g., [11]).

When one passes from the public protocol specification to its *implementation* in some language (e.g. Java, DyLOG), a program is obtained which, by definition, relies on the information contained in the internal "state" of the agent for deciding which action to execute [20]. In this perspective, the use of a declarative language is helpful because it allows the proof of properties of the *specific implementation* in a straightforward way. In particular, the use of a language that explicitly represents and uses the agent internal state is useful for proving to which extent certain properties depend on the agent mental state or on the semantics of the speech acts. For instance, in our work we perform hypothetical reasoning about the effects of conversations on the agent mental state, in order to find conversation plans which are proved to respect the implemented protocols, achieving at the same time some desired goal, and we can prove the conformance of an implemented protocol w.r.t. its specification in AUML.

3.1   DyLOG in Brief

Intuitively, DyLOG [9, 7] allows the specification of rational agents that reason about their own behavior, choose courses of actions conditioned by their mental state and can use sensors and communication for obtaining fresh knowledge. The agent behavior is described by a *domain description*, which includes, besides a specification of the agent initial beliefs, a description of the agent behavior plus a *communication kit* (denoted by $CKit^{ag_i}$), that encodes its *communicative behavior*. Atomic actions are either world actions, affecting the world, or mental actions, i.e., sensing and communicative actions producing new beliefs and then affecting the agent mental state. Complex actions are defined through (possibly recursive) definitions, given by means of Prolog-like clauses and by action operators from dynamic logic, like sequence ";", test "?" and non-deterministic choice "∪". The action theory allows coping with the problem of reasoning about complex actions with incomplete knowledge and in particular to address the temporal projection and planning problem in presence of sensing and communication.

Communication is supported both at the level of *primitive speech acts* and at the level of *interaction protocols*. Thus, the communication kit of an agent ag_i is defined as a triple $(\Pi_C, \Pi_{CP}, \Pi_{Sget})$: Π_C is a set of laws defining precondition and effects of the agent speech acts; Π_{CP} is a set of procedure axioms, specifying a set of interaction protocols, and can be intended as a library of *conversation policies*, that the agent follows when interacting with others; Π_{Sget} is a set of sensing axioms for acquiring information by messages reception.

Speech acts are represented as atomic actions with preconditions and effect on ag_i's mental state, of form speech_act(ag_i, ag_j, l), where ag_i (sender) and ag_j (receiver) are agents and l (a fluent) is the object of the communication. Effects and preconditions are modeled by a set of effect and precondition laws. We use the modality □ to denote such laws, i.e., formulas that hold *always*, after every (possibly empty) arbitrary action sequence.

A DyLOG agent has a twofold representation of each a speech act: one holds when it is the sender, the other when it is the receiver. As an example, let us define the semantics of the *inform* speech act within the DyLOG framework:

a) $\Box(\mathcal{B}^{Self} l \wedge \mathcal{B}^{Self} \mathcal{U}^{Other} l \supset \langle \text{inform}(Self, Other, l) \rangle \top)$

b) $\Box([\text{inform}(Self, Other, l)] \mathcal{M}^{Self} \mathcal{B}^{Other} l)$

c) $\Box(\mathcal{B}^{Self} \mathcal{B}^{Other} authority(Self, l) \supset [\text{inform}(Self, Other, l)] \mathcal{B}^{Self} \mathcal{B}^{Other} l)$

d) $\Box(\top \supset \langle \text{inform}(Other, Self, l) \rangle \top)$

e) $\Box([\text{inform}(Other, Self, l)] \mathcal{B}^{Self} \mathcal{B}^{Other} l)$

f) $\Box(\mathcal{B}^{Self} authority(Other, l) \supset [\text{inform}(Other, Self, l)] \mathcal{B}^{Self} l)$

In general, for each action a and agent ag_i, $[a^{ag_i}]$ is a universal modality ($\langle a^{ag_i} \rangle$ is its dual). $[a^{ag_i}]\alpha$ means that α holds after every execution of action a by agent ag_i, while $\langle a^{ag_i} \rangle \alpha$ means that there is a possible execution of a (by ag_i) after which α holds. Therefore clause (a) states *executability preconditions* for the action inform($Self, Other, l$): it specifies the mental conditions that make the action executable in a state. Intuitively, it states that $Self$ can execute an inform act only if it believes l (we use the modal operator $\mathcal{B}^{ag_i}$ to model the beliefs of agent ag_i) and it believes that the receiver ($Other$) does not know l. It also considers possible that the receiver will adopt its belief (the modal operator $\mathcal{M}^{ag_i}$ is defined as the dual of $\mathcal{B}^{ag_i}$, intuitively $\mathcal{M}^{ag_i} \varphi$ means the ag_i considers φ possible), clause (b), although it cannot be certain about it -autonomy assumption-. If agent $Self$ believes to be considered a trusted *authority* about l by the receiver, it is also confident that $Other$ will adopt its belief, clause (c). Since executability preconditions can be tested only on the $Self$ mental state, when $Self$ is the receiver, the action of informing is considered to be *always* executable (d). When $Self$ is the receiver, the effect of an inform act is that

Self will believe that l is believed by the sender (*Other*), clause (e), but *Self* will adopt l as an own belief only if it thinks that *Other* is a trusted authority, clause (f).

DyLOG supports also the representation of *interaction protocols* by means of procedures, that build on individual speech acts and specify communication patterns guiding the agent communicative behavior during a protocol-oriented dialogue. Formally, protocols are expressed by means of a collection of procedure axioms of the action logic of the form $\langle p_0 \rangle \varphi \subset \langle p_1 \rangle \langle p_2 \rangle \dots \langle p_n \rangle \varphi$, where p_0 is the procedure name the p_i's can be i's speech acts, special sensing actions for modeling message reception, test actions (actions of the form $Fs?$, where Fs is conjunction of belief formulas) or procedure names [1]. Each agent has a subjective perception of the communication with other agents; for this reason, given a protocol specification, we have as many procedural representations as the possible roles in the conversation (see example in the next section).

Message reception is modeled as a special kind of sensing action, what we call *get message actions*. Indeed, from the point of view of an individual agent receiving a message can be interpreted as a query for an external input, whose outcome cannot be predicted before the actual execution, thus it seems natural to model it as a special case of sensing. The *get message actions* are defined by means of inclusion axioms, that specify a finite set of (alternative) speech acts expected by the interlocutor.

DyLOG allows reasoning about agents' communicative behavior, by supporting techniques for proving existential properties of the kind "given a protocol and a set of desiderata, is there a specific conversation, respecting the protocol, that also satisfies the desired conditions?". Formally, given a DyLOG domain description Π_{ag_i} containing a CKit^{ag_i} with the specifications of the interaction protocols and of the relevant speech acts, a *planning* activity can be triggered by *existential queries* of the form $\langle p_1 \rangle \langle p_2 \rangle \dots \langle p_m \rangle Fs$, where each p_k $(k = 1, \dots, m)$ may be a primitive speech act or an interaction protocol, executed by our agent, or a get message action (in which our agent plays the role of the receiver). Checking if the query succeeds corresponds to answering to the question "is there an execution of $p_1, \dots, p_m$ leading to a state where the conjunction of belief formulas Fs holds for agent ag_i?". Such an execution is a plan to bring about Fs. The procedure definition constrains the search space.

Actions in the plan can be speech acts performed or received by ag_i, the latter can be read as the *assumption* that certain messages will be received from the interlocutor. The ability of making assumptions about which message (among those foreseen by the protocol) will be received is necessary in order to actually build the plan. Depending on the task that one has to execute, it may alternatively be necessary to take into account all of the possible alternatives that lead to the goal or just to find one of them. In the former case, the extracted plan will be *conditional*, because for each get_message it will generally contain

---

[1] For sake of brevity, sometimes we will write these axioms as $\langle p_0 \rangle \varphi \subset \langle p_1; p_2; \dots; p_n \rangle \varphi$.

many branches. Each path in the resulting tree is a linear plan that brings about *Fs*. In the latter case, instead, the plan is linear.

4   Integrating DyLOG into DCaseLP to Reason About Communicating Agents

Let us now illustrate, by means of examples, the advantages of adding to the current interaction design tools of DCaseLP the possibility of converting AUML sequence diagrams into a DyLOG program. In the first DCaseLP release, AUML interaction protocols could be only translated into Jess code, which could not be formally verified but just executed. The use of DyLOG bears some advantages: on the one hand it is possible to automatically verify that a DyLOG implementation is *conformant* to the AUML specification (see below), moreover, it is also possible to *verify properties* of the so obtained DyLOG program. Property proof can be carried out using the existing DyLOG interpreter, implemented in Sicstus [1].

Besides the methodological integration, DyLOG can be also integrated in a *physical way*. Recently we have begun a new implementation in Java of the language, based on *tuProlog* [36]. A visual editor based on *Eclipse* is also being implemented; the editor will allow the designer to write DyLOG programs in a graphical and intuitive way, the designer will also have the possibility of exporting them in OWL [33] for realizing Semantic Web applications like the one described hereafter. Once the physical integration will be completed, it will be possible to animate complete DyLOG agents into DCaseLP. This will mean that agents specified in Jess, Java, DyLOG, will be able to interact with each other inside a single prototype whose execution will be monitored using JADE.

In the rest of this section, however, we deal with the *methodological integration*. Let us suppose, for instance, to be developing a set of interaction protocols for a restaurant and a cinema that, for promotional reasons, will cooperate in this way: a customer that makes a reservation at the restaurant will get a free ticket for a movie shown by the cinema. By restaurant and cinema we here mean two generic service providers and not a specific restaurant and a specific cinema. In this scenario the same customer will interact with both providers. The developer must be sure that the customer, by interacting with the composition (by sequentialization) of the two protocols, will obtain what desired. Figure 2 shows an example of AUML protocols, for the two services; (i) and (ii) are followed by the cinema, (iii) by the restaurant. This level of representation does not allow any proof of properties because is lacking of a formal semantics. Supposing that the designed diagrams are correct, the protocols are to be implemented. It is desirable that the correctness of the implementation w.r.t. the AUML specification can be verified. If the protocols are implemented in DyLOG, this can actually be done. In [8] we, actually, show that, given an AUML protocol specification and a DyLOG implementation, it is possible to prove if the latter will never produce conversations that are not foreseen by the protocol. This problem is known as *conformance verification*. Briefly, with reference to Figure 3, this can be done by turning the problem into a problem of verification of the inclusion of

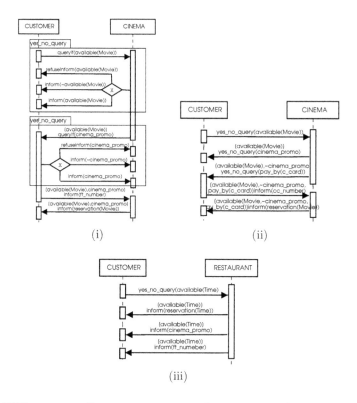

Fig. 2. AUML sequence diagrams representing the interactions between customer and provider: (i) and (ii) are followed by the cinema service, (iii) is followed by the restaurant. Formulas in square brackets represent preconditions to speech act execution

the language of all the sequences generated by the implementation $L(G_{p_{DyLOG}})$ in the language of all the sequence generated by the AUML sequence diagram $L(G_{p_{AUML}})$. In particular, we have studied the dependence of conformance on the agent private mental state and on the semantics of speech acts, proposing three degrees of conformance, at different levels of abstraction. The strongest of the three, *protocol conformance*, is proved to be decidable and tractable, and if it holds also the other degrees (which depend at some extent on the the agent mental state) hold.

Let us describe one possible implementation of the two protocols in a Dy-LOG program. Each implemented protocol will have two complementary views (customer and provider) but for the sake of brevity, we report only the view of the customer. It is easy to see how the structure of the procedure clauses corresponds to the sequence of AUML operators in the sequence diagrams. The subscripts next to the protocol names are a writing convention for representing the role that the agent plays; so, for instance, Q stands for *querier*, and C for *customer*. The customer view of the restaurant protocol is the following:

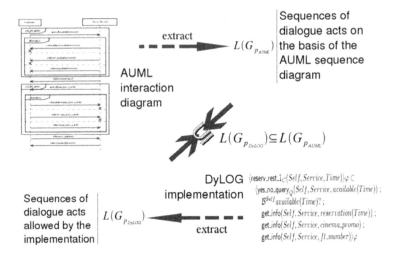

Fig. 3. Conformance verification of a DyLOG implementation w.r.t. an AUML protocol: the problem is interpreted as the verification of language inclusion

(a) $\langle$reserv_rest$_C(Self, Service, Time)\rangle \varphi \subset$
    $\quad\langle$yes_no_query$_Q(Self, Service, available(Time))$;
    $\quad\quad\mathcal{B}^{Self} available(Time)?$;
    $\quad\quad$get_info$(Self, Service, reservation(Time))$;
    $\quad\quad$get_info$(Self, Service, cinema\_promo)$;
    $\quad\quad$get_info$(Self, Service, ft\_number)\rangle \varphi$

(b) $[$get_info$(Self, Service, Fluent)] \varphi \subset [$inform$(Service, Self, Fluent)] \varphi$

Procedure (a) is the protocol procedure: the customer asks if a table is available at a certain time, if so, the restaurant informs it that a reservation has been taken and that it gained a promotional free ticket for a cinema (*cinema_promo*), whose code number (*ft_number*) is returned. Clause (b) shows how get_info can be implemented as an inform act executed by the service and having as recipient the customer. The question mark amounts to check the value of a fluent in the current state; the semicolon is the sequencing operator of two actions. The cinema protocol, instead, is:

(c) $\langle$reserv_cinema$_C(Self, Service, Movie)\rangle \varphi \subset$
    $\quad\langle$yes_no_query$_Q(Self, Service, available(Movie))$;
    $\quad\quad\mathcal{B}^{Self} available(Movie)?$;
    $\quad\quad$yes_no_query$_I(Self, Service, cinema\_promo)$;
    $\quad\quad\quad\neg\mathcal{B}^{Self} cinema\_promo?$;
    $\quad\quad\quad$yes_no_query$_I(Self, Service, pay\_by(c\_card))$;
    $\quad\quad\quad\quad\mathcal{B}^{Self} pay\_by(c\_card)?$;
    $\quad\quad\quad\quad$inform$(Self, Service, cc\_number)$;
    $\quad\quad\quad\quad$get_info$(Self, Service, reservation(Movie))\rangle \varphi$

(d) $\langle$reserv_cinema$_C$$(Self, Service, Movie)\rangle\varphi \subset$
    $\langle$yes_no_query$_Q$$(Self, Service, available(Movie))$;
      $\mathcal{B}^{Self}$available$(Movie)$? ;
      yes_no_query$_I$$(Self, Service, cinema_promo)$;
      $\mathcal{B}^{Self}$cinema_promo? ;
      inform$(Self, Service, ft\_number)$;
      get_info$(Self, Service, reservation(Movie))\rangle\varphi$

Supposing that the desired movie is available, the cinema alternatively accepts credit card payments (c) or promotional tickets (d). *We can verify if the two implementations can be composed with the desired effect*, by using the reasoning mechanisms embedded in the language and answering to the query:

$\langle$reserv_rest$_C$$(customer, restaurant, dinner)$;
  reserv_cinema$_C$$(customer, cinema, movie)\rangle$
  $(\mathcal{B}^{customer}cinema\_promo \wedge \mathcal{B}^{customer}reservation(dinner)\wedge$
  $\mathcal{B}^{customer}reservation(movie) \wedge \mathcal{B}^{customer}\mathcal{B}^{cinema}ft\_number)$

This query amounts to determine if it is possible to compose the interaction so to reserve a table for dinner ($\mathcal{B}^{customer}reservation(dinner)$) and to book a ticket for the movie *movie* ($\mathcal{B}^{customer}reservation(movie)$), exploiting a promotion ($\mathcal{B}^{customer}cinema\_promo$). The obtained free ticket is to be spent ($\mathcal{B}^{customer}$ $\mathcal{B}^{cinema}$ ft_number), i.e., *customer* believes that after the conversation the chosen cinema will know the number of the ticket given by the selected restaurant. If the customer has neither a reservation for dinner nor one for the cinema or a free ticket, the query succeeds, returning the following linear plan:

queryIf$(customer, restaurant, available(dinner))$;
   | inform$(restaurant, customer, available(dinner))$; |
inform$(restaurant, customer, reservation(dinner))$;
inform$(restaurant, customer, cinema\_promo)$;
inform$(restaurant, customer, ft\_number)$;
queryIf$(customer, cinema, available(movie))$;
   | inform$(cinema, customer, available(movie))$; |
queryIf$(cinema, customer, cinema\_promo)$;
inform$(customer, cinema, cinema\_promo)$;
inform$(customer, cinema, ft\_number)$;
inform$(cinema, customer, reservation(movie))$

This means that there is first a conversation between *customer* and *restaurant* and, then, a conversation between *customer* and *cinema*, that are instances of the respective conversation protocols, after which the desired condition holds. The linear plan, will, actually lead to the desired goal given that some *assumptions* about the provider's answers hold. In the above plan, assumptions have been outlined with a box. For instance, an assumption for reserving a seat at a cinema is that there is a free seat, a fact that can be known only at execution time. Assumptions occur when the interlocutor can respond in different ways depending on its internal state. It is not possible to know in this phase which the answer will be, but since the set of the possible answers is given by the protocol, it is possible to identify the subset that leads to the goal. In the example they are answers foreseen by a yes_no_query protocol (see Figure 2 (i) and [7]). Returning such assumptions to the designer is also very important to understand the correctness of the implementation also with respect to the chosen speech act ontology.

Using DyLOG as an implementation language is useful also for other purposes. For instance, if a library of protocol implementations is available, a designer might will to search for one that fits the requirements of some new project. Let us suppose, for instance, that the developer must design a protocol for a restaurant where a reservation can be made, not necessarily using a credit card. The developer will, then, search the library of available protocol implementations, looking for one that satisfies this request. Given that *search_service* is a procedure for searching in a library for a given category of protocol, a protocol fits the request if there is at least one conversation generated by it after which $\neg \mathcal{B}^{service} cc\_number$; such a conversation can be found by answering to the existential query:

$$\langle search\_service(restaurant, Protocol) \,;\, Protocol(customer, service, time)\rangle$$
$$(\mathcal{B}^{customer} \neg \mathcal{B}^{service} cc\_number \wedge \mathcal{B}^{customer} reservation(time))$$

which means: find a protocol with at least one execution after which the customer is sure that the provider does not know his/her credit card number and a reservation has been taken.

5   Generating and Executing Jess Agents That Adhere to the AUML Protocols

From the AUML sequence diagrams represented in Figure 4, and by defining two more AUML diagrams that provide information on the classes and instances of agents that will be involved in the MAS ("class diagram" and "agent diagram", see [4, 29]) we can automatically generate the Jess code for the given agent classes. Here, by "agent class" we mean a group of agents that share the same role (in the *restaurant + cinema* example the roles are customer, cinema and restaurant) and the same internal structure (in the *restaurant + cinema* example agents are conceptualized using mental attitudes, thus we can assume that their internal structure is based on a BDI-style architecture). The code for the program that characterizes each class must be completed by adding the conditions under which a message can be sent. In the diagrams in Figure 4, these conditions appear just above the message which labels each arrow, thus the developer can easily add them to the Jess code. Once the code is completed, the developer must define the initial state of the agent instances. The information about the initial state cannot be found in the diagrams in Figure 4, since these diagrams describe general patterns of interaction between roles, rather than between instances of agents, and they abstract from the details that characterize the agents' state.

As an example, the Jess rule shown in Table 1 is taken from the program of the agents that play the Cinema role. It manages the situation in which the Cinema agent has received a queryIf(available(Movie)) message from an agent playing the role of Customer, and that there are seats available for Movie. In this case an inform(available(Movie)) message is to be sent to the Customer agent[2]. The bold font indicates the part of code added by the developer. The added code, **(seats ?movie ?s)** and **(> ?s 0)**, allows to retrieve the seats available for movie, and to verify that they are more than zero.

Table 1. Jess rule for the Cinema agent class

```
(defrule E_2_1_1
   (state E_1 ?cid)
   (seats ?movie ?s)
   (¿ ?s 0)
=>
   (assert (state E_2_1_1 ?cid))
   (retract-string
      (str-cat "(state E_1 " ?cid " )"))
   (send (assert (ACLMessage
      (communicative-act inform)
      (role-sender Cinema) (role-receiver Customer)
      (conversation-id ?cid) (content (available ?movie))))) )))
```

The developer will be interested in configuring simulation runs which differ from the initial state of the agents involved, and check that, whatever the initial state may be, the interaction protocols are always followed and the properties verified using DyLOG are always satisfied. For each simulation run, once the initial state of the agents has been defined, the Java classes for interfacing Jess and JADE can be automatically created and the resulting JADE prototype can be executed.

The agent's state determines the protocol diagram branch that will be followed in a simulation run. As an example, let us suppose that the customer agent Customer_1 sends a queryIf(available(the_lord_of_the_rings)) request to the cinema agent Cinema_1. If the current state of Cinema_1 includes the information (seats ?the_lord_of_the_rings 2), the client request can be accepted and the number of available seats for the "The Lord of the Rings" movie is updated consequently. Cinema_1 will then ask to Customer_1 if it adheres to the promotional offer of a free ticket. Since Customer_1 adheres to the offer, it will issue an inform(cinema_promo) message followed by the number of its free ticket. The interaction ends when Cinema_1 confirms the reservation by sending an inform(reservation(the_lord_of_the_rings)) message to Customer_1.

---

[2] The syntax of messages used in both Figure 4 and this paragraph is Prolog-like, while Jess uses a Lisp-like syntax with variables preceeded by a question mark. Messages can be easily converted from the Prolog-like syntax to the Lisp-like one, and vice-versa.

Let us also suppose that, besides Customer_1, in the MAS there are two more customer agents, namely Customer_2, which does not adhere to the promotional offer, and Customer_3, which adheres to the promotional offer. Both of them want to buy a ticket for the "The Lord of the Rings" movie. Customer_2 asks if there are available seats to Cinema_1 and gets the information that there is one. Cinema_1 considers this seat as reserved, and thus, when Customer_3 asks for available seats, it answers that there are no more left: the ones initially possessed by Cinema_1 have already been issued to Customer_1 and Customer_2.

The performatives of messages exchanged between Cinema_1 and Customer_1 can be seen in Figure 4 which shows the output of the JADE Sniffer agent. Figure 5 shows the details of the message that Cinema_1 sends to Customer_3 to inform it that there are no seats left.

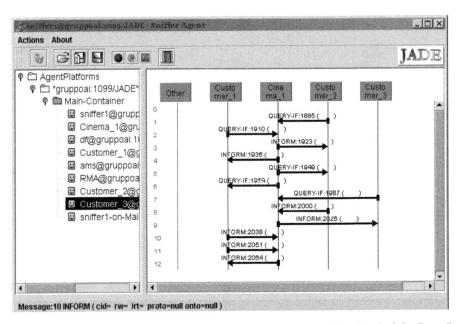

Fig. 4. Interactions between three customers interested in the "The Lord of the Rings" movie, and a cinema

By running the prototype a sufficient number of times starting from as many different agents' initial states as possible, all the possible evolutions of the MAS should be observed. If the software engineer who captured the requirements of the system using the AUML diagrams of Figure 4 forgot to describe some interaction patterns or described them incorrectly, and the verification carried out by means of DyLOG did not allow to discover these deficiencies, the prototype execution may help the developer in completing (resp. correcting) the missing (resp. incorrect) interaction patterns.

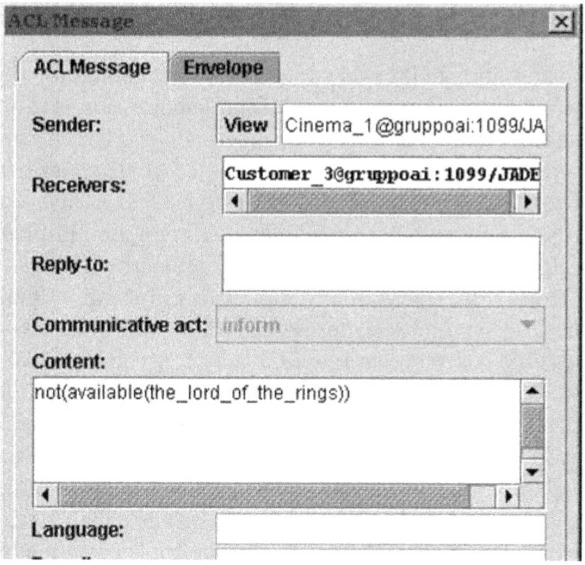

Fig. 5. Details of the last message sent by Cinema_1 to Customer_3

The possibility to both verify some properties of a set of AUML diagrams by means of their translation into DyLOG, and *animate* the diagrams by creating a simulation of a MAS, helps the MAS engineer in the task of developing a *real MAS* that is correct w.r.t. the initial requirements. Once the simulation of the MAS works properly, the real MAS can be obtained by substituting the agents developed using Jess, with agents that show the same behavior but are developed using Java[3]. A prototype of the MAS that includes only Java agents, is very close to a final implementation. Java agents can easily act as interfaces towards existing services, databases or the Web thus allowing the integration of legacy software and data and the interaction with Web services.

The integration of DyLOG inside DCaseLP, although just methodological, is a step forward towards achieving the goal of making DCaseLP a truly *multi lingual* environment, where agents that are *heterogeneous* in both the language they are specified/implemented and in their internal architecture[4] are used in the different stages of the engineering process.

---

[3] The substitution should be carried out in such a way that the internal and social behavior of the Java agents is exactly the same as the one of the Jess agents. For the moment, techniques and tools for proving the correctness of the substitution are not provided with the DCaseLP environment: the MAS developer must ensure this correctness by him-/herself.

[4] The agents of the *restaurant + cinema* example have a BDI-like architecture, but simpler reactive or proactive agents could be specified/implemented as well using Jess and Java.

6   Conclusions and Related Work

AOSE does not yet supply solid and complete environments for the seamless integration of *heterogeneous* specification and implementation languages, nonetheless, some interesting results have already been achieved with the development of prototypical environments for engineering *heterogeneous agents*. Just to cite some of them, the AgentTool development system [2] is a Java-based graphical development environment to help users analyze, design, and implement MASs. It is designed to support the Multiagent Systems Engineering (MaSE) methodology [14], which can be used by the system designer to graphically define a high-level system behavior. The system designer defines the types of agents in the system as well as the possible communications that may take place between them. This system-level specification is then refined for each type of agent in the system. To refine the specification of an agent, the designer either selects or creates an agent's architecture and then provides detailed behavioral specification for each component in such architecture. Zeus [38] is an environment developed by British Telecommunications for specifying and implementing collaborative agents, following a clear methodology and using the software tools provided by the environment. The approach of Zeus to the development of a MAS consists of analysis, design, realization and runtime support. The first two stages of the methodology are described in detail in the documentation, but only the last two stages are supported by software tools. The description of other prototyping environments can be found starting from the UMBC Web Site (http://agents.umbc.edu) and following the path Applications and Software, Software, Academic, Platforms. The reader can refer to [15] for a comparison between some of them, including the predecessor of DCaseLP (CaseLP).

In respect to the existing MAS prototyping environments, DCaseLP stresses the aspect of *multi-language support* to cope with the heterogeneity of both the views of the MAS and the agents. This aspect is usually not considered in depth, and this is the reason why we opted to work with DCaseLP rather than with other existing environments. In particular, in this paper we have focused on the *methodological* integration of the agent logic-based implementation language DyLOG into the MAS prototyping environment DCaseLP, with the main aim of exploiting the formal methods supported by DyLOG in order to reason about agent protocol-driven interactions.

A methodology for integrating DyLOG into DCaseLP has been proposed that is based on the semi-automatic generation of a DyLOG implementation from an AUML sequence diagram, in a similar way as it has been done for the AUML → Jess translation [4]. Such an integration allows to support the MAS developer in many ways. In fact, by means of this integration we add to DCaseLP the ability of verifying properties of the implemented protocols during the *design phase* of the MAS; this feature is not offered by DCaseLP (without DyLOG) since protocols can only be translated into Jess code and executed. The ability of reasoning about possible interactions is very useful in many practical tasks. In this paper we have shown a couple of examples of use: *selection* of already developed protocols from a library and verification of *compositional properties*.

In recent work, part of the authors have used formal methods for proving other kinds of properties of the interaction protocols implemented in DyLOG. In particular, we have faced the *conformance* problem, which amounts to determine if a given protocol implementation respects a protocol specification (in our case the specification language is AUML). In [8] we have, in fact, proposed three definitions of conformance, characterized by different levels of abstraction from the agent private mental state, we have shown that by interpreting the conformance test as a problem of language inclusion, protocol conformance (the strongest of the three) is actually decidable and tractable (see Figure 3).

In the future, we mean to study the application of other techniques derived from the area of logic-based protocol verification [18] where the problem of proving universal properties of interaction protocols (i.e., properties that hold after every possible execution of the protocol) is faced. Such techniques could be exploited to perform the *validation stage* [25] in order to check the coherence of the AUML description with the specifications derived from the analysis. This is usually done by defining a model of the protocol (AUML) and expressing the specification by a temporal logic formula; thus model checking techniques test if the model satisfies the temporal logic formula.

Acknowledgement

This research is partially supported by MIUR Cofin 2003 "Logic-based development and verification of multi-agent systems (MASSiVE)" national project.

References

1. Advanced logic in computing environment. Available at http://www.di.unito.it/~alice/.
2. AgentTool development system. http://www.cis.ksu.edu/ sdeloach/ai/projects/agentTool/agentool.htm.
3. K. Arisha, T. Eiter, S. Kraus, F. Ozcan, R. Ross, and V.S. Subrahmanian. IMPACT: a platform for collaborating agents. *IEEE Intelligent Systems*, 14(2):64–72, 1999.
4. E. Astesiano, M. Martelli, V. Mascardi, and G. Reggio. From Requirement Specification to Prototype Execution: a Combination of a Multiview Use-Case Driven Method and Agent-Oriented Techniques. In J. Debenham and K. Zhang, editors, *Proceedings of the 15th International Conference on Software Engineering and Knowledge Engineering (SEKE'03)*, pages 578–585. The Knowledge System Institute, 2003.
5. E. Astesiano and G. Reggio. Knowledge Structuring and Representation in Requirement Specification. In *Proceedings of SEKE 2002*. ACM Press, 2002.
6. AUML Home Page. http://www.auml.org.
7. M. Baldoni, C. Baroglio, A. Martelli, and V. Patti. Reasoning about self and others: communicating agents in a modal action logic. In C. Blundo and C. Laneve, editors, *Theoretical Computer Science, 8th Italian Conference, ICTCS'2003*, volume 2841 of *LNCS*, pages 228–241, Bertinoro, Italy, October 2003. Springer.

8. M. Baldoni, C. Baroglio, A. Martelli, V. Patti, and C. Schifanella. Verifying protocol conformance for logic-based communicating agents. In J. Leite and P. Torroni, editors, *Pre-Proc. of 5th Int. Workshop on Computational Logic in Multi-Agent Systems, CLIMA V*, pages 82–97, Lisbon, Portugal, September 2004.

9. M. Baldoni, L. Giordano, A. Martelli, and V. Patti. Programming Rational Agents in a Modal Action Logic. *Annals of Mathematics and Artificial Intelligence, Special issue on Logic-Based Agent Implementation*, 41(2-4):207–257, 2004.

10. J. Bentahar, B. Moulin, J. J. Ch. Meyer, and B. Chaib-Draa. A computational model for conversation policies for agent communication. In J. Leite and P. Torroni, editors, *Pre-Proc. of 5th Int. Workshop on Computational Logic in Multi-Agent Systems, CLIMA V*, pages 66–81, Lisbon, Portugal, September 2004.

11. A. Bracciali, P. Mancarella, K. Stathis, and F. Toni. On modelling declaratively multiagent systems. In *Proceedings of the Workshop on Declarative Agent Languages and Technologies (DALT'04)*, LNCS 3476, Springer-Verlag (2005). In this volume.

12. L. Cabac and D. Moldt. Formal semantics for AUML agent interaction protocol diagrams. In *Proceedings of Agent-Oriented Software Engineering (AOSE), 2004.*

13. G. De Giacomo, Y. Lespérance, and H. J. Levesque. CONGOLOG, a concurrent programming language based on situation calculus. *Artificial Intelligence*, 121:109–169, 2000.

14. S. A. DeLoach. *Methodologies and Software Engineering for Agent Systems*, chapter The MaSE Methodology. Kluwer Academic Publisher, 2004. To appear.

15. T. Eiter and V. Mascardi. Comparing Environments for Developing Software Agents. *AI Communications*, 15(4):169–197, 2002.

16. FIPA Specifications. http://www.fipa.org.

17. M. Fisher. A survey of concurrent METATEM - the language and its applications. In D. M. Gabbay and H.J. Ohlbach, editors, *Proc. of the 1st Int. Conf. on Temporal Logic (ICTL'94)*, LNCS 827, pages 480–505. Springer-Verlag, 1994.

18. L. Giordano, A. Martelli, and C. Schwind. Specifying and Verifying Systems of Communicating Agents in a Temporal Action Logic. In A. Cappelli and F. Turini, editors, *Proc. of the 8th Conf. of AI*IA*, LNAI 2829, Springer-Verlag, 2003.

19. L. Giordano, A. Martelli, and C. Schwind. Verifying communicating agents by model checking in a temporal action logic. In J. Alferes and J. Leite, editors, *9th European Conference on Logics in Artificial Intelligence (JELIA'04)*, LNAI 3229, pages 57–69, Lisbon, Portugal, Sept. 2004. Springer-Verlag.

20. F. Guerin and J. Pitt. Verification and Compliance Testing. In M.P. Huget, editor, *Communication in Multiagent Systems*, LNAI 2650, pages 98–112. Springer-Verlag, 2003.

21. I. Gungui and V. Mascardi. Integrating tuProlog into DCaseLP to engineer heterogeneous agent systems. Proceedings of CILC 2004. Available at http://www.disi.unige.it/person/MascardiV/Download/CILC04a.pdf.gz.

22. G. Gutnik and G. Kaminka. A scalable Petri Net representation of interaction protocols for overhearing. In *Proceedings of the Third International Joint Conference on Autonomous Agents and Multiagent Systems (AAMAS)*, volume 3, pages 1246–1247, 2004.

23. G. Gutnik and G.A. Kaminka. A comprehensive Petri Net representation for multi-agent conversations. Technical Report 2004/1, Bar-Ilan University, 2004.

24. M-P. Huget. Model checking agent UML protocol diagrams. Technical Report ULCS–02–012, CS Department, University of Liverpool, UK, 2002.

25. M.P. Huget and J.L. Koning. Interaction Protocol Engineering. In M.P. Huget, editor, *Communication in Multiagent Systems*, LNAI 2650, pages 179–193. Springer, 2003.
26. JADE Home Page. `http://jade.cselt.it/`.
27. Jess Home Page. `http://herzberg.ca.sandia.gov/jess/`.
28. J. Leite, A. Omicini, P. Torroni, and P. Yolum, editors. *Proceedings of the Workshop on Declarative Agent Languages and Technologies (DALT'04)*, LNCS 3476, Springer-Verlag (2005). This volume.
29. M. Martelli and V. Mascardi. From UML diagrams to Jess rules: Integrating OO and rule-based languages to specify, implement and execute agents. In F. Buccafurri, editor, *Proceedings of the 8th APPIA-GULP-PRODE Joint Conference on Declarative Programming (AGP'03)*, pages 275–286, 2003.
30. H. Mazouzi, A. El Fallah Seghrouchni, and S. Haddad. Open protocol design for complex interactions in multi-agent systems. In C. Castelfranchi and W. L. Johnson, editors, *Proceedings of the First International Joint Conference on Autonomous Agents and Multiagent Systems (AAMAS 2002)*, pages 517–526. ACM Press, 2002.
31. J. Odell, H. V. D. Parunak, and B. Bauer. Extending UML for agents. In *Proceedings of the Agent-Oriented Information System Workshop at the 17th National Conference on Artificial Intelligence*. 2000.
32. L. R. Pokorny and C. R. Ramakrishnan. Modeling and verification of distributed autonomous agents using logic programming. In *Proceedings of the Workshop on Declarative Agent Languages and Technologies (DALT'04)*, LNCS 3476, Springer-Verlag (2005). In this volume.
33. C. Schifanella, L. Lusso, M. Baldoni, and C. Baroglio. Design and development of a visual environment for writing dylog, 2004. Submitted.
34. M. P. Singh. A social semantics for agent communication languages. In *Proc. of IJCAI-98 Workshop on Agent Communication Languages*, Berlin, 2000. Springer.
35. F. Stolzenburg and T. Arai. From the specification of multiagent systems by statecharts to their formal analysis by model checking: Towards safety-critical applications. In M. Schillo, M. Klusch, J. Müller, and H. Tianfield, editors, *Proceedings of the First German Conference on Multiagent System Technologies*, LNAI 2831, pages 131–143. Springer-Verlag, 2003.
36. tuProlog Home Page. `http://lia.deis.unibo.it/research/tuprolog/`.
37. C. Walton. Model checking agent dialogues. In *Proceedings of the Workshop on Declarative Agent Languages and Technologies (DALT'04)*, LNCS 3476, Springer-Verlag (2005). In this volume.
38. ZEUS Home Page. `http://more.btexact.com/projects/agents.htm`.

Model Checking Agent Dialogues

Christopher D. Walton

Centre for Intelligent Systems and their Applications (CISA),
School of Informatics, University of Edinburgh, UK
Tel: +44-(0)131-650-2718
cdw@inf.ed.ac.uk

Abstract. In this paper we address the challenges associated with the verification of correctness of communication between agents in Multi-Agent Systems. Our approach applies model-checking techniques to protocols which express interactions between a group of agents in the form of a dialogue. We define a lightweight protocol language which can express a wide range of dialogue types, and we use the SPIN model checker to verify properties of this language. Our early results show this approach has a high success rate in the detection of failures in agent dialogues.

1   Introduction

A popular basis for agent communication in Multi-Agent Systems (MAS) is the theory of *speech acts*, which is generally recognised to have come from the work of the philosopher John Austin [1]. This theory recognises that certain natural language utterances have the characteristics of physical actions in that they change the state of the world (e.g., declaring war). Austin identified a number of *performative verbs* which correspond to different types of speech acts, e.g., inform, promise, request. The theory of speech acts has been adapted for expressing interactions between agents by many MAS researchers, and this is most visible in the development of Agent Communication Languages (ACLs). The two most popular ACLs are currently the Knowledge Query and Manipulation Language (KQML) [2] and the Foundation for Intelligent Physical Agents ACL (FIPA-ACL) [3]. In these languages, the model of interaction between agents is based on the exchange of *messages*. KQML and FIPA-ACL define sets of performatives (message types) that express the intended meaning of the messages. These languages do not define the actual content of the messages and they assume a reliable method of message exchange.

In order to connect the theory of speech acts with the rational processes of agents, Cohen and Levesque defined a general theory of *rational action* [4]. This theory is itself based upon the theory of *intentional reasoning*, developed by the philosopher Michael Bratman [5], which introduced the notion that human behaviour can be predicted and explained through the use of attitudes (mental states), e.g., believing, fearing, hoping. In the general theory, speech acts are modelled as actions performed by agents to satisfy their intentions. The FIPA-ACL specification recognises this theory by providing a formal semantics for the performatives expressed in Belief-Desire-Intension (BDI) logic [6]. A BDI semantics for KQML has also been developed [7]. The combination

J. Leite et al. (Eds.): DALT 2004, LNAI 3476, pp. 132–147, 2005.

of speech acts and intentional reasoning provides an appealing theoretical basis for the specification and verification of MAS [8]. Similarly, the KQML and FIPA standards provide useful frameworks for the implementation of MAS based upon these theories, e.g., JADE [9].

Nonetheless, there is a growing dissatisfaction with the mentalistic model of agency as a basis for defining *inter-operable* agents between different agent platforms [10, 11]. Inter-operability requires that agents built by different organisations, and using different software systems, are able to reliably communicate with one another in a common language with an agreed semantics. The problem with the BDI model as a basis for inter-operable agents is that although agents can be defined according to a commonly agreed semantics, it is not generally possible to verify that an agent is acting according to these semantics. This stems from the fact that it is not known how to assign mental states systematically to arbitrary programs. For example, we have no way of knowing whether an agent actually believes a particular fact. For the semantics to be verifiable it would be necessary to have access to an agents' internal mental states. This problem is known as the *semantic verification* problem and is detailed in [12].

To understand why semantic verification is a highly-desirable property for an inter-operable agent system it is necessary to view the communication between agents as part of a coherent *dialogue* between the agents. According to the theory of rational action, the dialogue emerges from a sequence of speech acts performed by an agent to satisfy their intentions. Furthermore, agents should be able to recognise and reason about the other agents intentions based upon these speech acts. For example, according to the FIPA-ACL standard, if an agent receives an `inform` message then it is entitled to believe that the sender believes the proposition in the message. There is an underlying *sincerity assumption* in this definition which demands that agents always act in accordance with their intentions. This assumption is considered too restrictive in an open environment as it will always be possible for an insincere agent to simulate any required internal state, and we cannot verify the sincerity of an agent as we have no access to is mental states.

In order to avoid the problems associated with the mentalistic model, and thereby express a greater range of dialogue types, a number of alternative semantics for expressing rational agency have been proposed. The two approaches that have received the most attention are a semantics based on social commitments, and a semantics based on dialogue games [13].

The key concept of the social commitment model is the establishment of shared commitments between agents. A social commitment between agents is a binding agreement from one agent to another. The commitment distinguishes between the creditor who commits to a course of action, and the debtor on whose behalf the action is done. Establishing a commitment constrains the subsequent actions of the agent until the commitment is discharged. Commitments are stored as part of the social state of the MAS and are verifiable. A theory which combines speech acts with social commitments is outlined in [14].

Dialogue games can trace their origins to the philosophical tradition of Aristotle. Dialogue games have been used to study fallacious reasoning, for natural language processing and generation, and to develop a game-theoretic semantics for various logics. These games can also be applied in MAS as the basis for interaction between autonomous agents. A group of agents participate in a dialogue game in which their utterances correspond to moves in this game. Different rules can be applied to the game, which correspond to different dialogue types, e.g., persuasion, negotiation, enquiry [15]. For example, a persuasion dialogue begins with an assertion and ends when the proponent withdraws the claim or the opponent concedes the claim. A framework which permits different kinds of dialogue games, and also meta-dialogues is outlined in [16].

There is an additional problem of verification of the BDI model, which we term the *concurrency verification* problem. A system constructed using the BDI model defines a complex concurrent system of communicating agents. Concurrency introduces *non-determinism* into the system which gives rise to a large number of potential problems, such as synchronisation, fairness, and deadlocks. It is difficult, even for an experienced designer, to obtain a good intuition for the behaviour of a concurrent protocol, primarily due to the large number of possible interleavings which can occur. Traditional debugging and simulation techniques cannot readily explore all of the possible behaviours of such systems, and therefore significant problems can remain undiscovered. The detection of problems in these systems is typically accomplished through the use of *formal verification* techniques such as theorem proving and model checking.

In order to address the concurrency verification problem, a number of attempts have been made to apply model checking to models of BDI agents [17, 18, 19, 20]. The model checking technique is appealing as it is an automated process, though it is limited to finite-state systems. A model checker normally performs an exhaustive search of the state space of a system to determine if a particular property holds and, given sufficient resources, the procedure will always terminate with a yes/no answer.

One of the main issues in the verification of software systems using model checking techniques is the *state-space explosion* problem. The exhaustive nature of model checking means that the state space can rapidly grow beyond the available resources as the size of the model increases. Thus, in order to successfully check a system it is necessary that the model is as small as possible. However, it is a fundamental concept of the BDI model that communicative acts are generated by agents in order to satisfy their intentions. Therefore, in order to model check BDI agents we must represent both rational and communicative processes in the model. This problem has affected previous attempts to model-check multi-agent systems e.g., [18], which use the BDI model as the basis for the verification process, limiting the applicability to very small agent models.

In this paper we do not adopt a specific semantics of rational agency, or define a fixed model of interaction between agents. Our belief is that in a truly heterogeneous agent system we cannot constrain the agents to any particular model. For example, *web-service* [21] agents are rapidly becoming an attractive alternative to BDI-based agents. Instead, we define a model of dialogue which separates the rational process and interactions from the actual dialogue itself. This is accomplished through the adoption of a *dialogue protocol* which exists at a layer between these processes. This approach has been adopted in the Conversation Policy [22] and Electronic Institutions [23, 24] formalisms, among others. The definition presented in this paper differs in that dialogue protocol specifications can be directly executed. We define a lightweight language of

Multi-Agent dialogue Protocols (MAP) as an alternative to the state-chart [25] representation of protocols. Our formalism allows the definition of infinite-state dialogues and the mechanical processing of the resulting dialogue protocols. MAP protocols contain only a representation of the communicative processes of the agents and the resulting models are therefore significantly simpler.

Dialogue protocols specify complex concurrent and asynchronous patterns of communication between agents. This approach does not suffer from the semantic verification problem as the state of the dialogue is defined in the protocol itself, and it is straightforward to verify that an agent is acting in accordance with the protocol. Nonetheless, our experiences with defining dialogue protocols in MAP have shown that it is a difficult task to define correct protocols, even for simple dialogues. The problem is not related to the internal states of the agent, but rather as a result of unexpected interactions between agents. For example, the receipt of a stale bid may adversely affect an auction. In general, the prediction of undesirable behaviour in our dialogue protocols is non trivial. Thus, the focus of this paper if on the verification of dialogue protocols specified in MAP.

We use the SPIN model checker [26] to verify our MAP protocols, as we have no desire to construct our own model checking system. The SPIN model checker has been in development for many years and includes a large number of techniques for improving the efficiency of the model checking, e.g., partial-order reduction, state-compression, and on-the-fly verification. SPIN accepts design specifications in its own language PROMELA (PROcess MEta-LAnguage), and verifies correctness claims specified as Linear Temporal Logic (LTL) formula. The verification of our dialogue protocols is achieved by a translation from the MAP language to an abstract representation in PROMELA. We use this representation in SPIN to check a number of properties of the protocols, such as termination, liveness, and correctness. Our approach to translation is similar to [19], though we are primarily interested in checking general properties of inter-agent communication rather than specific BDI properties.

Our presentation in this paper is structured as follows: in Section 2 we define the syntax of the Multi-Agent Protocol (MAP) language. In Section 3 we specify the essential features of a translation from MAP to PROMELA which enables us to perform model checking of our protocols, and discuss our initial model checking results. We conclude in Section 4 with a discussion of future work.

2   The MAP Language

The MAP language is a lightweight dialogue protocol language which provides a replacement for the state-chart representation of protocols found in Electronic Institutions. The underlying semantics of our language is derived from process calculus. In particular MAP can be considered a sugared variant of the π-calculus [27]. We have redefined the core of the Electronic Institutions framework to provide an executable specification, while retaining the concepts of *scenes*, and *roles*.

The division of agent dialogues into *scenes* is a key concept in our protocol language. A scene can be thought of as a bounded space in which a group agents interact on a single task. The use of scenes divides a large protocol into manageable chunks. For example, a negotiation scene may be part of a larger marketplace institution. Scenes also add a measure of security to a protocol, in that agents which are not relevant to the task are excluded from the scene. This can prevent interference with the protocol and limits the number of exceptions and special cases that must be considered in the design of the protocol. Additional security measures can also be introduced into a scene, such as placing entry and exit conditions on the agents, though we do not deal with these here. However, we assume that a scene places barrier conditions on the agents, such that a scene cannot begin until all the agents are present, and the agents cannot leave the scene until the dialogue is complete.

$$
\begin{array}{lll}
P & ::= n(r\{\mathcal{M}\})^{+} & \text{(Scene)} \\[4pt]
M & ::= \texttt{method}(\phi^{(k)}) = op & \text{(Method)} \\[8pt]
op & ::= \alpha & \text{(Action)} \\
& \mid\ op_1 \ \texttt{then}\ op_2 & \text{(Sequence)} \\
& \mid\ op_1 \ \texttt{or}\ op_2 & \text{(Choice)} \\
& \mid\ \texttt{waitfor}\ op_1 \ \texttt{timeout}\ op_2 & \text{(Iteration)} \\
& \mid\ \texttt{call}(\phi^{(k)}) & \text{(Recursion)} \\[8pt]
\alpha & ::= \epsilon & \text{(No Action)} \\
& \mid\ v = p(\phi^{(k)}) & \text{(Decision)} \\
& \mid\ M \texttt{ => agent}(\phi^1, \phi^2) & \text{(Send)} \\
& \mid\ M \texttt{ <= agent}(\phi^1, \phi^2) & \text{(Receive)} \\[8pt]
M & ::= \rho(\phi^{(k)}) & \text{(Performative)} \\[8pt]
\phi & ::= \_ \mid a \mid r \mid c \mid v & \text{(Terms)}
\end{array}
$$

Fig. 1. MAP Abstract Syntax

The concept of an agent *role* is also central to our definition of a dialogue protocol. Agents entering a scene assume a fixed role which persists until the end of the scene. For example, a negotiation scene may involve agents with the roles of *buyer* and *seller*. The protocol which the agent follows in a dialogue will typically depend on the role of the agent. For example, an agent acting as a seller will typically attempt to maximise profit and will act accordingly in the negotiation. A role also identifies capabilities which the agent must provide. For example, the buyer must have the capability to make buying decisions and to purchase items. Capabilities are related to the rational processes of the agent and are encapsulated by *decision procedures* in our definition.

The abstract syntax of MAP is presented in Figure 1. We have also defined a corresponding concrete XML-based syntax for MAP which is used in our implementation. A scene protocol P is uniquely named n and defined as a (non-empty) sequence of roles r, each of which define a set of methods $\mathcal{M}$. Agents have a fixed role for the duration of the protocol, and are individually identified by unique names a. A method M can be considered a procedure where $\phi^{(k)}$ are the arguments. The initial protocol for an agent is specified by setting $\phi^{(k)}$ to be empty (i.e., $k = 0$). Protocols are constructed from operations op which control the flow of the protocol, and actions α which have side-effects, and can fail. The interface between the protocol and the rational process of the agent is achieved through the invocation of decision procedures p. Interaction between agents is performed by the exchange of messages M which contain performatives ρ. Procedures and performatives are parameterised by terms ϕ, which are either variables v, agent names a, role names r, constants c, or wild-cards _. Variables are bound to terms by unification which occurs in the invocation of procedures, the receipt of messages, or through recursive calls.

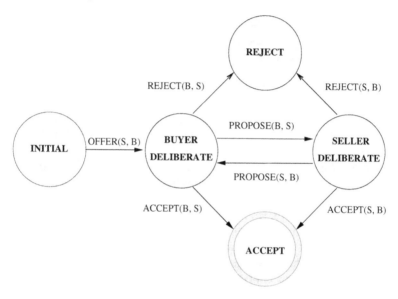

Fig. 2. Negotiation Protocol

We will now define a simple negotiation protocol, which will illustrate the MAP language and act as an example for model-checking. Before we present the definition of this protocol in MAP, we consider a state-based description of the protocol, as shown in Figure 2. The state-based description is similar to a specification of the protocol in the Electronic Institutions framework, e.g., [24].

Our negotiation protocol is an attempt to simulate a standard bargaining process between two parties (a buyer and a seller). We do not impose artificial constraints, such as turns or rounds, on the participants in the protocol. The negotiation begins with an offer from the seller to the buyer, which we denote with the message OFFER(S, B). Upon receipt of the initial offer, the buyer enters a deliberative state, in which a decision is required. The buyer can accept or reject the offer in which case the protocol terminates. The buyer can also make a proposal to the seller PROPOSE(B, S), e.g., an offer at a lower price. If a proposal is made to the seller, then the seller enters a deliberative state. The seller can in turn accept or reject the proposal, or make a counterproposal. If a counterproposal is made, the buyer deliberates further. Thus, the negotiation is effectively captured by a sequence of proposals and counter-proposals between the buyer and the seller.

A definition of the negotiation protocol in MAP syntax is presented in Figure 3. For convenience, we distinguish between the different types of terms by prefixing variables names with $, and role names with %. We define two roles: %buyer and %seller. Each of these roles has three associated methods which define the protocol states for the roles.

When exchanging messages through send and receive actions, a unification of terms in the definition agent(ϕ^1, ϕ^2) is performed, where ϕ^1 is matched against the agent name, and ϕ^2 against the agent role. For example, when the buyer receives the initial offer, in line 5 of the protocol, the terms will match any agent whose role is a %seller, and $seller will be bound to the name of the seller.

The semantics of message passing corresponds to reliable, buffered, non-blocking communication. Sending a message will succeed immediately if an agent matches the definition, and the message M will be stored in a buffer on the recipient. Receiving a message involves an additional unification step. The message M supplied in the definition is treated as a template to be matched against any message in the buffer. For example, in line 19 of the protocol, a message must match accept($sellvalue), and the variable $sellvalue will be bound to the content of the message if the match is successful. Sending a message will fail if no agent matches the supplied terms, and receiving a message will fail if no message matches the message template.

The send and receive actions complete immediately and do not delay the agent. For this reason, all of the receive actions are wrapped by waitfor loops to avoid race conditions. For example, in line 18 the agent will loop until a message is received. If this loop was not present the agent may fail to find a response and the protocol would terminate prematurely. The advantage of non-blocking communication is that we can check for the receipt of a number of different messages. For example, in lines 19, 20, and 21 the protocol, the agent waits for either an accept, reject, or propose message respectively. The waitfor loop includes a timeout condition which is triggered after a certain interval has elapsed. The timeout is defined to restart the loop (in lines 23 and 37), though we could define an alternative behaviour, such as withdrawing from the negotiation. Timeouts give us a measure of fault tolerance in the presence of delays or failures.

At various points in the protocol, an agent is required to perform various tasks, e.g., making a decision, or retrieving some information. This is achieved through the use of decision procedures. As stated earlier, a decision procedure provide an interface between the dialogue protocol and the rational processes of the agent. In our language, a decision procedure p takes a number of terms as arguments and returns a single result in a variable v. The actual implementation of the decision procedure is external to the dialogue protocol. For example, the acceptOffer decision procedure in line 31 of the dialogue refers to an external decision procedure, which can be arbitrarily complex, e.g., based on reputation, or according to some negotiation strategy.

The operations in the protocol are sequenced by the then operator which evaluates op_1 followed by op_2, unless op_1 involved an action which failed. The failure of actions is handled by the or operator. This operator is defined such that if op_1 fails, then op_2 is evaluated, otherwise op_2 is ignored. External data is represented by constants c in our language. We do not attempt to assign types to this data, rather we leave the

```
1   negotiate[
2     %buyer{
3       method() =
4         waitfor
5          (offer($value) <= agent($seller, %seller) then
6           call(deliberate, $value, $seller))
7         timeout (e)
8
9       method(deliberate, $value, $seller) =
10          ($newvalue = acceptOffer($value, $seller) then
11           accept($value) => agent($seller, %seller))
12        or ($newvalue = counterPropose($value, $seller) then
13            propose($newvalue) => agent($seller, %seller) then
14            call(wait, $newvalue))
15        or  reject($value) => agent($seller, %seller)
16
17      method(wait, $value) =
18        waitfor
19           (accept($sellvalue) <= agent($seller, %seller)
20         or reject($oldvalue) <= agent($seller, %seller)
21         or (propose($newvalue) <= agent($seller, %seller)
22             then call(deliberate, $newvalue, $seller)))
23        timeout (call(wait, $value))}
24
25    %seller{
26      method() =
27        $value = getValue() then
28        offer($value) => agent(_, %buyer) then
29        call(wait, $value)
30
31      method(wait, $value) =
32        waitfor
33           (accept($sellvalue) <= agent($buyer, %buyer)
34         or reject($oldvalue) <= agent($buyer, %buyer)
35         or (propose($newvalue) <= agent($buyer, %buyer) then
36             call(deliberate, $newvalue, $buyer)))
37        timeout (call(wait, $value))
38
39      method(deliberate, $value, $buyer) =
40          ($newvalue = acceptOffer($value, $buyer) then
41           accept($value) => agent($buyer, %buyer))
42        or ($newvalue = counterPropose($value, $buyer) then
43            propose($newvalue) => agent($buyer, %buyer) then
44            call(wait, $newvalue))
45        or reject($value) => agent($buyer, %buyer)} ]
```

Fig. 3. MAP Negotiation Protocol

interpretation of this data to the decision procedures. For example, in line 27 the starting value is returned by the getValue procedure, and interpreted by the acceptOffer procedure in line 10. Constants can therefore refer to complex data-types, e.g., currency, flat-file data, XML documents.

It should be clear that MAP is a powerful language for expressing multi-agent dialogues. It is important to note that MAP is only intended to express protocols, and is not intended to be a general-purpose language for computation. Therefore, the relative paucity of features, e.g., no user-defined data-types, is entirely appropriate. Furthermore, MAP is designed to be a lightweight protocol language and only a minimal set of operations has been provided. It is intended that MAP protocols will be automatically generated, e.g., from a planning system, or from visual tools such as ISLANDER [28].

$$
\begin{array}{rcll}
n(r\{\mathcal{M}\})^+ & \rightsquigarrow & [\![\mathcal{M}^1]\!] \wedge \cdots \wedge [\![\mathcal{M}^k]\!] & \text{(Scene)} \\
\texttt{method}(\phi^{(k)}) = op & \rightsquigarrow & [\![op]\!] \quad \Delta \cup \{\phi^{(k)} \mapsto op\} & \text{(Protocol)} \\
\alpha & \rightsquigarrow & \bot \mid \top & \text{(Action)} \\
op_1 \text{ then } op_2 & \rightsquigarrow & [\![op_1]\!] \wedge \Diamond[\![op_2]\!] & \text{(Sequence)} \\
op_1 \text{ or } op_2 & \rightsquigarrow & [\![op_1]\!] \vee [\![op_2]\!] & \text{(Choice)} \\
\texttt{waitfor } op_1 \text{ timeout } op_2 & \rightsquigarrow & \Diamond([\![op_1]\!] \vee [\![op_2]\!]) & \text{(Iteration)} \\
\texttt{call}(\phi^{(k)}) & \rightsquigarrow & [\![\Delta(\phi^{(k)})]\!] & \text{(Recursion)}
\end{array}
$$

Fig. 4. MAP Denotational Semantics

A formal operational semantics for the MAP language has previously been presented in [29], together with an encoding of an auction protocol. It is also helpful to define the semantics of MAP denotationally to show what is being computed mathematically. Thus, we now sketch the semantics of MAP in a modal temporal logic. We require only one modal construct: the term $\Diamond\varphi$ denotes that the expression φ is true at some future time. Figure 4 illustrates the translations into this form for the operations of MAP. The square brackets indicate that the translation should be applied recursively. The environment Δ stores mappings from method arguments to operations. For each action α, we must make a judgement as to whether the action is true $\top$ or false $\bot$. We note that the semantics are for a stricter variant of the language, where the choice operations are evaluated non-deterministic, rather than in left-to-right order. This behaviour is useful for exposing errors in the protocols which may otherwise remain hidden.

We have used our language to specify a wide range of other protocols, including a range of popular negotiation and auction protocols. We have also restated the semantics of the FIPA-ACL performatives in MAP. Figure 5 gives a flavour of this transformation, with a (simplified) encoding of the FIPA inform performative. We also outline an encoding of the dialogue-games model in [30].

FIPA Semantics: $< i, \text{inform}(j, \Phi) >$
                    $FP: \quad B_i\Phi \wedge \neg B_i(Bif_j\Phi \vee Uif_j\Phi)$
                    $RE: \quad B_j\Phi$

MAP Encoding:

```
method(inform, $p, $i, $j) =
  believe($i, $p) then
  not(believe($i, bif($j, $p))) then
  not(believe($i, uif($j, $p))) then
  inform(p) => agent($j, _) then
  assert(believe, $j, $p)
```

Fig. 5. Encoding of FIPA `inform` Performative

3   Model Checking MAP

The first step in the application of SPIN model checking to MAP protocols is the construction of an appropriate system model. The underlying framework for modelling in SPIN is the Kripke structure, though this is well hidden underneath its own process meta-language PROMELA. SPIN translates the PROMELA language into Kripke structures, through a (loose) mapping of processes to states and channels to transitions. To generate the appropriate model for our MAP protocols, we perform a a translation from the MAP language to an abstract representation in PROMELA. Of particular importance in this translation is the level of abstraction of the model on which the verification is performed. If the level of abstraction is too low-level, the state space will be too large and verification will be impossible. For example, it would be possible to construct a meta-interpreter for MAP protocols in PROMELA, but this would be unlikely to yield a sufficiently compact representation. Conversely, if the level of abstraction is too high then important issues will be obscured by the representation. Our chosen method of representation is a syntax-directed translation of the MAP protocols into PROMELA.

At an intuitive level there are a number of apparent similarities between MAP and PROMELA. For example, both are based on the notion of asynchronous sequential processes (or agents), and both assume that communication is performed via message passing. These high-level similarities significantly simplify the translation as we can translate MAP agents directly into PROMELA processes and agent communication into message passing over buffered channels. Nonetheless, the translation of the low-level details of MAP is not so straightforward as there are significant semantic differences in the execution behaviour of the languages.

There are three key points of semantic mismatch between MAP and PROMELA which we must address. The first of these concerns the order of execution of the statements. In MAP, we assume a depth-first execution order, while PROMELA is based on guarded commands [31]. The MAP language makes use of unification for the invocation of decision procedures, for recursion, and in message passing, while PROMELA has a call-by-value semantics. Furthermore, MAP assumes that messages can be   retrieved in an arbitrary order (by unification), while PROMELA enforces a strict queue of messages. Finally, we must consider how to represent MAP decision procedures in our specification. We will now sketch how these semantic differences are handled in our translation system.

We cannot readily represent the MAP execution tree in PROMELA as the language does not permit the definition of complex data structures. Our adopted solution involves flattening the execution tree through the translations shown in Figure 6. The templates shown are applied recursively, where $T(op)$ denotes a further translation of the operation op. We use a reserved variable `fail` to indicate whether a failure has occurred. This variable is tested on the execution of `then` and `or` operations. If a failure occurs, we skip all of the intermediate operations until an `or` node is encountered at which point the execution resumes. In this way we simulate the essential behaviour of the depth-first algorithm.

MAP: op_1 then op_2 op_1 or op_2

```
PROMELA:    fail = false ;              fail = false ;
            T(op₁) ;                    T(op₁) ;
            if                          if
            :: (fail == false) ->       :: (fail == true) ->
               T(op₂)                      fail = false ; T(op₂)
            :: else -> skip             :: else -> skip
            fi                          fi
```

Fig. 6. Control Flow Translation

Pattern matching is an essential part of the MAP language as it is used in method invocation, and in the exchange of messages. Pattern matching is achieved through the unification of terms, which may bind variables to values. As PROMELA does not support pattern matching, we must perform a *match compilation* step in order to unfold the unification into a sequence of conditional tests. We do not describe the match compilation further here as there are many existing algorithms for performing this task.

We previously stated that messages are stored in buffered channels in PROMELA, and we define a separate message buffer for each agent. However, a message buffer acts as a FIFO queue, and the messages must be retrieved in a strict order from the front of the queue. By contrast, messages in MAP are retrieved by unification and any message in the queue may be returned as a result. To simulate the required behaviour, we must remove all of the messages in the queue in turn and compare them with the required message by unification. The first message that is successfully matched is stored and the remaining messages are returned to the queue. We note that it is not enough simply to examine all the messages in the queue in-place, as we must also remove a matching message.

A remaining issue in the translation process is the treatment of decision procedures, which are references to external rational processes. For example, in our negotiation the buyer may make a counterproposal, expressed in line 12: $newvalue

= `counterPropose($value, %seller)`. The separation of rational processes from the communicative processes is a key feature in MAP. Nonetheless, the decision procedures are ultimately responsible for controlling the protocol and must be represented in some manner by our translation to PROMELA. To address this issue we make the observation that the purpose of a decision procedure is to make a yes/no decision. Similarly, the purpose of the model checking process is to detect errors in the protocol and not in the decision procedures. Thus, based on these observations we can in principle replace a decision procedure with any code that returns a yes/no decision. Furthermore, if this code returns a non-deterministic decision, the exhaustive nature of the model checking process will mean that all possible behaviours of the protocol will be explored. In other words, the model checker will explore all consequences for the protocol where the decision was yes, and where the decision was no.

Our translation of decision procedures into PROMELA is achieved by exploiting the non-determinism of guarded commands in the language. The semantics of guarded commands is such that if more than one guard is executable in a given situation, a non-deterministic choice is made between the guards. Therefore, the code fragment presented in Figure 7 can act as a suitable substitute for the `counterPropose` decision procedure. The decision is marked as `atomic` as this improves the efficiency of the model checking operation.

```
1   /* Decision: counterPropose */
2   atomic {
3     if
4       :: true -> fail = true
5       :: true -> newvalue = PROC_COUNTERPROPOSE
6     fi }
```

Fig. 7. Translation of `counterPropose` Decision Procedure

We have now sketched the essence of the translation from MAP to PROMELA. There are a number of residual implementation issues, such as the implementation of parallel composition, but these can be readily represented in PROMELA. The result of the translation is an specification of a protocol in PROMELA which replicates the semantics of the protocol as defined in MAP.

Our initial model checking experiments with the SPIN model checker have focused on the *termination* of MAP protocols. This is an important consideration in the design of protocols, as we do not (normally) want to define scenes that cannot conclude. Non-termination can occur as a result of many different issues such as deadlocks, live-locks, infinite recursion, and message synchronisation errors. We also want to ensure that protocols do not simply terminate due to failure within the protocol. The termination condition is the most straightforward to validate. Given that progress is a requirement in almost every concurrent system, the SPIN model checker automatically verifies this property by default. Every PROMELA process has one or more associated *end* states, which denote the valid termination points. The final state of a process is implicitly an end state. The termination condition states that every process eventually reaches a valid end state. This can be expressed as the following LTL formula, where `end1` is the end state for the first process, and `end2` is the end state for the second process, etc: $\Box(\Diamond(\text{end1} \wedge \text{end2} \wedge \text{end3} \wedge \cdots))$. We append the PROMELA code in Figure 8 to the end of each translated process. The test in line 2 will block if a failure has occurred, and the process will be prevented from reaching the end-state in line 3, i.e., the process will not terminate.

```
1   /* Check For Failure */
2   fail == false ;
3   end: skip
```

Fig. 8. Test for Protocol Failure

One of the main pragmatic issues associated with model checking is producing a state space that is sufficiently small to be checking with the available resources (1GB memory in our case). Hence, it is frequently necessary to make a number of simplifying assumptions in order to work within these limits. The negotiation protocol which we have defined does not place any restriction on the length of the deliberation process and is therefore in effect an infinite protocol. Model checking is restricted to finite models, and therefore we must set a limit on the length of the negotiation. We therefore set a limit of 50 cycles before the negotiation if forced to terminate.

An issue that was uncovered in the verification of the negotiation protocol is the treatment of certain decision procedures. Our protocol was designed under the assumption that the `getValue()` procedure would always return a value to be used as the starting value of the negotiation. However, our translation makes no such assumption as it substitutes a non-deterministic choice for each decision procedure. Therefore, the result is that if the `getValue()` procedure fails, then the seller agent will terminate with a failure, and the buyer will timeout. The issue with decision procedures was resolved by introducing a new type of procedure into the MAP language, corresponding to a simple procedure that does not fail. We have found that it is often useful in the design of MAP protocols to have simple procedures which perform basic tasks, such as recording or returning values, and performing calculations. Amending the negotiation protocol with a simple `getValue()` procedure resulted in a model which successfully passed the model checking process.

4   Results and Conclusions

In this paper we have presented a novel language for representing Multi-Agent Dialogue Protocols (MAP), and we have outlined a syntax-directed translation from MAP into PROMELA for use in conjunction with the SPIN model checker. Our translator has been applied to a number of protocols, including the negotiation example in this paper. We were pleased to find that the model checking process uncovered issues in these protocols which had remained hidden during simulation. We believe that this is a significant achievement in the design of reliable agent dialogue protocols. In contrast with existing approaches to model checking MAS, our protocols remain acceptable in terms of memory and time consumption. Furthermore, we verify the actual protocol that will be executed, rather than an abstract version of the system.

Our MAP protocol language was designed to be independent of any particular model of rational agency. This makes the verification applicable to heterogeneous agent systems. Nonetheless, we recognise that the BDI model is still of significant importance to the agent community. To address this issue, we are currently defining a system which translates FIPA-ACL specifications into MAP protocols. We believe this will allow us to overcome the problems of the BDI model highlighted in the introduction, and will yield models that do not suffer from state-space explosion.

The translation system which we have outlined in this paper is designed to perform *automatic* checking of MAP protocols. This makes the system suitable for use by non-experts who do not need to understand the model checking process. However, this approach places restrictions on the kinds of properties of the protocols that we can check. In our negotiation example, we can check that the protocol terminates, but we cannot check for a particular outcome. This is a result of our abstraction of decision procedures to non-deterministic entities.

Our current research is aimed at extending the range of properties of dialogue protocols that can be checked with model checking. In order to check a greater range of properties we must augment the PROMELA translation with additional information about the protocol. This information, and the resulting properties that we can check, are specific to the protocol under verification. We have been able to verify protocol-specific properties with a hand-encoding of the decision procedures as PROMELA macros, but this relies on a detailed knowledge of the translation system. The provision of a general solution to the specification of protocol-specific properties remains as further work.

Acknowledgements

This work is sponsored by the UK Engineering and Physical Sciences Research Council (EPSRC Grant GR/N15764/01) Advanced Knowledge Technologies Interdisciplinary Research Collaboration (AKT-IRC).

References

1. Austin, J.L.: How to Do Things With Words. Oxford University Press, Oxford, UK (1962)
2. Patil, R., Fikes, R.F., Patel-Schneider, P.F., McKay, D., Finin, T., Gruber, T., Neches, R.: The DARPA Knowledge Sharing Effort: Progress Report. In Nebel, B., Rich, C., Swartout, W., eds.: KR'92. Principles of Knowledge Representation and Reasoning: Proceedings of the Third International Conference. Morgan Kaufmann, San Mateo, California (1992) 777–788
3. Foundation for Intelligent Physical Agents: Fipa specification part 2 - agent communication language. Available at: www.fipa.org (1999)
4. Cohen, P.R., Levesque, H.J.: Rational interaction as the basis for communication. Intentions in Communication (1990) 221–256
5. Bratman, M.E.: Intention, Plans, and Practical Reason. Harvard University Press, Cambridge, MA (1987)

6. Rao, A.S., Georgeff, M.: Decision procedures for BDI logics. Journal of Logic and Computation **8** (1998) 293–344
7. Labrou, Y., Finin, T.: Semantics and conversations for an agent communication language. In: Proceedings of the FIfteenth International Joint Conference of Artificial Intelligence (IJCAI-97), Nagoya, Japan (1997) 584–591
8. Wooldridge, M.: Reasoning about Rational Agents. MIT Press (2000)
9. Bellifemine, F., Poggi, A., Rimassa, G.: JADE: A FIPA-compliant agent framework. In: Proceedings of the 1999 Conference on Practical Application of Intelligent Agents and Multi-Agent Technology (PAAM'99), London, UK (1999) 97–108
10. Singh, M.P.: Agent Communication Languages: Rethinking the Principles. IEEE Computer (1998) 40–47
11. Labrou, Y., Finin, T.: Comments on the specification for FIPA '97 Agent Communication Language. Available at: www.cs.umbc.edu/kqml/papers/ (1997)
12. Wooldridge, M.: Semantic issues in the verification of agent communication languages. Autonomous Agents and Multi-Agent Systems **3** (2000) 9–31
13. Maudet, N., Chaib-draa, B.: Commitment-based and Dialogue-game based Protocols–News Trends in Agent Communication Language. The Knowledge Engineering Review **17** (2002) 157–179
14. Flores, R.A., Kremer, R.C.: Bringing Coherence to Agent Conversations. In: Proceedings of Agent-Oriented Software Engineering (AOSE 2001). Volume 2222 of Lecture Notes in Computer Science., Montreal, Canada, Springer-Verlag (2002) 50–67
15. Walton, D.N., Krabbe, E.C.W.: Commitment in Dialogue: Basic Concepts of Interpersonal Reasoning. SUNY Press (1995)
16. McBurney, P., Parsons, S.: Games that agents play: A formal framework for dialogues between autonomous agents. Journal of Logic, Language and Information **11** (2002) 315–334
17. Benerecetti, M., Giunchiglia, F., Serafini, L.: Model Checking Multiagent Systems. Journal of Logic and Computation **8** (1998) 401–423
18. Wooldridge, M., Fisher, M., Huget, M.P., Parsons, S.: Model Checking Multiagent systems with MABLE. In: Proceedings of the First International Conference on Autonomous Agents and Multiagent Systems (AAMAS-02), Bologna, Italy (2002)
19. Bordini, R.H., Fisher, M., Pardavila, C., Wooldridge, M.: Model Checking AgentSpeak. In: Proceedings of the Second International Joint Conference on Autonomous Agents & Multiagent Systems (AAMAS), Melbourne, Australia, ACM (2003) 409–416
20. Bordini, R.H., Fisher, M., Visser, W., Wooldridge, M.J.: State-space Reduction Techniques in Agent Verification. In: Proceedings of the Third International Conference on Autonomous Agents and Multiagent Systems (AAMAS-04), New York, USA, ACM Press (2004) 896–903
21. Booth, D., Haas, H., McCabe, F., Newcomer, E., Champion, M., Ferris, C., Orchard, D.: Web Services Architecture. World-Wide-Web Consortium (W3C). (2003) Available at: www.w3.org/TR/ws-arch/.
22. Greaves, M., Holmback, H., Bradshaw, J.: What is a Conversation Policy? In: Proceedings of the Workshop on Specifying and Implementing Conversation Policies, Autonomous Agents '99, Seattle, Washington (1999)
23. Esteva, M., Rodríguez, J.A., Sierra, C., Garcia, P., Arcos, J.L.: On the Formal Specification of Electronic Institutions. In: Agent-mediated Electronic Commerce (The European AgentLink Perspective). Number 1991 in Lecture Notes in Artificial Intelligence (2001) 126–147
24. Vaconcelos, W.: Norm Verification and Analysis of Electronic Institutions. In: 2004 Workshop on Declarative Agent Languages and Technologies (DALT-04), New York, USA (2004) 141–155
25. Harel, D.: Statecharts: A Visual Formalism for Computer System. Science of Computer Programming **8** (1987) 231–274

26. Holzmann, G.J.: The SPIN Model Checker: Primer and Reference Manual. Addison Wesley (2003)
27. Milner, R., Parrow, J., Walker, D.: A Calculus of Mobile Processes (Part 1/2). Information and Computation **100** (1992) 1–77
28. Esteva, M., Cruz, D., Sierra, C.: ISLANDER: an electronic institutions editor. In: Proceedings of the First International Joint Conference on Autonomous Agents & Multiagent Systems (AAMAS), Bologna, Italy, ACM press (2002) 1045–1052
29. Walton, C.: Multi-Agent Dialogue Protocols. In: Proceedings of the Eighth International Symposium on Artificial Intelligence and Mathematics, Fort Lauderdale, Florida (2004)
30. McGinnis, J.P., Robertson, D., Walton, C.: Using Distributed Protocols as an Implementation of Dialogue Games. In: Proceedings of the 1st European Workshop on Multi-Agent Systems (EUMAS-03), Oxford, UK (2003)
31. Dijkstra, E.W.: Guarded commands, nondeterminacy and formal derivation of programs. Communications of the ACM **18** (1975) 453–457

Modeling and Verification of Distributed Autonomous Agents Using Logic Programming

L. Robert Pokorny and C.R. Ramakrishnan

Department of Computer Science,
State University of New York at Stony Brook,
Stony Brook, New York, 11794-4400, U.S.A.
pokorny@xsb.com, cram@cs.sunysb.edu

Abstract. Systems of autonomous agents providing automated services over the Web are fast becoming a reality. Often these agent systems are constructed using procedural architectures that provide a framework for connecting agent components that perform specific tasks. The agent designer codes the tasks necessary to perform a service and uses the framework to connect the tasks into an integrated agent structure. This bottom up approach does not provide an easy mechanism for confirming global properties of constructed agent systems. In this paper we propose a declarative methodology based on logic programming for modeling such procedurally constructed agents and specifying their global properties as temporal logic formulas. This methodology allows us to bring to bear a body of work for using logic programming based model checking to verify certain global properties of procedurally constructed Multi-Agent Systems.

1 Introduction

The Internet is fast becoming a venue for automated services. The advent of the Semantic Web and Web Services fosters an environment where complex services can be provided that are composed of a number of tasks. The tasks that compose the service are often accomplished by a group of autonomous agent programs. These agents communicate asynchronously over a LAN or the Internet to provide the desired service. Ideally, specifying agents as programs in a declarative logic programming language facilitates the implementation of agent systems for desired service. It also provides a formal model for proving that the implemented agent system performs the service with expected results.

While a number of high-level formalisms for specifying multi-agent systems have been proposed (see, e.g. [23, 3, 20]), many agent systems are currently being implemented in a procedural language such as Java. Development and deployment of agent systems using traditional languages such as Java has been simplified by the presence of frameworks that provide a rich array of services. These range from communication and database interfaces to persistence and fault-tolerance (e.g., the Cognitive Agent Architecture, *Cougaar* [2]). It should be noted that the standardization efforts in the web services community

J. Leite et al. (Eds.): DALT 2004, LNAI 3476, pp. 148–165, 2005.

(e.g. BPEL4WS [1]) have been oriented towards languages for specifying agent interfaces (e.g. the services offered and the types of data exchanged). These facilitate service discovery and composition, while leaving the implementation of the agents themselves unspecified. Although these developments alleviate some of the drudgery involved in constructing agents and provide facilities to compose agent systems, they do not provide mechanisms to give formal assurances about the behavior of agent systems.

The interesting problem here is to develop methods and techniques to ensure that agent systems built in this manner exhibit certain desired properties. We outline here a declarative approach to addressing this problem. This approach models the procedural agent framework as a logic program. The program captures the generic structure of the framework as a state transition system and can be easily customized to reflect specific agents built in the framework. Properties of the MAS can be expressed as temporal logic formulas that can be checked using model checking techniques.

Using a procedural agent architecture such as Cougaar, described in Section 2, agent systems are most easily developed in a bottom-up fashion. Individual agent programs are first built to perform specific tasks and then the allowable communications between agents are defined. The key to formally verifying the behavior of agent systems implemented in this manner is to first develop a formal model of the agent architecture itself. The main contribution of this paper is the development of a formal model of the main parts of the Cougaar architecture, including its persistence and fault-tolerance features. We then develop a framework, based on this model, to formally describe an agent system by specifying the behavior of the individual agent programs. The internal behavior of an agent is modeled as an extended finite-state automaton (EFSA), i.e., an automaton where states may be associated with variables and transitions may be guarded by constraints on values of the variables). In particular, the EFSA models a state transition system where there are a finite number of control states but potentially an infinite number of data states that can be partitioned into a finite number of data types. This is outlined in Section 3.

The intra-agent processes of an agent are presented as Horn clauses representing state transitions between control states in the EFSA. The EFSA for an agent describes the intra-agent actions. The behavior of the agent system can then be obtained as a concurrent composition of individual agent EFSAs and the architecture model that accounts for the possible synchronizations due to inter-agent communications.

The service being provided by an agent system is most easily described as a temporal process in which certain changes occur to a set of objects in a certain order. This is a workflow-centric view of the service where its global properties are enumerated. The workflow describes the desired or, at least, anticipated outcomes of the service without making any explicit statements about the implementation details of the system of agents providing the service. While a graph-based workflow formalism can be used to easily specify certain required (or prohibited) behaviors of an agent system at a high-level, we find it better to use a more expressive temporal logic formalism to describe complex properties such as availability, resilience to failure, etc.

We choose to represent workflow properties as temporal logic formulas for two reasons. First, temporal logic formulas make statements about infinite executions of EFSAs and, in particular, Linear Temporal Logic (LTL) [16] can represent fairness properties. Second, this formulation allows us to directly use the logic-based model checking techniques that have been developed in the past few years, (in which properties expressed in temporal logics can be directly verified for state transition models). Model checking allows us to determine whether an agent implementation possesses certain high-level behavioral properties. Therefore in this paper, we use generalized linear temporal logic (GLTL), described in Section 4, which allows for statements about properties of states and labels on state transitions. GLTL is extended with data variables as the formalism for specifying behavioral properties. In Section 5 we present workflow properties represented in GLTL. We have developed model checkers for verifying GLTL properties for transition systems expressed as logic programs [18]. We can use this model checker to verify GLTL properties that depend on the control structure or data types in the model as long as the the GLTL formula being checked does not make statements that depend on the values of specific data objects. There have been many languages based on the Beliefs-Desires-Intensions (BDI) model for describing agent systems and their properties. This paper does not directly address the addition of modalities needed to model BDI properties in GLTL; we discuss issues related to this in Section 6.

In summary, there are three main contributions of this paper. First of all, we develop a formal operational model of the Cougaar framework in terms of a transition relation. The encoding of the transition relation as a logic program makes the model amenable to verification. The key technical contribution here is the modeling of persistence and recovery features of the Cougaar architecture. Secondly, we propose a simple formalism, based on definite-clause grammar notation, for specifying the behaviour of Cougaar agents. Finally, we show the usefulness of parameterized temporal formulas in GLTL to specify properties of Cougaar agents.

2   Cougaar, an Implementation Architecture for Distributed Autonomous Agents

Cougaar is a Java based procedural implementation architecture for building systems of autonomous agents. It was originally funded by DARPA and is now maintained by an open-source community. It uses a design framework that handles both intra-agent data manipulation and inter-agent communications in a manner that provides transparency to the agent system designer. The architecture uses a distributed blackboard for inter-agent as well as intra-agent communication. This design framework provides persistence and recovery for individual agents and also system resilience against the loss of agents.

Data is stored and persisted at the agent level. Each agents keeps only the data necessary to perform its own functions. Data needed by more than one agent is shared by copying data objects from one agent to another. This distributed data model has the advantage that data is only stored where needed and dose not have to be made continuously available to all agents in the system. The disadvantage is that agents needing to share data are responsible for maintaining synchronization of that data. It is the responsibility of the agent designer to insure this synchronization.

At the agent level, all data is stored in a communal blackboard. The blackboard contains objects that are instantiations of Java classes representing items of interest to the agent. Objects are added to the blackboard either through communication with another agent or by an agent subprocess called a plugin. Plugins can also change or delete objects on the blackboard. Plugins are designed to be stateless processes that handle the computation required of the agent. Plugins subscribe to objects on the blackboard and execute a defined procedure in response to changes in those objects. The executed procedure can query the blackboard about objects; add, change, or delete objects and publish these changes to the blackboard; change the plugin's subscription; or interact with the environment outside the agent system. Data on the blackboard is changed by the plugins, but the data changes are persisted by the agent control structure.

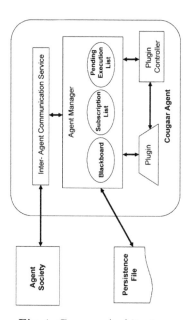

Fig. 1. Cougaar Architecture

The agent control structure is illustrated in Figure 1. When an agent starts up, it first instantiates an inter-agent communication service and an agent manager which contains a blackboard, subscription list, and plugin pending execution list. It then instantiates its component plugins. When a plugin is instantiated, it runs a subscribe method which notifies the agent manager about the objects in which it is interested. Once all plugins have been instantiated and have run their subscribe methods, the agent checks to see if any objects have been added to the blackboard which match a plugin's subscription. If so, that plugin is queued to run an execute method which can publish changes that add, modify, or delete blackboard objects. Whenever a change is published to the blackboard, plugin subscriptions are checked and the plugins affected by the change are added to the pending execution list and scheduled to run by the plugin controller.

Blackboard objects can also be communicated to other agents. The inter-agent messenger service sends copies of these objects as messages to other agents and also publishes added objects to the blackboard when they are received as messages from other agents. The state of the blackboard, subscription list, and plugin pending execution list is persisted by saving to a file before every sent message and after every received message.

If an agent crashes and is then restored, the restoration proceeds in a similar fashion to agent initialization. The main difference is that agent state is restored from the persisted state file written during the last inter-agent communication before the crash. This method of restoring an agent coupled with the fact that copies of data objects are passed between agent blackboards means that when an agent is restored, it will have internal consistency but its blackboard might be out of synchronization with other agents in the system. In the Cougaar implementation it is up to the agent designer to provide inter agent synchronization if needed. Also Cougaar assumes that any state information that individual plugins need is embodied in data objects that the plugins publish to the blackboard.

We will use an order processing system as a running example of a Cougaar-based multi-agent system. In this example, a simple Cougaar agent would contain order objects on its blackboard. New orders would be received from other agents and cause order objects to be added to the blackboard. The order objects would contain a status flag that is set to received when the order is added. This order agent might have a capacity setting so that when the number of orders on the blackboard reaches a certain level no more orders will be accepted. Processing of orders in the agent would be handled by plugins. In the simplest case, a plugin would subscribe to order objects on the blackboard and be notified when orders are added. When notified, the plugin would execute and check an external database for credit and inventory information and change the status of the order to shipped, rejected, or back-ordered. The agent would then communicate these revised statuses to other agents in the system by sending a copy of the order object to the appropriate agent. An order with a shipped status might go to a billing agent, a rejected order to a customer notification agent, and a back-ordered order to a production scheduling agent. Once copies of the order objects are sent to these other agents the objects would then be removed from the processing agent's blackboard. As order objects are removed the capacity to receive and process new orders is correspondingly increased.

In summary, the plugins in each agent can be considered as *actions* taken by an agent with each plugin representing a specific action. The agent system is developed by specifying, albeit in a procedural form, the behavior of each plugin. Note that the development of an agent focuses on the detailed behaviors of the plugins. Combining the models of behaviors of each plugin with a detailed formal model of the behavior of the Cougaar architecture itself, we can derive the agent-wide and system-wide behaviors. Note, however, that the Cougaar architecture itself does not directly support the specification of global agent-wide and system-wide behaviors. Hence it is possible that the actual agent or system behavior deviates from its expected behavior. In the next section we introduce a declarative model of the Cougaar Agent Architecture.

3 A Declarative Model of the Cougaar Architecture

We now develop a high-level model of the Cougaar architecture. The model for an agent consists of a set of concurrent automata, one automaton for each component: the blackboard and agent manager, the communication interface, and the components representing plug-ins. The automata have a finite number of control locations with local variables, and transitions in the automaton may be guarded by conditions on the valuation of these variables. Each automaton, formalized as an *extended finite-state automaton* (EFSA) can be simply described by a logic program that represents its transition relation [22].

We represent the transition relation of an automaton in our model using the ternary relation `trans`. A tuple in this relation of the form `trans(S, A, T)` represents a transition from state `S` to state `T` labeled with action `A`. The states may be in general be *terms* representing both the control information (e.g. the program counter value at an agent state) and data values at a state. The action labels represent *events*: communication with other automata, or simply computation steps internal to the automaton. The labels for internal computations may specify additional parameters that qualify the computation. Labels for communication operations are written as terms either of the form $f(t_1, \ldots t_n)$ where f is a function symbol, or of the form $\overline{f(t_1, \ldots, t_n)}$. The two are usually taken to represent an *input* action (where f stands for the channel or port over which the communication takes place), and an *output* action, respectively. In our case we do not distinguish between input and output actions; rather than considering communication as a transmission of data from one automaton to another, we generalize the approach of CCS [17] and view communication as an agreement of data values in two automata. Two concurrent automata synchronize by simultaneously taking transitions with complemenary labels: e.g. $f(t_1)$ and $\overline{f(t_2)}$. At synchronization, the terms t_1 and t_2 are unified. In general, synchronization takes place only when the labels of the two transitions unify.

The transition relation model captures the details of the operational behavior of a Cougaar agent. However, such an explicit representation may become tedious to develop (and consequently, error-prone) when used to model large systems.

Hence we represent the transition relation by a set of Horn clauses defining the relation, rather than as an explicit set of tuples.

We divide agent models into two parts: a generic part consisting of services provided by the Cougaar architecture, such as the blackboard service, communication service, etc; and a part specific to a particular agent instance, which is described by the behaviors of the plug-ins in the agent. The Cougaar architecture provides a rich variety of common services to simplify agent development and deployment. In terms of the behavioral models, this means that an agent model can be obtained by composing models of generic services (developed once and subsequently reused for all agents) with models describing the behaviors of the specific plugins. We first describe the models for Cougaar's generic services.

3.1   A Model of Cougaar's Generic Sevices

The blackboard service is central to a Cougaar agent. The blackboard serves as a storehouse for passive information— the objects manipluated by the different plugins within the agent. At the same time actively participates in agent behaviours such as serving object change notifications to plug-ins, handling persistance, scheduling certain communication operations, etc.

The storage used by the blackboard service comprises of the following components:

1. the set of objects in the agent's blackboard (data)
2. the set of plugins pending execution in response to changes to data objects (pending)
3. the set of object subscriptions in which each plugin is interested (subscription)

We represent these three areas collectively by store(D,P,S) where D, P and S represent the above three storage areas respectively. In addition, to enable recovery from faults, an agent checkpoints its execution by saving the blackboard state at each intra-agent communication point. We model this persistence by representing a blackboard's state by state(Current, Saved) where Current is the representation of the current storage (a term of the form store(...)) and Saved is the representation of the storage at the last checkpoint.

The data part of a blackboard's storage is simply a set of objects. We use a notation borrowed from F-logic [15] to denote objects and use F-logic's mechanisms for representing an object store using attribute-value, subclass and instance relations. For instance, an object Obj belonging to class Cls and whose status field holds the value new, represented in F-logic by Obj:Cls[status->new], will be stored in the blackboard's storage as tuples instance(Obj, Cls) and attr(Obj, status, new). Evaluation of attribute values follow F-logic's inheritance mechanisms.

The pending list is a set of pairs of the form (plugin, object) where a change to the object matches the plugin subscription. The set of subscriptions associates a plugin with subscription patterns which are of the form (class, change), where class is the class of objects and change is the change flag for this subscription.

The blackboard is the arbiter of data and communication between the plugins and other Cougaar services in an agent. Plugins communicate synchronously with the blackboard using the following four primitives:

1. **query**: check the presence or absence of an object in the `data` area, and to retrieve information from objects in the `data` area
2. **modify**: add/delete objects to/from the `data` area
3. **subscribe**: add/remove self from subscription lists
4. **publish**: notify the rest of the agent system about changes made to the blackboard objects by this plugin

Apart from the data access operations from the agent's plugins, the blackboard also services communication requests from other agents. Although the Cougaar implementation separates the data service provided by the blackboard from the communication services, it vastly simplifies the model to combine the two. A Cougaar agent may receive a `put` request to place an object in its blackboard from another agent; and may send objects, when requested to do so by its plugins, to other agents. Each of these requests (from plugins or other agents) represent events; the behavior of the generic services of Cougaar in response to these events (or when generating these events) is captured by the Horn clause rules in Figure 2 defining the `trans` relation.

Plugins are executed under the control of a plugin scheduler. Initially, the plugin scheduler invokes the `subscribe` method of each plugin which enables them to register with the blackboard service for object modification notifications. After the initialization phase is complete, the scheduler enters a loop, nondeterministically selecting a plugin to execute from the pending set in the blackboard, and invoking the corresponding plugin. The plugins, may in general, be run on a separate thread from the scheduler. We model the simpler and more common case where the plugins are sequentialized in the same thread as the scheduler. The transition relation of the scheduler's automaton can then be written as illustrated in Figure 3.

In the above, we assume that the `subscribe(Pin,C)` and and `execute((Pin, Obj),C)` correpond to the entry points of the subscribe and execute methods of a plugin `Pin`. The second argument `C` is the *continuation*: the state to which the methods return.

States of a system composed of two concurrent automata are represented by terms of the form `par(P1, P2)` where `P1` and `P2` represent the *local* states of the component automata. Operationally, an interleaving of the executions of two concurrent automata is an execution of the composition. In addition, the two automata may synchronize by unifying their action labels. The behavior of the concurrent composition of two automata is captured by the transition rules in Figure 4. It should be noted that synchronization by unification generalizes CCS's agreement-based synchronization for non-value-passing systems and synchronization by substitution for value-passing systems.

Note that with the above notation, it is straightforward to extend the model to deal with agents with multi-threaded plugins: instead of the *sequential* composition encoded by `execute((Pin,Obj),C)`, the scheduler loop will spawn `Pin`

```
% QUERY
trans(S, present(Q), S) :-
   S = state(store(Data,_,_),_), Q ∈ Data.
trans(S, absent(Q), S) :-
   S = state(store(Data,_,_),_), Q ∉ Data.
% MODIFY
trans(S, add(Q), T) :-
   S = state(store(Data,P,Subs), Saved),
   Data' = Data ∪ {Q},
   T = state(store(Data',P,Subs), Saved).
trans(S, delete(Q), T) :-
   S = state(store(Data,P,Subs), Saved),
   Data' = Data − {Q},
   T = state(store(Data',P,Subs), Saved).
% SUBSCRIBE
trans(S, subscribe(Pin, Class, Change), T) :-
   S = state(store(D,P,Subs), Saved),
   Subs' = Subs ∪ {sub(Pin, Class, Change)},
   T = state(store(D,P,Subs), Saved).
trans(S, unsubscribe(Pin, Class, Change), T) :-
   S = state(store(D,P,Subs), Saved),
   Subs' = Subs − {sub(Pin, Class, Change)},
   T = state(store(D,P,Subs), Saved).
% PUBLISH
trans(S, publish(Obj, Change), T) :-
   S = state(store(D,Pending,Subs), Saved),
   Notify = {Pin | subs(Pin, Class, Change) ∈ Subs, Obj:Class},
   Pending' = Pending ∪ Notify,
   T = state(store(D,Pending',Subs), Saved).
% PENDING_EXECUTION
trans(S, select(Pin, Obj), T) :-
   S = state(store(D,Pending,Subs), Saved),
   Pending' = Pending − {Pin},
   T = state(store(D,Pending',Subs), Saved).
% PUT
trans(S, put(Obj), T) :-
   S = state(store(Data,Pending,Subs), _),
   Data' = Data ∪ {Obj}
   Notify = {Pin | subs(Pin, Class, add) ∈ Subs, Obj:Class},
   Pending' = Pending ∪ Notify,
   SavedStore = store(Data', Pending',Subs),
   T = state(SavedStore, SavedStore).
% SEND
trans(S, put(Obj), T) :-
   S = state(Current, _),
   Current = store(Data,P,Subs),
   Data' = Data − {send(Obj)}
   NewStore = store(Data',P,Subs)
   T = state(NewStore, Current).
```

Fig. 2. Transition Relation for Generic Cougaar Services

```
% INITIALIZE
trans(scheduler, initialize, init(Pins, scheduler_loop)) :-
    initial_plugins(Pins).
trans(init([], S), A, T) :- trans(S, A, T).
trans(init([Pin|Pins], S), A, T) :-
    trans(subscribe(Pin, init(Pins, S)), A, T).
% EXECUTE
trans(scheduler_loop, select(Pin, Obj), execute((Pin, Obj), scheduler_loop)).
```

Fig. 3. Transition Relation for the Plugin Scheduler

```
% INTERLEAVE
trans(par(P1, P2), A, par(Q1, P2)) :-
    trans(P1, A, Q1).
trans(par(P1, P2), A, par(P1, Q2)) :-
    trans(P2, A, Q2).
% SYNCHRONIZE
trans(par(P1, P2), tau, par(Q1, Q2)) :-
    trans(P1, A, Q1),
    trans(P2, B, Q2),
    complement(A, B).

complement(L(X), L̄(X)).
complement(L̄(X), L(X)).
```

Fig. 4. Transition Relation for Parallel Composition

in an available concurrent thread and return immediately to picking up another plugin to notify.

When an agent crashes, the current state of the blackboard and other generic services is lost, and so are the local states of the plugins and the scheduler. When the agent recovers, it refreshes its state from the one saved at the last checkpoint, and resumes the scheduler loop. Thus, the crash and the eventual recovery of an agent can be captured by the transition rules given in Figure 5.

```
% CRASH
trans(agent(par(state(_,Saved), _)), crash, agent_crashed(Saved)).
% RECOVER
trans(agent_crashed(Saved), recover,
      agent(par(state(Saved,Saved), scheduler_loop))).
```

Fig. 5. Transition Relation for Crash and Recovery

The **crash** and **recover** labels can be used in the model checker to specify properties representing fair behaviors, considering only paths where **crash** occurs only finitely often, or those where **recover** occurs infinitely often.

3.2   Modeling Specific Cougaar Agents

Having developed a detailed model for the generic Cougaar services, we can instantiate an agent by simply specifying (a) the set of plugins in the agent, and (b) the behaviors of their subscribe and execute methods. We illustrate such an instantiation by considering a simple order processing agent with a plugin process_order which takes an object of class order whose status field is new, and changes the order status field to one of shipped, back_ordered or rejected. For the purposes of this illustration, we will replace the logic for determining the status field with a nondeterministic choice. Orders processed by the agent then need to be transmitted to the other agents. The transition system for the execute method of this plugin can be written as:

```
trans(execute((process_order,order(Order)), C),
      delete(Order[status->new]), order_1(Order, C)).
trans(order_1(Order, C)), add(Order[status->NS]), order_2(Order, C)) :-
   choose_status(NS).
trans(order_2(Order, C)), send(Order), order_3(Order, C)).
trans(order_3(Order, C)), publish(Order, modify), C).

choose_status(shipped).
choose_status(back_ordered).
choose_status(rejected).
```

Since plugins typically have a simple structure (e.g. no thread creation, and usually no loops), we can simplify the specification of plugin behaviors by using a DCG-like notation that makes the states implicit. For instance, the above order plugin may be written as:

```
order(Order) -->
    [ delete(Order[status->new]) ],
    {choose_status(NS)},
    [ add(Order[status->NS]) ],
    [ send(Order) ],
    [ publish(Order, modify) ].
```

Each terminal symbol in the above DCG specifies only the action label of a transition, leaving the source and destination states implicit. It is easy to convert the above specification to the explicit transition rules given earlier. We can thus derive models of agent systems by modeling each plugin separately and combining these models with the models of generic services.

4   Linear Temporal Logic

We now review Linear Temporal Logic (LTL) and its extensions that are used for specifying temporal properties of finite-state systems. In particular we describe Generalized LTL (GLTL) which can make statements about properties of system states as well as action labels on transitions between states. GLTL has the following syntax (P is the finite set of propositions and A is the finite set of action labels):

$$\Psi \rightarrow A\Phi \mid E\Phi$$
$$\Phi \rightarrow p \mid \neg p \mid \alpha \mid \neg\alpha \mid \Phi \wedge \Phi \mid \Phi \vee \Phi \mid \Phi \text{ U } \Phi \mid \Phi \text{ R } \Phi \mid X\Phi \qquad p \in P, \alpha \subseteq A$$

Formulas derived from Φ are called *path* formulas and formulas derived from Ψ are state formulas Traditionally, GLTL is defined to include only $A\Phi$; we consider the trivial addition of $E\Phi$ since the model checking procedure we discuss is based on such formulae.

The semantics of GLTL is given in terms of infinite paths (called *runs*) of a Labeled Transition System (LTS). Runs are infinite sequences of states of the LTS. The formal definition of GLTL semantics is standard (see, e.g. [7, 6]) and is omitted. Briefly, the semantics expresses how a run can satisfy a path formula. A formula Φ is true if Φ is true in the first state of a run. If Φ is p then p is a proposition that must hold in this state for Φ to be true. If Φ is α then the transition from the first state to the second state in the run must be labelled with an element in α for Φ to be true. For $\neg p$ and $\neg\alpha$, p must be false and the transition label must not be an element of α respectively to make Φ true. $X\Phi$ is true if Φ is true in the next state of a run, $\Phi_1 \wedge \Phi_2$ is true if both Φ_1 and Φ_2 are true for a given run. Φ_1 U Φ_2 is true of a run if Φ_1 holds in every state until a state where Φ_2 holds. Φ_1 R Φ_2 is true of a run if Φ_2 holds in every state or until a state where Φ_1 holds. $A\Phi$ is true for state s if Φ is true for all runs originating in s and $E\Phi$ is true if Φ is true for some run originating in s.

$\wedge$ and $\vee$ are duals. Similar to $\wedge$ and $\vee$, U and R are duals (i.e., $\neg(\phi_1 \text{ U } \phi_2) = \neg\phi_1 \text{ R } \neg\phi_2$), E and A are duals (i.e., $\neg A\psi = E\neg\psi$), and X is its own dual (i.e., $\neg X\phi = X\neg\phi$). It is easy to see that the standard semantics respects this duality.

To write more legible GLTL formulae, we define the following shorthand constructs for common GLTL formulas:

$$G\phi \equiv false \text{ R } \phi$$
$$F\phi \equiv true \text{ U } \phi$$
$$\phi \Rightarrow \psi \equiv \neg\phi \vee \psi$$

G is the global temporal quantifier. It is used to describe a property that is always true along a given path. F is the eventual temporal operator and describes a property that eventually becomes true along a path. The third shorthand is the standard logical implication.

Finally, GLTL can be enhanced by allowing terms containing logical variables to replace propositions. In the next section we describe the encoding of workflow properties about the expected global behaviors of agent systems in GLTL.

5   Workflows as Property Specifications

Agents and systems of communicating agents are built to provide specific services. Often these services are explicitly described by a workflow. Even when such an explicit definition is lacking, there is an implicit workflow which describes the anticipated outcome from invoking a service. The standard view of a workflow with respect to agents is that the workflow is a specification for the agent. In contrast, we consider the workflow as a specification of a property that the agent must exhibit.

Workflows have been directly represented in Transaction Logic [11]. One approach to showing that an agent system possesses a behavior expressed as a workflow would be to use Theorem Proving Techniques to show that the Transaction Logic representation of the workflow and the agent were equivalent. We believe a better approach is to express the workflow property in GLTL and use Logic Programming based model checking to show that the GLTL formula holds for the EFSA model of the agent system. Also Linear Temporal Logics (LTL) and their extensions are well suited to represent fairness properties [16]. Fairness is important in real world systems because there are always certain system conditions that cause failure and fairness properties explicity state the boundries of such failure.

GLTL is uniquely suited for representing workflow properties and more expressive than Transaction Logic for temporal properties. Workflows, in essence are temporal graphs that express sequences of events. Consider a simple workflow in which an order is first received and then shipped. The workflow implies an order to these two events, but no absolute time period between them. This is precisely the type of property that is easy to describe in GLTL.

To aid in writing properties that are easier to understand, a mechanism similar to macro replacement in a programming language can be used. In this mechanism a "named" formula acts as a replacement for an underlying GCTL* formula. While GCTL* does not directly support this idea of "named" formulas, this can easily be implemented with a macro interpreter in the GCTL* model checker logic program. Using this mechanism, if we let $dependency(\phi, \psi)$ stand for the GLTL state formula

$$G(\phi \Rightarrow X(F\psi))$$

We can write the following GLTL formula to describe the ordering property expressed in the above workflow as:

$$\texttt{A}(dependency(\{received\}, \{shipped\}))$$

This states that along all paths if a *received* action occurs it is eventually followed by a *shipped* action.

Since the Cougaar agent model described above can crash, this property would not hold for it. The agent could crash between the *received* and *shipped* actions and never recover. This leads to describing fairness properties for which GLTL is also well suited. Fairness essentially states that some good result will always occur providing some condition occurs infinitely often. Paths for which such a condtion holds are considered fair execution paths. We would like to have the above received-shipped dependency property hold as long as the agent recovers from crashes infinitely often (the fairness condition). This can be written as:

$$\texttt{A}(GF(recover) \Rightarrow dependency(\{received\}, \{shipped\}))$$

Notice that neither the workflow or the above formulas say anything about what purchase order is received or shipped. Implicit in the workflow is the idea that the workflow describes the events for a specific purchase order. This can be handled by parameterizing the *received* and *shipped* actions, leading to:

$$A(GF(recover) \Rightarrow dependency(\{received(order1)\}, \{shipped(order1)\})$$

Finally, the agent system is designed to run multiple instances of the specifying workflow so that we could be interested in properties that express ordering between workflow instances. For instance, we may want orders to be shipped in the order they were received. Enhancing GLTL with logical variables allows us to express these type of properties. We define *ordered_events*(ϕ, ψ) to stand for the GLTL formula:

$$F\phi \wedge F\psi \wedge \neg\psi \; \mathsf{U} \; \phi$$

which express that ϕ occurs before ψ. Note that *ordered_events*(ϕ, ψ) is not as strong a property as *dependency*(ϕ, ψ) defined above. The first indicates that one occurance of the second event occurs after one occurance of the first event. The second indicates that an occurance of the second event happens after every occurance of the first event. We can now express the property that orders are shipped in the order they are received as:

$$A(ordered\_events(\{received(order(X))\}, \{received(order(Y))\}) \Rightarrow$$
$$ordered\_events(\{shipped(order(X))\}, \{shipped(order(Y))\}))$$

This shows that GLTL is a logic that is well suited for specifying global properties of agent systems either as specifications of workflow properties or directly as fairness properties. GLTL also allows us to take advantage of logic programming for verification of these properties.

6 Ongoing Work and Concluding Remarks

Having been able to declaratively model a real world agent architecture as an EFSA and also express specifications for that system as temporal logic properties, we are now in a position to apply model checking techniques to verifying properties of agent systems.

We have been developing and using model checkers for finite and several classes of infinite systems based on logic programming [19, 12, 5]. We have also developed a model checker that can verify GLTL properties of labeled transition systems [18]. This model checker, implemented as a logic program, first constructs a Büchi automaton from a given GLTL formula, constructs the product of the given system model and the automaton, and performs good-cycle detection, i.e. cycles that meet the acceptance conditions of the automaton, to complete the model checking. Subsequently, we have also developed a constraint-based model checker where system models as well as properties are expressed using EFSAs [22]. This model checker can be directly used to verify properties of a Cougaar-based agent system. This model checker can verify certain class of infinite-state systems called data independent systems: those whose control behavior is independent of the domain of the data values. This is especially useful for the verification of agent systems since many aspects of their behaviors are data independent. For instance, the behavior of the ordering agent is independent of the domain of identifiers associated with different order objects. Thus we can use a constraint-based model checker to verify properties like the order of receiving and shipping of a specific order object with or without a fairness constraint on the agent crashing. It also allows us to check properties about the ordering of events. There is a complexity price to pay for this added capability. Standard model checking of finite-state systems runs in time linear in the size of the model. The constraint-based model checker in in the worst case exponential. Our future work will explore the limits and efficiency of using Logic Programming-based Model Checking to verify global behaviors of procedurally constructed MAS.

The main limitation of our approach is the representation of the blackboard. The blackboard is a part of an agent's state and we have to bound the number of objects that may be present simultaneously in the blackboard in order to ensure termination of verification runs.

The main contribution of this paper is the development of a logic-based high-level model of agent systems built using a procedural framework such as Cougaar. Since there are many such frameworks being proposed and implemented to address providing Web Services, this concept could have significant application. A secondary contribution of this modeling technique is that it allows us to verify properties of MAS that are data independent infinite-state systems with finite control structures.

We want to point out how our work compares to other efforts in the field. There have been a number of presentations of applying model checking to verifying properties of MAS including [9, 26], These presentations model MAS in languages that have a direct translation to a finite-state labelled transition system and express properties to be verified in Belief-Desire-Intention (BDI) logics which can be transformed into propositional LTL properties. Our goal was to be able to verify properties of MAS developed in a procedural framework like Cougaar where global behavior is emergent and non-obvious. Also, by modelling such systems as EFSAs we do not need to limit our model to finite-state systems, but can consider properties of infinite-state data independent systems. This allows us to verify properties concerned with the general ordering of events. Our model also allows us to investigate fault tolerance of MAS expressed as GLTL fairness properties. There is an interesting parallel between Cougaar agents and BDI agents. Data on the Cougaar blackboard is similar to BDI beliefs, plugin subscriptions have a similar flavor to BDI desires, and plugins pending execution are similar BDI intentions. We feel that this similarity should be investigated, especially since properties expressed in BDI logics can easily be incorporated into an expansion of GLTL and be directly verified using our model checker. We see this as an important area for future work.

Among the works presented at DALT 2004, the ones most closely related to our work are those that deal with temporal logic model checking or logic-based modeling [25, 21, 4, 24, 10, 14]. Walton [25] defines MAP, a language for defining multi-agent protocols (in a CCS-like fashion), its translation to Promela, and proposes the use of the model checker SPIN to verify properties of protocols written in MAP. Robertson [21] introduces LCC, a language for describing social norms of distributed processes. Specifications in LCC can then be subject to simulation or model checking (via MAP). Baldoni *et al* [4] describe the addition, to DCaseLP, a framework for converting AUML sequence diagrams to DyLOG and then verifying the interactions between the diagrams by querying. Vasconcelos [24] describes a methodology for investigating properties of descriptions called *electronic institutions* which define virtual environments in which agents interact. The state-chart-like notation used to specify electronic institutions are encoded as facts in a logic program. The constraints on their behavior, called their *norms*, which are specified by sets of actions are also represented as facts. Queries are then described over this intentional database to infer properties such as the set of feasible actions, feasible norms etc. In contrast, we develop a model, in terms of a transition relation, for the Cougaar architecture, and describe how models of individual Cougaar agents can be developed. We then use model checking techniques we have previously developed to verify temporal properties of these models.

Chopra *at al* [10] develop a methodology to build processes from declarative commitment-based protocol specifications and to enact them in a declarative manner. The operational semantics of protocols and commitments are specified using the pi-calculus. Fan *et al* [14] Gives an operational (transition system) semantics of a team-oriented agent programming language called MALLET for specifying teamwork knowledge and behaviors. These works do not address issues related to verification.

There has also been a considerable amount of work addressing workflows as specifications. Workflows have been represented in Transaction Logic [8] and their properties as theorems that satisfy these models [11]. In addition, [13] presents workflows modeled as UML Activity Diagrams and using LTL model checking to verify properties of these models. These approaches look at workflows as the model about which properties are stated. In our work we view the workflow as specifying global properties for a model of an independently constructed agent system. There are also a number of efforts to declaratively specify connectivity of autonomous agents using XML such as BPEL4WS cited earlier. These are primarily focused on finding and connecting agents that can compose a service, but they do not provide any method of verifying the behavior of the composition. What we propose allows the agent designer to use a procedural framework like Cougaar to build an agent system and gain some assurance about the conditions under which that system will exhibit expected behaviors.

Acknowledgements

The authors are grateful to the anonymous reviewers for their valuable comments and suggestions. The research reported in this paper was supported in part by NSF grants CCR-9876242, IIS-0072927, CCR-0205376, and CCR-0311512.

References

1. Business process execution language for web sevices (BPEL4WS). http://www.ibm.com/developerworks/library/ws-bpel/.
2. Cougaar: Cognitive agent architecture. http://www.cougaar.org.
3. J. Alferes, A. Brogi, J. A. Leite, and L. M. Pereira. Logic programming for evolving agents. In *Intl. Workshop on Cooperative Information Agents (CIA'03)*, number 2782 in LNAI, pages 281–297. Springer Verlag, 2003.
4. M. Baldoni *et al.* Reasoning about communicating agents inside DCaseLP. In *Proceedings of the Workshop on Declarative Agent Languages and Technologies (DALT'04)*, LNCS 3476, Springer-Verlag (2005). In this volume.
5. S. Basu, K. N. Kumar, L. R. Pokorny, and C. R. Ramakrishnan. Resource-constrained model checking of recursive programs. In *TACAS*, volume 2280 of *LNCS*, pages 236–250, 2002.
6. G. Bhat, R. Cleaveland, and A. Groce. Efficient model checking via beuchi tableau automata. In *Computer Aided Verification (CAV)*, 2001.
7. G. Bhat, R. Cleaveland, and O. Grumberg. Efficient on-the-fly model checking for CTL*. In *IEEE Symposium on Logic in Computer Science*. IEEE Press, 1995.
8. A. Bonner and M. Kifer. An overview of transaction logic. *Theoretical Computer Science*, 133:205–265, 1994.
9. R. H. Bordini, M. Fisher, C. Pardavila, and M. Wooldridge. Model checking AgentSpeak. In *Second Internatonal Joint Conference on Autonomous Agents and Multi-Agent Systems (AAMAS)*, 2003.
10. A. K. Chopra, A. U. Mallya, N. V. Desai, and M. P. Singh. Modeling flexible business processes. In *Preproceedings of the Workshop on Declarative Agent Languages and Technologies (DALT)*, 2004.
11. H. Davulcu, M. Kifer, C. R. Ramakrishnan, and I. V. Ramakrishnan. Logic based modeling and analysis of workflows. In *ACM Symposium on Principles of Database Systems (PODS)*, pages 25–33. ACM, 1998.
12. X. Du, C. R. Ramakrishnan, and S. A. Smolka. Tabled resolution + constraints: A recipe for model checking real-time systems. In *IEEE Real Time Systems Symposium (RTSS)*, Orlando, Florida, 2000.
13. R. Eshuis. *Semantics and Verification of UML Activity Diagrams for Workflow Modelling*. PhD thesis, University of Twente, 2002.
14. X. Fan, J. Yen, M. Miller, and R. Volz. The semantics of MALLET — an agent teamwork encoding language. In *Proceedings of the Workshop on Declarative Agent Languages and Technologies (DALT'04)*, LNCS 3476, Springer-Verlag, 2005. In this volume.
15. M. Kifer, G. Lausen, and J. Wu. Logical foundations of object-oriented and frame-based languages. *Journal of the ACM*, 42(4):741–843, 1995.
16. Z. Manna and A. Pnueli. *The Temporal Logic of Reactive and Concurrent Systems: Specification*. Springer Verlag, 1991.

17. R. Milner. *Communication and Concurrency*. International Series in Computer Science. Prentice Hall, 1989.
18. L. R. Pokorny and C. R. Ramakrishnan. Model checking linear temporal logic using tabled logic programming. In *Workshop on Tabling in Parsing and Deduction (TAPD)*, 2000.
19. Y. S. Ramakrishna, C. R. Ramakrishnan, I. V. Ramakrishnan, S. A. Smolka, T. L. Swift, and D. S. Warren. Efficient model checking using tabled resolution. In *CAV*, 1997.
20. A. S. Rao. AgentSpeak(L): BDI agents speak out in a logical computable language. In *Seventh Workshop on Modelling Autonomous Agents in a Multi-Agent World (MAAMAW)*, number 1038 in LNAI, pages 42–55. Springer Verlag, 1996.
21. D. Robertson. A lightweight coordination calculus for agent social norms. In *Proceedings of the Workshop on Declarative Agent Languages and Technologies (DALT'04)*, LNCS 3476, Springer-Verlag, 2005. In this volume.
22. B. Sarna-Starosta and C. R. Ramakrishnan. Constraint based model checking of data independent systems. In *Intl. Conf. on Formal Engineering Methods (ICFEM)*, LNCS, 2003.
23. V. S. Subrahmanian, P. Bonatti, J. Dix, T. Eiter, S. Kraus, and F. Ozcan. *Heterogenous Agent Systems*. MIT Press, 2000.
24. W. W. Vasconcelos. Norm verification and analysis of electronic institutions. In *Proceedings of the Workshop on Declarative Agent Languages and Technologies (DALT'04)*, LNCS 3476, Springer-Verlag, 2005. In this volume.
25. C. Walton. Model checking agent dialogues. In *Proceedings of the Workshop on Declarative Agent Languages and Technologies (DALT'04)*, LNCS 3476, Springer-Verlag, 2005. In this volume.
26. M. Wooldridge, M. Fisher, M.-P. Huget, and S. Parsons. Model checking multi-agent systems with MABLE. In *First Internatonal Joint Conference on Autonomous Agents and Multi-Agent Systems (AAMAS)*, pages 952–959. ACM Press, 2002.

Norm Verification and Analysis of Electronic Institutions

Wamberto W. Vasconcelos

Department of Computing Science, University of Aberdeen,
Aberdeen AB24 3UE, United Kingdom
wvasconcelos@acm.org

Abstract. Electronic institutions are a formalism to define and analyse protocols among agents with a view to achieving global and individual goals. In this paper we propose a definition of norms for electronic institutions and investigate how these norms can be employed for verification and analysis. We offer automatic means to perform the extraction of sub-parts of an electronic institution in which norms hold true or can safely be avoided. These sub-parts can be used to synthesise norm-aware agents that will pursue or avoid commitments to norms.

1 Introduction

An important aspect in the design of heterogeneous multiagent systems (MAS, henceforth) concerns the *norms* that should constrain and influence the behaviour of its individual components [1, 2, 3]. Electronic institutions have been proposed as a formalism to define and analyse protocols among agents with a view to achieving global and individual goals [4, 5]. In this paper we propose a definition for norms and a means of using this definition to verify properties of electronic institutions. We also describe means to help designers analyse an electronic institution with a view to extracting alternative and restricted versions of it in which norms are guaranteed to be fulfilled or versions in which norms will never be adopted. We observe that restricted versions of an electronic institution can be used to synthesise agents that will either pursue norms or avoid commitments to norms.

Electronic institutions define *virtual environments* in which agents interact. Designers specify their electronic institutions which may become arbitrarily complex. Tools and mechanisms ought to ensure that certain properties of electronic institutions hold before they can be enacted (*i.e.* agents interact following the specified order and kind of messages of an electronic institution). Some such properties are well-formedness and reachability of all parts of the specification by agents (*i.e.*, absence of "dead parts" that are never used) [6].

Norms, as defined in this work, provide means to check for additional properties of electronic institutions. Our norms are of the kind: if agent x says M_x and agent y says M_y then agent z is *obliged* to say M_z. Given an electronic institution and a set of norms, we want to check if the agents taking part in an enactment

J. Leite et al. (Eds.): DALT 2004, LNAI 3476, pp. 166–182, 2005.

of it will indeed abide by the norms prescribed and whether the norms will have any effect on them. We observe that the machinery required for the verification of such properties can also be used to help designers analyse their specification with a view to *extracting* sub-parts of it in which norms are guaranteed to hold (or, alternatively, sub-parts in which agents will not commit to the norms).

Ours is a formal declarative approach. Declarative formal specifications have many advantages [7, 8] over procedural notations. We capitalise on the ability to use the very same specification to check for properties as well as to obtain execution models of future systems to be devised using the specification [6, 9]. We employ logic programming (in particular, Prolog) [10] to describe all our concepts and proposed functionalities. Although we could have employed "cleaner" formalisms to represent our concepts and solutions, Prolog is a good compromise between a detailed implementation and abstract mathematical formulations.

In Section 2 we introduce a lightweight definition of electronic institutions and a declarative representation for them. In Section 3 we introduce a definition of norms and explain their incorporation to electronic institutions; we also show how norms can be used to check if the agents of an electronic institution will ever commit to a norm and, if they do, whether a norm will eventually be fulfilled. In Section 4 we show how we can analyse electronic institutions with respect to norms in order to extract sub-parts in which norms are fulfilled or never committed to by any agents. We present our conclusions in Section 5, compare our research with related work and give directions for future research.

2   Lightweight Electronic Institutions

Electronic institutions (e-institutions, for short) can be viewed as a variation of non-deterministic finite state machines [11]. We present e-institutions here in a "lightweight" version: those features not essential to our investigation have been omitted. We refer readers to [4, 5] for a complete description of e-institutions.

Our lightweight e-institutions are defined as sets of *scenes* related by *transitions*. We shall assume the existence of a communication language CL among the agents of an e-institution as well as a shared ontology which allow them to interact and understand each other. We first define a scene:

Definition 1. *A scene is a tuple* $\mathbf{S} = \langle R, W, w_0, W_f, WA, WE, \Theta, \lambda \rangle$ *where*

- $R = \{r_1, \ldots, r_n\}$ *is a finite, non-empty set of roles;*
- $W = \{w_0, \ldots, w_m\}$ *is a finite, non-empty set of states;*
- $w_0 \in W$ *is the initial state;*
- $W_f \subseteq W$ *is the non-empty set of final states;*
- WA *is a set of sets* $WA = \{ WA_r \subseteq W,\ r \in R \}$ *where each* $WA_r,\ r \in R$, *is the set of access states for role* r;
- WE *is a set of sets* $WE = \{ WE_r \subseteq W,\ r \in R \}$ *where each* $WE_r,\ r \in R$, *is the set of exit states for role* r;
- $\Theta \subseteq W \times W$ *is a set of directed edges;*
- $\lambda : \Theta \mapsto CL$ *is a labelling function associating edges to messages in the agreed language* CL.

A scene is a protocol specified as a finite state machine where the states represent the different stages of the conversation and the directed edges connecting the states are labelled with messages of the communication language. A scene has a single initial state (non-reachable from any other state) and a set of final states representing the different possible endings of the conversation. There should be no edges connecting a final state to any other state. Because we aim at modelling multi-agent conversations whose set of participants may dynamically vary, scenes allow agents to join or leave at particular states during an ongoing conversation, depending on their role[1]. For this purpose, we differentiate for each role the sets of access and exit states.

To illustrate this definition, in Figure 1 we provide a simple example of a scene for an agora room in which an agent willing to acquire goods interacts with a number of agents intending to sell such goods. This agora scene has been simplified – no auctions or negotiations are contemplated. The buyer announces the goods it wants to purchase, collects the offers from sellers (if any) and chooses the best (cheapest) of them. The simplicity of this scene is deliberate, in

Fig. 1. Simple Agora Room Scene

order to make the ensuing discussion and examples more accessible. A more friendly visual rendition of the formal definition is employed in the figure. Two roles, buyer and seller, are defined. The initial state w_0 is denoted by a thicker circle (top left state of scene); the only final state, w_3, is represented by a pair of concentric circles (bottom left state). Access states are marked with a "▶" pointing towards the state with a box containing the roles of the agents that are allowed to enter the scene at that point. Exit states are marked with a "▶" pointing away from the state, with a box containing the roles of the agents that may leave the scene at that point. The edges are labelled with the messages to be sent/received at each stage of the scene. A special label "nil" has been used to denote edges that can be followed without any action/event.

We now provide a definition for e-institutions:

Definition 2. *An e-institution is the tuple* $\mathcal{E} = \langle SC, T, \mathbf{S}_0, \mathbf{S}_\Omega, E, \lambda_E \rangle$ *where*
- $SC = \{\mathbf{S}_1, \ldots, \mathbf{S}_n\}$ *is a finite, non-empty set of scenes;*

---

[1] Roles in e-institutions are more than labels: they help designers abstract from individual agents thus defining a *pattern of behaviour* that any agent adopting that role ought to conform to. Moreover, all agents with the same role are guaranteed the same rights, duties and opportunities [4].

- $T = \{t_1, \ldots, t_m\}$ *is a finite, non-empty set of transitions;*
- $\mathbf{S}_0 \in SC$ *is the root scene;*
- $\mathbf{S}_\Omega \in SC$ *is the output scene;*
- $E = E^I \cup E^O$ *is a set of arcs such that* $E^I \subseteq WE^{\mathbf{S}} \times T$ *is a set of edges from all exit states* $WE^{\mathbf{S}}$ *of every scene* $\mathbf{S}$ *to some transition* T, *and* $E^O \subseteq T \times WA^{\mathbf{S}}$ *is a set of edges connecting all transitions to an access state* $WA^{\mathbf{S}}$ *of some scene* $\mathbf{S}$;
- $\lambda_E : E \mapsto p(x_1, \ldots, x_k)$ *maps each arc to a predicate representing the arc's constraints.*

Transitions are special connections between scenes through which agents move, possibly changing roles and synchronising with other agents. We illustrate the definition above with an example comprising a complete virtual agoric market. This e-institution has more components than the above scene: before agents can take part in the agora they have to be admitted; after the agora room scene is finished, buyers and sellers must proceed to settle their debts. In Figure 2 we show a graphic rendition of an e-institution for our market. The

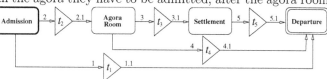

Fig. 2. E-Institution for Simple Agoric Market

scenes are shown in the boxes with rounded edges. The root scene is represented as a thicker box and the output scene as a double box. Transitions are represented as triangles. The arcs connect exit states of scenes to transitions, and transitions to access states. The labels of the arcs have been represented as numbers. The same e-institution is, of course, amenable to different visual renditions.

The predicates $p(x_1, \ldots, x_k)$ labelling the arcs, shown above as numbers, typically represent constraints on roles that agents ought to have to move into a transition, how the role changes as the agent moves out of the transition, as well as the number of agents that are allowed to move through the transition and whether they should synchronise their moving through it. In the Agoric Market above, the arc label 3 is:

$$p_3(x, y) \leftarrow id(x) \wedge role(y) \wedge y \in \{seller, buyer\} \wedge \langle x, y \rangle \in Ags \qquad (3)$$

that is, transition t_3 is restricted to those agents x whose role y is either *seller* or *buyer* – information on such agents is recorded in the set *Ags*. The complementary arc label 3.1 leaving transition t_3 is:

$$p_{3.1}(x, z) \leftarrow \langle x, y \rangle \in Ags \wedge y/z \in \{seller/receiver, buyer/payer\} \qquad (3.1)$$

that is, those agents $\langle x, y \rangle \in Ags$ that moved into t_3 may move out of the transition provided they change their roles: *seller* agents in the **Agora Room** scene should become *receiver* agents in the **Settlement** scene, *buyer* agents should become *payer* agents.

2.1   Representing E-Institutions

We have represented our e-institutions in a logical formalism [6] implemented in Prolog [10], making them computer-processable. We show in Figure 3 our Prolog representation for the agora room scene graphically depicted in Figure 1 above.

```
roles(agora,[buyer,seller]).
states(agora,[w0,w1,w2,w3]).
initial_state(agora,w0).
final_states(agora,[w3]).
access_states(agora,buyer,[w0]).
access_states(agora,seller,[w0,w2]).
exit_states(agora,buyer,[w3]).
exit_states(agora,seller,[w1,w3]).
theta(agora,[w0,request(B:buyer,all:seller,buy(I)),w1]).
theta(agora,[w1,offer(S:seller,B:buyer,sell(I,P)),w2]).
theta(agora,[w1,nil,w2]).
theta(agora,[w2,offer(S:seller,B:buyer,sell(I,P)),w2]).
theta(agora,[w2,inform(B:buyer,S:seller,accept(I,P)),w3]).
theta(agora,[w2,inform(B:buyer,S:seller,reject(I,P)),w3]).
theta(agora,[w2,nil,w3]).
theta(agora,[w3,inform(B:buyer,S:seller,reject(I,P)),w3]).
```

Fig. 3. Representation of Agora Room Scene

Each component of the formal definition has its corresponding representation. Since many scenes may coexist within one e-institution, the components are parameterised by a scene name (first parameter). The Θ and λ components of the definition are represented together in `theta/2`, where the second argument holds a list containing the directed edge as the first and third elements of the list and the label as the second element.

Any scene can be conveniently and economically described in this fashion. E-institutions are collections of scenes in this format, plus the extra components of the tuple comprising its formal definition. In Figure 4 we present a Prolog representation for the agora market e-institution. Of particular importance are the arcs connecting scenes to transitions and vice-versa. In definition 2 arcs E are defined as the union of two sets $E = E^I \cup E^O$, E^I connecting (exit states of) scenes to transitions, and E^O connecting transitions to (access states of) scenes. We represent the E^I arcs as `arc/3` facts: its first argument is a list which holds a scene and one of its exit

```
scenes([admission,agora,settlement,departure]).
transitions([t1,t2,t3,t4,t5]).
root_scene(admission).          output_scene(departure).
arc([admission,w3],p_1,t1).   arc(t1,p_{1.1},[departure,w0]).
arc([admission,w3],p_2,t2).   arc(t2,p_{2.1},[agora,w0]).
                                arc(t2,p_{2.1},[agora,w2]).
arc([agora,w3],p_3,t3).        arc(t3,p_{3.1},[settlement,w0]).
arc([agora,w1],p_4,t4).        arc(t4,p_{4.1},[departure,w0]).
arc([agora,w3],p_4,t4).
arc([settlement,w3],p_5,t5).  arc(t5,p_{5.1},[departure,w0]).
```

Fig. 4. Representation of E-Institution

states, the second argument holds the predicate (constraint) p_i which enables the arc, and the third argument is the destination transition. For simplicity, we choose to represent the arcs of E^O also as `arc/3` facts, but with different arguments: the first argument holds the transition, the second argument holds the constraint that enables the arc, and the third argument holds (as a list) a scene and one of its access states.

3   Norms in E-Institutions

We adopt a pragmatic notion of norm as the prescription of a set of actions that an agent is obliged to carry out during its participation in an e-institution enactment. In our definition below, the actions contemplated by our norms concern utterances that agents ought to issue, that is, messages that ought to be sent[2].

As identical utterances in different contexts (*e.g.*, saying "yes" to a waiter serving you more wine and saying "yes" to a police officer asking if you committed a crime) serve very different purposes and cause rather disparate obligations, our actions will be uniquely identified as the pair $(\mathbf{S}, \gamma)$ where $\mathbf{S}$ is a scene and $\gamma \in CL$ is an illocution from the agreed communication language [4]. The complete set of actions of an e-institution is given by the union of all utterances labelling the edges of each of its scenes [12]. Formally, given an e-institution $\mathcal{E} = \langle SC, T, \mathbf{S}_0, \mathbf{S}_\Omega, E, \lambda_E \rangle$, then $Actions^{\mathcal{E}}$, its set of actions, is defined as

$$\left\{ (\mathbf{S}, \gamma) \,\middle|\, \begin{array}{l} \mathbf{S} \in SC, \mathbf{S} = \langle R, W, w_0, W_f, WA, WE, \Theta, \lambda \rangle, \\ (w, w') \in \Theta, \lambda((w, w')) = \gamma \end{array} \right\}$$

That is, all labels $\lambda((w, w')) = \gamma$ on edges $(w, w') \in \Theta$ of each one of its scenes $\mathbf{S} \in SC$.

Our norms are defined as two finite sets of actions, one the set of preconditions, that is what causes the norm to be triggered, and the other the set of actions that agents are obliged to perform:

Definition 3. *A norm is the pair $N^{\mathcal{E}} = \langle Pre, Obls \rangle$ where:*

- *$Pre \subseteq Actions^{\mathcal{E}}$ is the set of actions which must be performed (the preconditions) in order for the norm to be triggered.*
- *$Obls \subseteq Actions^{\mathcal{E}}$ is the set of actions that agents are obliged to perform after the norm has been triggered.*

This definition is a simplification of that introduced in [13] – in particular we have dropped the boolean expression over variables. Another distinct feature of our formulation is the implicit logical operators in our norms: a norm $N^{\mathcal{E}} = \langle Pre, Obls \rangle$ where $Pre = \{a_1^{Pre}, \ldots, a_n^{Pre}\}$ and $Obls = \{a_1^{Obls}, \ldots, a_m^{Obls}\}$ is, implicitly, $(a_1^{Pre} \wedge \cdots \wedge a_n^{Pre}) \rightarrow (a_1^{Obls} \wedge \cdots \wedge a_m^{Obls})$.

Our norms represent the preconditions that ought to hold (*i.e.*, the *Pre* actions) in order for the obligations (*i.e.*, the *Obls* actions) to become in effect. By removing additional constraints (*i.e.*, boolean expressions over variables) we can provide, as we shall see below, a useful suite of automatic checks on e-institutions and their norms. It is possible, however, to enhance both the syntax of norms and the automatic checks to accommodate constraints over variables, as we depict in [12].

---

[2] Other actions, such as manipulating data structures, updating internal beliefs, or moving the arm of a robot, can easily be accommodated if we associate a message (sent to an administrative agent) reporting that the action has been performed.

Designers associate a possibly empty set of norms $\mathbf{N}^{\mathcal{E}} = \{N_0^{\mathcal{E}}, \ldots, N_m^{\mathcal{E}}\}$ to their e-institutions. For the pair $\langle \mathcal{E}, \mathbf{N}^{\mathcal{E}} \rangle$ we introduce the term *normatised e-institituion*. We show in Figure 5 below a sample norm for our e-institution of Figure 2. The norm prescribes the implications of an agent B playing the role

$$\left\langle \begin{array}{l} \{(agora, inform(B : buyer, S : seller, accept(Item, Price)))\} \\ \{(settlement, inform(B : payer, S : receiver, pay(Price)))\} \end{array} \right\rangle$$

Fig. 5. A Sample Norm

of a buyer in the *agora* scene and sending a message to an agent S playing the role of a seller: the message informs that B accepts the offered *Price* for *Item*. If this holds then agent B is obliged to pay and should send a message in scene *settlement* informing S that *Price* will have been paid. We show our sample norm above represented in Prolog in Figure 6. We use the term `norm(Name,Pre,Obls)`

```
norm(n1,[(agora,inform(B:buyer,S:seller,accept(Item,Price)))],
        [(settlement,inform(B:payer,S:receiver,pay(Price)))]).
```

Fig. 6. Sample Norm in Prolog

to represent our norms in Prolog, where `Name` is a label to identify the norm, `Pre` and `Obls` are lists of pairs (`Scene,Illocution`) storing the actions of the preconditions and obligations, respectively.

3.1   Norm Verification of E-Institutions

An initial test designers need to perform is the well-formedness of a set of norms. This is straightforward: all we need to do is to check if the actions in the sets *Pre* and *Obls* of every $N_i^{\mathcal{E}}$ appear as labels on the edges of a scene in $\mathcal{E}$. We also need to check if all scenes referred to indeed have been defined in $\mathcal{E}$.

A more useful check concerns the *feasibility* of a norm, that is, given an e-institution we want to know if the *Pre* actions of a norm will ever take place and if its *Obls* obligation actions will ever be fulfilled. We can verify this property by checking for paths within the scenes and transitions of an e-institution, thus trying to find at least one path connecting the initial state of the root scene to a final state of the output scene in which the actions of a norm appear as labels. The order of actions in norms is not important in our approach[3]: as long as the action takes place (*i.e.*, there is a label in a path) then we can tick the action off as being performable.

We show in Figure 7 a straightforward implementation of this approach.

---

[3] We are aware that in some situations the order of actions is essential. In [12] we put forth a more expressive definition of norms in which the order of events is taken into account. Our functionalities could be enhanced to account for the ordering of actions since the dialogues are followed in the order that they take place.

```
 1 feasible_actions(_,[]).
 2 feasible_actions(Path,Actions):-
 3     Path = [(Scene,State)|_],
 4     theta(Scene,[State,M,NewState]),
 5     \+ member((Scene,NewState),Path),
 6     member((Scene,M),Actions),
 7     delete(Actions,(Scene,M),RestActions),
 8     feasible_actions([(Scene,NewState)|Path],RestActions).
 9 feasible_actions(Path,Actions):-
10     Path = [(Scene,State)|_],
11     theta(Scene,[State,M,NewState]),
12     \+ member((Scene,NewState),Path),
13     \+ member((Scene,M),Actions),
14     feasible_actions([(Scene,NewState)|Path],Actions).
15 feasible_actions(Path,Actions):-
16     Path = [(Scene,State)|_],
17     arc([Scene,State],_,Transition),
18     arc(Transition,[NewScene,NewState]),
19     feasible_actions([(NewScene,NewState)|Path],Actions).
```

Fig. 7. Program to Check Feasibility of Actions

Predicate feasible_actions/2 builds a path in its first argument and gradually removes from the list of actions in its second argument those elements it finds labelling edges within the scenes of the e-institution. The path in the first argument is required to avoid loops. Line 1 shows the condition for successful termination: the list of actions is empty (and the contents of the path are irrelevant).

Clause 2 (lines 2–8) addresses the case when a Θ edge is to be followed but whose associated λ label is an illocution in one of the actions – in this case the matching action is removed (via built-in predicate delete/3) from the list of actions and the remaining actions are recursively examined. Clause 3 (lines 9–14) exploits a similar situation, but the illocution labelling the Θ edge does not occur in the list of actions – in this case, feasible_actions/2 simply updates the path and carries on examining the list of actions. Finally, clause 4 (lines 15–19) follows a transition from one scene to a new scene, carrying on the check for feasibility into the new scene.

Termination is guaranteed: either the program stops at line 1, when all actions are removed from the list Actions (2nd argument of feasible_actions/2) or the program terminates because it cannot find an alternative path (all paths are recorded in the 1st argument of feasible_actions/2) in which the actions in Actions may take place. Correctness is also guaranteed: if at least one action is not found in any of the dialogues of an institution, then the program fails – no new edges can be found and the list Actions is not empty, causing a failure. On the other hand, if the given list of actions is to be found in dialogues of the institution, clause 2–8 will remove each of them, one at a time.

The fragment of code above must be used twice for each norm: once to check the *Pre* actions and another time to check for the *Obls* actions. An initial value ought to be assigned to the path consisting of the root scene and its initial state. A top-level definition of the check for the feasibility of a norm is shown in Figure 8. Predicate `feasible/1` takes as its only parameter the name of a norm and returns "yes" if that norm is feasible or "no" otherwise. It works by retrieving the definition of `Norm` (line 2), the root scene (line 3) and its initial state (line 4), then calling predicate `feasible_actions` for the action list `Pre` and `Obls`. Only if *both* `Pre` and `Obls` are feasible is that `Norm` is considered feasible.

```
1 feasible(Norm):-
2     norm(Norm,Pre,Obls),
3     root_scene(Scene),
4     initial_state(Scene,State),
5     feasible_actions([(Scene,State)],Pre),
6     feasible_actions([(Scene,State)],Obls).
```

Fig. 8. Predicate to Check Feasibility of Norms

Although the code above always terminates, its complexity is exponential in the worst case, as it tries all possible paths. This complexity can be reduced, however, via simple heuristics such as checking for all actions of each scene, using the scenes' definitions to control the checking loop. For instance, if we check for all actions of a norm that should take place in a certain scene and we find that at least one of them is not found, then we can stop the verification as the norm is unfeasible.

We envisage two likely scenarios for norm verification. In the first scenario designers willing to create norms for an existing e-institution can verify if these new norms are feasible: designers may alter and change norms until they achieve feasibility. In the second scenario designers in possession of a norm which captures a desirable property of agents and their illocutions may "tinker" with an e-institution until it complies with the norm. The same feasibility verification can thus lead to changes in the norm, in the e-institution or in both, depending on the designers' intention.

If we consider our actions to be ordered, then the code above has to reflect this. The execution control should be guided by the list of actions to be searched in the dialogues: for each action, check that it takes place in a dialogue, *in the order* they appear in the list `Actions`.

4   Norm Analysis of E-Institutions

Normatised e-institutions provide a hitherto unexplored approach to the analysis and engineering of multiagent systems: designers manipulate the normatised e-institution with a view to *extracting* sub-portions of it. These sub-portions are guaranteed to avoid or indeed cause specific obligations on those agents taking part in the original e-institution. The more limited e-institution(s) can be used as a guideline to synthesise agents which conform to the specification (as introduced in [6, 9]) but have restricted forms of behaviour.

Clearly, the removal of parts of an e-institution is a difficult and error-prone task and designers need support to perform it. We propose the use of *meta-programming* [14, 15] to help designers analyse and manipulate e-institutions with a view to extracting sub-portions of it in which certain properties hold. A meta-program is a program whose data denotes another (object) program, both of which are in the same language.

We have designed a meta-interpreter, shown in Figure 9, to build a list with those portions of the original e-institution used to compute a result. Predicate meta/3 builds in its third argument a list with the components of the e-institution that were used in the proof of its first argument. The second argument is a temporary list with the components used so far in the proof and is initially assigned the empty list.

The first clause (lines 1–3) caters for a conjunction of goals (G,Gs) and recursively builds its list of goals used in the proof of G and uses it to build the list of goals of Gs. The second clause (lines 4–6) addresses the built-in predicates, those goals G that satisfy the built-in test system/1. The third clause (lines 7–10) handles user-defined predicates: a clause from the program is selected via the clause/2 built-in (line 8) whose head matches G and its body is returned in Body. The goal G is then used to update (line 9) the list EITmp containing the portions of the e-institution used so far – predicate update/3 defined in lines 1–14 inserts G as the head of its third argument if it is a collectable goal and does not yet appear in the list. The body of the clause is recursively used with the updated result (line 10).

```
1 meta((G,Gs),TmpEI,EI):-
2     meta(G,TmpEI,NewTmpEI),
3     meta(Gs,NewTmpEI,EI).
4 meta(G,EI,EI):-
5     system(G),
6     call(G).
7 meta(G,EITmp,EI):-
8     clause(G,Body),
9     update(EITmp,G,NewEITmp),
10    meta(Body,NewEITmp,EI).

11 update(EI,G,[G|EI]):-
12    collectable(G),
13    \+ member(G,EI).
14 update(EI,_,EI).

15 collectable(roles(_,_)).
16 collectable(states(_,_)).
      . . .
```

Fig. 9. Program to Collect Portions of E-Institution

The collectable goals defined via the collectable/1 predicate (lines 15 onwards) are all those used in the definition of an e-institution, such as roles/2, states/2, and so on. These are the goals required to completely define an e-institution and are the ones that should be collected during the execution of the meta-interpreter. If a goal is not collectable, then the second clause of update/3 returns the same input e-institution.

4.1   Norm-Based Extraction

In order to extract sub-parts of the e-institution that make up a coherent whole, we ought to make sure an agent can join it and find its way from an initial state of the root scene to a final state of the output scene.

We have designed a program which captures the behaviours of a generic agent within an e-institution. This program is shown in Figure 10: predicate loop/1 (lines 1–4) gathers information and makes an initial call to its auxiliary loop/2 (lines 5–19) predicate. Predicate loop/1 has only one argument Ag, an agent

```
 1 loop(Ag):-
 2    root_scene(Scene), initial_state(Scene,State),
 3    role_scenes(Scene,Roles), member(Role,Roles),
 4    loop([Scene,State,Role,nil],Ag).
 5 loop([(Scene,State,_,_)|_],_):-
 6    output_scene(Scene),
 7    final_states(Scene,States),
 8    member(State,States).
 9 loop(Path,Ag):-
10    Path = [(Scene,State,Role,_)|_],
11    theta(Scene,[State,M,NewState]),
12    illocution(Role,Ag,M,AcM),
13    \+ member((Scene,State,Role,AcM),Path),
14    loop([(Scene,NewState,Role,AcM)|Path],Ag).
15 loop(Path,Ag):-
16    Path = [(Scene,State,Role,_)|_],
17    arc([Scene,State],_,Tr), arc(Tr,_,[NewScene,NewState]),
18    roles(NewScene,Roles), member(Role,Roles),
19    loop([(NewScene,NewState,Role,nil)|Path],Ag).

20 illocution(Role,Ag,M,M):-
21    M =.. [_,Ag:Role,_,_] ; M =.. [_,_,Ag:Role,_].
22 illocution(_,_,_,nil).
```

Fig. 10. Generic E-Institituion Agent

identifier. It obtains the initial state in the root scene (line 2), then selects a role (line 3) from the possible roles of the root scene. It then makes an initial call to its auxiliary predicate loop/2 which defines a loop.

The first argument of predicate loop/2 is a list of tuples (Scene,State,Role, Illocution) storing a path an agent can follow within the e-institution and the second argument is the unique identification of the agent. The first clause (lines 5–8) captures the termination condition when a final state of the output scene is reached. The second clause (lines 9–14) addresses Θ edges within a scene, making sure that the new state and message are not part of the current path built. Finally, the third clause (lines 15–19) caters for transitions between two scenes: the transitions out of the current scene and into the new scene are followed in line 13, a role is picked for the new scene (line 14) and the loop carries on recursively.

The second clause of predicate loop/2 makes use of an auxiliary predicate illocution/4 (lines 20–22). This predicate obtains in its fourth argument the actual message sent or received by an agent incorporating role Role: it may send the message (first case of line 21), receive the message (second case of line 21) or none of them (line 22 – a "nil" illocution is returned), depending on whether its role matches the one specified in the λ label.

We can put our meta-interpreter above to use in order obtain the parts of an e-institution that guarantee that a norm will hold, by using the query

```
?- meta((loop(ag1),feasible(n1)),[],EI).
```

asking for the portions EI of the e-institution in which both loop(ag1) and feasible(n1) hold, that is, the subparts of the e-institution required for an agent to find its way into and out of it and such that norm n1 (defined in Fig. 6) holds.

If we use the query above with the definitions of Figures 3 and 4, then we obtain in EI the parts of the e-institution definition required to prove that norm n1 is feasible, that is, the portions of the e-institution required to allow an agent to correctly navigate its way into and out of it and, in addition to that, the parts ensure that the norm has both its preconditions and obligations fulfilled. We show in Figures 11 and 12 the visual rendition of the fragments of, respectively,

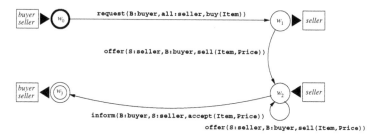

Fig. 11. Portion of Agora Room Scene

the agora scene and the agoric market e-institution obtained with the query above. The scene fragment shows the edges and labels that should be followed

Fig. 12. Portion of Agoric Market E-Institution

by agents in order for the pre-conditions of the norm to hold. The fragment of the e-institution shows those scenes that ought to take place in order for the obligations to be fulfilled – the alternative paths that bypass the agora room are eliminated.

Alternatively, we can obtain the portions of an e-institution that allow agents to join in and leave, but *avoiding* the conditions that would bind them to a norm. In order to do that, we ought to get hold of a proper portion of the e-institution (*i.e.* one that allows an agent join in and leave it) and in which the pre-conditions of the norm does not hold. The auxiliary definition of Figure 13 captures the conditions when a

```
1 untriggered(Norm):-
2     norm(Norm,Pre,Obls),
3     root_scene(Scene),
4     initial_state(Scene,State),
5     \+ feasible_actions([(Scene,State)],Pre).
```

Fig. 13. Test for Untriggered Norms

norm cannot be triggered. The definition is similar to that in Figure 8, but here the feasible_actions/2 predicate is used in its negated form. Moreover, only the preconditions of the norm are tested: an untriggered norm is one whose preconditions do not occur in the e-institution.

The query below obtains the portions of the e-institution that allow an agent to join in and leave it, but avoids triggering the norm by causing its preconditions:

$$\text{?- meta((loop(ag1),untriggered(n1)),[],EI).}$$

that is, it obtains in `EI` the parts of the e-institution used to allow agent `ag1` to navigate it but these parts do not trigger the preconditions of norm `n1`. If we use the query above with the e-institution of Figures 3 and 4, then we get the fragments shown in Figures 14 and 15 (represented in their visual form).

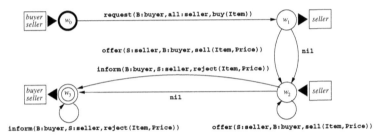

Fig. 14. Another Portion of the Agora Room Scene

Figure 14 shows the agora scene but the edge labelled with the message that

Fig. 15. Another Portion of the E-Institution

would trigger norm `n1` has been removed. This fragment of the agora scene becomes part of the e-institution depicted in Figure 12. We have obtained only those parts used to go from the root scene to the output scene via one of the many existing paths.

Our formalisation of e-institutions exploits non-determinism to represent the many different behaviours agents are allowed to have. When an e-institution is analysed using our queries above, only *one* path in and out of the e-institution is actually pursued. We can, however, exhaustively examine all paths obtaining all sub-parts of the e-institution in which a norm is fulfilled or avoided. Our approach allows any combination of any number of norms to be fulfilled and/or avoided.

4.2   Norm-Aware Synthesis of Agents

In [6, 9] we have shown how we can synthesise simple agents conforming to a given specified e-institution. We have also shown how these simple agents can be further customised into more sophisticated software. We notice that the restricted e-institutions obtained via our approach explained above can be used to synthesise agents – these agents will correctly follow the e-institution but will pursue paths in which norms can be triggered (and fulfilled) or paths in which norms cannot be triggered.

We envisage a scenario in which an initial normatised e-institution is manipulated using the approach described above, giving rise to a number of alternative e-institutions. Each of these alternative e-institutions is fully compatible with the original one but they offer particular "views" in which norms are fulfilled or avoided. The alternative e-institutions can be used to synthesise agents that will adopt norm-avoiding or norm-fulfilling behaviour.

This approach is depicted in the diagram of Figure 16 below: an initial e-institution $\mathcal{E}$ is used to extract (simple arrow) a repertoire of e-institutions $\mathcal{E}'_i$ each of which has particular features of avoiding or fulfilling norms. Each of these extracted e-institutions is used to synthesise agents $\Pi_{[i]}$ (double arrows). The synthesised initial agents are then customised differently as $\Pi_{[i,j]}$ (triple arrows). The customised agents can take part in

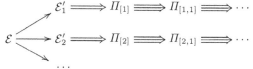

Fig. 16. Extraction, Synthesis & Customisation

an enactment of e-institution $\mathcal{E}$ as they will be in full compliance with it, but the agent will be adverse to particular norms or eager to fulfil them.

5   Conclusions, Related Work and Directions of Research

We have presented a formal definition of norms and shown how norms can be incorporated in electronic institutions and employed to verify properties both of norms and electronic institutions. We have also introduced automatic means to obtain portions of an e-institution in which norms are guaranteed to hold and portions in which norms can be safely avoided.

Clearly, not all kinds of norms can be represented in our approach. In particular, we focus on utterances: the only events we consider are those of issuing messages. Additional events associated to, for instance, sensors or data structures, although important in many applications of multiagent systems, are not considered in our approach. Directed norms (*i.e.*, norms between two people [3]) are captured via the *roles* of those agents sending (and receiving) messages. Ours is a less expressive notion of norms and we are aware that there are limitations on what we can represent with this notion. However, alternative (more expressive) definitions of norms will inevitably require more sophisticated (and computationally expensive) mechanisms to verify properties.

The scenario we contemplate is one in which an electronic institution is endowed with a layer of administrative (or institutional) agents, the *governor agents.* These agents work as proxies of heterogeneous (external) agents that will join in in the enactment of the institution. The governor agents guarantee that the external agents will follow the specifications of the institution, sending the appropriate messages in the prescribed order. The governor agents, plus a team of other administrative agents, form a *social layer* to the institution [16]. Issues of trust and sincerity are confined to the communication between the governor agent and its external agent. Various mechanisms can be put in place to prevent these issues from spreading to other parts of the institution. For instance, if an external agent refuses to send a message it is required to within a certain period, then its governor agent takes over and sends an appropriate exception message (contemplated by the scene's protocol).

Electronic institutions provide an ideal scenario within which alternative definitions and formalisations of norms can be proposed and studied. In [13] we find an early account of norms relating illocutions of an e-institution. In [17] we find a first-order logic formulation of norms for e-institutions: an institution conforms to a set of norms if it is a logical model for them.

Our work is an adaptation and extension of [13] but our approach differs in that we do not explictly employ any deontic notions of obligations [1]. Our norms are of the form $Pre \rightarrow Obls$, that is, if Pre holds then $Obls$ ought to hold. The components of Pre and $Obls$ are utterances, that is, messages the agents participating in the e-institution send. This more pragmatic definition fits in naturally with the view of e-institutions as a specification of virtual environments which can be checked for properties and then used for synthesising agents [6, 9].

We represent e-institutions in a non-deterministic fashion: all possible behaviours of agents that will perform within it are captured. However, this feature causes an exponential number of possibilities to be considered when verifying and analysing e-institutions – the behaviours of the agents are paths of a non-deterministic finite-state machine. The functionalities described in this paper all have the same undesirable property: in the worst case, their computational complexity is exponential as they have to consider *all* possible behaviours.

Rather than extracting a complete e-institution as explained in Section 4.1, we can offer a similar functionality that collects just a single path (or a set of paths) that agents may follow in order to fulfil a norm or avoid it. Such a path can be supplied (in various alternative formats) to heterogenous agents wanting to join the e-institution or to institutional agents looking over the enactment of an e-institution. The paths provide an agenda to help agents deliberate when given choices of behaviour.

We would like to include *prohibitions* in our norms as a set of actions that ought not to take place in an e-institution. Prohibitions would allow norms and e-institutions to be checked for *consistency*: an agent cannot be obliged to perform an action and simultaneously be prohibited from doing it. Furthermore, we have explored in [12] a more expressive notion of norms in which the ordering of the events is taken into account and there can be arbitrary constraints on the variables of our illocutions. Ideally this richer formalisation should be accompanied by algorithms and tools to verify properties and perform distinct analyses in electronic institutions. We are currently working on means to automate the verification and analysis of these more expressive norms.

Acknowledgements. Thanks to J. Rodríguez-Aguillar and M. Esteva for their comments and suggestions, and to Seumas Simpson for proofreading earlier versions of this document. Thanks are also due to the anonymous reviewers whose comments helped improving this paper. Any remaining mistakes are the author's responsibility only.

References

1. Dignum, F.: Autonomous Agents with Norms. Artificial Intelligence and Law **7** (1999) 69–79
2. López y López, F., Luck, M., d'Inverno, M.: Constraining Autonomy Through Norms. In: Proceedings of the 1st Int'l Joint Conf. on Autonomous Agents and Multiagent Systems (AAMAS), ACM Press (2002)
3. Verhagen, H.: Norm Autonomous Agents. PhD thesis, Stockholm University (2000)
4. Esteva, M., Rodríguez-Aguilar, J.A., Sierra, C., Garcia, P., Arcos, J.L.: On the Formal Specification of Electronic Institutions. Volume 1991 of LNAI. Springer-Verlag (2001)
5. Rodríguez-Aguilar, J. A.: On the Design and Construction of Agent-mediated Electronic Institutions. PhD thesis, IIIA-CSIC, Spain (2001)
6. Vasconcelos, W.W., Robertson, D., Sierra, C., Esteva, M., Sabater, J., Wooldridge, M.: Rapid Prototyping of Large Multi-Agent Systems through Logic Programming. Annals of Mathematics and Artificial Intelligence **41** (2004) 135–169
7. Fuchs, N.E.: Specifications are (Preferably) Executable. Software Engineering Journal (1992) 323–334
8. Lloyd, J.W.: Practical Advantages of Declarative Programming. In: Joint Conference on Declarative Programming, GULP-PRODE'94. (1994) Invited Paper.
9. Vasconcelos, W.W., Sierra, C., Esteva, M.: An Approach to Rapid Prototyping of Large Multi-Agent Systems. In: Proc. 17th IEEE Int'l Conf. on Automated Software Engineering (ASE 2002), Edinburgh, UK, IEEE Computer Society, U.S.A (2002) 13–22
10. Apt, K.R.: From Logic Programming to Prolog. Prentice-Hall, U.K. (1997)
11. Hopcroft, J.E., Motwani, R., Ullman, J.D.: Introduction to Automata Theory, Languages and Computation. 2nd edn. Addison-Wesley, U.S.A (2001)
12. Esteva, M., Vasconcelos, W., Sierra, C., Rodríguez-Aguilar, J.A.: Verifying Norm Consistency in Electronic Institutions. In: Proc. AAAI-04 Workshop on Agent Organizations: Theory and Practice, San Jose, California, U.S.A., AAAI Press (2004)
13. Esteva, M., Padget, J., Sierra, C.: Formalizing a Language for Institutions and Norms. Volume 2333 of LNAI. Springer-Verlag (2001)
14. Hill, P.M., Gallagher, J.: Meta-Programming in Logic Progamming. In: Handbook of Logic in Artificial Intelligence and Logic Programming. Volume 5., Oxford University Press (1998) 421–498
15. Sterling, L.S., Beer, R.D.: Meta-Interpreters for Expert System Construction. Journal of Logic Programming **6** (1989) 163–178

16. Esteva, M., Rosell, B., Rodríguez-Aguilar, J.A., Arcos, J.L.: AMELI: an Agent-Based Middleware for Electronic Institutions. In: Proc. 3rd Int'l Joint Conf. on Autonomous Agents & Multi-Agent Systems (AAMAS), New York, U.S.A., ACM Press (2004)
17. Ibrahim, I.K., Kotsis, G., Schwinger, W.: Mapping Abstractions of Norms in Electronic Institutions. In: 12th. Int'l Workshop on Enabling Technologies: Infrastructure for Collaborative Enterprise (WETICE'03), Linz, Austria, IEEE Computer Society (2003)

A Lightweight Coordination Calculus for Agent Systems

David Robertson

Informatics, University of Edinburgh, UK

Abstract. The concept of a social norm is used in multi-agent systems to specify behaviours required of agents interacting in a given social context. We describe a method for specifying a class of social norms that is more compact than existing methods without loss of generality and permits simple but powerful mechanisms for analysis and deployment. We explain the method and how to compute with it. Specifically, we show how it relates to a well known system for enforcing social norms - the ISLANDER system - and compare it to performative languages.

1 Introduction: A Broad View of Social Norms

The Internet raises the prospect of engineering large scale systems that are not engineered in the traditional way, by tightly integrating modest numbers of components familiar to a single design team, but are assembled opportunistically from components built by disparate design teams. Ideally such systems would make it easy for new components to be designed and deployed in competition with existing components, allowing large systems to evolve through competitive design and service provision. That requires standardisation of the languages used for description of the interfaces between components - hence Web service specification efforts such as DAML-S (in the Semantic Web community) and performative-based message passing protocols such as FIPA-ACL and KQML (in the agent systems community). Although helpful these are, in themselves, insufficient to coordinate groups of disparate components in a way that allows substantial autonomy for individual agents while maintaining the basic rules of social interaction appropriate to particular coordinated tasks. This is especially difficult in unbounded, distributed systems (like the Internet) because coordination depends on each component "being aware" of the state of play in its interaction with others when performing a shared task and being able to continue that interaction in a way likely to be acceptable to those others. This is the broad sense in which "social norm" is used in this paper, recognising that it possesses more specific connotations for part of the multi-agent systems community.

Solving coordination problems requires some description of the focus of coordination. One way of doing this is by the use of policy languages (*e.g.* [1]). By enforcing appropriate policies we may provide a safe envelope of operation within which services operate. This is useful but not the same as specifying more directly the interactions required between services. For this it has been more natural to use concepts from temporal reasoning to represent the required behaviours of individual services (*e.g.* [2]); shared models for coordinating services (*e.g.* [3]) or the process of composing services

J. Leite et al. (Eds.): DALT 2004, LNAI 3476, pp. 183–197, 2005.

(*e.g.* [4, 5]). As recognised in earlier studies on conversation policies [6] the constraints on interaction between agents often are more "fine grained" than those anticipated in standard performative languages like FIPA-ACL. One solution to this problem is the concept of an electronic institution [7, 8] to which we return in the next section.

In what follows we shall present an approach to coordination that we intend to be consistent with the views described above but which is also comparatively lightweight to use. The language we shall present is intended to be understood by programmers (since this is the one skill common to most engineers of multi-agent systems) but is also declarative (in the sense that it can be understood independently of a specific execution architecture). It also contains as few operators as possible - the idea being to make this a core language for interaction. A consequence of this decision is that some of the conceptual notions that are important to coordination (such as commitment and sanction) do not feature explicitly in the language but must be constructed by assembling the protocol in an appropriate way. In other words, if you want to enforce something like commitment using our approach then you must write a definition in which failure to commit breaks the protocol.

We begin, in Section 2, by summarising the concept of social norms as we understand it using the Islander system as an example. In Section 3 we introduce the Lightweight Coordination Calculus (LCC) which is a process calculus for specifying multi-agent coordination. A basic example of its use is in Section 4. LCC is a comparatively simple but flexible language and can be supplied with a straightforward method for constraining the behaviour of an individual agent in a collaboration, as described in Section 5. It is then possible to construct simple, general-purpose mechanisms for multi-agent coordination that harness this method (see Section 6). LCC is intended as a practical, executable specification language and has been used for a variety of purposes which we summarise in Section 7. Finally, in Section 8 we return to mainstream performative languages and show how LCC may be used to describe the coordination aspects of those types of system.

2   Islander: A Means of Enforcing Social Norms

The Islander system [8] is sketched here as an example of a traditional means of enforcing social norms. In this section we introduce the approach and main representational features of Islander. In Section 3 we shall return to these when introducing the LCC notation. The framework for describing agent interactions in Islander relies upon a (finite) set of state identifiers representing the possible stages in the interaction. Agents operating within this framework must be allocated roles and may enter or leave states depending on the illocutions (via message passing) that they have performed. In order to structure the description, states are grouped into scenes. An institution is then defined by a set of scenes and a set of connections between scenes with constraints determining whether agents may move across these connections. A scene is defined as a collection of the following sets: roles; state identifiers; an initial state identifier; final state identifiers; access state identifiers for each role; exit state identifiers for each role; and cardinality constraints on agents per role. A social norm for an agent is defined by an antecedent (defined as a list of scene-illocution pairs) and a consequent (the predicates obliged to be true if the antecedent illocutions have taken place). This thumbnail sketch of the main components of an institution model suffices to give the reader an overview of the approach. Later we shall revisit these components in more detail.

This sort of state transition model has been shown to be adequate for constraining multi-agent dialogue in situations, such as auctions, where social norms are essential for reliable behaviour. It also permits a style for enforcement of the model during deployment, in which the state-based model of interaction is used to check that the agents involved do indeed conform to the model. It suffers, however, from two weaknesses. The first weakness is its reliance on representing the entire model of interaction as a single (albeit structured) state transition model. This makes enforcement of the model difficult except via some form of representation of the global state of the interaction as it applies to the group of agents involved in it.

Thus far, the only solutions to this problem have been to maintain a single institution model with which all agents must synchronise or to have synchronised distribution of a single model. Both these solutions undermine the distributed nature of the computation by enforcing centralised control over interactions between agents. The second weakness (related to the first) is that its focus on global state of multi-agent interaction makes it difficult to disentangle the specification of constraints on individual agent processes contributing to that state. This is of practical importance because all current efforts on large scale agent deployment via standardised Web services (*e.g.* DAML-S) use process models specific to individual agents. The relevance of LCC to the modelling and deployment of semantic web services has previously been argued in [9, 10]. In the current paper we concentrate on the related but separable issue of its relevance to multi-agent coordination. The system described in the remainder of this paper is a process calculus that can be used to describe social norms as complex as those of state-based systems such as Islander, with the advantage that these can be deployed without requiring centralised control.

3   LCC Syntax

LCC borrows the notion of role from institution based systems, as described in the previous section but reinterprets this as a form of typing on a process in a process calculus. Process calculi have been used before to specify social norms (see for example [7]) but LCC is, to our knowledge, the first to be used directly in computation for multi-agent systems. Following [11] we understand that "following a social law corresponds to choosing strategies within the set of lawful behaviours allowed by the law". The clauses of LCC describe the lawful behaviours for agents undertaking roles in a collaborative interaction. For each individual agent, following a social law means obeying the message passing sequence stipulated by the clause it currently is using, and deciding how it satisfies any constraints associated with the messages it sends or receives. Thus, the most basic behaviours in LCC are to send or receive messages, where sending a message may be conditional on satisfying a constraint and receiving a message may imply constraints on the agent accepting it. The choice of constraint language depends on the constraint solvers used, although the LCC constraints used in current implementations are in first order predicate calculus. More complex behaviours are specified using the connectives *then, or* and *par* for sequence, choice and parallelisation respectively. A set of such behavioural clauses specifies the message passing behaviour expected of a social norm. We refer to this as the interaction framework. Its syntax is given in Figure 1.

$$
\begin{aligned}
Framework &:= \{Clause, \ldots\} \\
Clause &:= Agent :: Def \\
Agent &:= a(Type, Id) \\
Def &:= Agent \mid Message \mid Def \text{ then } Def \mid Def \text{ or } Def \mid Def \text{ par } Def \mid \\
null &\leftarrow C \\
Message &:= M \Rightarrow Agent \mid M \Rightarrow Agent \leftarrow C \mid M \Leftarrow Agent \mid M \Leftarrow Agent \leftarrow C \\
C &:= Term \mid C \wedge C \mid C \vee C \\
Type &:= Term \\
M &:= Term
\end{aligned}
$$

Where *null* denotes an event which does not involve message passing; $Term$ is a structured term in Prolog syntax and Id is either a variable or a unique identifier for the agent. The operators $\leftarrow$, $\wedge$ and $\vee$ are the normal logical connectives for implication, conjunction and disjunction. $M \Rightarrow A$ denotes that a message, M, is sent out to agent A. $M \Leftarrow A$ denotes that a message, M, from agent A is received. The implication operator dominates the message operators, so for example $M \Rightarrow Agent \leftarrow C$ is scoped as $(M \Rightarrow Agent) \leftarrow C$

Fig. 1. Syntax of LCC interaction framework

Although LCC looks different to state-based systems like Islander it provides all the representational features we saw in Section 2. These are:

Role and scene identification: These are described by the agent type definition ($Type$ in Figure 1) which permits any structured term to be used to describe the agent type, hence this structure could include the agent's scene and role.

Initial state: Although LCC does not require a single initial state we can choose to have one of the clauses (an instance of $Clause$ in Figure 1) determine the scene and role of the agent that initiates the interaction.

Final and exit states: Although states are not labelled in LCC each agent can determine its current position in the interaction protocol by using the definition of protocol closure described in Figure 3.

Movement between states: Each agent moves between states by following its clause in the protocol. LCC allows changes of scene/role and recursion over scenes/roles (recall that states and roles are described in LCC using structured terms so these can be used to describe recursive orderings).

Access to protocol for agents: Agents can access a protocol by selecting an appropriate clause. The means of distributing protocols described in Section 6 allow agents hitherto unaware of a protocol to be "invited into" an interaction, so LCC-enabled agents may either initiate interaction or reactively join interactions.

Constraints on individual agents: Constraints can be applied to sending messages, accepting messages and to change of scene/role (see use of C in Figure 3). In order to keep the LCC language simple there is no special notation in LCC for representing temporal constraints (such as timeouts or temporal prohibitions) so one must construct these from normal first-order expressions.

Constraints on groups of agents: Although LCC clauses are used by individual agents it is easy to "thread" information through a group of interacting agents via arguments in the structured terms defining each agent's type ($Type$ in Figure 1). Constraints relevant to the group (such as cardinality constraints on the set of agents participating in an interaction) can then be checked by constraints on the individual agents. Simple temporal constraints (such as timeouts or prohibition periods) can be handled similarly, although there is the perennial issue of what a time interval means if communicated between agents on different processors with different clocks.

In Section 7 we describe aspects of LCC that go beyond current abilities of systems such as Islander. First we give an illustrative example of LCC in use.

4   Example LCC Interaction Framework

Figure 2 shows an example of a protocol in LCC for a basic multi-agent auction. There are two initial roles - a bidder and an auctioneer - with the auctioneer's role changing during the interaction between that of a caller of bids and a vendor collecting offers from bidders (notice the use of mutual recursion between auctioneer and vendor in clauses 2 and 4). The list of bidders known to the auctioneer (the variable named S in clauses 1 to 4) is assumed to be fixed throughout the auction but it is straightforward to extend the protocol to allow new bidders to join - for example we could add a clause for an introductory bidder that would ask for entry to the auction and then become a bidder; then extend clause 4 to allow acceptance of an invitation to bid.

The point of Figure 2 is not to describe an optimal auction protocol but to give the reader a flavour of what it is like to describe protocols in LCC. For those familiar with logic programming the style of description should be reassuringly familiar, since each clause of the protocol can be read similarly to a Horn clause with the "head" of the clause being the agent role and the "body" being the definition of its behaviour when discharging that role. Our preliminary efforts at teaching this language to first year postgraduate students encourages us to believe that teaching LCC as a form of declarative programming language is comparable in difficulty to teaching other declarative languages, such as Prolog. LCC is, however, a language for coordinating distributed processes (which we could not do using a straightforward rule based model of computation - we need to include asynchronous roles and message passing) so forms of debugging and analysis appropriate to asynchronous systems also are required to support LCC engineers. For example, model checking has been performed for a variant of LCC [10], analogous to model checking applied to systems like Islander [12]. A more

The role of an auctioneer, A, is performed by performing the role of an auctioneer for an item, X, with a set of bidders, S, at initial reserve price, R, and an initial empty list, $[]$, of bids. The constraint $item(X, R)$ determines the initial reserve price for the item and the constraint $bidders(S)$ determines the set of bidding agents.

$$a(auctioneer, A) \quad :: \quad a(auctioneer(X, S, R, []), A) \leftarrow item(X, R) \wedge bidders(S) \quad (1)$$

An auctioneer is first a caller for bids and then becomes a vendor.

$$a(auctioneer(X, S, R, Bids), A) \quad :: \quad \begin{array}{l} a(caller(X, S, R), A) \; then \\ a(vendor(X, S, R, Bids), A) \end{array} \quad (2)$$

A caller recurses through the list, S, of bidders, sending each an invitation to bid.

$$a(caller(X, S, R), A) \;\; :: \;\; \left(\begin{array}{l} invite\_bid(X, R) \Rightarrow a(bidder, B) \leftarrow S = [B|Sr] \; then \\ a(caller(X, Sr, R), A) \\ or \; null \leftarrow S = [] \end{array} \right)$$
$$(3)$$

A vendor receives a bid which is added to its current collection of bids, C, to give the updated set, C_n. It then does one of the following: sells to the highest bidder if there is one at the current reserve price; continues as a vendor if not all of the bids are collected; reverts to being an auctioneer if all the bids are in but there is no highest bidder or the highest bid exceeds the current reserve.

$$a(vendor(X, S, R, C), A) \quad :: \quad add\_bid(B_b, V_b, C, C_n) \leftarrow bid(X, V_b) \Leftarrow a(bidder, B_b) \\ then$$

$$\left(\begin{array}{l} \left(\begin{array}{l} sold(X, V_s) \Rightarrow a(bidder, B_s) \leftarrow all\_bid(S, C_n) \wedge \\ \qquad\qquad\qquad\qquad highest\_bid(C_n, B_s, V_s) \wedge V_s = R \end{array} \right) \; or \\ (a(vendor(X, S, R, C_n), A) \leftarrow not(all\_bid(S, C_n))) \; or \\ \left(\begin{array}{l} a(auctioneer(X, S, R, []), A) \leftarrow all\_bid(S, C_n) \wedge \\ \qquad\qquad\qquad\qquad not(highest\_bid(C_n, \_)) \end{array} \right) \; or \\ \left(\begin{array}{l} a(auctioneer(X, S, Rn, []), A) \leftarrow all\_bid(S, C_n) \wedge \\ \qquad\qquad\qquad\qquad highest\_bid(C_n, Rn) \wedge Rn > R \end{array} \right) \end{array} \right)$$
$$(4)$$

A bidder receives an invitation to bid from an auctioneer agent; then sends a bid to that agent (in its role as vendor); then either receives a message informing it that the item has been sold to it or it reverts to being a bidder again.

$$a(bidder, B) \quad :: \quad \begin{array}{l} invite\_bid(X, R) \Leftarrow a(auctioneer(X, \_, \_, \_), A) \; then \\ bid(X, V_b) \Rightarrow a(vendor(X, \_, \_, \_), A) \leftarrow bid\_at(X, R, V_b) \; then \\ (sold(X, V_s) \Leftarrow a(vendor(X, \_, \_, \_), A) \; or \; a(bidder, B)) \end{array}$$
$$(5)$$

Fig. 2. LCC framework for an auction example

extensive discussion of the relationship between mechanism design and distributed protocols appears in [13].

Although analytical techniques like model checking help support engineers, a simple and predictable computational model of the behaviour of protocols in deployment is fundamental to good engineering. In the next two sections we describe this model for LCC, beginning in Section 5 with the most basic computational step of accessing and updating the protocol; then in Section 6 showing how this is harnessed to provide flexible styles of multi-agent coordination.

5   Clause Expansion

To enable an agent to conform to a LCC protocol it is necessary to supply it with a way of unpacking any protocol it receives; finding the next moves that it is permitted to take; and recording the new state of dialogue. There are many ways of doing this but perhaps the most elegant way is by applying rewrite rules to expand the dialogue state. In this section we describe an expansion algorithm, showing in Section 6 how to use it with a selection of coordination systems.

The mechanism described below for coordinating agents using LCC assumes some means by which messages may be sent to a message exchange system and some means by which messages may be read from that system. The means of transmitting messages is not prescribed by LCC so this could be done using any appropriate distributed communication infrastructure. LCC does, however, make the following assumptions related to the format of messages:

- A message must contain (at least) the following information, which can be encoded and decoded by the sending and receiving mechanisms attached to each agent:
  - An identifier, I, for the social interaction to which the message belongs. This identifier must be unique and is chosen by the agent initiating the social interaction.
  - A unique identifier, A, for the agent intended to receive the message.
  - The role, R, assumed of the agent with identifier A with respect to the message.
  - The message content, M, in the syntax defined in Section 3.
  - The protocol, $\mathcal{P}$, for continuing the social interaction. This consists of: a set, $\mathcal{C}$, of LCC clauses defining the dialogue framework (see Section 3); and a set, $\mathcal{K}$, of axioms defining any common knowledge assumed during the social interaction. This provides a way of preserving information context as the protocol moves between agents. It also allows the common knowledge to be adapted during an interaction, so agents may add information for others to use, although we shall not be discussing this facility in the current paper.
- The agent must have a mechanism for satisfying any constraints associated with its clause in the dialogue framework. Where these can be satisfied from common knowledge (the set K above) it is possible to supply standard constraint solvers with the protocol. Otherwise, this is the responsibility of the agent.

Given these assumptions about message format, the basic operation an agent must perform when interacting via LCC is to decide what its next steps for its role in the interaction should be, using the protocol information carried with the message it obtains from some other agent. Recall that the behaviour of an agent in a given role is determined by the appropriate LCC clause. Figure 3 gives a set of rewrite rules that are applied to give an expansion of a LCC clause C_i in terms of protocol $\mathcal{P}$ in response to the set of received messages, M_i, producing: a new LCC clause C_n; an output message set O_n and remaining unprocessed messages M_n (a subset of M_i). These are produced by applying the protocol rewrite rules above exhaustively to produce the sequence:

$$\langle C_i \xrightarrow{M_i, M_{i+1}, \mathcal{P}, O_i} C_{i+1}, \ldots, C_{n-1} \xrightarrow{M_{n-1}, M_n, \mathcal{P}, O_n} C_n \rangle$$

We refer to the rewritten clause, C_n, as an expansion of the original clause, C_i. In the next section this basic expansion method is used for multi-agent coordination.

6   Coordination Mechanisms

Figure 4 depicts two methods of distributed coordination using LCC. Both use the clause expansion mechanism given in Section 5, the only difference between them being in the way the state of the interaction is preserved during interactions. In both cases there are two distinct (but interacting) uses of the LCC clauses. The first is the general protocol, which one might understand intuitively as the script for the whole interaction. The second is the set of specific clauses for each interacting agent (each copied from the general protocol and then progressively instantiated as described below) that store the state of that agent's interaction with respect to the general protocol. For simplicity, the diagrams of Figure 4 depict an interchange between only two agents (Agent 1 and Agent 2), with a message (Message 1) being sent from Agent 1 to Agent 2 and another message (Message 2) being returned in response. We describe below the first coordination mechanism in detail, then explain the second as a special case of the first.

Method 1 of Figure 4 depicts an instance of the coordination method described in detail as follows (from the point of view of Agent 2 in the diagram):

- An agent with unique identifier, A, retrieves a message of the form $(I, M, R, A, \mathcal{P})$ where: I is a unique identifier for the coordination; M is the message; R the role assumed of the agent when receiving the message; A the agent's unique identifier; and $\mathcal{P}$ the attached protocol consisting of a set of clauses, $\mathcal{C}$, and a set of axioms, $\mathcal{K}$, describing common knowledge. The message is added to the set of messages currently under consideration by the agent - giving the message set M_i.
- The agent checks its internal store of dialogue clauses to see if it already has a clause, C_i, indexed under coordination identifier I. If so, it selects it. If not it makes a copy of C_i as an element of $\mathcal{C}$, thus determining its part of the dialogue.
- The rewrite rules of Figure 3 are applied to give an expansion, C_n, of C_i in terms of protocol $\mathcal{P}$ in response to the set of received messages, M_i, producing: a new dialogue clause C_n; an output message set O_n and remaining unprocessed messages M_n (a subset of M_i).

The following ten rules define a single expansion of a clause. Full expansion of a clause is achieved through exhaustive application of these rules. Rewrite 1 (below) expands a protocol clause with head A and body B by expanding B to give a new body, E. The other nine rewrites concern the operators in the clause body. A choice operator is expanded by expanding either side, provided the other is not already closed (rewrites 2 and 3). A sequence operator is expanded by expanding the first term of the sequence or, if that is closed, expanding the next term (rewrites 4 and 5). A parallel operator expands on both sides (rewrite 6). A message matching an element of the current set of received messages, M_i, expands to a closed message if the constraint, C, attached to that message is satisfied (rewrite 7). A message sent out expands similarly (rewrite 8). A null event can be closed if the constraint associated with it can be satisfied (rewrite 9). An agent role can be expanded by finding a clause in the protocol with a head matching that role and body B - the role being expanded with that body (rewrite 10).

$$A :: B \xrightarrow{M_i, M_o, \mathcal{P}, O} A :: E \qquad\qquad if\ B \xrightarrow{M_i, M_o, \mathcal{P}, O} E$$

$$A_1\ or\ A_2 \xrightarrow{M_i, M_o, \mathcal{P}, O} E \qquad\qquad if\ \neg closed(A_2)\ \wedge$$
$$A_1 \xrightarrow{M_i, M_o, \mathcal{P}, O} E$$

$$A_1\ or\ A_2 \xrightarrow{M_i, M_o, \mathcal{P}, O} E \qquad\qquad if\ \neg closed(A_1)\ \wedge$$
$$A_2 \xrightarrow{M_i, M_o, \mathcal{P}, O} E$$

$$A_1\ then\ A_2 \xrightarrow{M_i, M_o, \mathcal{P}, O} E\ then\ A_2 \qquad if\ A_1 \xrightarrow{M_i, M_o, \mathcal{P}, O} E$$
$$A_1\ then\ A_2 \xrightarrow{M_i, M_o, \mathcal{P}, O} A_1\ then\ E \qquad if\ closed(A_1) \wedge A_2 \xrightarrow{M_i, M_o, \mathcal{P}, O} E$$
$$A_1\ par\ A_2 \xrightarrow{M_i, M_o, \mathcal{P}, O_1 \cup O_2} E_1\ par\ E_2 \qquad if\ A_1 \xrightarrow{M_i, M_n, \mathcal{P}, O_1} E_1\ \wedge$$
$$A_2 \xrightarrow{M_n, M_o, \mathcal{P}, O_2} E_2$$

$$C \leftarrow M \Leftarrow A \xrightarrow{M_i, M_i - \{M \Leftarrow A\}, \mathcal{P}, \emptyset} c(M \Leftarrow A)\ if\ (M \Leftarrow A) \in M_i\ \wedge\ satisfy(C)$$
$$M \Rightarrow A \leftarrow C \xrightarrow{M_i, M_o, \mathcal{P}, \{M \Rightarrow A\}} c(M \Rightarrow A) \qquad if\ satisfied(C)$$
$$null \leftarrow C \xrightarrow{M_i, M_o, \mathcal{P}, \emptyset} c(null) \qquad if\ satisfied(C)$$
$$a(R, I) \leftarrow C \xrightarrow{M_i, M_o, \mathcal{P}, \emptyset} a(R, I) :: B \qquad if\ clause(\mathcal{P}, a(R, I) :: B)\ \wedge$$
$$satisfied(C)$$

A protocol term is decided to be closed, meaning that it has been covered by the preceding interaction, as follows:

$$closed(c(X))$$
$$closed(A\ or\ B) \leftarrow closed(A)\ \vee\ closed(B)$$
$$closed(A\ then\ B) \leftarrow closed(A)\ \wedge\ closed(B)$$
$$closed(A\ par\ B) \leftarrow closed(A)\ \wedge\ closed(B)$$
$$closed(X :: D) \leftarrow closed(D)$$

$satisfied(C)$ is true if C can be solved from the agent's current state of knowledge.
$satisfy(C)$ is true if the agent's state of knowledge can be made such that C is satisfied.
$clause(\mathcal{P}, X)$ is true if clause X appears in the dialogue framework of protocol $\mathcal{P}$, as defined in Figure 1.

Fig. 3. Rewrite rules for expansion of a protocol clause

Method 1: LCC clauses distributed with protocol (carried with message); used and retained on appropriate agent.

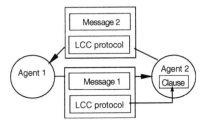

Method 2: LCC clauses distributed with protocol (carried with message); used by appropriate agent but stored with protocol.

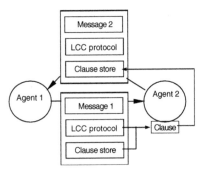

Fig. 4. Two methods of coordination

- The agent's original clause, C_i, is then replaced in $\mathcal{P}$ by C_n to produce the new protocol, $\mathcal{P}_n$.
- The agent can then send the messages in set O_n, each accompanied by a copy of the new protocol $\mathcal{P}_n$.

In Method 1 the clauses determining the behaviours of the interacting agents are distributed among the agents as the protocol is passed between them - these are the clauses named C_i in the algorithm above. The state of the interaction is described by the set of these distributed clauses. Notice that each agent must retain only the clause (or clauses if it has multiple roles) appropriate to it. Agents do not need to retain the whole protocol because this is passed with the message, so will return to the agent if other messages arrive as part of the appropriate interaction.

Method 1 is comparatively lightweight because it requires only that an agent can perform clause expansion, as described in Section 5, and that it can store its own copies of LCC clauses. It is possible, however, to place even less burden on individual agents if we have interactions that are linear, in the sense that (regardless of how many agents interact) at any given time exactly one agent alters the state of the interaction. An example of a linear interaction is a dialogue between two agents where each agent takes alternate turn in the interaction. An example of a non-linear interaction is an auction involving a broadcast call for bids (like the one in Figure 2). When the interaction is linear then we can store agents' clauses (named C_i in the algorithm above) with the message rather than with the agent. This is the "Clause store" depicted in the lower diagram of Figure 4. Agents then look up their clauses from this clause store, and the state of the whole interaction is preserved by the message as it passes between agents.

7   Computing with LCC

LCC can be used to tackle a variety of different forms of coordination problem, from those in which agents' behaviours are tightly constrained by the protocol to those in which agents are constrained only in terms of the message sequences they may send. The difference between these two extremes is made by the number and rigidity of the constraints included with the protocol. A tightly constrained protocol has many constraints, all of which have a precise interpretation determined by the protocol designer (Figure 2 is an example), in which case the interaction is similar to a traditional distributed computation with the participating agents acting as processors for the computation described by the LCC protocol. A loosely constrained protocol has few constraints, any of which may have an interpretation given to it by the agent designers, in which case the agents involved may have a greater degree of autonomy within the message passing framework set by the protocol.

Since constraints attach to messages or roles, it has proved most natural in practice for those writing LCC protocols to begin by specifying the (unconstrained) sequences of messages and changes of role for each of the roles in an interaction. Then, once this skeletal structure is in place, constraints can be added to tighten the protocol in whatever way suits the application. The form of refinement is similar to the style of design used in conventional relational and functional programming where a skeletal control structure often is described as a precursor to detailed design. This is why it is advantageous for LCC to resemble these kinds of traditional language, despite being also a process calculus.

Although recent, LCC has been used for a variety of practical purposes:

– In simulation, where we have built simulators for empirical comparison of LCC protocols under controlled conditions. For example, we have compared the performance of different protocols for resource mediation under varying supply and demand regimes. The simulators needed for this sort of empirical analysis have been simple to construct for LCC because we re-use the expansion algorithm of Section 5 within the simulation harnesses.
– In model checking, where we have written a translator from a variant of LCC (Walton's MAP language) to the Promela language which can then be fed into the SPIN model checker.
– In constraint solving, where we have extended the basic clause expansion mechanism to preserve the ranges of finite-domain constraints on variables. This allows agents to restrict rather than simply instantiate constraints when interacting, thus allowing a less rigid interaction.

- To permit human interaction, where we have built a generic user interface (in Tcl-TK interacting with SICStus Prolog) for accepting, viewing and replying to LCC messages. This is intended for prototyping to get a feel for the sort of interaction occurring between agents.

8   LCC and Performative Languages

Although LCC was not intended for direct comparison to performative languages such as FIPA-ACL or KQML, there is a relationship that may be of practical value. Performative languages provide a language for communication between agents that is oriented to the demands of dialogue. They provide ways of describing basic "speech acts" such as asking for information or telling an agent some new information, via performative expressions. This is of benefit because an agents receiving a message with content "wrapped" within performative expressions can have some idea of the role of that message in dialogue. Such languages are, however, limited in the extent to which they can describe dialogue:

- When an agent receives a message this is wrapped only in a single performative, so it can know for example that the message is a "tell" but it is not given any further reference to the broader dialogue of which this message may be a part.
- The semantics of performatives is defined (more or less formally depending on the performative language) in documents describing the language but it is entirely up to the engineers of individual agents to ensure that they adhere to an appropriate semantics. Thus, the sender of a performative has no way of helping the recipient to understand what is meant by it, nor of checking that it was used appropriately.

The remainder of this section shows how LCC overcomes these limitations, offering comparable precision in description of semantics plus the practical benefit of linking these more closely to the mechanics of actual agent dialogue.

There are various ways of describing the semantics of performatives but a common form of description is by defining preconditions and postconditions on the performative message. Preconditions "indicate the necessary states for an agent to send a performative and for the receiver to accept it and successfully process it". Postconditions "describe the states of the sender after the successful utterance of a performative, and of the receiver after the receipt".

An example of this sort of definition is the $tell(A, B, X)$ performative in KQML which describes the act of agent A telling agent B some information, X. Below are the constraints given for this in [14] (ignoring the issue of how the agent knows what it should be telling another agent about). We use the predicates: $k(A, X)$ to denote that A knows X; $b(A, X)$ to denote that A believes X; $i(A, X)$ to denote that A intends X and $w(A, X)$ to denote that A wants X. These correspond to the predicates $know$, bel, $intend$ and $want$ in [14].

- Preconditions:
  - Agent A believes X and knows that agent B wants to know about X:

$$b(A, X) \wedge$$
$$k(A, w(B, k(B, X))) \tag{6}$$

  - Agent B intends to know that B knows X:

$$i(B, k(B, X)) \tag{7}$$

- Postconditions:
  - Agent A knows that agent B knows that A believes X:

$$k(A, k(B, b(A, X))) \tag{8}$$

  - Agent B knows that agent A believes X:

$$k(B, b(A, X)) \tag{9}$$

These are the basic constraints on $tell$ according to [14]. A more sophisticated set of constraints (described informally in [14]) would accommodate refusal of a $tell$ message by the recipient agent (for example by replying with a $sorry$ or $error$ performative). This allows for more sophisticated dialogue constraints than in expressions 8 and 9 above but is a similar specification task so, to save space, we limit ourselves to the basic interaction.

A difficulty in practice when constraining the use of performatives such as '$tell$', above, is in ensuring that the constraints set in the specification of these performatives actually hold during the course of a dialogue. How, for example, can both agents (A and B) ensure that B wants to know about X (as preconditions 6 and 7 require)? How can agent A be sure, after it sent the message $tell(A, B, X)$, that postcondition 9 holds, since (for instance) its message may by accident never have been delivered to B. Using LCC we can tackle this problem as follows.

First, it is necessary to define the dialogue associated with the '$tell$' performative. In order to provide acknowledgement of receipt of this message we require a confirmatory response from the recipient (B). For this we add a '$heard$' performative. The message passing framework for the '$tell$' protocol is then as shown in expressions 10 and 11, with the first clause requiring the agent doing the telling (in role T_a) to tell the recipient (in role T_b) and await confirmation that the recipient has heard. KQML pre- and post-conditions 6 and 8 are added to apply the appropriate constraints on Agent A's beliefs. The second clause obliges the recipient to receive the information and confirm that it has heard, again with appropriate constraints 7 and 9.

$$a(T_a, A) :: tell(X) \Rightarrow a(T_b, B) \leftarrow \tag{10}$$
$$\begin{pmatrix} b(A, X) \wedge \\ k(A, w(B, k(B, X))) \end{pmatrix} then$$
$$k(A, k(B, b(A, X))) \leftarrow heard(X) \Leftarrow a(T_b, B)$$

$$a(T_b, B) :: i(B, k(B, X)) \leftarrow \mathit{tell}(X) \Leftarrow a(T_a, A) \mathit{\ then} \qquad (11)$$
$$\mathit{heard}(X) \Rightarrow a(T_a, A) \leftarrow k(B, b(A, X))$$

In the example above we included the constraints imposed on the semantics of a performative in the definition of the constraints embedded in our dialogue protocol. This makes them explicit so, if the application demands high reliability, they could be part of a system of automatic checking or endorsement. This is not intrinsic to traditional performative languages.

9   Conclusions

LCC is a language for describing social norms as interacting, distributed processes. Although it is comparatively simple in design (comparable to traditional logic programming languages) it is able to represent concepts generally considered to be essential for representing and reasoning about social norms. A primary aim of LCC (as with other social norm systems) is to interfere as little as possible with the design and operation of individual agents. We have coded (separately for Prolog and Java) compact algorithms for unpacking LCC protocols to yield the illocutions implied by them in whatever is the current state of interaction (see Section 5). Little more than this is required beyond a method for parsing incoming and outgoing LCC-enabled messages (on whatever is the chosen message passing infrastructure) and for satisfying the constraints (if any) associated with appropriate clauses in the protocol.

LCC protocols are modular in the sense that they can be understood separately from the agents participating in the interactions they describe and are neutral to the implementation of those agents. The clauses within an LCC protocol also are modular, so individual roles within an interaction are easy to identify. This makes it comparatively straightforward to design different models of coordination for LCC depending on the demands of the problem. Section 6 describes three such models.

Since LCC is an executable specification language, work continues on both aspects of the system. On the specification side we have translations from LCC to other more traditional styles of temporal specification, currently a modal logic and a form of situation calculus. On the deployment side we are investigating ways of making the LCC protocols adaptable in ways which preserve the intent of the social norms they describe. We are also investigating how LCC may be adapted to support workflow in computational grids.

Acknowledgements

This work is supported under the Advanced Knowledge Technologies Interdisciplinary Research Collaboration, which is sponsored by the UK Engineering and Physical Sciences Research Council under grant number GR/N15764/01.

References

1. Kagal, L., Finin, T., Joshi, A.: A policy language for pervasive systems. In: Fourth IEEE International Workshop on Policies for Distributed Systems and Networks. (2003)
2. Decker, K., Pannu, A., Sycara, K., Williamson, M.: Designing behaviors for information agents. In: Proceedings of the First International Conference on Autonomous Agents. (1997)
3. Giampapa, J., Sycara, K.: Team-oriented agent coordination in the retsina multi-agent system. Technical Report CMU-RI-TR-02-34, Robotics Institute, Carnegie Mellon University (2002)
4. McIlraith, S., Son, T.: Adapting golog for composition of semantic web services. In: Proceedings of the Eighth International Conference on Knowledge Representation and Reasoning. (2002) 482–493
5. Sheshagiri, M., desJardins, M., Finin, T.: A planner for composing services described in daml-s. In: International Conference on Automated Planning and Scheduling. (2003)
6. Greaves, M., Holmback, M., Bradshaw, J.: What is a conversation policy? In Dignum, F., Greaves, F., eds.: Issues in Agent Communication. Springer-Verlag (1999) 118–131
7. Esteva, M., Padget, J., Sierra, C.: Formalizing a language for institutions and norms. In: Intelligent Agents VIII, Lecture Notes in Artificial Intelligence. Volume 2333. Springer-Verlag (2002) 348–366
8. Esteva, M., de la Cruz, D., Sierra, C.: Islander: an electronic institutions editor. In: Proceedings of the 1st International Joint Conference on Autonomous Agents and MultiAgent Systems. (2002) 1045–1052
9. Robertson, D.: A lightweight method for coordination of agent oriented web services. In: Proceedings of AAAI Spring Symposium on Semantic Web Services, California, USA (2004)
10. Walton, C.: Model checking multi-agent web services. In: Proceedings of AAAI Spring Symposium on Semantic Web Services, California, USA (2004)
11. Fitoussi, D., Tennenholtz, M.: Choosing social laws for multi-agent systems: Minimality and simplicity. Artificial Intelligence **119** (2000)
12. Huget, M., Esteva, M., Phelps, S., Sierra, C., Wooldridge, M.: Model checking electronic institutions. In: Proceedings of ECAI Workshop on Model Checking and Artificial Intelligence, Lyon, France (2002)
13. Monderer, D.,Tennenholtz, M.: Distributed games: From mechanisms to protocols. In: Proceedings of the Sixth National Conference on Artificial Intelligence. (1999)
14. Labrou, Y., Finin, T.: A semantics approach for KQML: a general purpose communication language for software agents. In: Third International Conference on Knowledge and Information Management. (1994)

Enhancing Commitment Machines

Michael Winikoff[1], Wei Liu[2], and James Harland[1]

[1] RMIT University, Melbourne, Australia
{winikoff,jah}@cs.rmit.edu.au
[2] University of Western Australia, Perth, Australia
wei@csse.uwa.edu.au

Abstract. Agent interaction protocols are usually specified in terms of permissible sequences of messages. This representation is, unfortunately, brittle and does not allow for flexibility and robustness. The *commitment machines* framework of Yolum and Singh aims to provide more flexibility and robustness by defining interactions in terms of the commitments of agents. In this paper we identify a number of areas where the commitment machines framework needs improvement and propose an improved version. In particular we improve the way in which commitments are discharged and the way in which pre-conditions are specified.

1   Introduction

Communications between software agents are typically regulated by interaction protocols. These include general communication protocols, such as the auction protocol and the contract net protocol, as well as more specific protocols such as the NetBill payment protocol [1, 2]. Traditional protocol representations such as Finite State Machines (FSM), Petri-Nets [3] and AUML sequence diagrams [4, 5] often specify protocols in terms of legal message sequences. Under such protocol specifications, agent interactions are pre-defined and predictable. However, the inevitable rigidity resulting from such protocols prevents agents from taking opportunities and handling exceptions in a highly dynamic and uncertain multi-agent environment.

Yolum and Singh's Commitment Machines [1] (CMs henceforth) define an interaction protocol in terms of actions that change the state of the system, which consists of not only the state of the world but also the *commitments* that agents have made to each other. It is the commitment made to an interaction partner that motivates an agent to perform its next action. In other words, an agent acts because it wants to comply with the protocol and provide the promised outcomes for another party. Actions in CMs not only change the values of state variables, but also may initiate new commitments and/or discharge existing commitments. In traditional protocol representations, agents are confined to perform some pre-defined sequence of actions, whereas in CMs, an agent is able to reason about the next action to be taken in accordance with the dynamics of the environment and the commitments. This fundamentally changes the process of protocol specification from a procedural approach (i.e., prescribing *how* an interaction is to be executed) to a declarative one (i.e., describing *what* interaction is to take place) [1].

Using commitments as the rationale for agent interactions allows protocols to be specified at a higher level, which then generates more flexible and robust interactions

J. Leite et al. (Eds.): DALT 2004, LNAI 3476, pp. 198–220, 2005.

than pre-defined sequences. For example, in the NetBill protocol (discussed in Section 2), a customer may wish to order goods without first receiving a quotation, or a merchant may be happy to send goods to a known reliable customer with less rigorous checking than normal.

In this paper we identify a number of areas where the Commitment Machine framework can be improved. Specifically, we show how the identification of undesirable states (such as omitting to provide a receipt, or receiving the goods before payment has been confirmed) can be incorporated into the design process in order to achieve acceptable outcomes for a wider variety of circumstances than is done in [1, 2]. We also show how certain anomalies in discharging commitments and in handling pre-conditions can be remedied.

We demonstrate the operation of the improved framework on some examples. This is necessarily limited to a small number of illustrative cases, but these suffice to demonstrate the generality of the improvements.

The paper is organized as follows: in Section 2 we introduce the commitment machine framework and a detailed example, both based on [1]. In Section 3 we identify a number of anomalies and issues with the commitment machines framework and in Section 4 we propose some improvements. In Section 5 we discuss further applications of the improved framework and in Section 6 we present our conclusions.

2   Background

We briefly introduce the commitment machines framework and the NetBill protocol. Both are based on the description in [1] and we refer the reader to [1, 2] for further details.

The key example used in [1] is the NetBill protocol [6]. In this protocol a customer buys a product from a merchant. To buy a desired product, the protocol begins with a customer (C) requesting a quote (message 1 in Figure 1) from the merchant (M), followed by the merchant sending the quote (message 2). If the customer accepts the quote (message 3), the merchant proceeds by sending the goods (message 4) and waits for the customer to pay by sending an electronic payment order (EPO). Note that it is assumed that the goods cannot be used until the merchant has sent the relevant decryption key, such as software downloaded from the internet, or sent on a CD. Once the customer has sent payment (via an EPO in message 5), the merchant will send the decryption key along with a receipt (message 6). This concludes the NetBill transaction.

As suggested by the name "commitment machine", a crucial concept is that of *commitment*. A (social) commitment is an undertaking by one agent (the *debtor*, x) to another agent (the *creditor*, y) to bring about a certain property p, written $C(x, y, p)$. A commitment of the form $C(x, y, p)$ is a *base-level* commitment. For example, in the NetBill protocol when the customer sends message 3 and then receives the goods, he or she has a commitment to pay the merchant, i.e., $C(C, M, pay)$.

When a party is willing to commit only if certain conditions hold (such as another party making a corresponding commitment), a *conditional commitment* can be used. A conditional commitment, denoted $CC(x, y, p, q)$, indicates that agent x is committed to achieving q for agent y if p becomes true. A conditional commitment is latent – it

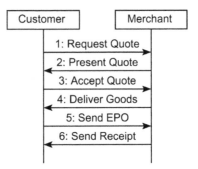

Fig. 1. Simplified Net Bill Protocol

doesn't commit x to do anything until p becomes true, at which point the conditional commitment is transformed to the base-level commitment $C(x, y, q)$. For example, in the NetBill protocol the customer may insist on his or her commitment to pay being conditional on the goods being sent, which would be represented as $CC(customer, merchant, goods, pay)$. Where the identity of the debtor and the creditor are obvious from the context we shall sometimes write $C(p)$ in place of $C(x, y, p)$ and $CC(p \rightsquigarrow q)$ in place of $CC(x, y, p, q)$.

Interactions are specified in the CM framework by defining the roles of the participants, the domain-specific fluents (i.e., boolean state variables), the (conditional) commitments that may arise during the interaction, and the rules for *initiating* and *terminating* commitments. Together, they define the preconditions and effects of (communicative) actions, and are used to regulate the choices of actions during protocol execution. The execution of a protocol is driven by the commitments that are in place: the desire to fulfil these commitments generates an action or actions to achieve them, which in turn may create new commitments or discharge existing ones. The NetBill protocol as a CM can be found in Figure 2.

A *state* in a CM is a triple $\langle F, CC, C \rangle$, where F is a set of fluents, CC is a set of conditional commitments and C is a set of base-level commitments. A *final state* is a state that does not have undischarged base-level commitments. A final state may contain conditional commitments, since they are latent commitments that have not been activated. Formally, a state in a CM is a final state if $C = \emptyset$. Note that a final state in a CM is one where the interaction *may* end. However, it is also possible for interaction to continue from a final state. A *protocol run* consists of a sequence of actions that results in a final state.

A commitment machine places constraints on the sequence of agent actions that constitute the interaction. For example, if an agent has a commitment, then it must at some point fulfil its commitment[1]. However, commitment machines do not dictate or require that agents perform particular actions.

Each commitment machine implicitly defines a corresponding Finite State Machine[2] (FSM) where the states of the FSM correspond to the states of the CM and the transi-

---

[1] Commitments can also be discharged in ways other than being fulfilled [1].
[2] Actually, a variation of finite state machines, since there is no defined initial state.

Roles: M (merchant), C (customer) **Fluents:**

- $request$ (the customer has requested a quote),
- $goods$ (the goods have been delivered to the customer),
- pay (the customer has paid),
- $receipt$ (the merchant has sent the receipt)

Commitments:

- $accept = \mathsf{CC}(C, M, goods, pay)$: a commitment by the customer (to the merchant) to pay once the goods have been delivered.
- $promiseGoods = \mathsf{CC}(M, C, accept, goods)$: a commitment by the merchant to send the goods if the customer accepts. Since $accept$ is itself a commitment this is a nested commitment: $promiseGoods = \mathsf{CC}(M, C, \mathsf{CC}(C, M, goods, pay), goods)$.
- $promiseReceipt = \mathsf{CC}(M, C, pay, receipt)$: a commitment by the merchant to send a receipt once the customer has paid.
- $offer = promiseGoods \wedge promiseReceipt$: an offer is a commitment by the merchant (a) to send the goods if the customer accepts the offer, and (b) to send a receipt after payment has been made.

Action Effects: the following (communicative) actions are defined:

- $sendRequest$: this action by the customer makes the fluent $request$ true.
- $sendQuote$: this action by the merchant creates the two commitments $promiseGoods$ and $promiseReceipt$ (i.e., $offer$) and terminates (makes false) the fluent $request$.
- $sendAccept$: this action by the customer creates the commitment $accept$.
- $sendGoods$: this action by the merchant makes the fluent $goods$ true and also creates the commitment $promiseReceipt$.
- $sendEPO$: this action by the customer makes the fluent pay true. This action is defined in [1] as having the pre-condition that the goods have been sent.
- $sendReceipt$: this action by the merchant makes the fluent $receipt$ true. This is defined in [1] as having the pre-condition that payment has been made.

Fig. 2. The NetBill Protocol as a Commitment Machine [1]

tions are defined by the effects of the actions. Figure 4 shows a (partial) view of the states and transitions corresponding to the CM defined in Figure 2. Final states (those with no undischarged base-level commitments) are shaded and dotted lines depict actions that are intended to be prevented by pre-conditions (but see Section 3.4). This figure is an extension of the figure given in [1, 2]. The table in Figure 3 gives the fluents and commitments that hold in each state.

3   Properties of CMs

In this section we discuss various properties of CMs as presented in [1, 2] and identify a number of areas where we propose improvements to the CM framework.

No.	State
1	-
2	$request$
3	M: $promiseReceipt \wedge promiseGoods$
4	M: $promiseReceipt \wedge$ C$(goods)$, C: $accept$
5	$goods$, M: $promiseReceipt$, C: C(pay)
6	$goods, pay$, M: C$(receipt)$
7	$goods, pay, receipt$
8	$goods$, M: $promiseReceipt$
9	C: $accept$
10	pay, M: C$(receipt) \wedge promiseGoods$
11	$pay, receipt$, M: $promiseGoods$
12	$goods, receipt$
13	$goods$, M: $promiseReceipt$, C: $accept$

Fig. 3. States and associated commitments and fluents

3.1   Explicit Labelling of Undesirable States

The presentation in [1, 2] presents protocols as defining states (in terms of the commitments of the agents and the fluents that hold). A query is then given and the reasoning module finds possible sequences of actions that lead to the requested state. For example, in [2] given the commitment machine defined in Figure 2, the reasoning module is asked to find sequences of actions that lead to a final state where goods have been received, payment has been made, and a receipt has been issued.

However, when designing interaction rules it is important to not only ensure that a desirable final state is possible, but also to ensure that undesirable states are not possible.

In this context when we talk about "desirable" and "undesirable" states we are talking from the perspective of the *designer* of the interaction, not from the perspective of an agent who will take part in the interaction. Roughly speaking, the designer should consider a state to be desirable if at least one agent desires it and no agents find it undesirable. A state should be considered undesirable if any agent finds it undesirable.

If an undesirable final state is determined to be possible then this can be fixed by either adding additional commitments so that the state is no longer final, or by adding pre-conditions so that the state can not be reached. It is *not* possible to fix undesirable final states by merely having the agents be aware of the undesirable state - if a state is undesirable to one agent, another agent may still perform an action that results in that state.

For example, in the NetBill protocol the desirable final states are those in which the goods have been delivered and paid for and a receipt has been given. Undesirable final states are those where only one or two of these three conditions hold; it is clearly undesirable to have the goods without payment, to have paid for the goods without getting a receipt, to have a receipt without payment, or to have paid without the goods being delivered. The final state where the goods have not been delivered, no payment has been made, and there is no receipt is acceptable, but not desirable (neutral). In Figure 4 state 7 is desirable, states 8,11,12 and 13 are undesirable, and states 1,2,3

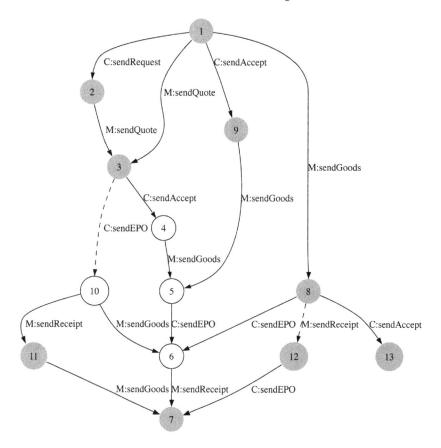

Fig. 4. Implied FSM for the NetBill CM (partial), final states are shaded and dotted lines depict actions that are intended to be prevented by pre-conditions

and 9 are neutral. Note that states 10, 11, 12 and 13 have been added to the machine discussed in [1, 2]. Note also that states 4,5,6 and 10 have undischarged commitments, and hence are not final states.

To illustrate why we need to identify and avoid undesirable states we consider an alternative protocol which seems quite reasonable. This protocol differs from the one presented in [1, 2] in that we remove the axiom:

$$Initiates(sendGoods, promiseReceipt, t)$$

This axiom is not needed in the "normal" expected sequence of actions (depicted in Figure 1) and it is quite possible that a naïve protocol designer would leave it out of an initial protocol specification.

Now suppose that the customer does not need a quote (perhaps the customer and merchant have interacted in the past), and begins the interaction with *sendAccept*. The merchant replies to the *sendAccept* with *sendGoods*. At this point in the interaction the customer's acceptance commitment CC($good \leadsto pay$) becomes a commitment to pay,

$C(pay)$, since the goods have been received. The customer then fulfils their obligation by paying. At this point we are in a final state — there are no remaining commitments — and goods have been received and payment made. However, this state is an undesirable one because the customer has not received a receipt.

The important point is that the omission of the *Initiates* rule is detected by checking whether undesirable (final) states are reachable, rather than by only checking whether desirable ones can be reached. If we had simply taken the variant protocol and asked for sequences which result in goods being delivered along with payment and a receipt then the problem would not have been noticed. In other words, the undesirable states can be used as a check on the interaction rules, which in this case results in the problem being easily found.

3.2   Failure to Discharge Conditional Commitments

There are anomalies in the rules that govern the discharge of conditional commitments. These anomalies can, in certain situations, result in conditional commitments not being discharged when, intuitively, they ought to be.

Consider the following sequence of steps:

1. The customer asks for a quote
2. The merchant replies with a quote. At this point the merchant has promised to send the goods if the customer accepts, and has promised to send a receipt if the customer pays.
3. The customer, misunderstanding the protocol perhaps, decides to accept but sends payment instead of an acceptance.

At this point the merchant becomes committed to sending a receipt, which it does, resulting in the following final state:

- fluents: pay, $receipt$
- commitments of merchant: $CC(CC(goods \rightsquigarrow pay) \rightsquigarrow goods)$

The crucial point here is that this is a final state and the merchant is not committed to sending the goods. The reason is that in order for $CC(CC(goods \rightsquigarrow pay) \rightsquigarrow goods)$ to become $C(goods)$ the commitment $CC(goods \rightsquigarrow pay)$ must hold: it is not enough according to the formal framework for pay to hold. This is counter-intuitive because pay is stronger than $CC(goods \rightsquigarrow pay)$ in that it discharges the commitment. The formal framework does recognise this, but only at the top level – the reasoning process that discharges $CC(goods \rightsquigarrow pay)$ when pay becomes true is not applied to nested commitments.

3.3   Commitment Discharge Is Not Symmetrical

The axiom/postulate defining the conditions when a commitment (or conditional commitment) is discharged says that the commitment is discharged when it already exists and its condition is brought about by an event.

A problem with this is that it is possible to create a commitment $C(p)$ when p already holds. This commitment will not be discharged unless an event takes place subsequently which re-initiates p.

For example, consider the following sequence:

1. The customer sends an accept. The customer has now committed to paying if the goods are received ($CC(goods \leadsto pay)$)
2. The merchant sends the goods. Since the goods have been sent, the customer now is committed to paying ($C(pay)$).

However, lets consider what happens if the two steps occur in the reverse order:

1. The merchant sends the goods to the customer[3]
2. The customer sends an accept.

What is the resulting state? When sending the acceptance the customer initiates the conditional commitment to pay if the goods are received. This conditional commitment, however, does *not* become a commitment to pay even though the goods have already been sent. Consequently, the resulting state has no base-level commitments and so is an (undesirable) final state (state 13 in Figure 4).

3.4   Pre-condition Mechanism Does Not Prevent Action

A standard view of actions that goes back to STRIPS is that an action definition contains a pre-condition and a post-condition. The formalization of actions in the CM framework uses these, but the way in which pre-conditions are handled has a slight problem.

Pre-conditions in a CM are defined by putting conditions on the action effect definitions. For example, in [1] the effects of the $sendEPO$ action are defined using the clause[4]

$$Initiates(sendEPO, pay, t) \leftarrow HoldsAt(goods, t)$$

The intended reading in line with traditional pre-conditions is that "the goods must have been delivered in order for payment to be possible"[5] However, what this formalization actually does is limit the *effects* of $sendEPO$ rather than the action itself. In the event calculus the causality between $sendEPO$ and pay is captured by the predicate $Intiates(sendEPO, pay, t)$, *not* by the implication. The implication only places a condition on when the *causality* holds, not on when the action may be performed. Thus, this does not prevent the event $sendEPO$ from occurring if $goods$ is false, it merely means that if the event $sendEPO$ occurs without $goods$ being true then the fluent pay does not become true as a result of $sendEPO$.

From the perspective of the reasoning mechanism, the formalisation of pre-conditions introduces an additional link from a state back to that state that corresponds to performing an action whose pre-conditions are not satisfied (see Figure 5).

This is a fairly subtle difference but it does have one significant implication: if we consider agents that use an implementation of commitment machines to reason about

---

[3] As discussed in [2–example 2], this may be a sensible strategy if the goods are cheap to copy - e.g., software.

[4] Notation has been slightly changed. The actual clause in [1] is: $Initiates(sendEPO(i, m), pay(m), t) \leftarrow HoldsAt(goods(i), t)$.

[5] Note that this is the only $Initiates$ clause concerning $sendEPO$.

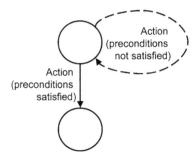

Fig. 5. Additional action link created by incorrect formalisation of pre-conditions

what actions to perform, then, for example, a customer agent who has not received the goods is not prevented from executing the *sendEPO* action. Although the reasoning module will, in this case, believe that the effects of payment have not taken place, if the *sendEPO* action is executed resulting in credit card details being sent, then in the real world the action's execution *will* have resulted in the undesired effect of payment.

3.5   Communication Mode Assumptions Not Clear

The state space defined by the available events (actions) includes sequences of events where an event representing an action by an agent (e.g., the merchant) is followed by an event representing another action by the same agent. This may not be desirable, if the intention is to define interactions where a message from M to C can only be followed by a response from C to M.

The point here is that in the CM framework, there is no explicit specification of how the conversation should be carried out between the two parties, i.e., whether it should follow a synchronous mode or an asynchronous mode. Were the synchronous communication mode clearly specified, the action *sendReceipt* by the Merchant would have been prevented in state 8 as the actors for the incoming and outgoing arc are the same.

However, there are situations where consecutive actions from the same agent *are* desirable. A typical CM state that may result in multiple actions from the same agent (or simultaneous actions from multiple agents) would have more than one base level commitment. See Section 4 for an example of a state with multiple base level commitments (state 10 in Figure 9).

A related issue is that the axioms allow an agent to perform actions that have no effect. For example, in the state where a request has been sent, sending another request has no effect on the state. In the FSMs that we show these arcs from a state S to itself have been elided.

We do not address these issues in this paper; we will return to them in subsequent work.

4   Proposed Extended CM Model

In this section we propose an extended CM model which addresses some of the concerns discussed in the previous section.

4.1   Labelling Undesirable States

This isn't a change to the model so much as an extension and a change to how it is used (the methodology). As part of developing the commitment machine the designer indicates which states are undesirable (bad), which are desirable (good) and which are acceptable but not desirable (neutral). Indicating the desirability of states can be done by specifying conditions. For example, one could specify that all final states which satisfy $pay \wedge \neg receipt$ are undesirable.

The indication of good/bad states is specific to a particular interaction and the preferences of the parties involved. For example, in [2–example 2] where the goods are cheap to copy, the merchant may not consider state 8 in Figure 4, which has $goods$ but not pay or $receipt$, to be a bad state.

The desirability of states, particularly of those states that are undesirable, is then used to perform safety checking.

4.2   Issues with Commitment Discharge

We now present a revised axiomatisation that remedies both anomalies associated with commitment discharge (Sections 3.2 and 3.3). We first consider the issue discussed in Section 3.2. Our proposed solution involves treating certain commitments as being "implied". For example, if pay is true, then any commitment of the form $CC(X \rightsquigarrow pay)$ that occurs as a condition can be treated as having implicitly held (and been discharged).

We introduce predicates $Implied$ and $Subsumes$ which capture when a commitment (base or conditional) holds implicitly or is subsumed by a condition. These are used in the rules that govern commitment dynamics. When checking whether a condition p holds, we also check whether it is implied or subsumed[6].

In [2], *fluents* are initiated directly by an action through the *initiates axioms* (e.g. $Initiates(sendGood, goods, t)$). On the other hand, *commitments*, both base-level and conditional, are created through the *Create* axioms. The *Create* axioms then initiate the commitments when the action happens according to the first axiom in Figure 6. However, this does not adequately distinguish commitments from other fluents. In particular, it makes no difference if we remove the first axiom in Figure 6 and replace all the *Create* axioms with *Initiates* axioms. In other words, according to the original commitment axioms and protocol specification, we can use *initiates* axioms for not only the fluents, but also all commitments. Such specifications dictate the action effects regardless of the current state of the world. However, an action should only initiate a base level commitment when the committed fluent is not already true, or when the premises but not the conclusion of a conditional commitment are true. An action should only initiate a conditional commitment when neither its premises nor conclusion are true. The axioms in Figure 6 fail to address this, which results in the asymmetrical discharge of commitments (Section 3.3).

In order to make commitment discharge symmetrical (Section 3.3) we de-couple intended causation from actual causation: instead of stating that an action initiates a

---

[6] $Implied(p, t)$ checks whether p is implied at time t and is used to check whether a condition (implicitly) holds at the current time. $Subsumes(p, p')$ checks whether p subsumes p' and is used to check whether an event would cause a condition to (implicitly) hold.

$Initiates(e, \mathsf{C}(x, y, p), t) \leftarrow Happens(e, t) \wedge Create(e, x, \mathsf{C}(x, y, p))$
$Initiates(e, \mathsf{CC}(x, y, p, q), t) \leftarrow Happens(e, t) \wedge Create(e, x, \mathsf{CC}(x, y, p, q))$

$Terminates(e, \mathsf{C}(x, y, p), t) \leftarrow Happens(e, t) \wedge Discharge(e, x, \mathsf{C}(x, y, p))$
$Discharge(e, x, \mathsf{C}(x, y, p)) \quad \leftarrow \quad HoldsAt(\mathsf{C}(x, y, p), t) \quad \wedge \quad Happens(e, t) \quad \wedge$
$Initiates(e, p, t)$

$Initiates(e, \mathsf{C}(x, y, p), t) \quad \leftarrow \quad HoldsAt(\mathsf{CC}(x, y, p, q), t) \quad \wedge \quad Happens(e, t) \quad \wedge$
$Initiates(e, p, t)$
$Terminates(e, \mathsf{CC}(x, y, p, q), t) \leftarrow HoldsAt(\mathsf{CC}(x, y, p, q), t) \wedge Happens(e, t) \wedge$
$\qquad Initiates(e, p, t)$
$Terminates(e, \mathsf{CC}(x, y, p, q), t) \leftarrow HoldsAt(\mathsf{CC}(x, y, p, q), t) \wedge Happens(e, t) \wedge$
$\qquad Initiates(e, q, t)$

Fig. 6. Commitment Machine Axiom 2,3,8,9,10 from [2]

commitment (e.g., $Initiates(sendGoods, promiseReceipt, t)$), we state that the action is *intended* to cause the initiation of the commitment (e.g., $Causes(sendGoods,$ $promiseReceipt)$). We then link the two notions by defining $Initiates$ in terms of $Causes$. When p is a fluent (not a commitment) then an event $Initiates$ the fluent p exactly when it $Causes$ it. However, for a base level commitment $\mathsf{C}(p)$ even though $Causes(e, \mathsf{C}(p))$, the event e will not make $\mathsf{C}(p)$ true if p already holds. Similarly, for $Causes(e, \mathsf{CC}(p \rightsquigarrow q))$, if p holds then e will create $\mathsf{C}(q)$, not $\mathsf{CC}(p \rightsquigarrow q)$, and if q holds then e will have no effect. The rules in Figure 7 realise these cases and Figure 8 illustrates the additional commitment discharge and creation rules. Note that the axioms of figure 7 have been implemented and can be found in the appendix.

We then have the following action effect rules for the NetBill CM (the roles, fluents and commitments remain unchanged):

$Causes(sendRequest, request)$
$Causes(sendQuote, offer)$
$Causes(sendAccept, accept)$
$Causes(sendGoods, goods)$
$Causes(sendGoods, promiseReceipt)$
$Causes(sendEPO, pay)$
$Causes(sendReceipt, receipt)$
$Terminates(sendQuote, request, t)$

We now explain how the revised axiomatisation and rules address the two commitment discharge anomalies. Let us begin with the first anomaly (Section 3.2). Consider the following sequence of steps:

1. The customer asks for a quote
2. The merchant replies with a quote. At this point the merchant has promised to send the goods if the customer accepts, and has promised to send a receipt if the customer pays.

$Implied(p, t) \leftarrow HoldsAt(p, t)$
$Implied(\mathsf{C}(x, y, p), t) \leftarrow Implied(p, t)$
$Implied(\mathsf{CC}(x, y, p, q), t) \leftarrow Implied(q, t)$
$Implied(\mathsf{CC}(x, y, p, q), t) \leftarrow Implied(\mathsf{C}(x, y, q), t)$

$Subsumes(p, p)$
$Subsumes(p, \mathsf{C}(x, y, p')) \leftarrow Subsumes(p, p')$
$Subsumes(p, \mathsf{CC}(x, y, q, p')) \leftarrow Subsumes(p, p')$
$Subsumes(\mathsf{C}(x, y, p), \mathsf{CC}(x, y, q, p')) \leftarrow Subsumes(p, p')$

$Happens(e, t) \leftarrow AgentTry(a, e, t) \wedge Precond(e, p) \wedge HoldsAt(p, t)$

$Initiates(e, p, t) \leftarrow Happens(e, t) \wedge Causes(e, p) \wedge isFluent(p)$
$Initiates(e, \mathsf{C}(x, y, p), t) \leftarrow Causes(e, \mathsf{C}(x, y, p)) \wedge Happens(e, t) \wedge \neg Implied(p, t)$
$Initiates(e, \mathsf{C}(x, y, p), t) \quad\leftarrow\quad Causes(e, \mathsf{CC}(x, y, q, p)) \quad\wedge\quad Happens(e, t) \quad\wedge$
$\qquad Implied(q, t)\wedge$
$\qquad\quad \neg Implied(p, t)$
$Initiates(e, \mathsf{CC}(x, y, p, q), t) \leftarrow Causes(e, \mathsf{CC}(x, y, p, q)) \wedge Happens(e, t)\wedge$
$\qquad\quad \neg Implied(q, t) \wedge \neg Implied(p, t)$
$Initiates(e, \mathsf{C}(x, y, q), t) \leftarrow HoldsAt(\mathsf{CC}(x, y, p, q), t) \wedge Happens(e, t)\wedge$
$\qquad\quad Subsumes(p', p) \wedge Initiates(e, p', t)$
$Terminates(e, \mathsf{C}(x, y, p), t) \quad\leftarrow\quad HoldsAt(\mathsf{C}(x, y, p), t) \quad\wedge\quad Happens(e, t) \quad\wedge$
$Subsumes(p', p)$
$\qquad\quad \wedge Initiates(e, p', t)$
$Terminates(e, \mathsf{CC}(x, y, p, q), t) \leftarrow HoldsAt(\mathsf{CC}(x, y, p, q), t) \wedge Happens(e, t)\wedge$
$\qquad\quad Subsumes(q', q) \wedge Initiates(e, q', t)$
$Terminates(e, \mathsf{CC}(x, y, p, q), t) \leftarrow HoldsAt(\mathsf{CC}(x, y, p, q), t) \wedge Happens(e, t)\wedge$
$\qquad\quad Subsumes(p', p) \wedge Initiates(e, p', t)$

Fig. 7. Revised Commitment Machine Framework

3. The customer, misunderstanding the protocol perhaps, decides to accept but sends payment instead of an acceptance.

Unlike previously, the payment causes the merchant to become committed to sending the goods (as well as a receipt). Through the postulate
$\qquad Implied(\mathsf{CC}(x, y, p, q), t) \leftarrow Implied(q, t),$
the fact that the *pay* fluent holds indicates that the conditional commitment $\mathsf{CC}(goods \rightsquigarrow pay)$ *implicitly* holds[7] at the same time. This implied conditional commitment discharges the *promiseGoods* ($\mathsf{CC}(\mathsf{CC}(goods \rightsquigarrow pay) \rightsquigarrow goods)$) conditional commitment and creates the base level commitment $\mathsf{C}(goods)$. Once the commitments $\mathsf{C}(goods)$ and $\mathsf{C}(receipt)$ are discharged we are in a desirable final state.

---

[7] More precisely, it could be considered to hold: there is no actual commitment, because it has been discharged, since *pay* is true.

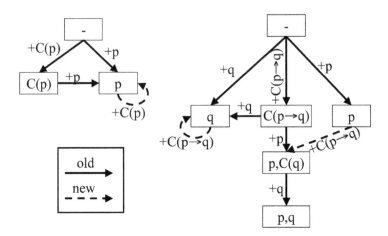

Fig. 8. Additional Commitment Transition Rules for base level commitment (left) and conditional commitment (right)

Consider now the second anomaly (non-symmetric commitment discharge, Section 3.3). Using the new predicate $Causes$, a conditional commitment is resolved to a base level commitment if the premise is already true using the clause

$Initiates(e, C(x, y, p), t) \leftarrow$

$Causes(e, CC(x, y, q, p)) \land Happens(e, t) \land Implied(q, t) \land \neg Implied(p, t)$

Consider the transition from state 8 to state 13, where the customer accepts after the goods have been sent. The customer's $sendAccept$ is meant to cause $accept$ ($CC(goods \rightsquigarrow pay)$), but because $goods$ already holds, sending the acceptance actually creates the (base level) commitment $C(pay)$.

Figure 9 shows (part of) the state machine implicitly defined by the revised Net-Bill protocol and CM axiomatisation. The differences are in states 10, 11 and 13. Whereas previously state 10 had pay, $C(receipt)$ and $promiseGoods$, now it has pay, $C(receipt)$ and $C(goods)$. As a result state 11 now includes a commitment to send the goods and is no longer a final state. State 13, which previously had $goods$, $promiseReceipt$ and $accept$ now has $goods$, $C(pay)$ and $promiseReceipt$ which is actually state 5, therefore state 13 no longer exists, and performing $sendAccept$ in state 8 leads to state 5. As before, final states are shaded. Also, dotted lines indicate actions that are affected by pre-conditions. Note that once pre-conditions are fixed (in the next sub-section) states 10, 11 and 12 will no longer be reachable. Note also that the resulting interaction space maintains the flexible interaction that is characteristic of the CM framework.

4.3   Issues with Pre-conditions

As discussed in Section 3.4 trying to capture pre-conditions by adding conditions to $Initiates$ clauses does not work.

Our proposed solution is to extend the agents with a proper notion of pre-condition that specifies when actions should not be performable (as opposed to preventing the

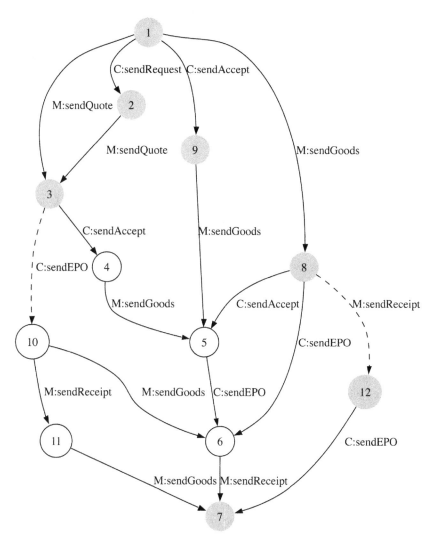

Fig. 9. Revised Transitions in example (partial), final states are shaded and dotted lines depict actions that are affected by pre-conditions

effects of the action from being caused). In the NetBill example we have the pre-conditions $Precond(sendEPO, goods)$ and $Precond(sendReceipt, pay)$.

We then need to de-couple an agent wanting to perform an action from the action actually occurring. This can be done by using a new predicate $AgentTry(a, e, t)$ to indicate that an agent a wants to perform an action e at time t. If the pre-conditions of the action e hold[8] at time t then this will imply that the event e happens.

---

[8] This assumes that p does not involve commitments. If it does then replace $HoldsAt(p, t)$ with $Implied(p, t)$.

$$Happens(e,t) \leftarrow AgentTry(a,e,t) \land Precond(e,p) \land HoldsAt(p,t)$$

Note that the definition of the interaction cannot prevent an agent from performing an action (any more than it can force an agent to honour its commitments). However, it can specify when an action should not be performed, and detect violations, in the same way that violations of commitments are detected.

5   Applications

Having proposed an improvement to the commitment machine framework, let us see how it works on another example of mutual commitment. This simple (and unrealistic) example is intended to show how the improved framework sharpens the interactions between the agents.

The example involves two roles, called "me" and "you". The two roles are friends who would like to negotiate with the outcome that both of them get an outrageous haircut for the last day of classes. It is highly undesirable that only one person have the haircut. There are two fluents (*yourscut* and *minecut*) representing who has had the haircut. We define two commitments: $Dare$ which is the conditional commitment $CC(you, me, Ok, yourscut)$, i.e., the commitment from you to me that if I agree (Ok) then you will get your hair cut;[9] and Ok, which is the conditional commitment $CC(me, you, yourscut, minecut)$, i.e., the commitment from me to you that if you get a haircut then I will get a haircut. There are four actions: *cutme* (which makes the fluent *minecut* true), *cutyou* (which makes the fluent *yourscut* true), *Offer* (which you can use to make $Dare$ true), and *Accept* (which I can use to make Ok true). The actions of me cutting my hair ($cutme$) and you cutting your hair ($cutyou$) have the precondition that I (respectively you) have a commitment to do so ($C(me, you, minecut)$, respectively $C(you, me, yourscut)$).

Figure 10 shows the complete finite state machine corresponding to this CM, derived using the old axioms, whereas Figure 11 shows the complete finite state machine derived using the new axioms. It should be immediately clear that the new axioms yield a much simpler behaviour that correctly reflects the intentions of this very simple example.

Note also the symmetry of Figure 11, reflecting that the order in which the *Offer* and *Accept* messages are sent is immaterial. Hence changing $Dare$ to $CC(me, you, Ok, minecut)$ and Ok to $CC(you, me, minecut, yourscut)$ will result in the same machine, except for the relabelling of me to you and vice-versa throughout.

On the other hand, using the old axioms (Figure 10), even this very simple example has anomalies. For example, consider the following sequence:

– *accept* from state 1 to state 25: $CC(me, you, yourscut, minecut)$

---

[9] This is the agent equivalent of "I will if you will".

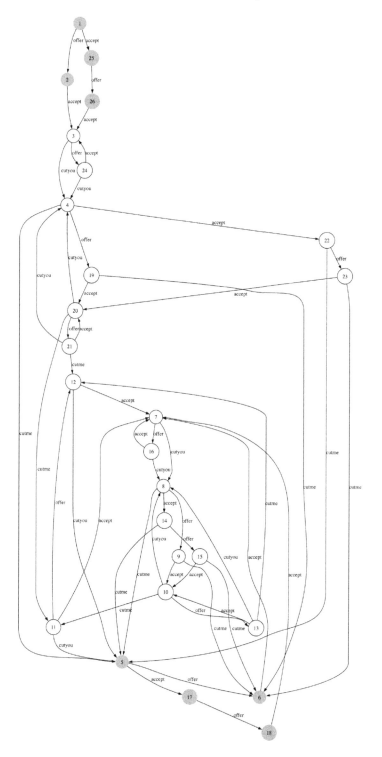

Fig. 10. Complete Finite State Machine for Haircut Example (old axioms)

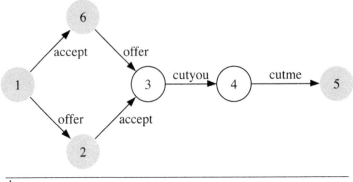

1 -
2 $Dare = CC(you, me, CC(me, you, your scut, minecut), your scut)$
3 $C(you, me, your scut), Ok = CC(me, you, your scut, minecut)$
4 $your scut, C(me, you, minecut)$
5 $your scut, minecut$
6 $Ok = CC(me, you, your scut, minecut)$

Fig. 11. Complete Finite State Machine for Haircut Example (new axioms)

- *offer* to state 26: $CC(me, you, your scut, minecut)$,
  $CC(you, me, CC(me, you, your scut, minecut), your scut)$

- *accept* (again) to state 3: $CC(me, you, your scut, minecut)$,
  $C(you, me, your scut)$

- *cutyou* to state 4: $your scut, C(me, you, minecut)$

- *accept* (again) to state 22: $your scut, C(me, you, minecut)$,
  $CC(me, you, your scut, minecut)$

- *offer* (again) to state 23: $your scut, C(me, you, minecut), CC(me, you, your scut, minecut)$, $CC(you, me, CC(me, you, your scut, minecut), your scut)$

- *accept* (again) to state 20: $your scut, C(me, you, minecut)$,
  $CC(me, you, your scut, minecut), C(you, me, your scut)$

- *cutme* to state 11: $your scut, C(you, me, your scut), minecut$

- *cutyou* (again) to state 5, which is a final state.

Because of anomalies with commitment creation and discharge, the action of accepting can be performed four times along this path, leading each time to a distinct state. Further, in order to fulfil the commitments, you have to cut you hair twice, which is counter-intuitive.

Note also the lack of symmetry in Figure 10. This reflects the fact that the order in which the commitments are expressed is not immaterial (i.e. that *Dare* is defined in terms of *Ok* means that the *Offer* and *Accept* actions are not entirely symmetric).

Let us now turn to the Net Bill example. Figure 12 shows the complete state machine for the interaction using the old axioms. This figure is not meant to be readable, but illustrates the size of the space and its complexity. By contrast, Figure 13 shows the same interaction, but using the new axioms[10]. The old axioms generate many more states (166 compared with 16) because of the discharge anomalies. For example, consider the following sequence of actions and resulting states:

1. sendQuote: results in the state with the two commitments *promiseGoods* and *promiseReceipt*.

   $CC(accept \rightsquigarrow goods), CC(pay \rightsquigarrow receipt)$

2. sendAccept: creates the commitment *accept*, which results in *promiseGoods* being transformed into the commitment to send the goods.

   $CC(goods \rightsquigarrow pay), C(goods), CC(pay \rightsquigarrow receipt)$

3. sendQuote: creates the two commitments *promiseGoods* and *promiseReceipts*. The latter makes no difference (since it already holds), but the former is re-introduced, even though it is redundant.

   $CC(goods \rightsquigarrow pay), C(goods), CC(pay \rightsquigarrow receipt), CC(accept \rightsquigarrow goods)$

6   Conclusion

We analyzed the reasoning process of commitment machines and identified several anomalies in the current reasoning mechanism. We then indicated how these anomalies could be remedied, giving detailed rules for fixing the anomalies involving commitment discharge and pre-conditions.

The aim of this work is to make agent interactions more flexible and robust. There is a range of other work that has similar aims.

The work of Fornara and Colombetti [7] also uses commitments, but they use them to define the meanings of speech acts, rather than defining protocols in terms of their effects on commitments.

Kumar et. al. [8] model interaction in terms of *landmarks* that need to be reached. They use the framework of joint intention theory to formalise both landmarks and speech acts. Given the complexity of the multi-modal logics used, implementation would seem to be a challenge, and no details of an implementation appear to be available. Baldoni et. al. [9] also use a multi-modal logic to formalise interaction, in their case within the DCaseLP environment using the DyLOG language.

---

[10] Note that the numbering of states has changed, since this figure was automatically generated.

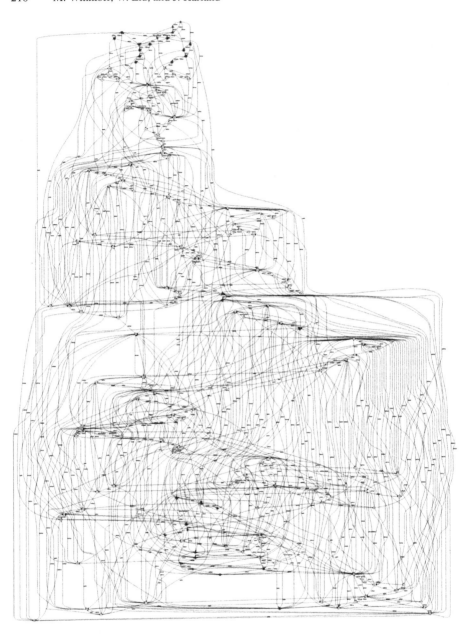

Fig. 12. Complete Finite State Machine for Net Bill using Old Axioms. This figure is not intended to be readable, but to illustrate the size and complexity of the interaction space

Hutchison and Winikoff [10] use belief-desire-intention agents and realise inter-action using goal-triggered plans, where a given goal may have many plans that can achieve it. This work is more implementation-oriented, but is not particularly well de-

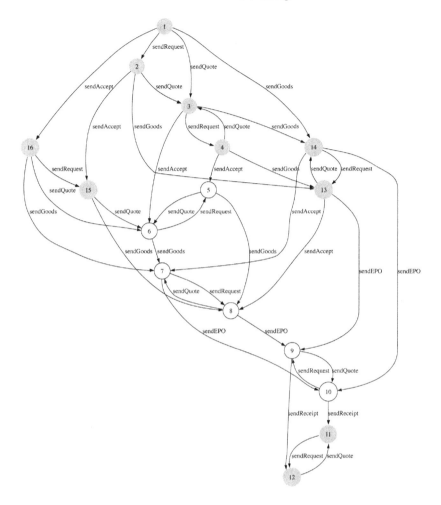

Fig. 13. Complete Finite State Machine for Net Bill using New Axioms, final states are shaded

veloped. It provides a set of guidelines for a human to follow when designing and implementing agent interaction, rather than a formally specified interaction mechanism.

Küngas and Matskin [11] use linear logic to formalise negotiation. Their approach has been implemented, but it is not clear whether it generalises to types of interaction other than negotiation.

Chopra et. al. [12] formalise the commitment machine framework using the π calculus. However, their formalisation is based on the axioms of [13] and suffers from the shortcomings discussed in this paper.

There are a number of papers in these proceedings that are concerned with verifying agent interactions in various ways [14, 15].

There are a number of areas for future work including extending the CM framework to deal with protocols involving open numbers of participants $(1 - N)$ such as auction protocols.

One area where we believe that commitment machines could be simplified concerns pre-conditions. In a sense pre-conditions and commitments are dual: the former state that a certain action must not be performed (under the prescribed conditions) whereas the latter state that a certain state must be brought about. It may be that the commitment machines framework could be simplified by merging the two concepts into a more generalised form of commitment. Specifically, pre-conditions could be replaced by commitments to *avoid* certain actions. These avoidance commitments, might be better termed *prohibitions*. A prohibition of the form $P(x, a)$ would state that agent x is prohibited from performing action a. A *conditional* prohibition of the form $CP(x, a, p)$ would state that agent x is *prohibited* from performing action a if p holds. For example, a merchant could have a conditional prohibition against sending a receipt if payment has not been made: $CP(M, sendReceipt, \neg pay)$. Prohibitions are more flexible than pre-conditions in that they can vary over time.

An additional issue in the CM framework concerns the termination of interactions. If an interaction reaches a state where there are no base-level commitments, but there are conditional commitments, then an agent, A, might decide that it wants to consider the interaction finished, and delete any record of it from its memory. However, after A drops the interaction, agent B might act in a way that changes a conditional commitment to a base-level commitment. The underlying issue is that a final state is only final in the sense that the interaction *could* end in that state, a final state does not require that the interaction *must* end there. As a result, an agent cannot consider the interaction to be completed if it could be continued.

Another area for future work would be applying our changes to the presentation of commitment machines in [13, 16]. Whereas the presentation of commitment machines in [1, 2] uses the event calculus to formalise commitment machines, the presentation of [13, 16] defines a process for compiling a commitment machine to a finite state machine.

Finally, the reasoning that each agent performs when deciding which action to do needs to be specified in more detail. The reasoning could resemble a form of game playing where an agent wants to ensure that states that it considers undesirable cannot be reached by other agents' actions while trying to achieve states that it considers desirable.

Acknowledgements

We would like to acknowledge the support of Agent Oriented Software and of the Australian Research Council under grant LP0218928. We would also like to thank the anonymous reviewers and Min Xu for their comments.

References

1. Yolum, P., Singh, M.P.: Flexible protocol specification and execution: Applying event calculus planning using commitments. In: Proceedings of the 1st Joint Conference on Autonomous Agents and MultiAgent Systems (AAMAS). (2002) 527–534
2. Yolum, P., Singh, M.P.: Reasoning about commitments in the event calculus: An approach for specifying and executing protocols. Annals of Mathematics and Artificial Intelligence (AMAI), Special Issue on Computational Logic in Multi-Agent Systems **42** (2004) 227–253

3. Reisig, W.: Petri Nets: An Introduction. EATCS Monographs on Theoretical Computer Science. Springer-Verlag (1985) ISBN 0-387-13723-8.

4. Huget, M.P., Odell, J., Haugen, Ø., Nodine, M.M., Cranefield, S., Levy, R., Padgham., L.: Fipa modeling: Interaction diagrams. On http://www.auml.org under "Working Documents" (2003) FIPA Working Draft (version 2003-07-02).

5. Odell, J., Parunak, H., Bauer, B.: Extending UML for agents. In: Proceedings of the Agent-Oriented Information Systems Workshop at the 17th National conference on Artificial Intelligence. (2000)

6. Sirbu, M.A.: Credits and debits on the internet. In Huhns, M.N., Singh, M.P., eds.: Readings in Agents. Morgan Kaufman (1998) 299–305 (Reprinted from *IEEE Spectrum*, 1997).

7. Fornara, N., Colombetti, M.: Operational specification of a commitment-based agent communication language. In: Proceeding of the First International Joint Conference on Autonomous Agents and Multi-Agent Systems, Bologna, Italy, ACM Press (2002) 535 – 542

8. Kumar, S., Huber, M.J., Cohen, P.R.: Representing and executing protocols as joint actions. In: Proceedings of the First International Joint Conference on Autonomous Agents and Multi-Agent Systems, Bologna, Italy, ACM Press (2002) 543 – 550

9. Baldoni, M., Baroglio, C., Gungui, I., Martelli, A., Martelli, M., Mascardi, V., Patti, V., Schifanella, C.: Reasoning about agents' interaction protocols inside DCaseLP. In *Proceedings of the Workshop on Declarative Agent Languages and Technologies (DALT'04)*, LNCS 3476, Springer-Verlag (2005). In this volume.

10. Hutchison, J., Winikoff, M.: Flexibility and robustness in agent interaction protocols. In: Workshop on Challenges in Open Agent Systems at the First International Joint Conference on Autonomous Agents and Multi-Agents Systems, Bologna, Italy, ACM Press (2002)

11. Küngas, P., Matskin, M.: Partial deduction for linear logic — the symbolic negotiation perspective. In *Proceedings of the Workshop on Declarative Agent Languages and Technologies (DALT'04)*, LNCS 3476, Springer-Verlag (2005). In this volume.

12. Chopra, A.K., Mallya, A.U., Desai, N.V., Singh, M.P.: Modeling flexible business processes. In Leite, J., Omicini, A., Torroni, P., Yolum, P., eds.: Preproceedings of Declarative Agent Languages and Technologies. (2004) 93–108

13. Yolum, P., Singh, M.: Commitment machines. In Meyer, J.J.C., Tambe, M., eds.: Agent Theories, Architectures, and Languages (ATAL). Volume 2333 of Lecture Notes in Computer Science., Springer (2002) 235–247

14. Vasconcelos, W.W.: Norm verification and analysis of electronic institutions. In *Proceedings of the Workshop on Declarative Agent Languages and Technologies (DALT'04)*, LNCS 3476, Springer-Verlag (2005). In this volume.

15. Walton, C.D.: Model checking agent dialogues. In *Proceedings of the Workshop on Declarative Agent Languages and Technologies (DALT'04)*, LNCS 3476, Springer-Verlag (2005). In this volume.

16. Yolum, P., Singh, M.: Synthesizing finite state machines for communication protocols. Technical Report TR-2001-06, North Carolina State University (2001) Available from http://www.csc.ncsu.edu/research/tech-reports/README.html.

A   Source Code for the Implemented Axioms

The complete source code is available from http://www.cs.rmit.edu.au/ winikoff/CM

New Axioms

```
implied(P,T) :- holdsAt(P,T).
implied(c(_,_,P),T) :- implied(P,T).
implied(cc(_,_,_,Q),T) :- implied(Q,T).
implied(cc(X,Y,_P,Q),T) :- implied(c(X,Y,Q),T).

subsumes(P,P).
subsumes(P,c(_,_,PP)) :- subsumes(P,PP).
subsumes(P,cc(_,_,_,PP)) :- subsumes(P,PP).
subsumes(c(X,Y,P),cc(X,Y,_Q,PP)) :- subsumes(P,PP).

happens(E,T) :- isAction(E), precond(E,P), holdsAt(P,T).

initiates(E,P,T) :- happens(E,T), isFluent(P), causes(E,P).
initiates(E,c(X,Y,P),T) :- causes(E,c(X,Y,P)),
  happens(E,T), \+(implied(P,T)).
initiates(E,c(X,Y,P),T) :- causes(E,cc(X,Y,Q,P)),
  happens(E,T), implied(Q,T), \+(implied(P,T)).
initiates(E,cc(X,Y,P,Q),T) :- causes(E,cc(X,Y,P,Q)),
  happens(E,T), \+(implied(Q,T)), \+(implied(P,T)).
initiates(E,c(X,Y,Q),T) :- holdsAt(cc(X,Y,P,Q),T), happens(E,T),
  subsumes(PP,P), initiates(E,PP,T).

terminates(E,c(X,Y,P),T) :- holdsAt(c(X,Y,P),T), happens(E,T),
  subsumes(PP,P), initiates(E,PP,T).
terminates(E,cc(X,Y,P,Q), T) :- holdsAt(cc(X,Y,P,Q),T),
  happens(E,T), subsumes(QP,Q), initiates(E,QP,T).
terminates(E,cc(X,Y,P,Q), T) :- holdsAt(cc(X,Y,P,Q),T),
  happens(E,T), subsumes(PP,P), initiates(E,PP,T).
```

Old Axioms

```
initiates(E,P,T) :- happens(E,T), causes(E,P).
initiates(E,c(X,Y,Q),T) :- holdsAt(cc(X,Y,P,Q),T), happens(E,T),
  initiates(E,P,T).

terminates(E,c(X,Y,P),T) :- holdsAt(c(X,Y,P),T), happens(E,T),
  initiates(E,P,T).
terminates(E,cc(X,Y,P,Q), T) :- holdsAt(cc(X,Y,P,Q),T),
  happens(E,T), initiates(E,Q,T).
terminates(E,cc(X,Y,P,Q), T) :- holdsAt(cc(X,Y,P,Q),T),
  happens(E,T), initiates(E,P,T).
```

A Protocol for Resource Sharing in Norm-Governed Ad Hoc Networks

Alexander Artikis[1], Lloyd Kamara[2], Jeremy Pitt[2], and Marek Sergot[1]

[1] Department of Computing, SW7 2BZ,
[2] Electrical & Electronic Engineering Department, SW7 2BT,
Imperial College, London
a.artikis@acm.org, {l.kamara, j.pitt, m.sergot}@imperial.ac.uk

Abstract. Ad hoc networks may be viewed as computational systems whose members may fail to, or choose not to, comply with the rules governing their behaviour. We are investigating to what extent ad hoc networks can usefully be described in terms of permissions, obligations and other more complex normative relations, based on our previous work on specifying and modelling open agent societies. We now propose to employ our existing framework for the management of ad hoc networks, exploiting the similarities between open agent societies and ad hoc networks viewed at the application level. We also discuss the prospects of modelling ad hoc networks at the physical level in similar terms. We demonstrate the framework by constructing an executable specification, in the event calculus, of a common type of protocol used to regulate the control of access to shared resources in ad hoc networks.

1 Introduction

Ad Hoc Network (*AHN*) is a term used to describe a transient association of network nodes which inter-operate largely independently of any fixed support infrastructure [17]. An AHN is typically based on wireless technology and may be short-lived, supporting spontaneous rather than long-term interoperation [18]. Such a network may be formed, for example, by the devices of the participants in a workshop or project meeting (for sharing and co-authoring documents); by consumers entering and leaving an 802.11 wireless hot spot covering a shopping mall (for buying/selling goods C2C-style by matching potential buyers and sellers); or by emergency or disaster relief workers, where the usual static support infrastructure is unavailable.

An AHN may be visualised as a continuously changing graph [17]: connection and disconnection may be controlled by the physical proximity of the nodes or, it may be controlled by the nodes' continued willingness to cooperate for the formation, and maintenance, of a cohesive (but potentially transient) community. An issue that typically needs to be addressed when managing and maintaining an AHN is that of resource sharing: the participating nodes compete over a set of limited resources such as bandwidth and power (for example, battery

J. Leite et al. (Eds.): DALT 2004, LNAI 3476, pp. 221–238, 2005.

consumption). Often AHNs are specifically set up for sharing a resource such as broadband Internet access, processor cycles, file storage, or a document in the project meeting example mentioned above. In all cases the limited resources are controlled by the participants of a network.

Due to its inherently transient nature, an AHN needs to be 'adaptable', that is, it should be able to deal with 'exceptions'. The aim of our present research is to investigate to what extent adaptability can be enhanced by viewing AHNs as instances of *norm-governed* systems. We want to examine this question both at the *application level* and at the *physical level*. At the application level, an AHN can be viewed as an *open agent society* [1–3], that is, a computational (agent) community exhibiting the following characteristics:

- Members are programmed by different parties — moreover, there is no direct access to a member's internal state and so we can only make inferences about that state.
- Members do not necessarily share a notion of global utility — they may fail to, or even choose not to, conform to the community specifications in order to achieve their individual goals.
- The members' behaviour and interactions cannot be predicted in advance.

In previous work [1–3] we presented a theoretical framework for specifying open agent societies in terms of concepts stemming from the study of legal and social systems. The behaviour of the members of an open agent society is regulated by rules expressing their *permissions, obligations* and other more complex normative relations that may exist between them [10]. Software tools enable formal specifications of these rules to be executed and analysed in various ways. We propose to use this framework for the management of AHNs. In this paper we focus on the issue of resource sharing and employ the theoretical framework to specify a common family of protocols for controlling access to shared resources.

We believe that there may also be value in viewing an AHN as an instance of a norm-governed system at the *physical level*. This is because it is possible, even likely, that system components will fail to behave as they ought to behave — not from wilfulness or to seek advantage over others but simply because of the inherently transient nature of the AHN. It is therefore meaningful to speak of system components failing to comply with their obligations, of permitted/forbidden actions, and even of 'sanctions' (though clearly not of 'punishments'). A secondary aim of our research is to investigate to what extent the methods we have previously used to model open agent societies can be applied to this new setting.

The remainder of this paper is divided into three main parts. First, we review a line of research on resource sharing, namely *floor control protocols*. Second, we present a specification of a protocol for resource sharing in norm-governed AHNs. The presentation of the protocol specification includes a description of the relevant parts of the theoretical framework mentioned above. Third, we summarise the presented work and outline directions for current and future research.

2   Floor Control Protocols

In the fields of Collaborative Multimedia Computing (CMC) and Computer-Supported Co-operative Work (CSCW), the term *floor control* denotes a service guaranteeing that at any given moment only a designated set of users (subjects) may simultaneously work with or on the same objects (shared resources), thus creating a temporary exclusivity for access on such resources [5].

> "[. . . F]loor control lets users attain exclusive control over a shared resource by being granted the floor, extending the traditional notion as the "right to speak" [20] to the multimodality of data formats in networked multimedia systems. We understand floor control as a technology to implement group coordination, but use both terms synonymously in this paper." [7, p.18]

Sharing a resource may be achieved by executing *Floor Control Protocols* (*FCPs*) and *Session Control Protocols* (*SCPs*). FCPs prescribe ways for mutually exclusive access to shared resources amongst the subjects. A number of properties of such protocols have been identified [5,6]: *safety* (each floor request is eventually serviced), *fairness* (no subject 'starves', each floor request is serviced based on a common metric), and so on. SCPs prescribe ways for, amongst other things, joining a FCP (or session), withdrawing from a session, inviting to join a session, determining the resources to be shared, and determining the *policy* of a session, that is, the ways in which a floor may be requested or granted. Example policies are *chair-designated* (an elected participant is the arbiter over the usage of specific floors), *election* (participants vote on the next subject holding the floor), and *lottery scheduling* (floor assignment operates on a probabilistic basis).

It is our assumption that the abstractions of floor control and session control are applicable to the issue of resource sharing in AHNs. Clarifying what 'being granted the floor' or 'holding the floor' implies is one of the aims of the formalisation presented in later sections. The concept of session control (or *conference management* [23]) is applicable to the formation of an AHN, and to the management and maintenance of such a network in general. In this paper, however, we will focus on the issue of floor control, assuming that an AHN and a FCP within that network have already been established. The issue of session control will be addressed elsewhere.

We will present a specification of a simple *chaired Floor Control Protocol* (*cFCP*). (We apologise for the unfortunate mixed metaphor.) The chair-designated policy was chosen simply to provide a concrete example of a FCP — we could have equally chosen an election, or some other policy type. Moreover, we have intentionally omitted to address several of the design issues set out in the literature on FCPs (for instance, that a protocol should provide mutually exclusive resource access in 'real-time' [5,6]). Our point here is to illustrate that, in settings in which subjects (or other system members) may fail to behave as they ought to behave, any protocol specification for resource sharing (following a chair-designated, lottery scheduling or any other policy type, stemming from the CSCW, CMC, or any other research field) needs to express what a member

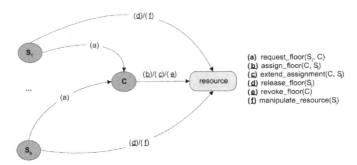

Fig. 1. A two-role chaired floor control protocol

is permitted to do, obliged to do, and, possibly, additional normative relations that may exist between them.

Two factors that characterise a FCP are [7]: (i) the mechanism and node topology that determine the ways in which floor information (for instance, floor requests, the status of the floor, and so on) is communicated amongst the participants, and (ii) the policy followed in the protocol. Factor (i) is the major design decision for a group coordination protocol and determines, amongst other things, which policies are established in a protocol. We adopt a high-level view of FCPs: we specify the rules prescribing the ways in which a floor is requested and granted without making any explicit assumptions about the node topology and distribution of floor information in general.

3   A Protocol for Resource Sharing in Ad Hoc Networks

In this section we present a chaired Floor Control Protocol (cFCP). For simplicity, we present a cFCP specification concerning a single resource, a single floor (associated with the resource), and a single chair, that is, a distinguished participant determining which other participant is actually given the floor. In this setting, the allocation of several resources in an AHN may be performed by several parallel executions of FCPs (following a chair-designated, election or any other policy type). Our cFCP specification includes the following roles:

- *Subject*, the role of designated participants performing the following actions: *request_floor* (requesting the floor from the chair), *release_floor* (releasing the floor), and *manipulate_resource* (physically manipulating the resource). Sometimes we will refer to the subject holding the floor as a 'holder'.
- *Chair*, the controller for the floor, that is, the participant performing the following actions: *assign_floor* (assigning the floor for a particular time period to a subject), *extend_assignment* (extending the time for which the floor may be held), and *revoke_floor* (revoking the floor from the holder).

The floor can be in one of the following states: (i) *granted*, denoting that a subject has been given exclusive access to the resource by the chair, or (ii) *free*, denoting that no subject currently holds the floor. In both cases, the floor may or may not be requested by a subject (for example, the floor may be granted to subject S' and requested by subject S'' at the same time). We make the following comments concerning our cFCP specification. First, there are no time-outs (deadlines) prescribing when a request should be issued, a floor should be assigned, or an assignment should be extended. Second, there is no termination condition signalling the end of the protocol. There is no particular difficulty in including timeouts and termination conditions in the formalisation but it lengthens the presentation and is omitted here for simplicity. See [2, 3] for example formalisations of deadlines and termination conditions in the context of protocol specifications.

Figure 1 provides an informal presentation of the possible interactions between the entities of a cFCP, that is, the subjects $S_1, \ldots, S_n$, the chair C, and the resource. The actions of our protocol specification may be classified into two categories: (i) communicative actions and, (ii) physical actions. The first category includes the *request_floor* action whereas the second category includes the *assign_floor*, *extend_assignment*, *release_floor*, *revoke_floor*, and *manipulate_resource* actions[1]). Consider an example in which the shared resource is hard disk space. In this setting, the action of assigning the floor could be realised as creating an account on the file server so that the holder can manipulate the resource, that is, store files.

4   An Event Calculus Specification

In previous work we employed three action languages with direct routes to implementation to express protocol specifications:

1. The Event Calculus (EC) [13], a formal, intuitive and well-studied action language (see [2] for an EC specification of a contract-net protocol).
2. The $C+$ language [9], a formalism with explicit transition systems semantics (see [3] for a $C+$ specification of a dispute resolution protocol).
3. The $(C+)^{++}$ language [25], an extended form of $C+$ specifically designed for modelling the normative and institutional aspects of multi-agent systems (see [25] for a $(C+)^{++}$ specification of a resource sharing protocol).

Each formalism has its advantages and disadvantages (see [1, Section 6.12] for a discussion about the utility of $C+$, $(C+)^{++}$ and EC on protocol specification). In this paper we will use EC because an EC implementation (in terms of logic programming) has proved to be more efficient than a $C+$ or $(C+)^{++}$ implementation (in terms of the *Causal Calculator*, a software tool supporting computational tasks regarding the $C+$ language) for the provision of 'run-time services' (a description of such services is presented in Section 6).

---

[1] The following convention is adopted in the figures of this paper: physical actions are represented by an underlined letter (for example, (b)) whereas communicative actions are represented with no underlining (for example, (a)).

Table 1. Main Predicates of the Event Calculus

Predicate	Meaning
happens(Act, T)	Action Act occurs at time T
initially($F = V$)	The value of fluent F is V at time 0
holdsAt($F = V$, T)	The value of fluent F is V at time T
initiates(Act, $F = V$, T)	The occurrence of action Act at time T initiates a period of time for which the value of fluent F is V
terminates(Act, $F = V$, T)	The occurrence of action Act at time T terminates a period of time for which the value of fluent F is V

First, we briefly present EC. Second, we specify the *social constraints* (or protocol rules) governing the behaviour of the cFCP participants. We maintain the standard and long established distinction between *physical capability, institutionalised power* and *permission* (see, for instance, [11, 15] for illustrations of this distinction). Accordingly, our specification of social constraints expresses: (i) the externally observable physical capabilities, (ii) institutional powers, and (iii) permissions and obligations of the cFCP participants; in addition, it expresses (iv) the *sanctions* and *enforcement policies* that deal with the performance of forbidden actions and non-compliance with obligations.

4.1   The Event Calculus

The Event Calculus (EC), introduced by Kowalski and Sergot [13], is a formalism for representing and reasoning about actions or events and their effects in a logic programming framework. In this section we briefly describe the version of the EC that we employ. EC is based on a many-sorted first-order predicate calculus. For the version used here, the underlying time model is linear and it may include real numbers or integers. Where F is a *fluent* (a property that is allowed to have different values at different points in time), the term $F = V$ denotes that fluent F has value V. Boolean fluents are a special case in which the possible values are true and false. Informally, $F = V$ holds at a particular time-point if $F = V$ has been *initiated* by an action at some earlier time-point, and not *terminated* by another action in the meantime.

An *action description* in EC includes axioms that define, amongst other things, the action occurrences (with the use of happens predicates), the effects of actions (with the use of initiates and terminates predicates), and the values of the fluents (with the use of initially and holdsAt predicates). Table 1 summarises the main EC predicates. Variables (starting with an upper-case letter) are assumed to be universally quantified unless otherwise indicated. Predicates, function symbols and constants start with a lower-case letter. The domain-independent definitions of the EC predicates are presented in the Appendix. In the following sections we present an EC action description expressing our cFCP specification.

4.2   Physical Capability

Table 2 displays a number of the fluents of the EC action description expressing the cFCP specification. The utility of these fluents will be explained during the presentation of the protocol specification. This section presents the specification of the externally observable physical capabilities of the cFCP participants. The second column of Table 3 presents the conditions that, when satisfied, enable the participants to perform the actions displayed in the first column of this table. We will refer to these conditions as expressing 'physical capability' though the term 'practical possibility' might have been employed instead. (In Table 3, C represents an agent occupying the role of the chair and S represents an agent occupying the role of the subject.)

Table 2. Main Fluents of the cFCP Specification

Fluent	Domain	Textual Description
$requested(S, T)$	boolean	subject S requested the floor at time T
$status$	$\{free, granted(S, T)\}$	the status of the floor: $status = free$ denotes that the floor is free whereas $status = granted(S, T)$ denotes that the floor is granted to subject S until time T
$best\_candidate$	agent identifiers	the best candidate for the floor
$can(Ag, Act)$	boolean	agent Ag is capable of performing Act
$pow(Ag, Act)$	boolean	agent Ag is empowered to perform Act
$per(Ag, Act)$	boolean	agent Ag is permitted to perform Act
$obl(Ag, Act)$	boolean	agent Ag is obliged to perform Act
$sanction(Ag)$	*	the sanctions of agent Ag

The chair is capable of assigning the floor to a subject if and only if the floor is free (see Table 3). The performance of such an action always changes the status of the floor as follows:

$$\begin{aligned} \mathsf{initiates}(assign\_floor(C, S), status = granted(S, T'), T) \leftarrow \\ role\_of(C, chair),\ role\_of(S, subject), \hspace{2cm} (1) \\ \mathsf{holdsAt}(status = free, T),\ (T' := T + 5) \hspace{1.5cm} \end{aligned}$$

After assigning the floor to a subject S at time T, the floor is considered granted until some future time (say $T+5$). The first two conditions of axiom (1) refer to the roles of the participants. We assume (in this version) that the participants of a cFCP do not change roles during the execution of a protocol, and so $role\_of$ is treated as an ordinary predicate and not as a time-varying fluent. Notice that the practical capability condition is included here as part of the initiates specification. There are other possible treatments of the practical capability conditions but we do not have space for discussion of alternative treatments here.

Table 3. Physical Capability and Institutional Power in the cFCP

Action	can	pow
$assign\_floor(C, S)$	$status = free$	−
$extend\_assignment(C, S)$	$status = granted(S, T)$	−
$revoke\_floor(C)$	$status = granted(S, T)$	−
$release\_floor(S)$	$status = granted(S, T)$	−
$manipulate\_resource(S)$	$status = granted(S, T)$	−
$request\_floor(S, C)$	$\top$	not $requested(S, T)$

Note also that the chair can assign the floor to a subject that has never requested it. In some systems, this type of behaviour may be considered 'undesirable' or 'wrong'. Section 4.4 presents how 'undesirable' behaviour in the cFCP is specified by means of the concept of *permitted* action.

If an assignment concerns a subject that has requested the floor, represented by the *requested* fluent (see Table 2), then this request is considered serviced, that is, the associated *requested* fluent no longer holds:

$$\begin{aligned}
\textsf{initiates}(assign\_floor(C, S), &requested(S, T') = \textsf{false}, T) \leftarrow \\
&role\_of(C, chair), \\
&\textsf{holdsAt}(status = free, T), \\
&\textsf{holdsAt}(requested(S, T') = \textsf{true}, T)
\end{aligned} \quad (2)$$

The chair can extend the assignment of the floor to a subject S if and only if S is holding the floor. Moreover, extending the assignment of the floor changes its status as follows:

$$\begin{aligned}
\textsf{initiates}(extend\_assignment(C, S), &status = granted(S, T''), T) \leftarrow \\
&role\_of(C, chair), \\
&\textsf{holdsAt}(status = granted(S, T'), T), \ (T'' := T' + 5)
\end{aligned} \quad (3)$$

In other words, if the floor was granted to S until time T', after the extension it will be granted until time $T' + 5$. Note that the chair is capable of extending the floor even if the holder has not requested such an extension.

A subject S can release the floor if and only if S is the holder (irrespective of whether or not the allocated time for the floor has ended). Releasing the floor changes its status as follows:

$$\begin{aligned}
\textsf{initiates}(release\_floor(S), &status = free, T) \leftarrow \\
&\textsf{holdsAt}(status = granted(S, T'), T)
\end{aligned} \quad (4)$$

In a similar manner we express when an agent is capable of performing the remaining physical actions of the protocol as well as the effects of these actions.

In this example cFCP there is only one communicative action, that of requesting the floor. We have specified that a subject is always physically capable of communicating a request for the floor to the chair. For the specification of the effects of this action, it is important to distinguish between the act of ('successfully') issuing a request and the act by means of which that request is issued. Communicating a request for the floor, by means of sending a message of a particular form via a TCP/IP socket connection, for example, is not necessarily 'successful', in the sense that the request is eligible to honoured by the chair. It is only if the request is communicated by an agent with the *institutional power* to make the request that it will be 'successful'. An account of institutional power is presented in the following section.

4.3   Institutional Power

The term institutional (or 'institutionalised') power refers to the characteristic feature of organisations/institutions — legal, formal, or informal — whereby designated agents, often when acting in specific roles, are empowered, by the institution, to create or modify facts of special significance in that institution — *institutional facts* — usually by performing a specified kind of act. Searle [24], for example, has distinguished between *brute facts* and institutional facts. Being in physical possession of an object is an example of a brute fact (it can be observed); being the owner of that object is an institutional fact.

According to the account given by Jones and Sergot [11], institutional power can be seen as a special case of a more general phenomenon whereby an action, or a state of affairs, A — because of the rules and conventions of an institution — counts, in that institution, as an action or state of affairs B (such as when sending a letter with a particular form of words counts as making an offer, or banging the table with a wooden mallet counts as declaring a meeting closed).

In some circumstances it is unnecessary to isolate and name all instances of the acts by means of which agents exercise their institutional powers. It is convenient to say, for example, that 'the subject S requested the floor from the chair C' and let the context disambiguate whether we mean by this that S performed an action, such as sending a message of a particular form via a TCP/IP socket connection, by means of which the request for the floor is signalled, or whether S actually issued a request, in the sense that this request is eligible to be honoured by C. We disambiguate in these circumstances by attaching the label 'valid' to act descriptions. We say that an action is *valid* at a point in time if and only if the agent that performed that action had the *institutional power* (or just 'power' or 'was empowered') to perform it at that point in time. So, when we say that 'the subject S requested the floor from the chair C' we mean, by convention, merely that S signalled its intention to request the floor; this act did not necessarily constitute the request eligible to be honoured. In order to say that a request is eligible to be honoured, we say that the action 'subject S requested the floor' was *valid*: not only did S signal its intention to request the floor, but also S had the institutional power to make the request. Similarly, *invalid* is used to indicate lack of institutional power: when we say that the action 'subject S

requested the floor' is invalid we mean that S signalled its intention to request it but did not have the institutional power to do so at that time (and so the attempt to make the request eligible to be serviced was not successful).

We express the institutional power to request the floor as follows:

$$
\begin{aligned}
\mathsf{holdsAt}(pow(S, request\_floor(S, C)) = \mathsf{true}, T) \leftarrow \\
role\_of(C, chair),\ role\_of(S, subject), \\
\mathsf{not}\ \mathsf{holdsAt}(requested(S, T') = \mathsf{true}, T)
\end{aligned}
\tag{5}
$$

Axiom (5) expresses that a subject S is empowered to request the floor from the chair C if S has no pending valid requests. not represents *negation by failure* [4].

The existence of a valid request is recorded with the use of the *requested* fluent:

$$
\begin{aligned}
\mathsf{initiates}(request\_floor(S, C), requested(S, T) = \mathsf{true}, T) \leftarrow \\
\mathsf{holdsAt}(pow(S, request\_floor(S, C)) = \mathsf{true}, T)
\end{aligned}
\tag{6}
$$

There is no corresponding fluent for invalid requests.

4.4   Permission and Obligation

Now we specify which of the cFCP acts are permitted or obligatory. Behaviour which does not comply with the specification is regarded as 'undesirable'. Such behaviour is not necessarily wilful. When an AHN member performs a non-permitted act or fails to perform an obligatory act, it could be deliberate, as when an agent (at the application level) seeks to gain an unfair advantage, but it could also be unintentional, and it could even be unavoidable, due to network conditions outside that member's control.

The definitions of permitted actions are application-specific. It is worth noting that there is no fixed relationship between powers and permissions. In some computational societies an agent is permitted to perform an action if that agent is empowered to perform that action. In general, however, an agent can be empowered to perform an action without being permitted to perform it (perhaps temporarily). The specification of obligations is also application-specific. It is important, however, to maintain the consistency of the specification of permissions and obligations: an agent should not be forbidden and obliged to perform the same action at the same time.

Table 4 displays the conditions that, when satisfied, oblige or simply permit the cFCP participants to perform an action. (In this table, *CurrentTime* represents the time that the presented conditions are evaluated.) There are other possible specifications of permitted and obligatory actions. The presented ones were chosen simply to provide a concrete illustration of cFCP.

The chair is permitted and obliged to assign the floor to a subject S provided that: (i) the floor is free, and (ii) S is the best candidate for the floor (see Table 4). The procedure calculating the best candidate for the floor at each point in time is application-specific. For the sake of this example, the best candidate is defined to be the one with the earliest (valid) request. In more realistic scenarios

Table 4. Permission and Obligation in the cFCP

Action	per	obl
$assign\_floor(C, S)$	$status = free,$ $best\_candidate = S$	$status = free,$ $best\_candidate = S$
$extend\_assignment(C, S)$	$status = granted(S, T),$ $best\_candidate = S$	$status = granted(S, T),$ $best\_candidate = S$
$revoke\_floor(C)$	$status = granted(S, T),$ $Current Time \geq T,$ $best\_candidate \neq S$	$status = granted(S, T),$ $Current Time \geq T,$ $best\_candidate = S',$ $S \neq S'$
$release\_floor(S)$	$\top$	$status = granted(S, T),$ $Current Time \geq T,$ $best\_candidate = S',$ $S \neq S'$
$manipulate\_resource(S)$	$status = granted(S, T),$ $Current Time < T$	$\bot$
$request\_floor(S, C)$	$\top$	$\bot$

the calculation of the best candidate would consider additional factors such as how urgent the request is, how many times the requesting subject had the floor in the past, and so on[2]. There is no difficulty in expressing such definitions in the formalism employed here. Indeed, the availability of the full power of logic programming is one of the main attractions of employing EC as the temporal formalism.

According to the above specification of permission, when the floor is free the chair is only permitted to assign it to the best candidate (if any). At the same time, however, the chair is capable of assigning it to any subject participating in the cFCP (see Table 3).

The chair is permitted to revoke the floor if: (i) the floor is currently granted to a subject, (ii) the allocated time for the floor has ended, and (iii) the subject holding the floor is currently not the best candidate for the floor. Note that the chair can revoke the floor even if the allocated time for the floor has not ended or if the subject holding the floor is currently the best candidate for it.

The chair is permitted to revoke the floor (after the allocated time for the holder has ended) even if there is no subject requesting the floor. If there is a subject requesting the floor, however, and that subject is the best candidate, then the chair is not only permitted, but obliged to revoke the floor:

$$\begin{aligned} \mathsf{holdsAt}(obl(C, revoke\_floor(C)) &= \mathsf{true}, T) \leftarrow \\ &role\_of(C, chair), \\ &\mathsf{holdsAt}(status = granted(S, T'), T), \ (T \geq T'), \\ &\mathsf{holdsAt}(best\_candidate = S', T), \ (S \neq S') \end{aligned} \quad (7)$$

---

[2] The best candidate is picked from the set of subjects having pending (valid) requests, not from the set of all subjects participating in a cFCP.

We have chosen to specify that a subject is always permitted to release the floor, although releasing the floor is not always physically possible. Alternatively, we could have specified that the permission to release the floor coincides with the physical capability to do so. In this example, we might guess that the alternatives are equivalent, in the sense that they produce protocols that always have the same outcome. This is a hypothesis that can be tested. One aim of the work presented here is to provide computational tools to support the automated testing of such hypotheses.

A subject S is permitted to manipulate the resource if S is holding the floor and the allocated time for it has not ended. Permitted or not, S is never obliged to manipulate the resource. Similarly, a subject is never obliged to request the floor — it is always permitted, however, to do so.

4.5   Sanction

Sanctions and enforcement policies are a means of dealing with 'undesirable' behaviour. In the cFCP, we want to reduce or eliminate the following types of 'undesirable' behaviour:

– the chair extending the assignment of, and revoking the floor when being forbidden to do so, and
– non-compliance with the obligation to assign, revoke and release the floor.

One possible enforcement strategy is to try to devise additional controls (physical or institutional) that will force agents to comply with their obligations or prevent them from performing forbidden actions. When competing for hard disk space, for example, a forbidden revocation of the floor may be physically blocked, in the sense that it is not possible to delete the holder's account on the file server. The general strategy of designing mechanisms to force compliance and eliminate non-permitted behaviour is what Jones and Sergot [10] referred to as *regimentation*. Regimentation devices have often been employed in order to eliminate 'undesirable' behaviour in computational systems. *Interagents* [21], for example, enforce the rules of the FishMarket auction house to the buyer and seller agents. *Sentinels* [12] monitor and, when necessary, modify some aspects of the agent interactions in order to provide 'exception handling' services. *Controllers* [16] enforce the 'law-governed interaction' coordination mechanism in open agent societies. (Lomuscio and Sergot [14] show how it is possible to determine formally whether the introduction of a controller does have the intended effect of eliminating unwanted system behaviour.) It has been argued [10], however, that regimentation is rarely desirable (it results in a rigid system that may discourage agents from entering it [19]), and not always practical. The practicality of regimentation devices is even more questionable when considering AHNs, due to the transient nature of these networks. In any case, violations may still occur even when regimenting a computational system (consider, for instance, a faulty regimentation device). For all of these reasons, we have to allow for sanctioning and not rely exclusively on regimentation mechanisms.

For the present example, we employ an additive fluent, *sanction(Ag)*, to express each participant's sanctions (see Table 2): initially, the value of this fluent is equal to zero and it is incremented every time a participant exhibits the type of 'undesirable' behaviour mentioned above. Consider the following example: the chair is sanctioned if it assigns the floor to a subject S while it is obliged to assign the floor to another subject S':

$$\begin{aligned}
\mathsf{initiates}(assign\_floor(C,S), sanction(C) = V', T) \leftarrow \\
role\_of(S, subject), \\
\mathsf{holdsAt}(obl(C, assign\_floor(C, S')) = \mathsf{true}, T), \ (S \neq S'), \\
\mathsf{holdsAt}(sanction(C) = V, T), \ (V' := V + 1)
\end{aligned} \tag{8}$$

According to axiom (8), every time the chair C fails to comply with its obligation to assign the floor the value of the associated $sanction(C)$ fluent is incremented by one. Similarly, we update the value of $sanction(Ag)$ when the remaining participants exhibit 'undesirable' behaviour. We would ordinarily also include a means for decreasing the value of a $sanction(Ag)$ fluent, for instance if Ag has not performed forbidden ('undesirable') actions for a specified period of time. We have omitted the details for simplicity of the presentation.

One way of discouraging the performance of forbidden actions and non-compliance with obligations (at the application level) is by penalising this type of behaviour. We specify the following penalties for the aforementioned sanctions (the presented specification is but one of the possible approaches, chosen here merely to provide a concrete illustration). Consider the following example:

$$\begin{aligned}
\mathsf{holdsAt}(pow(S, request\_floor(S,C)) = \mathsf{true}, T) \leftarrow \\
role\_of(C, chair), \ role\_of(S, subject), \\
\mathsf{not} \ \mathsf{holdsAt}(requested(S, T') = \mathsf{true}, T), \\
\mathsf{holdsAt}(sanction(S) = V, T), \ (V < 5)
\end{aligned} \tag{5'}$$

The above formalisation is a modification of the axiom expressing the power to request the floor (that is, axiom (5)), in the sense that it considers the sanctions associated with a subject S: when the value of $sanction(S)$ is greater or equal to five (say) then S is no longer empowered to request the floor. One may argue that once that happens, S is no longer an 'effective' participant of the protocol, in the sense that S may no longer 'successfully' request the floor. It may be the case, however, that the chair does not abide by the protocol rules and assigns (and even extends the assignment of) the floor to S, even though S has not 'successfully' requested the floor.

We anticipate applications in which agents participate in a Session Control Protocol (SCP) before taking part in a cFCP in order to acquire a set of roles that they will occupy while being part of that cFCP. Given the value of $sanction(C)$, a chair C may be:

- *suspended*, that is, C is temporarily disqualified from acting as a chair in future cFCPs. More precisely, C may not 'effectively' participate, for a specified period, in a SCP and, therefore, may not acquire the role of the chair.
- *banned*, that is, C is permanently disqualified from acting as a chair.

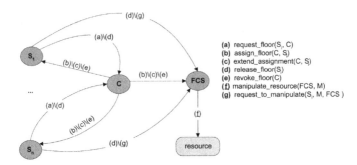

Fig. 2. A three-role chaired floor control protocol

Being deprived of the role of the chair means, in this example, being deprived of the permission and, more importantly, the physical capability to assign, extend the assignment of, and revoke the floor. Alternatively, a sanctioned chair may be suspended or banned from acting as a subject in future FCPs (not necessarily chaired-designated ones), thus not being able to compete for, and access other shared resources in an AHN. The axiomatisation of the penalties associated with a sanctioned chair and a detailed discussion about SCPs in general will be presented elsewhere (see, however, [2, Section 3.2], [1, Section 4.5]) for a brief presentation of role-assignment in open agent societies).

At the physical level, where the members of the AHN are network devices, the question of imposing penalties clearly does not arise. There is a possible role for 'sanctions' nevertheless. In the present example, the value of the $sanction(Ag)$ fluent can be seen as a measure of Ag's 'reliability'. When the value of that fluent passes the specified threshold, floor assigning capabilities (say) may be suspended (and usually passed to another network member) not as a 'punishment' but as a way of adapting the network organisation. To what extent this view gives useful insights in practice is a topic of our current research.

5   A Few Notes on cFCP

In the FCP literature, a cFCP usually includes a third role, that of the *Floor Control Server* (*FCS*) [23]. Figure 2 provides an informal presentation of the possible interactions between the entities of a three-role cFCP. In such a setting, only the FCS can physically manipulate the resource. A subject holding the floor may only *request* from the FCS to manipulate the resource, describing the type of manipulation M — it is up to the FCS whether this request will be honoured or not. The chair still assigns, extends the assignment of, and revokes the floor. These actions, however, are now communicative ones, they are multi-casted to the holder and the FCS. Similarly, releasing the floor is now a communicative action, multi-casted to the chair and the FCS.

In order to illustrate the difference between the two-role and three-role cFCP, we outline the physical capabilities and institutional powers associated with a holder in each setting. In a two-role cFCP, a holder S has the physical capability to manipulate the shared resource. In a three-role cFCP, a holder S has the institutional power to request (from the FCS) to manipulate the shared resource. Unlike the two-role setting, in a three-role cFCP a holder may not succeed in manipulating the shared resource (for example, if the FCS disregards S's valid requests for manipulation of the resource, thus not complying with the protocol rules). Developing a complete specification of a three-role cFCP and comparing that with a specification of a two-role cFCP is another topic of our current research.

6   Discussion

We have presented a specification of a simple protocol for resource sharing in norm-governed AHNs. The specification of norm-governed computational systems has been the focus of several studies stemming from various research fields. A few examples are [8, 16, 21, 26–28]. Generally, work on the specification of norm-governed computational systems does not explicitly represent the institutional powers of the member agents. This is one key difference between our work and related approaches in the literature: our specification of social constraints explicitly represents the institutional powers of the agents, differentiates between institutional power, permission, physical capability and sanction, and employs formalisms with a declarative semantics and clear routes to implementation to express these concepts. (A detailed comparison between our work and related approaches in the literature can be found in [1, Section 4.10].)

The cFCP specification is expressed as a logic program and is therefore directly executable providing a clear route to (prototype) implementations. In previous work [2] we presented ways of executing an EC action description expressing a protocol specification. The cFCP executable specification may inform the agents' decision-making at run-time, for example, by allowing the powers, permissions, obligations, and sanctions current at any time to be determined.

At design-time, agents may wish to prove various properties of the protocol specification in order to decide whether or not they should participate in the protocol. Such properties may include, for instance, that a protocol specification is 'safe' and 'fair' (see Section 2), that no agent is forbidden and obliged to perform an action at the same time, non-compliance with the obligation to assign the floor always leads to a sanction, and so on. We have been experimenting [3,25] with the use of various techniques (for example, planning query computation and model checking) to prove properties of a protocol specification expressed in the $C+$ language. (Our theoretical framework for specifying norm-governed systems is not dependent on any particular action language or temporal structure.) We aim to investigate the feasibility and practicality of the application of some of the aforementioned techniques to an EC-formalised protocol specification in order to prove properties of such a specification.

Sadighi and Sergot [22] argue that when dealing with resource access control in heterogeneous computational systems in which 'undesirable' behaviour may arise (such as AHNs), the concepts of permission and prohibition are inadequate and need to be extended with that of *entitlement*: "entitlement to access a resource means not only that the access is permitted but also that the controller of the resource is obliged to grant the access when it is requested" [22]. We are currently working towards a treatment of this and related senses of 'entitlement' as they arise in the context of our cFCP specification (entitlement is concept that arises naturally in a three-role cFCP). More precisely, we are identifying the conditions in which a subject holding the floor can be said to be 'entitled' to it, and what the consequences are, and the circumstances in which it is meaningful to say that a subject not holding the floor is 'entitled'/not 'entitled' to it, and what the consequences are.

We believe that viewing AHNs as instances of norm-governed systems enhances their 'adaptability' both at the application level and at the physical level. By specifying the permissions, obligations, entitlements, and other more complex normative relations that may exist between the members of an AHN, one may precisely identify 'undesirable' behaviour, such as performance of forbidden actions and non-compliance with obligations, and, therefore, introduce enforcement strategies in order to adapt to such behaviour. To what extent this view gives useful insights in practice remains to be investigated.

Acknowledgements

This work has been supported by the EPSRC project "Theory and Technology of Norm-Governed Self-Organising Networks" (GR/S74911/01).

References

1. A. Artikis. *Executable Specification of Open Norm-Governed Computational Systems*. PhD thesis, University of London, November 2003. Retrieved April 8, 2004, from http://www.doc.ic.ac.uk/~aartikis/publications/artikis-phd.pdf, also available from the author.

2. A. Artikis, J. Pitt, and M. Sergot. Animated specifications of computational societies. In *Proceedings of Conference on Autonomous Agents and Multi-Agent Systems (AAMAS)*, pages 1053–1062. ACM Press, 2002.

3. A. Artikis, M. Sergot, and J. Pitt. An executable specification of an argumentation protocol. In *Proceedings of International Conference on Artificial Intelligence and Law (ICAIL)*, pages 1–11. ACM Press, 2003.

4. K. Clark. Negation as failure. In H. Gallaire and J. Minker, editors, *Logic and Databases*, pages 293–322. Plenum Press, 1978.

5. H.-P. Dommel and J. J. Garcia-Luna-Aceves. Design issues for floor control protocols. In *Proceedings of Symposium on Electronic Imaging: Multimedia and Networking*, volume 2417, pages 305–316. IS&T/SPIE, 1995.

6. H.-P. Dommel and J. J. Garcia-Luna-Aceves. Floor control for multimedia conferencing and collaboration. *Multimedia Systems*, 5(1):23–38, 1997.

7. H.-P. Dommel and J. J. Garcia-Luna-Aceves. Efficacy of floor control protocols in distributed multimedia collaboration. *Cluster Computing Journal, Special issue on Multimedia Collaborative Environments*, 2(1):17–33, 1999.

8. M. Esteva, J. Rodriguez-Aguilar, C. Sierra, P. Garcia, and J. Arcos. On the formal specifications of electronic institutions. In F. Dignum and C. Sierra, editors, *Agent Mediated Electronic Commerce*, LNAI 1991, pages 126–147. Springer, 2001.

9. E. Giunchiglia, J. Lee, V. Lifschitz, N. McCain, and H. Turner. Nonmonotonic causal theories. *Artificial Intelligence*, 153(1–2):49–104, 2004.

10. A. Jones and M. Sergot. On the characterisation of law and computer systems: the normative systems perspective. In *Deontic Logic in Computer Science: Normative System Specification*, pages 275–307. J. Wiley and Sons, 1993.

11. A. Jones and M. Sergot. A formal characterisation of institutionalised power. *Journal of the IGPL*, 4(3):429–445, 1996.

12. M. Klein, J. Rodriguez-Aguilar, and C. Dellarocas. Using domain-independent exception handling services to enable robust open multi-agent systems: the case of agent death. *Journal of Autonomous Agents and Munti-Agent Systems*, 7(1–2):179–189, 2003.

13. R. Kowalski and M. Sergot. A logic-based calculus of events. *New Generation Computing*, 4(1):67–96, 1986.

14. A. Lomuscio and M. Sergot. A formulation of violation, error recovery, and enforcement in the bit transmission problem. *Journal of Applied Logic*, 2:93–116, 2004.

15. D. Makinson. On the formal representation of rights relations. *Journal of Philosophical Logic*, 15:403–425, 1986.

16. N. Minsky and V. Ungureanu. Law-governed interaction: a coordination and control mechanism for heterogeneous distributed systems. *ACM Transactions on Software Engineering and Methodology (TOSEM)*, 9(3):273–305, 2000.

17. A. Murphy, G.-C. Roman, and G. Varghese. An exercise in formal reasoning about mobile communications. In *Proceedings of Workshop on Software Specification and Design*, pages 25–33. IEEE Computer Society, 1998.

18. C. Perkins. *Ad Hoc Networking*, chapter 1. Addison Wesley Professional, 2001.

19. H. Prakken. Formalising Robert's rules of order. Technical Report 12, GMD – German National Research Center for Information Technology, 1998.

20. H. Robert. *Robert's Rules of Order: The Standard Guide to Parliamentary Procedure*. Bantam Books, 1986.

21. J. Rodriguez-Aguilar, F. Martin, P. Noriega, P. Garcia, and C. Sierra. Towards a test-bed for trading agents in electronic auction markets. *AI Communications*, 11(1):5–19, 1998.

22. B. Sadighi and M. Sergot. Contractual access control. In *Proceedings of Workshop on Security Protocols*, 2002.

23. H. Schulzrinne. Requirements for floor control protocol. Internet Engineering Task Force, January 2004. Retrieved April 8, 2004, from `http://www.ietf.org/internet-drafts/draft-ietf-xcon-floor-control-req-00.txt`.

24. J. Searle. What is a speech act? In A. Martinich, editor, *Philosophy of Language*, pages 130–140. Oxford University Press, third edition, 1996.

25. M. Sergot. Modelling unreliable and untrustworthy agent behaviour. In *Proceedings of Workshop on Monitoring, Security, and Rescue Techniques in Multiagent Systems (MSRAS)*, Advances in Soft Computing. Springer-Verlag, 2004.

26. M. Singh. A social semantics for agent communication languages. In F. Dignum and M. Greaves, editors, *Issues in Agent Communication*, LNCS 1916, pages 31–45. Springer, 2000.

27. W. Vasconcelos. Norm verification and analysis of electronic institutions. In J. Leite, A. Omicini, P. Torroni, and P. Yolum, editors, *This Volume*. 2005.
28. M. Winikoff, W. Liu, and J. Harland. Enhancing commitment machines. In J. Leite, A. Omicini, P. Torroni, and P. Yolum, editors, *This Volume*. 2005.

Appendix: The Event Calculus

The domain-independent definition of the holdsAt predicate is as follows:

$$
\begin{aligned}
\text{holdsAt}(F = V, T) \leftarrow & \\
& \text{initially}(F = V), \\
& \text{not broken}(F = V, 0, T)
\end{aligned} \tag{9}
$$

$$
\begin{aligned}
\text{holdsAt}(F = V, T) \leftarrow & \\
& \text{happens}(Act, T'), \\
& T' < T, \\
& \text{initiates}(Act, F = V, T'), \\
& \text{not broken}(F = V, T', T)
\end{aligned} \tag{10}
$$

According to axiom (9) a fluent holds at time T if it held initially (time 0) and has not been 'broken' in the meantime, that is, terminated between times 0 and T. Axiom (10) specifies that a fluent holds at a time T if it was initiated at some earlier time T' and has not been terminated between T' and T. not represents negation by failure. The domain-independent predicate broken is defined as follows:

$$
\begin{aligned}
\text{broken}(F = V, T_1, T_3) \leftarrow & \\
& \text{happens}(Act, T_2), \\
& T_1 \leq T_2, \ T_2 < T_3, \\
& \text{terminates}(Act, F = V, T_2)
\end{aligned} \tag{11}
$$

$F = V$ is 'broken' between T_1 and T_3 if an event takes place in that interval that terminates $F = V$. A fluent cannot have more than one value at any time. The following domain-independent axiom captures this feature:

$$
\begin{aligned}
\text{terminates}(Act, F = V, T) \leftarrow & \\
& \text{initiates}(Act, F = V', T), \\
& V \neq V'
\end{aligned} \tag{12}
$$

Axiom (12) states that if an action Act initiates $F = V'$ then Act also terminates $F = V$, for all other possible values V of the fluent F. We do not insist that a fluent must have a value at every time-point. In this version of EC, therefore, there is a difference between initiating a Boolean fluent $F = \text{false}$ and terminating $F = \text{true}$: the first implies, but is not implied by, the second.

We make two further comments regarding this version of EC. First, the domain-independent EC axioms, that is, axioms (9)–(12), specify that a fluent does not hold at the time that was initiated but holds at the time it was terminated. Second, in addition to their domain-independent definitions, the holdsAt and terminates predicates may be defined in a domain-dependent manner (see, for example, axioms (5) and (7)). The happens, initially and initiates predicates are defined only in a domain-dependent manner.

Intensional Programming for Agent Communication*

Vasu S. Alagar, Joey Paquet, and Kaiyu Wan

Department of Computer Science,
Concordia University,
Montreal, Quebec H3G 1M8, Canada
{alagar,paquet,ky_wan}@cs.concordia.ca

Abstract. This article investigates the intensional programming paradigm for agent communication by introducing *context* as a first class object in the intensional programming language *Lucid*. For the language thus extended, a *calculus of contexts* and a *logic of contexts* are provided. The paper gives definitions, syntax, and operators for context, and introduces an operational semantics for evaluating expressions in extended Lucid. It is shown that the extended Lucid language, called Agent Intensional Programming Language(AIPL), has the generality and the expressiveness for being an Agent Communication Language(ACL).

Keywords: Intensional Programming, Context, Lucid, Agent Communication Language, KQML performatives, FIPA.

1   Introduction

The goal of this paper is the investigation of Intensional Programming for agent communication by introducing *contexts* as a first class object in the intensional programming language *Lucid* [12]. We provide a *calculus of contexts*, and introduce the *semantics of contexts as values* in the language to add the expressive power required to write non-trivial application programs. We demonstrate that Lucid, extended with contexts, has the generality and the expressibility for being an *Agent Communication Language* (ACL) [5]. We also briefly discuss an implementation framework for agent-based distributed programs written in the extended Lucid.

Intensional programming is a powerful and expressive paradigm based on Intensional Logic. The notion of context is *implicit* in intensional programs, i.e., contexts are not ubiquitous in programs, as in most other declarative or procedural languages. *Intension*, expressed as Lucid programs, can be interpreted to yield values (its *extension*) using demand-driven *eduction* [12]. In this way, intensional programming allows a cleaner and more declarative way of programming without loss of accuracy of interpreting the meaning of programs. Moreover, intensional programming deals with *infinite entities* which can be any ordinary data values such as a stream of numbers, a tree of strings, multidimensional streams, etc. These infinite entities are first class objects in

---

* This work is supported by grants from Natural Sciences and Engineering Research Council, Canada.

J. Leite et al. (Eds.): DALT 2004, LNAI 3476, pp. 239–255, 2005.

Lucid and functions can be applied to these infinite entities. Information and their computation can be abstracted and expressed declaratively, while providing the support for their interpretation in different streams. Such a setting seems quite suitable to hide the internal details of agents while providing them the choice to communicate their internal states, if necessary, for cooperative problem solving in a community of agents. Intensional programming is also suitable for applications which describe the behaviour of systems whose state is changing with time, space, and other physical phenomena or external interaction in multidimensional formats. Agent communication where intensions of agents have to be conveyed is clearly one such application.

The notion of *context* was introduced by McCarthy and later used by Guha [7] as a means of expressing assumptions made by natural language expressions in Artificial Intelligence (AI). Hence, a formula, which is an expression combining a sentence in AI with contexts, can express the exact meaning of the natural language expression. The major distinction between contexts in AI and in intensional programming is that in the former case they are *rich objects* that are not *completely expressible* and in the later case they are *implicitly* expressible, i.e., one can write Lucid expressions whose evaluation is context-dependent, but where the context is not explicitly manipulated. In extended Lucid we add the possibility to explicitly manipulate contexts, and introduce contexts as first class objects. That is, contexts can be declared, assigned values, used in expressions, and passed as function parameters. In this paper we give the syntax for declaring contexts, and a partial list of operators for combining contexts into complex expressions. A full discussion on the syntax and semantics of the extended language appears in [1]. The ACL that we introduce in this paper uses context expressions in messages exchanged between communicating agents. The structure of message is similar to the structure of performatives in KQML [4].

The paper is organized as follows: In Section 2 we review briefly the intensional programming paradigm. Section 3 discusses the basic operators of Lucid and illustrates the style of programming and evaluation in Lucid with simple examples. In Section 4 we discuss software agents and communication language for agents as standardized by FIPA [5]. We discuss the extended Lucid language for agent communication as well. The GIPSY [9], which provides a platform for implementation of extended Lucid is briefly discussed in Section 5.

2   Intensional Programming Paradigm

Intensional Logic came into being from research in natural language understanding. According to Carnap, the real meaning of a natural language expression whose truth-value depends on the context in which it is uttered is its *intension*. The *extension* of that expression is its actual truth-value in the different possible contexts of utterance [10], i.e., the different *possible worlds* into which this expression can be evaluated. Hence the statement *"It is snowing"* has meaning in itself (its intension), and its valuation in particular contexts (i.e., its extention) will depend on each particular context of evaluation, which includes the exact time and space when the statement is uttered.

Basically, intensional logics add dimensions to logical expressions, and non-intensional logics can be viewed as *constant* in all possible dimensions, i.e., their valuation does not vary according to their context of utterance. Intensional operators are defined to *navigate* in the context space. In order to navigate, some dimension *tags* (or indexes) are required to provide placeholders along dimensions. These dimension tags, along with the dimension names they belong to, are used to define the context for evaluating intensional expressions. For example, we can have an expression:

E: the average temperature for this month here is greater than $0°\,C$.

This expression is intensional because the truth value of this expression depends on the context in which it is evaluated. The two intensional operators in this expression are *this month* and *here*, which refer respectively to the time and space dimension. If we "freeze" the space context to the city of Montreal, we will get the yearly temperature at this space context, for an entire particular year (data is freely given by the authors). So along the time dimension throughout a particular year, we have the following valuation for the above expression, with T and F respectively standing for *true* and *false*, where the time dimension tags are the months of the year :

$$E' = \frac{\text{Ja Fe Mr Ap Ma Jn Jl Au Se Oc No De}}{\text{F \ F \ F \ F \ T \ T \ T \ T \ T \ F \ F \ F}}$$

So the intension is the expression E itself, and a part of its extension related to this particular year is depicted in the above table. According to Carnap, we are restricting the possible world of intensional evaluation to Montreal, and extending it over the months of a particular year. Furthermore, the intension of E can be evaluated to include the spatial dimension, in contrast with the preceding, where space was made constant to Montreal. Doing so, we extend the possible world of evaluation to the different cities in Canada, and still evaluate throughout the months of a particular year. The extension of the expression varies according to the different cities and months. Hence, we have the following valuation for the same expression :

		Ja	Fe	Mr	Ap	Ma	Jn	Jl	Au	Se	Oc	No	De
	Montreal	F	F	F	F	T	T	T	T	T	F	F	F
$E'' =$	Ottawa	F	F	F	T	T	T	T	T	T	F	F	F
	Toronto	F	F	T	T	T	T	T	T	T	T	F	F
	Vancouver	F	T	T	T	T	T	T	T	T	T	T	T

The Lucid intensional programming language retains two aspects from intensional logic: first, at the syntactic level, are context-switching operators, called *intensional operators* ; second, at the semantic level, is the use of *possible worlds semantics* [10].

3   Lucid

Lucid was invented as a tagged-token dataflow language by William Wadge and Edward Ashcroft [12]. In the original version of Lucid, the basic intensional operators were *first*, *next*, and *fby*. The following is the definition of three popular operators of the original Lucid [10]:

Definition 1. If $X = (x_0, x_1, \ldots, x_i, \ldots)$ and $Y = (y_0, y_1, \ldots, y_i, \ldots)$, then

$$(1)\ \underline{\text{first}}\ X \overset{\text{def}}{=} (x_0, x_0, \ldots, x_0, \ldots)$$
$$(2)\ \underline{\text{next}}\ X \overset{\text{def}}{=} (x_1, x_2, \ldots, x_{i+1}, \ldots)$$
$$(3)\ X\ \underline{\text{fby}}\ Y \overset{\text{def}}{=} (x_0, y_0, y_1, \ldots, y_{i-1}, \ldots)$$

Clearly, analogues can be made to list operations, where `first` corresponds to hd, next corresponds to `tl`, and fby corresponds to `cons`.

Lucid has eventually gone through several generalization steps and has evolved into a multidimensional intensional programming language which enables functions and dimensions as first-class values [10]. To support this, two basic intensional operators are added, which are used respectively for intensional navigation (@) and for querying the current context of evaluation of the program (#). Doing this, the Lucid language went apart from its dataflow nature to the more general intensional programming paradigm (often referred to as *multidimensional indexical paradigm*).

The following example 1 is to extract a value from the stream representing the natural numbers, beginning from the ubiquitous number 42. We arbitrarily pick the third value of the stream, which is assigned tag number two (indexes starting at 0). We also set the stream's variance in the *d* dimension.

Example 1.
```
N @.d 2
where
      dimension d;
      N = 42 fby.d (N+1);
end;
```

Intuitively, we can expect the program to return the value 44. To see how the program is evaluated, we rewrite it in terms of the basic @ and # intensional operators as shown in Example 2. The translation rules used for the rewriting of the program are presented in [10]. It is also interesting to note that Lucid forms a family of languages, and that we have identified a generic form (the one presented in this paper) into which all the other languages can be syntactically translated without loss of meaning.

Example 2.
```
N @.d 2
   where
        dimension d;
        N = if (#.d <= 0)  then 42
                 else (N+1) @.d (#.d-1);
   end;
```

The implementation technique of evaluation for Lucid programs is an interpreted mode called *eduction*. Eduction can be described as *tagged-token demand-driven dataflow*, in which data elements (tokens) are computed on demand following a dataflow network defined in Lucid. Data elements flow in the normal flow direction (from producer to consumer) and *demands* flow in the reverse order, both being *tagged* with their current context of evaluation.

Evaluation takes place by generating successive demands for the appropriate values of N in different contexts, until the final computation can be affected. The demand for N @.d 2 generates a demand for N @.d 1 which in turn generates a demand for N @.d 0. The definition of the program explicitly states that the value of N @.d 0 is 42. Once this is found, the successive addition operations are made on the demand results, as required by the equation N = 42 fby.d N+1, giving a final result of 44. The examples can be clearly understood from the syntax and semantics of Lucid, whose in-depth descriptions are shown in Section 4.4.

Lucid has been extended in several ways. Its variants have been used to specify 3D spreadsheets, real-time systems using Lustre (a variant of Lucid), database systems and GLU (Granular Lucid) run-time system which illustrates how the multidimensional structure of a problem expressed in Lucid can be harnessed to produce efficient parallel implementations of problems. Currently, we are in the process of implementing the GIPSY (General Intensional Programming System), which is an investigation platform (compiler, run-time environment, etc) for all members of the Lucid family of intensional programming languages [9].

4   Agent Communication in Intensional Programming Language

Software agents, according to Chen et al [2], are personalized, continuously running and semi-autonomous, driven by a set of beliefs, desires, and intentions (BDI). Agent technology is being standardized by FIPA [5] with the goal of seamlessly integrating their architectures and languages with various commercial application systems such as *network management*, *E-commerce*, and *mobile computing* [2]. In such applications agents should have capabilities to exchange complex objects, their intentions, shared plans, specific strategies, business and security policies. An Agent Communication Language (ACL) must be declarative and have a small number of primitives that are necessary to construct the structures required for achieving the above capabilities.

4.1   KQML and FIPA Languages

An ACL must support *interoperability* in an agent community while providing the freedom for an agent to hide or reveal its internal details to other agents. The two existing ACLs are *Knowledge Query and Manipulation Language* (KQML) [4] and the FIPA [5] communication language. The FIPA language includes the basic concepts of KQML, yet they have slightly different semantics. We summarize below the major points of contrasts between KQML and FIPA ACL, from the work of Labrou, Finin, and Peng [8].

KQML has a *predefined* set of *reserved performatives*. It is neither a minimal required set nor a closed set. That is, an agent may use only those primitives that it needs in a communication, and a community of agents may agree either to use the union of the sets of primitives required by each one of them or use some additional performatives with a consensus on the semantics and protocols for using them. In the latter case, it is not clear as to how the agents will construct the additional performatives and how a semantics can be dynamically worked out. As an example of the former case, a KQML message representing a query from agent joe about the price of a share of IBM stock might be encoded as "ask-one" performative in Example 3, and the STOCK-SERVER's reply is encoded as "tell" performative in Example 3 [8]:

Example 3.

```
(ask-one                          (tell
  :sender joe                       :sender STOCK-SERVER
  :content (PRICE IBM ?price)       :content (PRICE IBM 14)
  :receiver STOCK-SERVER            :receiver joe
  :reply-with IBM-STOCK             :in-reply-to IBM-STOCK
  :language LPROLOG                 :language LPROLOG
  :ontology NYSE-TICKS )            :ontology NYSE-TICKS )
```

KQML also provides a small number of performatives that the agents can use to define meta data. A semantics of KQML in a style similar to Hoare logic is given in [8].

The syntax of the FIPA ACL resembles KQML, however its semantics is formally given by a quantified multi-modal logic [13]. The communication primitives in FIPA ACL are called *communicative acts* (CA), yet they are the same as KQML primitives.

In order to achieve cooperation and interoperability, both KQML and FIPA ACL need to predefine a set of performatives, which is neither a minimal required set nor a closed one. This creates a big problem for maintaining and extending the agents to face the fast evolution of performatives. However, if we design the communication language from a higher level and in a more abstract way in which the performatives become *first class objects*, we will be able to create additional performatives as contextual expressions. In the AIPL, which we discuss next, we define contexts as first class objects and encapsulate performatives in them. We define operators on contexts, that can be used to create new contexts from existing contexts. Informally, when an agent A sends a communicative act CA x to an agent B, we view x as a collection (may be a sequence) of objects, where each object is bound to some description on its interpretation, evaluation criteria, temporal properties, constraints, and any other information that can be encoded in the language. We view this collection as a context.

4.2   Contexts in AIPL

The approach of using intensional programming for agent communication is to make a conservative extension of Lucid by introducing context as a first class object in Lucid [1]. In our approach, the name of a performative is considered as an expression, and the rest of the performative constitute a *context* which can be understood as a *communication context*; each field except the name in the message is a *micro context*. The communication context will be evaluated by the receiver, by evaluating the expression at the context obtained by combining the micro contexts. In some cases, the receiver may combine the communication context with its *local context* to generate a new context.

Definitions of Contexts in AIPL. In extended Lucid contexts are defined as *a subset of a finite union of relations*. Let $DIM = \{d_1, d_2, \ldots, d_n\}$ denote a finite set of dimension names. With each dimension d_i, a unique index set X_i and a domain D_i

are associated. A domain is a non-empty set of values. For instance, a domain may be $\mathbb{N}$, the set of natural numbers, or $\mathbb{R}$, the set of real numbers, or any arbitrary set of named objects. Let $IND = \{X_1, \ldots, X_r\}$, and $DOM = \{D_1, D_2, \ldots, D_m\}$ denote the set of index and domains. There exists functions $f_{dimtoindex} : DIM \rightarrow IND$, and $f_{indextodom} : IND \rightarrow DOM$, such that every $d_i \in DIM$ to an index set $f_{dimtoindex}(d_i)$ in IND, and every $X_i \in IND$ is mapped to a domain $f_{indextodom}(X_i)$ in DOM.

Definition 2. Consider the relations

$$P_i = \{d_i\} \times f_{dimtoindex}(d_i) \qquad 1 \le i \le n$$

A context C, given $(DIM, f_{dimtoindex})$, is a finite subset of $\bigcup_{i=1}^{n} P_i$. The *degree* of the context C is $| \ \Delta \ |$, where $\Delta \subset DIM$ includes the dimensions that appear in C.

A context is written using *enumeration* syntax. The set enumeration syntax of a context C is $C = \{(d, x) \mid d \in \Delta, x \in f_{dimtoindex}(d)\}$. We use the syntax $[d_{i_1} : x_{j_1}, \ldots, d_{i_k} : x_{j_k}]$ in Lucid to explicitly denote the aggregation of dimension, index pairs. Note that the d_{i_r}s need not be distinct, and

$$C \subseteq \bigcup_{i=1}^{n} P_i \subset DIM \times I, \quad I = \bigcup_{i=1}^{m} X_i$$

Consequently, every subset of $\bigcup_{i=1,n} P_i$ is a context, but not every subset of $DIM \times I$ is a context. However, if $X_1 = X_2 \ldots, = X_n$, every subset of $DIM \times I$ is a context. This follows from the fact that $f_{dimtoindex}(d_i) = X_i, i = 1, \ldots, n$ implies that

$$\bigcup_{i=1}^{n} P_i = \bigcup_{i=1}^{n} (\{d_i\} \times I) = (\bigcup_{i=1}^{n} \{d_i\}) \times I = DIM \times I$$

We say a context C is *simple* (s_context), if $(d_i, x_i), (d_j, x_j) \in C \Rightarrow d_i \ne d_j$. A simple context C of degree 1 is called a *micro* (m_context) context.

Example 4. Let $DIM = \{X, Y, Z, U\}$, $DOM = \{\mathbb{N}, \mathbb{R}\}$, $IND = \{\mathbb{N}, \{blue, red\}\}$, $f_{dimtoindex}(X) = f_{dimtoindex}(Y) = \mathbb{N}$, $f_{dimtoindex}(U) = f_{dimtoindex}(Z) = \{blue, red\}$. Compute $P_1 = X \times \mathbb{N}$, $P_2 = Y \times \mathbb{N}$, $P_3 = Z \times \{blue, red\}$, and $P_4 = U \times \{blue, red\}$.

1. $C_1 = [X : 1.5, Y : red]$ is not a context.
2. $C_2 = [Z : blue]$ is a m_context.
3. $C_3 = [X : 3, Y : 2]$ is a s_context of degree 2.
4. $C_4 = [X : 3, X : 4, Y : 3, Y : 2, U : blue]$ is a context of degree 3.

Several functions on contexts are predefined. The basic functions dim and tag are to extract the set of dimensions and their associate indexes from a set of contexts.

Definition 3. Let M denote a set of m_contexts. We define functions

$$dim_m : M \rightarrow DIM \qquad tag_m : M \rightarrow IND_m,$$

where $IND_m = \bigcup_{m \in M} tag_m(m)$, such that for $m = [x : y] \in M$, $dim_m(m) = x$, and $tag_m(m) = y \in f_{dimtoindex}(dim_m(m))$.

Definition 4. Let S denote a set of contexts. We use functions dim_m and tag_m to define the functions dim and tag on a set of contexts.

$$dim : S \to \mathbb{P}\,DIM \qquad tag : S \to \mathbb{P}\,IND,$$

where $IND = \bigcup_{s \in S} \bigcup_{m \in s} tag_m(m)$ such that for $s \in S$, $dim(s) = \{dim_m(m) \mid m \in s\}$, and $tag(s) = \{tag_m(m) \mid m \in s\}$.

Example 5. Consider the contexts introduced in Example 4. An application of dim and tag functions to these contexts produces the following results:

1. dim and tag are not defined for context C_1.
2. $dim_m(C_2) = Z$, $tag_m(C_2) = blue$.
3. $dim(C_3) = \{X, Y\}$, $tag(C_3) = \{3, 2\}$.
4. $dim(C_4) = \{X, Y, U\}$, $tag(C_4) = \{3, 4, 2, blue\}$.

In general, a set of contexts may include contexts of different degrees. We use the syntax $Box[\Delta \mid p]$ to introduce a finite set of contexts in which all contexts are defined over $\Delta \subseteq DIM$ and have the same degree $\mid \Delta \mid$.

Definition 5. Let $\Delta = \{d_{i_1}, \ldots, d_{i_k}\}$, where $d_{i_r} \in DIM$ $r = 1, \ldots, k$, and p is a k-ary predicate defined on the tuples of the relation $\Pi_{d \in \Delta}\,f_{dimtoindex}(d)$. The syntax

$$Box[\Delta \mid p] = \{s \mid s = [d_{i_1} : x_{i_1}, \ldots, d_{i_k} : x_{i_k}]\},$$

where the tuple $(x_{i_1}, \ldots, x_{i_k})$, $x_{i_r} \in f_{dimtoindex}(d_{i_r})$, $r = 1, \ldots k$ satisfy the predicate p, introduces a set S of contexts of degree k. For each context $s \in S$ the values in $tag(s)$ satisfy the predicate p.

Example 6. The set of contexts defined by $Box[X, U \mid \frac{x}{4} + \frac{u}{5} \leq 1]$, $f_{dimtoindex}(X) = \mathbf{N}$, and $f_{dimtoindex}(U) = \mathbf{N}$ is given by
$\{[X : 0, U : 0], [X : 0, U : 1], [X : 0, U : 2], [X : 0, U : 3],$
$[X : 0, U : 4], [X : 0, U : 5], [X : 1, U : 0], [X : 1, U : 1],$
$[X : 1, U : 2], [X : 1, U : 3], [X : 2, U : 0], [X : 2, U : 1],$
$[X : 2, U : 2], [X : 3, U : 0], [X : 3, U : 1], [X : 4, U : 0]\}$

4.3   Context Calculus

We provide a set of operators which can be applied on contexts to produce many kinds of contexts according to the requirements of different applications. These operators include: *constructor* $[\_ : \_]$, *override* $\oplus$, *difference* $\ominus$, *choice* $\mid$, *conjunction* $\sqcap$, *disjunction* $\sqcup$, *undirected range* $\rightleftharpoons$, *directed range* $\rightharpoonup$, *projection* $\downarrow$, *hiding* $\uparrow$, *substitution* $/$, and *comparison* $=, \supseteq, \subseteq$. The language allows user defined functions on contexts. The definitions, properties, and examples of these operators are discussed in [1]. The following are the definitions and examples of some of them. In the following definitions G denotes a finite set of contexts, and M denotes a set of m_contexts.

Definition 6. Constructor operator constructs a *m_context* for a given dimension d, and index t:

$$[\_ : \_] : \{d\} \times f_{dimtoindex}(d) \longrightarrow M,$$

$[d : t] = m \in M$. Using the set notation and the definitions for contexts, we construct contexts.

Definition 7. Override operator takes two contexts c_1, $c_2 \in G$, and returns a context $c \in G$, which is the result of the conflict-free union of c_1 and c_2, as defined below:

$$\_ \oplus \_ : G \times G \rightarrow G,$$

$$c = c_1 \oplus c_2 = \{ m \mid (m \in c_1 \wedge \neg m \in c_2) \vee m \in c_2\}$$

Definition 8. Choice operator accepts a finite number of $c_1, \ldots, c_k$ of contexts and nondeterministically returns one of the c_is. The definition $c = c_1 \mid c_2 \mid \ldots, \mid c_k$ implies that c is one of the c_i, where $1 \leq i \leq k$:

$$\_ \mid \_ : G \times G \times \ldots \times G \rightarrow G,$$

Definition 9. Hiding operator enables a set of dimensions D to be applied on a context $c \in G$, and the result removes all the m_contexts in c whose dimensions are in D:

$$\_ \uparrow \_ : G \times D \rightarrow G,$$

$$c \uparrow D = \{c' \mid dim(c') \subseteq dim(c) \wedge dim(c') \cap D = \varnothing\}$$

Definition 10. Projection operator is the result of projecting a context c on a set of dimensions D to filter only those pairs in c that match the dimension in set D.

$$\_ \downarrow \_ : G \times D \rightarrow G,$$

$$c \downarrow D = \{c' \mid dim(c') \subseteq dim(c) \wedge dim(c') \subseteq D\}$$

Example 7. Let $c_1 = [d : 3, \ d : 4]$, $c_2 = [e : 1, \ d : 1, \ f : 2]$, $c_3 = [e : 3, \ d : 3]$, $\Delta = \{ e, \ f\}$. Then $c_1 \oplus c_2 = [d : 1, \ e : 1, \ f : 2]$, $c_2 \mid c_3 = c_2$ or c_3, $c_2 \uparrow \Delta = [d : 1]$, $c_2 \downarrow \Delta = [e : 1, \ f : 2]$

In order to provide a precise meaning for a context expression, we define the precedence rules for all the operators. The precedence rules for the operators are shown as follows: 1.$\downarrow$, $\uparrow$, $/$; 2.$\mid$; 3.$\sqcap$, $\sqcup$; 4.$\oplus$, $\ominus$; 5.$\rightleftharpoons$, $\rightarrow$; 6. $=$, $\subseteq$, $\supseteq$; (from the highest precedence to the lowest). Parentheses will be used to override this precedence when needed. Operators having the same precedence will be applied from left to right.

As an illustration, consider the context expression $c_1 \mid c_2 \oplus c_3 \uparrow D$. Applying the precedence rules, this expression is equivalent to $(c_1 \oplus (c_3 \uparrow D)) \mid (c_2 \oplus (c_3 \uparrow D))$.

4.4   Syntax and Semantics of Extended Lucid

The abstract syntax of the extended Lucid is defined below:

$$E ::= id \qquad\qquad\qquad\qquad Q ::= \texttt{dimension } id$$
$$| \; E(E_1, \ldots, E_n) \qquad\qquad\quad | \; id = E$$
$$| \; \texttt{if } E \texttt{ then } E' \texttt{ else } E'' \qquad | \; id(id_1, \ldots, id_n) = E$$
$$| \; \#E \qquad\qquad\qquad\qquad | \; Q \; Q$$
$$| \; \mathbf{E \; @ \; E'}$$
$$| \; \mathbf{[E_1 : E'_1, \; \ldots, \; E_n : E'_n]}$$
$$| \; E \texttt{ where } Q$$

The operator @ is the navigation operator, which evaluates an expression E in context E', where E' is an expression evaluating to a context. The operator # is the context query operator, operating on the current evaluation context. The non-terminals E and Q respectively refer to *expressions* and *definitions*. The only change applied to the syntax of the language in order to achieve contexts as first class objects comes in the syntactic rules presented in bold. The older syntax for the @ operator was of the form: $E \; @ \; E' E''$ where, semantically speaking, E' evaluated to a dimension, and E'' evaluated to a dimension tag (as depicted in its semantic rule presented in Figure 2). In fact, the $E' E''$ part of this syntactic construct represents a *m_context*, even though E' and E'' were evaluated as separate semantic entities, and not to a context. In contrast, the E' part of the new $E \; @ \; E'$ semantically evaluates to a *m_context*, thus introducing contexts as first class objects. The syntactic construct $[E_1 : E'_1, \ldots, E_n : E'_n]$ is representing how *s_contexts* are syntactically introduced in the language. The E' part of the $E \; @ \; E'$ rule shall be eventually evaluating to something of this form, as is reflected in the $\mathbf{E_{at(c)}}$ and $\mathbf{E_{context}}$ semantic rules. As for the operational semantics of Lucid, the general form of evaluating in Lucid is as follows: $\mathcal{D}, \mathcal{P} \vdash E : v$, which means that in the definition environment $\mathcal{D}$, and in the evaluation context $\mathcal{P}$, expression E evaluates to v. The definition environment $\mathcal{D}$ retains the definitions of all of the identifiers that appear in a Lucid program. It is therefore a partial function: $\mathcal{D} : \mathbf{Id} \rightarrow \mathbf{IdEntry}$, where $\mathbf{Id}$ is the set of all possible identifiers and $\mathbf{IdEntry}$ has five possible kinds of value such as: *Dimensions, Constants, Data Operators, Variables*, and *Functions* [10]. The evaluation context $\mathcal{P}$, associates a tag to each relevant dimension. It is therefore a partial function: $\mathcal{P} : \mathbf{Id} \rightarrow \mathbf{N}$.

The complete operational semantics is defined in Figure 1 [10]. The rule for the navigation operator is $\mathbf{E_{at(c)}}$, which corresponds to the syntactic expression $E @ E'$, evaluates E in context E'. The function $\mathcal{P}' = \mathcal{P}\dagger[id \mapsto v'']$ means that $\mathcal{P}'(x)$ is v'' if $x = id$, and $\mathcal{P}(x)$ otherwise. For example, the evaluation of the expression $E @ E_1 \oplus E_2 \ominus E_3$ is done in the following order:

  – compute $E' = E_1 \oplus E_2$
  – compute $E'' = E' \ominus E_3$
  – evaluate $E @ E''$.

4.5   Message Structure and Evaluation in AIPL

The syntax of a message in AIPL is $\langle E, E' \rangle$, where E is the message name and E' is a context. The message name in a Communicative Act CA of FIPA ACL or the name of a performative in KQML is captured in AIPL by E. In an implementation E corresponds to a function. The context E' includes all the information that an agent wants to convey in an interaction to another agent. Thus, a query from an agent A to an agent B is of the form $\langle E_A, E'_A \rangle$. A response from agent B to agent A will be of the form $\langle E_B, E''_B \rangle$, where E''_B will include the reference to the query for which this is a response in addition to the contexts in which the response should be understood.

Query Evaluation. The operational semantics in extended Lucid is the basis for query evaluation in AIPL. The query from agent A $\langle E_A, E'_A \rangle$ to agent B is evaluated as follows:

- agent B obtains the context $F_B = E'_A \oplus L_B$, where L_B is the local context for B.
- agent B evaluates $E_A @ F_B$
- agent B constructs the new context E''_B that includes the evaluated result and information suggesting the context in which it should be interpreted by agent A, and
- sends the response $\langle E_B, E''_B \rangle$ to agent A.

Example 8. The query in Example 3 is represented in AIPL as the expression $E @ E'$, $E' = E_1 \oplus E_2 \oplus E_3 \oplus E_4 \oplus E_5 \oplus E_6$.

```
E @ [ E1 ⊕ E2 ⊕ E3 ⊕ E4 ⊕ E5 ⊕ E6]
where
E = "ask-one";
E1 = [ sender : joe];
E2 = [ content : (PRICE IBM ?price)];
E3 = [ receiver : STOCK-SERVER ];
E4 = [ reply-with : IBM-STOCK ];
E5 = [ language: LPROLOG ];
E6 = [ ontology: NYSE-TICKS ];
end
```

Example 9. The reply in Example 3 is represented in AIPL as the expression $E' @ E''$, $E'' = E'_1 \oplus E'_2 \oplus E'_3 \oplus E'_4 \oplus E'_5 \oplus E'_6$.

```
E' @ [ E1' ⊕ E2' ⊕ E3' ⊕ E4' ⊕ E5' ⊕ E6']
where
E' = "tell";
E1' = [ sender : STOCK-SERVER];
E2' = [ content : (PRICE IBM 14)];
E3' = [ receiver : joe ];
E4' = [ in-reply-to : IBM-STOCK ];
E5' = [ language: LPROLOG ];
E6' = [ ontology: NYSE-TICKS ];
end
```

The implementation will assure that the local context of B is sufficient to evaluate the query and respond to A within an acceptable time delay. This is an important issue

$$\mathbf{E_{cid}} : \frac{\mathcal{D}(id) = (\mathtt{const}, c)}{\mathcal{D}, \mathcal{P} \vdash id : c} \qquad\qquad \mathbf{E_{did}} : \frac{\mathcal{D}(id) = (\mathtt{dim})}{\mathcal{D}, \mathcal{P} \vdash id : id}$$

$$\mathbf{E_{opid}} : \frac{\mathcal{D}(id) = (\mathtt{op}, f)}{\mathcal{D}, \mathcal{P} \vdash id : id} \qquad\qquad \mathbf{E_{fid}} : \frac{\mathcal{D}(id) = (\mathtt{func}, id_i, E)}{\mathcal{D}, \mathcal{P} \vdash id : id}$$

$$\mathbf{E_{vid}} : \frac{\mathcal{D}(id) = (\mathtt{var}, E) \qquad \mathcal{D}, \mathcal{P} \vdash E : v}{\mathcal{D}, \mathcal{P} \vdash id : v}$$

$$\mathbf{E_{op}} : \frac{\mathcal{D}, \mathcal{P} \vdash E : id \qquad \mathcal{D}(id) = (\mathtt{op}, f) \qquad \mathcal{D}, \mathcal{P} \vdash E_i : v_i}{\mathcal{D}, \mathcal{P} \vdash E(E_1, \ldots, E_n) : f(v_1, \ldots, v_n)}$$

$$\mathbf{E_{fct}} : \frac{\mathcal{D}, \mathcal{P} \vdash E : id \qquad \mathcal{D}(id) = (\mathtt{func}, id_i, E') \qquad \mathcal{D}, \mathcal{P} \vdash E'[id_i \leftarrow E_i] : v}{\mathcal{D}, \mathcal{P} \vdash E(E_1, \ldots, E_n) : v}$$

$$\mathbf{E_{cT}} : \frac{\mathcal{D}, \mathcal{P} \vdash E : \mathit{true} \qquad \mathcal{D}, \mathcal{P} \vdash E' : v'}{\mathcal{D}, \mathcal{P} \vdash \mathtt{if}\ E\ \mathtt{then}\ E'\ \mathtt{else}\ E'' : v'}$$

$$\mathbf{E_{cF}} : \frac{\mathcal{D}, \mathcal{P} \vdash E : \mathit{false} \qquad \mathcal{D}, \mathcal{P} \vdash E'' : v''}{\mathcal{D}, \mathcal{P} \vdash \mathtt{if}\ E\ \mathtt{then}\ E'\ \mathtt{else}\ E'' : v''}$$

$$\mathbf{E_{tag}} : \frac{\mathcal{D}, \mathcal{P} \vdash E : id \qquad \mathcal{D}(id) = (\mathtt{dim})}{\mathcal{D}, \mathcal{P} \vdash \#E : \mathcal{P}(id)}$$

$$\mathbf{E_{at(c)}} : \frac{\mathcal{D}, \mathcal{P} \vdash E' : P' \qquad \mathcal{D}, \mathcal{P}' \vdash E : v}{\mathcal{D}, \mathcal{P} \vdash E @ E' : v}$$

$$\mathbf{E_{context}} : \frac{\mathcal{D}, \mathcal{P} \vdash E_{d_j} : id_j \quad \mathcal{D}(id_j) = (\mathtt{dim}) \quad \mathcal{D}, \mathcal{P} \vdash E_{i_j} : v_j \quad v = [id_j \mapsto v_j]}{\mathcal{D}, \mathcal{P} \vdash [E_{d_1} : E_{i_1}, E_{d_2} : E_{i_2}, \ldots, E_{d_n} : E_{i_n}] : v}$$

$$\mathbf{E_w} : \frac{\mathcal{D}, \mathcal{P} \vdash Q : \mathcal{D}', \mathcal{P}' \qquad \mathcal{D}', \mathcal{P}' \vdash E : v}{\mathcal{D}, \mathcal{P} \vdash E\ \mathtt{where}\ Q : v}$$

$$\mathbf{Q_{dim}} : \frac{}{\mathcal{D}, \mathcal{P} \vdash \mathtt{dimension}\ id : \mathcal{D}\dagger[id \mapsto (\mathtt{dim})], \mathcal{P}\dagger[id \mapsto 0]}$$

$$\mathbf{Q_{id}} : \frac{}{\mathcal{D}, \mathcal{P} \vdash id = E : \mathcal{D}\dagger[id \mapsto (\mathtt{var}, E)], \mathcal{P}}$$

$$\mathbf{Q_{fid}} : \frac{}{\mathcal{D}, \mathcal{P} \vdash id(id_1, \ldots, id_n) = E : \mathcal{D}\dagger[id \mapsto (\mathtt{func}, id_i, E)], \mathcal{P}}$$

$$\mathbf{QQ} : \frac{\mathcal{D}, \mathcal{P} \vdash Q : \mathcal{D}', \mathcal{P}' \qquad \mathcal{D}', \mathcal{P}' \vdash Q' : \mathcal{D}'', \mathcal{P}''}{\mathcal{D}, \mathcal{P} \vdash Q\ Q' : \mathcal{D}'', \mathcal{P}''}$$

Fig. 1. Semantic rules for Lucid

$$\mathbf{E_{at(old)}} : \frac{\mathcal{D}, \mathcal{P} \vdash E' : id \quad \mathcal{D}(id) = (\mathtt{dim}) \quad \mathcal{D}, \mathcal{P} \vdash E'' : v'' \quad \mathcal{D}, \mathcal{P}\dagger[id \mapsto v''] \vdash E : v}{\mathcal{D}, \mathcal{P} \vdash E @ E'\ E'' : v}$$

Fig. 2. Semantic rule for for the old @ operation

because we want the agents to be reactive (responds within acceptable time limits) while the eduction is allowed to continue. The choice operator helps in achieving such a goal. For example, the query:

```
E @ [ E1 ⊕ E2 ⊕ E3 ⊕ E4 ⊕ E5 | E6 ⊕ E7 ]
where
E  = "ask-one";
E1 = [ sender : joe];
E2 = [ content : (PRICE IBM ?price)];
E3 = [ receiver: STOCK-SERVER ];
E4 = [ reply-with : IBM-STOCK ];
E5 = [ language: LPROLOG ];
E6 = [ language: STANDARD_PROLOG ];
E7 = [ ontology: NYSE-TICKS ];
end
```

gives the receiver, depending on its local context, choose either LPROLOG or STAN-DARD_PROLOG to ensure timeliness. The fields in the performative in Example 3 can not be dynamically changed in either FIPA or KQML. In our language, we form the context expression $E'' = E' \uparrow \{language\} \oplus [language : Java]$ to dynamically replace the language requirement and construct a new query. The meaning of the examples shown in this section can be clearly understood from the semantics of the context calculus presented in the Section 4.3.

4.6   Semantics of Conversation

In [8], the semantics of KQML performatives is provided in terms of *preconditions*, *postconditions*, and *completion conditions*. Preconditions, postconditions, and completion conditions involve action descriptors, such as $PROC(A, M)$ and $SENDMSG(A,-B, M)$, and describe states of agents in a language of mental attitudes such as belief, knowledge, want, and intention. Building on pre- and postcondition semantics they have devised the conversation policies for agent conversation. Conversation policies describe both the sequences of KQML performatives and the constraints and dependencies on the values of the reserved parameters of the performatives involved in the conversations. The semantics of FIPA ACL is given in the formal language SL, which provides the modal operators for beliefs (B), desires (D), intentions (persistent goals PG), and uncertain goals (U). Actions of objects, object descriptions, and propositions can be described in the language. Each formula in SL defines a constraint that the sender of the message must satisfy in order for the sender to conform to the FIPA ACL standard [13].

Our approach to semantics is different from the above two approaches. We have shown in [11] that a constraint can be represented as a set of contexts. We continue this method here to represent pre- and postconditions. We introduce special simple contexts having four dimensions B(Belief), K(Know), W(Want), and I(Intention). The tags along these dimensions are natural numbers. The domain $\mathcal{D}_B$ attached to dimension B is a set of predicates, and the respective domains $\mathcal{D}_K$, $\mathcal{D}_W$, and $\mathcal{D}_I$ attached to the dimensions K, W, and I are sets of expressions. Each performative is bound to a context $c = [B : i_1, K : i_2, W : i_3, I : i_4]$ over the dimensions B, K, W, I. The context c is suggested as the precondition to act upon the performative. If a dimension is not specified in c then it is equivalent to a "don't care" condition.

We define a *dialogue* initiated by agent X with agent Y as a pair $\langle \alpha, \beta \rangle$, where α is sent from X to Y and β is the response from Y to X. The agent X constructs the special context $Pre_Y(M_X)$ for message M_X and sends the pair $\alpha = (Pre_Y(M_X), M_X)$ to Y. The agent Y evaluates its local state at $Pre_Y(M_X)$. The result of evaluation is a tuple $\langle b_1, k_1, w_1, i_1 \rangle$. The tuple corresponding to an empty Pre_Y is $\langle NONE, NONE, NONE, NONE \rangle$, interpreted as *true*. That is, the agent X has not indicated any preference as to when agent Y should evaluate the performative M_X. If at least one component of the tuple is not $NULL$, then the special context $Pre_Y(M_X)$ is said to be *satisfied* at some local state of Y. If all components of the tuple are $NULL$ the context is not satisfiable at any local state of Y. If the outcome of evaluation is either *true* or *satisfied*, the agent Y will act upon the performative M_X. For instance, in Example 8, the agent X constructs the special context $E_7 = [I : i_4]$ and attaches it to the performative in a conversation with Y. The agent Y evaluates $\mathcal{D}_B \times \mathcal{D}_K \times \mathcal{D}_W \times \mathcal{D}_I$, the local repository on its belief, desire, want and intentions, at the context E_7. The result of evaluation is the tuple $\langle NONE, NONE, NONE, PROC(Y, M) \rangle$, implying that the agent Y has the intention to process the message M. The semantics of a dialogue initiated by X with Y is as follows:

1. Agent X creates a special context $Pre_X(M_X)$, the weakest precondition that enables to send a message to agent Y. When $Pre_X(M_X)$ is true in its local state, it constructs $Pre_Y(M_X)$, a precondition based on the information that it shares with agent Y.
2. Agent X sends $\alpha = (Pre_Y(M_X) \oplus M_X)$ to Y.
3. Agent Y disassembles it into the message part M and the special context $Pre_Y(M_X)$. This is done by computing $Pre_Y(M_X) = \alpha \downarrow \{B, K, W, I\}$, and $M_X = \alpha \uparrow \{B, K, W, I\}$.
4. Agent Y evaluates its local state at $Pre_Y(M_X)$.
5. If *satisfied* it does the following:
   (a) creates the post condition $Post_Y(M_X)$ that satisfies the task completion;
   (b) acts upon the message M_X;
   (c) composes the reply as a performative M_Y;
   (d) creates $Post_X(M_Y)$, the special context in which agent X should evaluate M_Y;
   (e) composes $\beta = (Post_X(M_Y), M_Y)$;
   (f) Agent Y sends β to agent X.
6. If NOT *satisfied*, more than one semantics can be given:
   - [1.] Agent Y responds immediately to X: composes an "unable to act" performative, constructs the special context $\langle NONE, NONE, NONE, NONE \rangle$, and sends the pair to agent X.
   - [2.] Agent Y delays the evaluation of M_X until the instant when the special context $Pre_Y(M_X)$ is either satisfied or not satisfied in its local state.
   - [3.] Agent Y abandons the message if the special context $Pre_Y(M_X)$ is either satisfied or not satisfied within a certain amount of time.

For the deterministic progress in the system, the first semantics is preferred. Under the first semantics of dialogue we can define the semantics of a *conversation*. A sequence $\langle(\alpha_1, \beta_1);\; \ldots;\; (\alpha_k, \beta_k), \ldots, \rangle$ of dialogues is a conversation if for every i, $i \geq 1$, there exists at least one local state of X in which the postcondition $Post_X(M_Y)$ in β_i is satisfied. In the language, a conversation can be represented as *tuple streams*, where each tuple is a pair of contexts.

5   Conclusion

The Agent Communication Language AIPL that we have introduced in this paper has a number of advantages:

- In KQML and FIPA, performatives, other than the primitive performatives defined in the language, can be agreed upon by the community of agents involved in a collaboration. That is, interoperability is proved. However, performatives are only static status and not first class objects in the language. As a consequence, performatives can not be changed dynamically, nor can they be used as a vehicle to communicate local state information of agents. In AIPL, by making context as first class objects, we have removed the above limitations. In addition, we can define functions on contexts and they can be used as parameters in programs. Thus, we have enhanced both *interoperability* and *flexibility* in agent communication.
- AIPL is declarative and has a formal semantics.
- AIPL uses multidimensional streams of objects, which can be used to represent plans and conversations in multiple streams.
- *Multiple formats of communication* can be supported since intensional programming language deals with any kind of ordinary data type. Even the multimedia streams between agents become feasible.

We create special contexts to provide a semantics for conversation. Performatives are constructed as context expressions. Contexts may be dynamically changed. Consequently in our approach performatives are not constants, and cannot be assigned *a priori* pre- and postconditions. This in turn requires creating dynamically the pre- and postconditions for performatives constructed by agents. An agent may share its belief, knowledge, wants, and intentions with those agents it wants to collaborate. However, an agent may share its resources only partially. Hence forcing agents to reveal their internal states in conversations is unsafe. The mechanism on which we have designed the agent communication protocol is known as *Publish-Subscribe*. An agent *publishes* what it wishes to share with other agents. An agent who wants to collaborate with another agents *subscribes* to that agent's publication. The semantics requires this mechanism to be fulfilled in agent systems. It seems that special contexts in our language have the same expressive power as the features in MALLET [6], a language for describing declarative and procedural aspects required for agent teamwork. Moreover, the ability to modify dynamically the belief, knowledge, wants, and intentions in our language is similar to the feature of the language in [3] to express dynamically changing goals. There is certainly some overhead in this approach. However, it is justified for the following reasons:

- dynamic creation and manipulation of performatives provide flexibility and expressiveness for programming agent systems in the language, and
- security policies can be enforced in the language as peer-to-peer agent communication with no central authority for enforcement.

Lately, we have undertaken the development of the GIPSY, which is designed as a framework in order to reach for maximal flexibility and generality of application [11, 14]. Being a functional language, Lucid programs can be evaluated in parallel or distributed execution mode. In such case, in order to augment the granularity of parallelism, GIPSY programs can be written as hybrid programs, allowing Java functions to be called by the Lucid part of the program. Interestingly, these Java functions can actually be the implementation of software agents. Then the Lucid part becomes a declarative specification describing the relationships between agents, implicitly describing how these agents are collaborating in a distributed execution. The AIPL described in this paper is then used as a formal ACL in order to achieve transparent contextual communication between agents. The semantics of the calculus of contexts being intrinsic to each agent through the eduction engine embedded in each node, there is no need to write agents that embed a parser and semantic analyzer and translator for the ACL primitives that are exchanged between agents at run time. These implementation issues are to be addressed as part of our ongoing work in GIPSY. Based on this system, communication between different categories of agents such as *interface agent*, *middle agent*, *task agent*, and *security agent* [2] can be used as case studies for AIPL. We will also investigate the use of AIPL for mobile agents communication and multimedia communication between agents.

References

1. Alagar, V.S., Paquet, J., Wan, K.: *Contexts in Intensional Programming.* Technical Report, Department of Computer Science, Concordia University, Montreal, Canada, April 2004.
2. Alagar, V.S., Holliday, J., Thiyagarajan, P.V., Zhou, B.: Agent Types and Their Formal Descriptions. Technical Report, Department of Computer Engineering, Santa Clara University, Santa Clara, CA, U.S.A., May 2002.
3. van Riemsdijk, M. B., Dastani, M., Dignum, F., Meyer, J.J.: *Dynamics of Declarative Goals in Agent Programming.* In: Proceedings of the Workshop on Declarative Agent Languages and Technologies (DALT'04), LNCS 3476, Springer-Verlag (2005). In this volume.
4. Finin, T., Fritzson, R., McKay, D., McEntire, R.: *KQML as an Agent Communication Language.* In: Proceedings of the 3rd International Conference on Information and Knowledge Management (CIKM'94), ACM Press, November 1994.
5. FIPA Semantic Language Specification.: *FIPA Specification repository*, FIPA-specification identifier XC00008G, September 2000 Foundation for Intelligent Physical Agents, Geneva, Switzerland.
6. Fan, X., Yen, J, Miller, M., Volz, R.: *The Semantics of MALLET - An Agent Teamwork Encoding Language.* In: Proceedings of the Workshop on Declarative Agent Languages and Technologies (DALT'04), LNCS 3476, Springer-Verlag (2005). In this volume.
7. Guha, R.V.: *Contexts: A Formalization and Some Applications.* PhD thesis, Stanford University, February 10,1995.

8. Labrou, Y., Finin, T., Peng, Y.: *Agent Communication Languages: The Current Landscape.* IEEE Journal on Intelligent Agents, Amrch/April 1999, pp. 45-52.
9. Paquet, J., Kropf, P.: *The GIPSY Architecture.* DCW 2000: 144-153
10. Paquet, J.: *Intensional Scientific Programming.* Ph.D. Thesis, Departement d'Informatique, Universite Laval, Quebec, Canada, 1999
11. Wan, K., Alagar, V.S., Paquet, J.: *Real Time Reactive Programming Enriched with Context.* ICTAC2004, Guiyang, China, September 2004, Lecture Notes in Computer Science,3407, Springer-Verlag.
12. Wadge, W.W., Ashcroft, E.A..: *Lucid, the dataflow programming language.*   Academic Press, 1985
13. Wooldridge, M.: *Verifiable Semantics for Agent Communication Languages.* In: Proceedings of the Third International Conference on Multi-Agent Systems (ICMAS'98).
14. Wu, A.H., Paquet, J., Grogono, P.: *Design of a compiler framework in the GIPSY system.* In Parallel and Distributed Computing and Systems - PDCS 2003, Marina Del Rey, California, USA, 2003.

The Logic of Communication Graphs

Eric Pacuit[1] and Rohit Parikh[2]

[1] Computer Science Department,
The Graduate Center of CUNY,
365 5th Avenue, New York City, NY 10016
epacuit@cs.gc.cuny.edu
www.cs.gc.cuny.edu/~epacuit[*]
[2] CS, Math and Philosophy,
Brooklyn College[**] and The Graduate Center of CUNY,
365 5th Avenue, New York City, NY 10016
rparikh@gc.cuny.edu
www.sci.brooklyn.cuny.edu/~rparikh

Abstract. In 1992, Moss and Parikh studied a bimodal logic of knowledge and effort called *Topologic*. In this current paper, *Topologic* is extended to the case of many agents who are assumed to have some private information at the outset, but may refine their information by acquiring information possessed by other agents, possibly via yet other agents.

Let us assume that the agents are connected by a *communication graph*. In the communication graph, an edge from agent i to agent j means that agent i can directly receive information from agent j. Agent i can then refine its own information by learning information that j has, including information acquired by j from another agent, k. We introduce a multi-agent modal logic with knowledge modalities and a modality representing communication among agents. We show that the validities of *Topologic* remain valid and that the communication graph is completely determined by the validities of the resulting logic. Applications of our logic to current political dilemmas are obvious.

1   Introduction

In [13], Moss and Parikh introduce a bimodal logic intended to formalize reasoning about points and sets. This new logic called *Topologic* can also be understood as an epistemic logic with an effort modality. Formally, the two modalities are: K and $\Diamond$. The intended interpretation of $K\phi$ is that ϕ is known; and the intended interpretation of $\Diamond\phi$ is that after some amount of effort ϕ becomes true. For example, the formula

$$\phi \rightarrow \Diamond K \phi$$

[*] Both authors would like to thank Hans van Ditmarsch and the Knowledge, Games and Beliefs Group of CUNY for their comments.

[**] 2900 Bedford Avenue, Brooklyn, NY 11210. Research of both authors supported under the PSC-CUNY FRAP program.

J. Leite et al. (Eds.): DALT 2004, LNAI 3476, pp. 256–269, 2005.
© Springer-Verlag Berlin Heidelberg 2005

means that if ϕ is true, then after some "work", $K\phi$ becomes true, i.e., ϕ is known. In other words, the formula says that if ϕ is true, then ϕ can be known with some effort. What exactly is meant by "effort" depends on the application. For example, we may think of effort as meaning taking a measurement, performing a calculation or observing a computation. In this paper we will think of effort as meaning consulting some agent's database of known formulas.

There is a temptation to think that the effort modality can be understood as (only) a temporal operator, reading $\Diamond\phi$ as "ϕ is true some time in the future". While there is a connection between the logics of knowledge and time and logics of knowledge and effort (see [8, 9] and references therein for more on this topic), following [13] we will assume that such effort leaves the base facts about the world unchanged. In particular, in any topologic model, if ϕ does not contain any modalities, then $\phi \leftrightarrow \Box\phi$ is valid. Thus, effort will not change the base facts about the world – it only change knowledge of these facts.

The family of logics introduced in [13] and later studied by Dabrowski, Moss and Parikh, Georgatos, Heinemann, and Weiss ([3, 4, 5, 6, 8, 21]) has a semantics in which the acquisition of knowledge is explicitly represented. Familiar mathematical structures such as subset spaces, topologies, intersection spaces and complete lattices of subsets corresponding to natural notions of knowledge acquisition are attached to standard Kripke structures.

Given a set W, a subset space is a pair $\langle W, \mathcal{O} \rangle$, where $\mathcal{O}$ is a collection of subsets of W. A point $x \in W$ represents a complete description of the world in which all ground facts are settled, whereas a set $U \in \mathcal{O}$ represents an *observation*. The pair (x, U), called a *neighborhood situation*, can be thought of as an actual situation together with an observation made about the situation. Formulas are interpreted at neighborhood situations. Thus the knowledge modality K represents movement within (consistent with) the current observation, while the effort modality $\Diamond$ represents a refining of the current observation.

Formally,

1. $x, U \models K\phi$ iff $(\forall y \in U)(y, U \models \phi)$
2. $x, U \models \Diamond\phi$ iff $(\exists V \in \mathcal{O})((x \in V \subseteq U) \text{ and } (x, V \models \phi))$

[13] provides a sound and complete axiomatization for all subset spaces. In [4] and [5], Georgatos provides a sound and complete axiomatization for subset spaces that are topological spaces and complete lattices. Dabrowski, Moss, and Parikh prove the same result using an embedding into **S4** ([3]). [6] provides a sound and complete axiomatization for treelike spaces, and Weiss ([21]) has provided a sound and complete axiomatization for intersection-spaces. Interestingly, it is shown in [21] that an infinite number of axiom schemes are necessary for any complete axiomatization of intersection spaces. More recently, Heinemann [8, 9] has looked at subset spaces and logics of knowledge and time, and the connection between hybrid logic and subset spaces [10, 12].

In this paper, we present a multi-agent topologic in which the effort modality $\Diamond$ is intended to mean communication among agents. In order for any communication to take place, we must assume that the agents understand a common language. Thus we assume a set At of propositional variables, understood by all the agents, but with only specific agents knowing their actual values at the start. Letters p, q, etc, will denote elements of At. The agents will have some information – knowledge of the truth values of some elements of At, but refine that information by acquiring information possessed by other agents, possibly via yet other agents. This implies that if agents are restricted in whom they can communicate with, then this fact will restrict the knowledge they can acquire.

Consider the current situation with Bush and Porter Goss, the director of the CIA. If Bush wants some information from a particular CIA operative, say Bob, he must get this information through Goss. Suppose that ϕ is a formula representing the exact whereabouts of Bin Laden, and that Bob, the CIA operative in charge of maintaining this information knows ϕ. In particular, $K_{\text{Bob}}\phi$, but suppose that at the moment, Bush does not know the exact whereabouts of Bin Laden ($\neg K_{\text{Bush}}\phi$). Presumably Bush *can* find out the exact whereabouts of Bin Laden ($\Diamond K_{\text{Bush}}\phi$) by going through Goss, but of course, *we* cannot find out such information ($\neg \Diamond K_e\phi \wedge \neg \Diamond K_r\phi$) since we do not have the appropriate security clearance. Clearly, then, as a *pre-requisite* for Bush learning ϕ, Goss will also have come to know ϕ. We can represent this situation by the following formula:

$$\neg K_{\text{Bush}}\phi \wedge \Box(K_{\text{Bush}}\phi \to K_{\text{Goss}}\phi)$$

where $\Box$ is the dual of diamond.

Let $\mathcal{A}$ be a set of agents. A **communication graph** is a directed graph $\mathcal{G}_{\mathcal{A}} = (\mathcal{A}, E)$ where $E \subseteq \mathcal{A} \times \mathcal{A}$. Intuitively $(i, j) \in E$ means that i can directly receive information from agent j, but *without* j knowing this fact. Thus an edge between i and j in the communication graph represents a one-sided relationship between i and j. Agent i has access to any piece of information that agent j knows. We have introduced this 'one sidedness' restriction in order to simplify our semantics, but also because such situations of one sided learning occur naturally. A common situation that is helpful to keep in mind is accessing a website. We can think of agent j as creating a website in which everything he *currently* knows is available, and if there is an edge between i and j then agent i can access this website without j being aware that the site is being accessed. Another important application is spying where one person accesses another's information without the latter being aware that information is being leaked. Naturally j may have been able to access some other agent k's website and had updated some of her own information. Therefore, it is important to stress that when i accesses j's website, he is accessing j's current information which may include what k knew initially.

The assumption that i can access all of j's information is a significant idealization from these common situations, but becomes more realistic if we think of this information as being confined to facts expressible as truth functional combinations of some small set of basic propositions. Thus our idealization rests on two assumptions:

1: All the agents share a common language, and
2: The agents make available all possible pieces of information which they know
   and which are expressible in this common language.

2   The Logic of Communication Graphs

In this section we will describe the logic of communication graphs, $\mathcal{K}(\mathcal{G})$. The language will be a multi-agent modal language with a communication modality. The formula $K_i\phi$ will be interpreted as "according to i's current information, i knows ϕ", and $\Diamond\phi$ will be interpreted as "after some communications (which respect the communication graph), ϕ becomes true". Thus for example, the multi-agent version of the formula $\phi \rightarrow \Diamond K\phi$, expressing that if ϕ is true then with some effort ϕ can be known, is

$$K_j\phi \rightarrow \Diamond K_i\phi$$

This formula expresses that if agent j (currently) knows ϕ, then after some communication agent i can come to know ϕ. Let At be a finite set of propositional variables. A well-formed formula of $\mathcal{K}(\mathcal{G})$ has the following syntactic form

$$\phi := p \mid \neg\psi \mid \phi \wedge \psi \mid K_i\phi \mid \Diamond\phi$$

where $p \in$ At. We abbreviate $\neg K_i \neg\phi$ and $\neg\Diamond\neg\phi$ by $L_i\phi$ and $\Box\phi$ respectively, and use the standard abbreviations for the propositional connectives ($\vee$, $\rightarrow$, and $\bot$). Let $\mathcal{L}_{\mathcal{K}(\mathcal{G})}$ denote the set of well-formed formulas of $\mathcal{K}(\mathcal{G})$. We also define $\mathcal{L}_0(\mathsf{At})$, (or simply $\mathcal{L}_0$ if At is fixed or understood), to be the set of ground formulas, i.e., the set of formulas constructed from At using $\neg, \wedge$ only.

2.1   Semantics

The semantics presented here combines ideas both from the subset models of [13] and the history based models of Parikh and Ramanajum (see [16,17]). Suppose that $\mathcal{G} = (\mathcal{A}, E)$ is a fixed communication graph. Given that the agents are initially given some private information and assumed to communicate according to the communication graph $\mathcal{G}$, the semantics in this section is intended to formalize what agents know and may come to know after some communication.

Initially, each agent i knows or is informed (say by nature) of the truth values of a certain subset At_i of propositional variables, and the At_i *as well as this fact are common knowledge.* Thus the other agents know that i knows the truth values of elements of At_i, but, typically, not what these values actually are. We do not need to assume that the At_i are disjoint, nor that the At_i together add up to all of At, although such sub-cases will be of interest. Thus if At_i and At_j intersect then agents i, j will share information at the very beginning. Let W be the set of boolean valuations on At. An element $v \in W$ is called a *state*. We use 1 for the truth value *true*. Initially each agent i is given a boolean valuation $v_i : \mathsf{At}_i \rightarrow \{0, 1\}$. This initial distribution of information among the agents can be represented by a vector $\boldsymbol{v} = (v_1, \ldots, v_n)$. Of course, since we are modeling knowledge and not belief, these initial boolean valuations must be compatible. I.e., for each i, j, v_i and v_j agree on $\mathsf{At}_i \cap \mathsf{At}_j$. Call any vector of partial boolean valuations $\boldsymbol{v} = (v_1, \ldots, v_n)$ **consistent** if for each $p \in dom(v_i) \cap dom(v_j)$, $v_i(p) = v_j(p)$ for all $i, j = 1, \ldots, n$. We shall assume that only such consistent vectors arise as initial information. All this information is common knowledge and only the precise values of the v_i are private.

Definition 1. *Let* At *be a finite set of propositional variables and* $\mathcal{A} = \{1, \ldots, n\}$ *a finite set of agents. Given the distribution of sublanguages* **At** $= (\mathsf{At}_1, \ldots, \mathsf{At}_n)$, *an* **initial information vector for At** *is any consistent vector* $\boldsymbol{v} = (v_1, \ldots, v_n)$ *of partial boolean valuations such that for each* $i \in \mathcal{A}$, $dom(v_i) = \mathsf{At}_i$.

We assumed that all initial vectors are consistent, although if we were dealing with beliefs rather than knowledge, then very interesting questions about *inconsistent* initial vectors could arise.

We assume that the only communications that take place are about the physical world. But we do allow agents to learn objective facts which are not atomic, but may be complex, like $p \vee q$ where $p, q \in \mathsf{At}$. Now note that if agent i learned some *literal* from agent j, then there is a simple way to update i's valuation v_i with this new information by just adding the truth value of another propositional symbol. However, if i learns a more general ground formula from agent j, then the situation will be more complex. For instance if the agent knows p and learns $q \vee r$ then the agent now has three valuations on the set $\{p, q, r\}$ which cannot be described in terms of a partial valuation on a subset of At.

Fix a communication graph $\mathcal{G}$ and suppose that agent i learns some ground fact ϕ from agent j. Of course, there must be an edge from agent i to agent j in $\mathcal{G}$. This situation will be represented by the tuple (i, j, ϕ) and will be called a **communication event**. Let $\Sigma_{\mathcal{G}}$ be the set of all possible events. Formally,

Definition 2. *Let* $\mathcal{G} = (\mathcal{A}, E_{\mathcal{G}})$ *be a communication graph. A tuple* (i, j, ϕ), *where* $\phi \in \mathcal{L}_0(\mathsf{At})$ *and* $(i, j) \in E_{\mathcal{G}}$ *is called a* **communication event**. *Then* $\Sigma_{\mathcal{G}} = \{(i, j, \phi) \mid \phi \in \mathcal{L}_0, (i, j) \in E_{\mathcal{G}}\}$ *is the set of all possible communication events (given the communication graph* $\mathcal{G}$).

Given the set of events $\Sigma_{\mathcal{G}}$, a **history** is a finite sequence of events. I.e., $H \in \Sigma_{\mathcal{G}}^*$. The empty history will be denoted ϵ. The following notions are standard (see [16, 17] for more information). Given two histories H, H', say $H \preceq H'$ iff $H' = HH''$ for some history H'', i.e., H is an initial segment of H'. Obviously, $\preceq$ is a partial order. If H is a history, and (i, j, ϕ) is a communication event, then H followed by (i, j, ϕ) will be written $H; (i, j, \phi)$. Given a history H, let $\lambda_i(H)$ be i's local history corresponding to H. I.e., $\lambda_i(H)$ is a sequence of events that i can "see". Formally, λ_i maps each event of the form (i, j, ϕ) to itself, and maps other events (m, j, ψ) with $m \neq i$ to the null character while preserving the order among events.

Fix a finite set of agents $\mathcal{A} = \{1, \ldots, n\}$ and a finite set of propositional variables At along with subsets $(\mathsf{At}_1, \ldots, \mathsf{At}_n)$. A **communication graph frame** is a pair $\langle \mathcal{G}, \mathbf{At} \rangle$ where $\mathcal{G}$ is a communication graph, and $\mathbf{At} = (\mathrm{At}_1, ..., \mathrm{At}_n)$ is an assignment of sub-languages to the agents. A **communication graph model** based on a frame $\langle \mathcal{G}, \mathbf{At} \rangle$ is a triple $\langle \mathcal{G}, \mathbf{At}, \boldsymbol{v} \rangle$, where $\boldsymbol{v}$ is a consistent vector of partial boolean valuations for $\mathbf{At}$.

Now we address two issues. One is that not all histories are legal. For an event (i, j, ϕ) to take place after a history H, it must be the case that after H, j knows ϕ. Clearly i cannot learn from j something which j did not know. Whether a history is justified depends not only on the initial valuation, but also on the set of communications that have taken place prior to each communication in the history.

The second issue is that the information which an agent learns by "reading" a formula ϕ may be *more* than just the fact that ϕ is true. For suppose that i learns $p \vee q$ from j, but j is not connected, directly or indirectly, to anyone who might know the initial truth value of q. In this case i has learned *more* than $p \vee q$, i has learned p as well. For the only way that j could have known $p \vee q$ is if j knew p in which case p must be true. Our definition of the semantics below will address both these issues.

Formulas will be interpreted at pairs (w, H) where w is a state (boolean valuation) and H is a finite sequence of communication events.

We first introduce the notion of i-equivalence among histories. Intuitively, two histories are i-equivalent if those communications which i takes active part in, are the same.

Definition 3. *Let w be a state and H a finite history. Define the relation $\sim_i$ as follows: $(w, H) \sim_i (v, H')$ iff $w_{|\mathrm{At}_i} = v_{|\mathrm{At}_i}$ and $\lambda_i(H) = \lambda_i(H')$.*

Before proceeding further, we summarize the uncertainty faced by each of the agents:

1. Agents may be uncertain about the actual state of the world.
2. Agents may be uncertain about which communications have taken place.

Example: *The Valerie Plame Affair:* In an earlier version of this paper we stated that if a formula ϕ was stable, agent j knew it, and agent i was connected either directly or indirectly to agent j, then agent i could also come to know ϕ. Here a formula ϕ is said to be stable if for all legal (w, H), $(w, H) \models_\mathcal{M} (\phi \rightarrow \Box\phi)$.

However, we were mistaken and an abstract example as well as the Valerie Plame/Judith Miller affair shows why. Suppose that agent i is connected directly to agent j who is connected directly to agents k, m, both of whom are connected to r who knows the value of p. Now m reads p, which is true, from r's website, and j reads p from m's website and thus knows not only that p but also $K_m(p)$. Now the formula $K_m(p)$ is stable, it will never again become false. But i cannot know this although i can know p. For *just by reading j's web page*, i cannot rule out the possibility that j learned about p from k.

The way in which this applies to the Plame-Miller affair is that the fact that Plame was a CIA covert operative was revealed by columnist Robert Novak in July 2003, possibly endangering her life, and this information seems to have come from Miller who is under a federal sentence for refusing to reveal who leaked the name of Valerie Plame to Novak. The point here is that while we know *what* Miller and Novak knew about Plame, we do not know *how* they knew it.

To deal with the notion of legal or justified history we introduce a propositional symbol L which is satisfied only by legal pairs (w, H). (We may also write $L(w, H)$ to indicate that the pair (w, H) is legal.) Since L can only be defined in terms of knowledge, and knowledge in turn requires quantification over legal histories we shall need mutual recursion.

Given a communication graph and the corresponding model $\mathcal{M} = \langle \mathcal{G}, \mathbf{At}, v \rangle$, and pair (w, H), we define the legality of (w, H) and the truth $\models_{\mathcal{M}}$ of a formula as follows:

- $w, \epsilon \models_{\mathcal{M}} L$
- $w, H; (i, j, \phi) \models_{\mathcal{M}} L$ iff $w, H \models_{\mathcal{M}} L$ and $w, H \models_{\mathcal{M}} K_j \phi$
- $w, H \models_{\mathcal{M}} p$ iff $w(p) = 1$, where $p \in \mathsf{At}$
- $w, H \models_{\mathcal{M}} \neg \phi$ iff $w, H \not\models_{\mathcal{M}} \phi$
- $w, H \models_{\mathcal{M}} \phi \wedge \psi$ iff $w, H \models_{\mathcal{M}} \phi$ and $w, H \models_{\mathcal{M}} \psi$
- $w, H \models_{\mathcal{M}} \Diamond \phi$ iff $\exists H'$, $H \preceq H'$, $L(w, H')$, and $w, H' \models_{\mathcal{M}} \phi$
- $w, H \models_{\mathcal{M}} K_i \phi$ iff $\forall (v, H')$ if $(w, H) \sim_i (v, H')$, and $L(v, H')$, then $v, H' \models_{\mathcal{M}} \phi$

Unless otherwise stated, we will only consider legal pairs (w, H), i.e., pairs (w, H) such that $w, H \models L$. We say ϕ is **valid in** $\mathcal{M}$, $\models_{\mathcal{M}} \phi$ if for all (w, H), $w, H \models_{\mathcal{M}} \phi$. ϕ is **valid in the communication graph frame** $\mathcal{F}$ if ϕ is valid in all models based on $\mathcal{F}$.

2.2   Surface Knowledge

Except for each agent's initial information, one may suspect that all information acquired by the agent i is just the sum of the ϕ which i learned from communications (i, j, ϕ). But we saw that this is not true. Given the assumption that both **At** and the structure of the communication graph are common knowledge, agents can come to know facts that are not explicitly contained in the communications.[1] We might still be interested in this 'surface' knowledge which the agents acquire.

Define the sets $X_i(w, H)$ as follows:

1. $X_i(w, \epsilon) = \{v \mid v_{|\mathsf{At}_i} = w_{|\mathsf{At}_i}\}$
2. $X_i(w, H; (i, j, \phi)) = X_i(w, H) \cap \hat{\phi}$
3. $i \neq m$ then $X_i(w, H; (m, j, \phi)) = X_i(w, H)$

---

[1] Here is an amusing story involving one of us, Parikh. Parikh had published a paper on pumping lemmas and regular sets jointly with A. Ehrenfeucht and G. Rozenberg. At some conference someone asked Parikh, *where* this paper would appear and Parikh did not remember. At this point Rao Kosaraju of Johns Hopkins who was standing by said, it was the *SIAM Journal of Computing*. Parikh then turned to Kosaraju and said, "*you* were the referee!" The point was that Kosaraju's information revealed the existence of an *edge* between him and the editor of *the SIAM journal*.

Intuitively, if $X_i(w, H) \subseteq \hat{\phi}$, then ϕ is implied (for i) by the sequence of communications. We first show a preliminary lemma which is needed to show that at (w, H), agents know at least the formulas implied by $X_i(w, H)$.

Lemma 1. *If* $(w, H) \sim_i (v, H')$, *then* $X_i(w, H) = X_i(v, H')$.

Proof. The proof is by induction on $\lambda_i(H) = \lambda_i(H')$. If $\lambda_i(H)$ was empty then H itself might as well be ϵ, and then we use the fact that $X_i(w, \epsilon) = \{u \mid u_{|At_i} = w_{|At_i}\}$ is the same as $X_i(v, \epsilon) = \{u \mid u_{|At_i} = v_{|At_i}\}$ since $w_{|At_i} = v_{|At_i}$. Otherwise we use the fact that since $\lambda_i(H) = \lambda_i(H')$, the initial set $X_i(w, \epsilon) = X_i(v, \epsilon)$ went through exactly the same intersections with various $\hat{\phi}$ when the ground facts ϕ were learned by i. Indeed $X_i(w, H)$ depends *only* on the *set* of ϕ which i learned in H and not on their order. In particular, If (i, j, ϕ) already occurs in H, then $X_i(w, H; (i, j, \phi)) = X_i(w, H)$. □

Lemma 2. *Let* $\mathcal{M} = \langle \mathcal{G}, \mathbf{At}, v \rangle$ *be any communication graph model and* ϕ *a ground formula. If* $X_i(w, H) \subseteq \hat{\phi}$, *then* $(w, H) \models_{\mathcal{M}} K_i(\phi)$.

Proof. Let $\mathcal{M} = \langle \mathcal{G}, \mathbf{At}, v \rangle$ be a communication graph model. Suppose that ϕ is a ground formula with $X_i(w, H) \subseteq \hat{\phi}$. Let $(v, H') \sim_i (w, H)$. We must show that $v, H' \models_{\mathcal{M}} \phi$. Since ϕ is a ground formula, this is equivalent to showing that $v(\phi) = 1$. Since $(w, H) \sim_i (v, H')$ by Lemma 1 $X_i(v, H') = X_i(w, H) \subseteq \hat{\phi}$. Thus we need only the following claim.

Claim: If $X_i(v, H') \subseteq \hat{\phi}$, then $v(\phi) = 1$.

Proof of claim: The proof is by induction on H'. If $H' = \epsilon$, then since $X_i(v, H') = \{y \mid y_{|At_i} = v_{|At_i}\}$ and, of course, $v_{At_i} = v_{|At_i}$, we have $v \in X_i(v, H') \subseteq \hat{\phi}$. Hence $v(\phi) = 1$. Suppose that $m \neq i$ and $H' = H_1; (m, j, \psi)$. Then by construction $X_i(v, H') = X_i(v, H_1)$, and so, since $X_i(v, H_1) = X_i(v, H') \subseteq \hat{\phi}$, by the induction hypothesis we have $v(\phi) = 1$.

Finally suppose that $H' = H_1(i, j, \psi)$. Then $X_i(v, H') = X_i(v, H_1) \cap \hat{\psi}$. Since we only consider justified state-history pairs, $X_j(v, H_1) \subseteq \hat{\psi}$. Hence, by the induction hypothesis $v(\psi) = 1$. Let θ be any formula such that $X_i(v, H_1) = \hat{\theta}$ (such a formula must exist since $\mathbf{At}$ is finite and so every set of states can be defined by a formula). By the induction hypothesis since $X_i(v, H_1) = \hat{\theta}$, $v(\theta) = 1$. Hence $\hat{\theta} \cap \hat{\psi} = X_i(v, H_1; (i, j, \psi)) \subseteq \hat{\phi}$. Since $v(\theta) = v(\psi) = 1$, $v(\phi) = 1$. This completes the proof of the claim and of the lemma. □

But as we saw, the converse is not true. That is, there are ground formulas that the agents may come to know that are not explicitly contained in their communications. Essentially, these are facts that the agents can derive given their knowledge of the structure of the communication graph and the initial distribution of facts. The sets $X_i(w, H)$ represent the knowledge which agents i would acquire after communication *if* they did not know the structure of the graph.

2.3   Axioms and Decidability

The following axioms and rules are known to be sound and complete with respect to the set of all subset spaces ([13]). Thus they represent the core set of axioms and rules for any topologic.

1. All propositional tautologies
2. $(p \rightarrow \Box p) \wedge (\neg p \rightarrow \Box \neg p)$, for $p \in \mathsf{At}$.
3. $\Box(\phi \rightarrow \psi) \rightarrow (\Box\phi \rightarrow \Box\psi)$
4. $\Box\phi \rightarrow \phi$
5. $\Box\phi \rightarrow \Box\Box\phi$
6. $K_i(\phi \rightarrow \psi) \rightarrow (K_i\phi \rightarrow K_i\psi)$
7. $K_i\phi \rightarrow \phi$
8. $K_i\phi \rightarrow K_iK_i\phi$
9. $\neg K_i\phi \rightarrow K_i\neg K_i\phi$
10. (Cross axiom) $K_i\Box\phi \rightarrow \Box K_i\phi$

We include the following rules: modus ponens, K_i and $\Box$ necessitation. We write $\vdash \phi$ if ϕ can be derived from any of the above schemes and rules. The soundness of axioms 1-9 and the rules are easy to verify also for our framework.

We now show that the cross axiom $K_i\Box\phi \rightarrow \Box K_i\phi$ is sound. It is easier to consider it in its contrapositive form: $\Diamond L_i\phi \rightarrow L_i\Diamond\phi$. This is interpreted as follows: if there is a sequence of updates that lead agent i to consider ϕ possible, then i already thinks it possible that there is a sequence of updates after which ϕ becomes true.

Proposition 1. $\Diamond L_i\phi \rightarrow L_i\Diamond\phi$ *is valid in all communication graph models.*

Proof. Let $\mathcal{M} = \langle \mathcal{G}, \mathbf{At}, v \rangle$ be a communication graph model and (w, H) any justified state-history pair. Suppose that $w, H \models \Diamond L_i\phi$. Then there exists H' with $H \preceq H'$ such that $w, H' \models L_i\phi$. Hence there is a pair (v, H'') such that $(v, H') \sim_i (w, H'')$ and $v, H'' \models_{\mathcal{M}} \phi$. Let H''' be any sequence such that $\lambda_i(H) = \lambda_i(H''')$ and $H''' \preceq H''$. Such a history must exist since $H \preceq H'$ and $H' \sim_i H''$. Since $H \preceq H', \lambda_i(H) \preceq \lambda_i(H') = \lambda_i(H'')$. Therefore, we need only let H''' be any initial segment of H'' containing $\lambda_i(H)$. By definition of L, all initial sequences of a legal history are legal. Therefore, since $v, H'' \models_{\mathcal{M}} \phi$, $v, H''' \models \Diamond\phi$; and since $H \sim_i H'''$, $w, H \models_{\mathcal{M}} L_i\Diamond\phi$. $\Box$

We leave the problem of finding a complete axiomatization for a future paper, and move to decidability. We show that the satisfiability problem is decidable by showing that a satisfiable formula has a model of bounded size. The main idea is to show that for any history H in which an event of the form (i, j, ϕ) occurs twice is "equivalent" to another history in which that event only occurs once. Here "equivalent" means satisfies the same formulas. We first need a definition. Given any history H, let $c(H)$ be the sequence of events of H generated by the order: e comes before e' iff the first occurrence of e in H occurred before the first occurrence of e' in H. Thus $c(H)$ is the compressed history obtained from H by deleting the second and subsequent occurrences of any event. Thus, for instance, if $H = e_2e_1e_2e_1e_3$ then $c(H) = e_2e_1e_3$.

Definition 4. *Let $w \in W$ be any state and suppose that H and H' are justified histories (for w). We say that H and H' are C-equivalent, written $C(H, H')$, iff $c(H) = c(H')$.*

Intuitively, for two histories H and H', $C(H, H')$ holds if their compressed versions are the same.

Lemma 3. *Fix a state w and suppose that H and H' are justified histories. Then*

1. *If $C(H, H')$ and $L(w, HH_1)$, then $L(w, H'H_1)$ and $C(HH_1, H'H_1)$. In particular, taking H_1 to be empty, $L(w, H)$ iff $L(w, H')$.*
2. *If $C(H, H')$ and $H \sim_i H_1$ for some i, then there is a legal history H'_1 such that $C(H_1, H'_1)$ and $H' \sim_i H'_1$.*

Proof. Let w be a state and H and H' two justified histories such that $C(H, H')$. To prove part 1, Let H_1 be any history such that HH_1 is legal. Now the legality of an event (i, j, ϕ) in H_1 as part of HH_1 depended on the fact that j knew ϕ. Now every (j, m, ψ) which occurred in H also occurred in H' and if it occurred in H_1 as part of HH_1 it would also occur in H_1 as part of $H'H_1$. Thus the same justifications for H_1 events are available in both cases and $H'H_1$ must also be legal. Clearly, $c(HH_1) = c(H'H_1)$. Therefore $C(HH_1, H'H_1)$.

For part 2, suppose that $H \sim_i H_1$ for some agent i and legal history H_1. Since $H \sim_i H_1$, $\lambda_i(c(H)) = \lambda_i(c(H_1))$. Also, since $c(H) = c(H')$, $\lambda_i(c(H)) = \lambda_i(c(H'))$. Therefore, $\lambda_i(c(H')) = \lambda_i(c(H_1))$.

That is, the sequence of first occurrence of i events in H' is the same as the sequence of first occurrence of i events in H_1. Thus, by adding extra i events to or removing excess i events from H_1, a history H'_1 can be constructed such that $H' \sim_i H'_1$. Clearly by construction $c(H_1) = c(H'_1)$. $\square$

Corollary 1. 1. *Let the relation D between state history pairs be defined by $D((w, H), (w, H'))$ iff $C(H, H')$. Then $L(w, H)$ iff $L(w, H')$ and D is a bisimulation.*
2. *with the same assumptions, for all formulas ϕ, $w, H \models \phi$ iff $w, H' \models \phi$.*
3. *For all formulas ϕ, $w, H \models \phi$ iff $w, c(H) \models \phi$.*
4. *If H contains (i, j, ψ) and $L(w, H)$ holds, then also $L(H; (i, j, \psi))$, and for all ϕ, $(w, H) \models \phi$ iff $(w, H; (i, j, \psi)) \models \phi$*

Corollary 2. *If a formula ϕ is satisfiable in some graph model $(\mathcal{G}, \textbf{At})$ then it is satisfiable in a history in which no communication (i, j, ϕ) occurs twice.*

This last result immediately gives us a decision procedure as we can limit the length of the history which might satisfy some given formula ϕ. Now there are only a finite number of ground formulas ϕ, thus only a finite number of learnings (i, j, ϕ), and hence only a finite number of histories we need to look at. Alas, this number is quite large and we hope to find a better decision procedure. Note that if we limited the agents to read *only* atomic formulas, a very natural restriction, then the number of possible communications would be smaller and the decision procedure would be faster, and indeed would be in non-deterministic exponential time. The logic *would* change as the formulas $K_i(p \vee q) \rightarrow K_i(p) \vee K_i(q)$ would be valid with such a restriction, but are not valid if non-atomic formulas can be read from another agent's website.

We now define a maximal history (relative to some w) as a history in which all possible (finitely many) communication events have taken place at least once. If H is a maximal history, then we will have, for all H', $C(H, HH')$ and hence for all H', all w, ϕ, $w, H \models \phi$ iff $w, HH' \models \phi$. In other words, a maximal w, H satisfies, for all ϕ, $\phi \leftrightarrow \Box \phi$.

Theorem 1. *The axiom $\Box \Diamond \phi \rightarrow \Diamond \Box \phi$ is valid in Logic of Communication Graphs.*

Proof. Fix w compatible with some history H which satisfies $\Box \Diamond \phi$. Let H' be a maximal history extending H, then w, H' satisfies $\Diamond \phi$ and hence ϕ and hence $\Box \phi$. Since H' extends H, w, H satisfies $\Diamond \Box \phi$. □

We strongly suspect that if H and H' are maximal histories (relative to w), then w, H and w, H' satisfy the same formulas. In this case, $\Diamond \Box \phi \rightarrow \Box \Diamond \phi$ would be valid. This and other issues related to a complete axiomatization will be left for another paper.

3   Connection with Communication Graphs

In this section we will investigate the close connection between formulas valid in a model based on the communication graph and the communication graph. We will prove that the valid formulas characterize the communication graph.

Theorem 2. *Let $\mathcal{G} = (\mathcal{A}, E)$ be a communication graph. Then $(i, j) \in E$ if and only if, for all $l \in \mathcal{A}$ such that $l \neq i$ and $l \neq j$ and all ground formulas ϕ, the scheme*

$$K_j \phi \wedge \neg K_l \phi \rightarrow \Diamond (K_i \phi \wedge \neg K_l \phi)$$

is valid in all communication graph models based on $\mathcal{G}$.

Proof. Suppose that $w, H \models_M K_j \phi \wedge \neg K_l \phi$. Then j knows ϕ and hence i can read ϕ directly from j's website. l is none the wiser as $\lambda_l(H) = \lambda_l(H; (i, j, \phi))$. Therefore, $w, H; (i, j, \phi) \models K_i \phi \wedge \neg K_l \phi$. □

4   Conclusions and Further Work

In this paper we have introduced a logic of knowledge and communication. Communication among agents is restricted by a communication graph, and idealized in the sense that the agents are unaware when their knowledge base is being accessed. We have shown that the communication graph is characterized by the validities of formulas in models based on that communication graph, and that our logic is decidable.

Related Work: This paper fits in with a growing body of work on social software ([14]). One of the main goals of the social software research program is to develop mathematical tools that can be used to study social procedures. Other work that falls into this category is [17] which studies the semantics of messages, [2] which studies voting strategies in the presence of knowledge, and [15] which studies a logic of knowledge with obligation.

Logics of knowledge acquisition through communication have been studied earlier, starting with [18] and more recently in [1, 11, 19, 7]. In chapter 4 of [11], Kooi provides an excellent overview of the current state of affairs of these dynamic epistemic logics. These logics use **PDL** style operators to represent an epistemic update. For example, if $!\phi$ is intended to mean a public announcement of ϕ, then $\langle!\phi\rangle K_i\phi$ is intended to mean that after ϕ is publically announced, agent i knows ϕ. From this point of view, the communication modality $\Diamond$ can be understood as existentially quantifying over a sequence of private epistemic updates. However, there are some important differences between the semantics presented in this paper and the semantics found in the dynamic epistemic logic literature. First of all, in our semantics communication is limited by the communication graph. Secondly, we do not consider general epistemic updates as is common in the literature, but rather study a specific type of epistemic update and its connection with a communication graph. Most important is the fact that the history of communications plays a key role in the deninition of knowledge in this paper. The general approach of dynamic epistemic semantics is to define update operations mapping Kripke structures to other Kripke structures intended to represent the effect of an epistemic update on the first Kripke structure. For example, a public announcement of ϕ selects the submodel of a Kripke structure in which ϕ is true at every state. The definition of knowledge after an epistemic update is the usual definition, i.e., ϕ is known by i at state w if ϕ is true in all states that i considers possible from state w in the updated Kripke structure. A closer analysis of the similarities and differences between these two approaches is an interesting topic for further study.

Further Work: We showed that the logic of communication graphs has the finite model property and so is decidable. Other standard questions such as finding an elegant complete axiomatization will also be studied. Another interesting extension would be to allow different types of updates, such as lying, conscious updates (where j is aware that his website is being read), updating to subgroups (creating common knowledge) and so on.

Another natural extension is to consider situations in which agents have a preference over which information they will read from another agent's website. Thus for example, if one hears that an English Ph.D. student and his advisor recently had a meeting, then one is justified in assuming that they probably did not discuss the existence of non-recursive sets, even though the advisor may conceivably know this fact. I.e., the advisor may have the fact, that there exists a non-recursive set, on her website, but there is a very good chance that the Ph.D. student did not ask about this particular fact. Given that this preference over the formulas under discussion among different groups of agents is common knowledge, each agent can regard some (legal) histories as being more or less likely than other (legal) histories. From this ordering over histories, we can define a defeasible knowledge operator for each agent. The operator is defeasible in the sense that agents may be wrong, i.e., it *is* after all possible that the English student and his advisor actually spent the meeting discussing the fact that there must be a non-recursive set.

Finally we remark that our framework and the logic can be seen as a demonstration of the need for cryptographic protocols. Two issues are important here. The first is that an agent may only want part of its knowledge base to be accessible by the public. This may be modeled in our framework by restricting for each agent j the set of formulas that the agent makes available, and so when i is directly connected to j, i can only update by facts in the accessible domain. The second issue is that we may not know the exact structure of the communication graph. For example, if Ann accesses some information from Bob's website, but unknown to Ann, Charles is listening in, then the communication graph has an edge between Charles and Bob, whose presence is not known to Ann or to Bob. Then clearly as a condition for Ann learning some information from Bob, Charles must be able to be informed of that same piece of information. Thus cryptographic protocols essentially intended to ensure that there are no undesired edges between agents in the communication graph. Thus, in that version of our model where the entire graph is not common knowledge, inferring the existence of edges *from* knowledge (as the Kosaraju example showed) is yet another, potentially important extension.

References

1. Baltag, A. and Moss, L., Logics for Epistemic Programs, *Knowledge, Rationality, and Action* section of *Synthese*, 139:**2**, pgs. 165-224, 2004,
2. Samir Chopra, Eric Pacuit and Rohit Parikh, *Knowledge-theoretic Properties of Strategic Voting*, Proceedings of 9th European Conference on Logics in Artifical Intelligence, Jos Jlio Alferes and Joo Leite editors, Lecture Notes in Artificial Intelligence, Springer, pgs. 18-30, 2004.
3. Dabrowski, A, Moss, L, and Parikh, R. Topolgical reasoning and the logic of knowledge. *Annals of Pure and Applied Logic*, **78**, (1996), pp. 73 - 110.
4. Georgatos, K, Modal Logics for Topological Spaces. PhD Dissertation. Graduate School and University Center. City University of New York, 1993.
5. Georgatos, K, Knowledge Theoretic Properties of Topological Spaces. In *Knowledge Representation and Uncertainty*. M. Masuch and L. Polos, Eds. Lecture Notes in Artificial Intelligence, vol. 808, pages 147-159, Springer-Verlag, 1994.
6. Georgatos, K, Knowledge on Treelike Spaces. *Studia Logica*, **59**, (1997), pp. 271 - 231.
7. Gerbrandy, J., *Bisimulations on Planet Kripke*, Ph.D. dissertation, University of Amsterdam, 1999.
8. Heinemann, B., Temporal Aspects of the Modal Logic of Subset Spaces, *Theoretical Computer Science*, **224(1-2)**:135-155, 1999.

9. Heinemann, B., Extending Topological Nexttime Logic. In S. D. Goodwin, A. Trudel, editors, *Temporal Representation and Reasoning*, TIME-00, Cape Breton, Nova Scotia, Canada, pages 87-94, IEEE Computer Society Press, Los Alamitos, CA, 2000.

10. Heinemann, B., A Hybrid Treatment of Evolutionary Sets. In C. A. Coello Coello, A. de Albornoz, L. E. Sucar, O. Cair Battistutti, editors, MICAI'2002: *Advances in Artificial Intelligence*, Mrida, Yucatn, Mexico. Volume 2313 of Lecture Notes in Artificial Intelligence, pages 204-213, Springer, Berlin, 2002.

11. Kooi, B., *Knowledge, Chance, and Change*, Ph.D. dissertation, University of Groningen, 2003.

12. Heinemann, B., A Hybrid Logic of Knowledge Supporting Topological Reasoning. In *Algebraic Methodology and Software Technology*, AMAST 2004, Stirling, United Kingdom. Lecture Notes in Computer Science, Springer, Berlin, 2004. *To appear*.

13. Moss, L. and Parikh, Topological Reasoning and the Logic of Knowledge, *TARK IV*, Ed. Y. Moses, Morgan Kaufmann, 1992.

14. Parikh, R., Social Software, *Synthese*, **132: 3**, Sep 2002, pp. 187-211.

15. Parikh, R., Pacuit, E. and Cogan, E., The logic of knowledge based obligation. Early version presented at DALT '04. Forthcoming in *Knowledge Rationality and Action*: Special Issue on the Knowledge and Games Workshop, 2005.

16. Parikh, R., and R. Ramanujam "Distributed Processing and the Logic of Knowledge", in *Logics of Programs*, Proceedings of a Conference at Brooklyn College, June 1985, Springer Lecture Notes in Computer Science #193., pp. 256-268.

17. Parikh, R. and Ramanujam, R., A knowledge based semantics of messages, in *J. Logic, Language, and Information*, **12**, pp. 453 - 467, 2003.

18. Plaza, J., Logics of public communications, *Proceedings, 4th International Symposium on Methodologies for Intelligent Systems*, 1989.

19. van Ditmarsch, H., *Knowledge Games*, Ph.D. dissertation, University of Groningen, 2000.

20. Vickers, S. *Topology Via Logic*, Cambridge University Press. 1989.

21. Weiss, M. A. and Parikh, R., "Completeness of Certain Bimodal Logics of Subset Spaces", *Studia Logica*, **71:1**, pp. 1 - 30, 2002.

Representational Content and the Reciprocal Interplay of Agent and Environment

Tibor Bosse[1], Catholijn M. Jonker[1], and Jan Treur[1,2]

[1] Vrije Universiteit Amsterdam, Department of Artificial Intelligence,
De Boelelaan 1081a, NL-1081 HV Amsterdam, The Netherlands
[2] Utrecht University, Department of Philosophy,
Heidelberglaan 8, 3584 CS Utrecht
{tbosse, jonker, treur}@cs.vu.nl
http://www.cs.vu.nl/~{tbosse, jonker, treur}

Abstract. Declarative modelling approaches in principle assume a notion of representation or representational content for the modelling concepts. The notion of representational content as discussed in literature in cognitive science and philosophy of mind shows complications as soon as agent and environment have an intense reciprocal interaction. In such cases an internal agent state is affected by the way in which internal and external aspects are interwoven during (ongoing) interaction. In this paper it is shown that the classical correlational approach to representational content is not applicable, but the temporal-interactivist approach is. As this approach involves more complex temporal relationships, formalisation was used to define specifications of the representational content more precisely. These specifications have been validated by automatically checking them on traces generated by a simulation model. Moreover, by mathematical proof it was shown how these specifications are entailed by the basic local properties.

1 Introduction

Declarative modelling approaches go hand in hand with some assumed notion of representation or representational content for the modelling concepts. Within cognitive and philosophical literature, classical approaches to representational content are based on correlations between an agent's internal state properties and external state properties. For example, the presence of a horse in the field is correlated to an internal state property that plays the role of a percept for this horse. One of the critical evaluations of this approach addresses the limitation that it is static: internal state properties are to be related to single external states, and cannot be related to processes involving multiple states or events over time. Especially in cases where the agent-environment interaction takes the form of an extensive reciprocal interplay in which both the agent and the environment contribute to the process in a mutual dependency, a classical approach to representational content is insufficient. Some authors even claim that it is a bad idea to aim for a notion of representation in such cases; e.g., [7; 12]. Therefore these cases can be considered a serious challenge to declarative methods.

J. Leite et al. (Eds.): DALT 2004, LNAI 3476, pp. 270–288, 2005.
© Springer-Verlag Berlin Heidelberg 2005

As an alternative, within Philosophy of Mind, the *interactivist* approach [1] is put forward. In [5] it is shown how a temporal-interactivist approach to representational content of an internal state property can be formalised based on sets of agent-environment past and future interaction trajectories or traces.

In this paper it is analysed how some non-classical approaches may be used to define representational content in the case of an extensive agent-environment interplay. In particular, for a case study it will be discussed how the temporal-interactivist approach and second-order approach to representational content can be used. These alternative notions involve more complex temporal relationships between internal and external states. Formalisation to define specifications of the representational content more precisely was used as a means to handle this complexity. This formalisation provided dynamic properties that can be (and actually have been) formally checked for given traces of the agent-environment interaction.

In Section 2 the modelling approach is briefly introduced. Section 3 introduces the case study and the language used to model this case study. In Section 4 a number of local dynamic properties describing basic mechanisms for the case study are presented; simulations on the basis of these local dynamic properties are discussed in Section 5. Section 6 presents global dynamic properties, describing the process as a whole and larger parts of the process. In Section 7 the interlevel relations between these nonlocal properties and the local properties are discussed. In Section 8 three different approaches to representational content are explored and formalised for the case study. In Section 9 it is shown how these formalisations can be validated against the simulation model, both by mathematical proof and by automated checks. Section 10 is a discussion.

2 Modelling Approach

To formally specify dynamic properties that express criteria for representational content from a temporal perspective an expressive language is needed. To this end the *Temporal Trace Language* is used as a tool; cf. [4]. In this paper for most of the occurring properties both informal or semi-formal and formal representations are given. The formal representations are based on the Temporal Trace Language (TTL), which is briefly defined as follows.

A *state ontology* is a specification (in order-sorted logic) of a vocabulary, i.e., a signature. A state for ontology Ont is an assignment of truth-values {true, false} to the set At(Ont) of ground atoms expressed in terms of Ont. The *set of all possible states* for state ontology Ont is denoted by STATES(Ont). The set of *state properties* STATPROP(Ont) for state ontology Ont is the set of all propositions over ground atoms from At(Ont). A fixed *time frame* T is assumed which is linearly ordered. A *trace* or *trajectory* γ over a state ontology Ont and time frame T is a mapping $\gamma : T \rightarrow$ STATES(Ont), i.e., a sequence of states γ_t ($t \in T$) in STATES(Ont). The set of all traces over state ontology Ont is denoted by TRACES(Ont). Depending on the application, the time frame T may be dense (e.g., the real numbers), or discrete (e.g., the set of integers or natural numbers or a finite initial segment of the natural numbers), or any other form, as long as it has a linear ordering. The set of *dynamic properties* DYNPROP(Σ) is the set of temporal statements that can be formulated with respect to traces based on the state ontology Ont in the following manner.

Given a trace γ over state ontology Ont, the input state of the organism (i.e., state of sensors for external world and body) at time point t is denoted by state(γ, t, input); analogously, state(γ, t, output), state (γ, t, internal) and state (γ, t, EW) denote the output state, internal state and external state (of the world, including the physical body) for the organism.

These states can be related to state properties via the formally defined satisfaction relation $\models$, comparable to the Holds-predicate in the Situation Calculus (see [11] for an introduction, and [10] for an example application): state(γ, t, output) $\models$ p denotes that state property p holds in trace γ at time t in the output state of the organism. Based on these statements, dynamic properties can be formulated in a formal manner in a sorted first-order predicate logic with sorts T for time points, Traces for traces and F for state formulae, using quantifiers over time and the usual first-order logical connectives such as $\neg, \wedge, \vee, \Rightarrow, \forall, \exists$.

To model direct temporal dependencies between two state properties, the simpler *leads to* format is used. This is an executable format defined as follows. Let α and β be state properties of the form "conjunction of literals" (where a literal is an atom or the negation of an atom), and e, f, g, h non-negative real numbers. In the *leads to* language $\alpha \twoheadrightarrow_{e, f, g, h} \beta$, means:

If   state property α holds for a certain time interval with duration g,
then   after some delay (between e and f) state property β will hold for a certain time interval of length h .

For a precise definition of the *leads to* format in terms of the language TTL, see [6]. A specification of dynamic properties in *leads to* format has as advantages that it is executable and that it can often easily be depicted graphically. The *leads to* format has shown its value especially when temporal or causal relations in the (continuous) physical world are modelled and simulated in an abstract, non-discrete manner; for example, the intracellular chemistry of *E. coli* [3].

3   The Case Study

In this Section the case study will be introduced and the internal state properties and their dynamics to model this example are presented.

3.1   Introduction of the Case Study

The case study addressed involves the processes to unlock a front door that sticks. Between the moment that the door is reached and the moment that the door unlocks the following reciprocal interaction takes place:

- the agent puts rotating pressure on the key,
- the door lock generates resistance in the interplay,
- the agent notices the resistance and increases the rotating pressure,
- the door increases the resistance,

- and so on, without any result.
- finally, after noticing the impasse the agent changes the strategy by at the same time pulling the door and turning the key, which unlocks the door.

This example shows different elements. The first part of the process is described in terms of Sun's sub-conceptual level, whereas the last part of the process is viewed in terms of the conceptual level [12; 13]. For both parts of the process the notion of representational content will be discussed and formalised.

3.2 State Properties

To model the example the following internal state properties are used:

s1	sensory representation for being at the door
s2(r)	sensory representation for resistance r of the lock
p1(p)	preparation for the action to turn the key with rotating pressure p (without pulling the door)
p2	preparation for combined pulling the door and turning the key
c	state for having learnt that turning the key should be combined with pulling the door

The interactions between agent and environment are defined by the following sensor and effector states:

o1	observing being at the door
o2(r)	observing resistance r
a1(p)	action turn the key with rotating pressure p (without pulling the door)
a2	action turn the key while pulling the door

In addition, the following state properties of the world are used:

arriving_at_door	the agent arrives at the door
lock_reaction(r)	the lock reacts with resistance r
door_unlocked	the door is unlocked
d(mr)	resistance threshold mr of the door (indicating that the door will continue to resist until pressure mr or more is used)
max_p(mp)	maximal force on the key that can be exercised by the agent.

4 Local Dynamic Properties

To model the dynamics of the example, the following local properties (in *leads to* format) are considered. They describe the basic parts of the process.

LP1 (observation of door)

The first local property LP1 expresses that the world state property arriving_at_door leads to an observation of being at the door. Formalisation:

arriving_at_door $\twoheadrightarrow$ o1

LP2 (observation of resistance)

Local property LP2 expresses that the world state property lock_reaction with resistance r leads to an observation of this resistance r.

lock_reaction(r) $\twoheadrightarrow$ o2(r)

Note that r is a variable here; the specification should be read as a schema for the set of all instances for r.

LP3 (sensory representation of door)

Local property LP3 expresses that the observation of being at the door leads to a sensory representation for being at the door.

o1 →» s1

LP4 (sensory representation of resistance)

LP4 expresses that the observation of resistance r of the lock leads to a sensory representation for this resistance.

o2(r) →» s2(r)

LP5 (action preparation initiation)

LP5 expresses that a sensory representation for being at the door leads to a preparation for the action to turn the key with pressure 1.

s1 →» p1(1)

LP6 (pressure adaptation)

LP6 expresses the following: if turning the key with a certain pressure p did not succeed (since the agent received a resistance that equals p), and the agent has not reached its maximal force (p<mp), and the agent has not learnt anything yet (not c), then it will increase its pressure.

p1(p) and s2(r) and p=r and p<mp and not c →» p1(p+1)

LP7 (birth of learning state)

LP7 expresses that, if turning the key with a certain pressure p did not succeed (since the agent received a resistance that equals p), and the agent has reached the limit of its force (p≥mp), then it will learn that should perform a different action.

p1(p) and s2(r) and p=r and p≥mp →» c

LP8 (learning state persistency)

LP8 expresses that the learning state property c persists forever.

c →» c

LP9 (alternative action preparation)

LP9 expresses that a sensory representation for resistance r of the lock together with the learning state property lead to a preparation for combined pulling of the door and turning the key.

c and s2(r) →» p2

LP10 (action performance)

LP10 expresses that a preparation for the action to turn the key with pressure p (without pulling the door) leads to the actual performance of this action.

p1(p) →» a1(p)

LP11 (alternative action performance)
LP11 expresses that a preparation for combined pulling of the door and turning the key leads to the actual performance of this action.

p2 —» a2

LP12 (negative effect of action)
LP12 expresses the following property of the world: if the key is turned with a certain pressure p that is smaller than the maximal resistance of the door (p<mr), and the agent is not pulling the door simultaneously, then the lock will react with resistance p.

a1(p) and not a2 and d(mr) and p<mr —» lock_reaction(p)

LP13 (positive effect of action)
LP13 expresses the following property of the world: if the key is turned with a certain pressure p that at least equals the maximal resistance of the door (p≥mr), then the door will unlock.

a1(p) and d(mr) and p≥mr —» door_unlocked

LP14 (positive effect of alternative action)
LP14 expresses the following property of the world: if the agent turns the key, and simultaneously pulls the door, then the door will unlock.

a2 —» door_unlocked

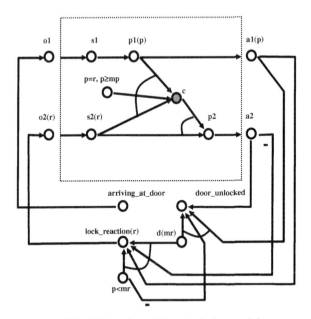

Fig. 1. Overview of the simulation model

In Figure 1 an overview of these properties is given in a graphical form. To limit complexity, local property LP6 is not depicted.

5 Simulation

A special software environment has been created to enable the simulation of executable models. Based on an input consisting of dynamic properties in *leads to* format, the software environment generates simulation traces. An example of such a trace can be seen in Figure 2. Time is on the horizontal axis, the state properties are on the vertical axis. A dark box on top of the line indicates that the property is true during that time period, and a lighter box below the line indicates that the property is false. This trace is based on all local properties identified above. In property LP6, the values (0,0,1,5) have been chosen for the timing parameters e, f, g, and h. In all other properties, the values (0,0,1,1) have been chosen. As can be seen in Figure 2, the presence of the agent at the door leads to a corresponding observation result (o1), followed by a sensory representation for being at the door. Next, the agent prepares for turning the key (initially with pressure 1), and subsequently performs this action. Since this pressure is insufficient to unlock the door (within this example, the resistant threshold of the door is 5), the door does not open, but a lock reaction (with resistance 1) occurs instead. As a consequence, the agent observes this resistance, and creates a sensory representation of it. At this point, the agent prepares to increase the pressure (see local property LP6), resulting in the action of turning the key with pressure 2. This loop is being activated once more: the agent even tries to turn the key with pressure 3, but then reaches the limit of its force (3 in this example, see LP7) and learns that it should perform a different action. In other words, internal state property c becomes true.

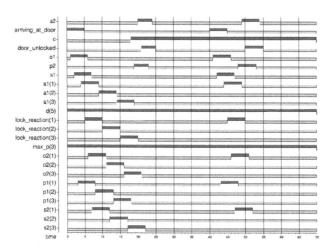

Fig. 2. Example simulation trace

Subsequently, the combination of this state property c and state property s2(3) leads to the preparation for an alternative action: combined pulling of the door and turning the key. As a result of this preparation, the action is actually performed and the door is unlocked. After that, to show that the agent has indeed learned something, the trace continues for a while. At time point 40, the agent again finds itself confronted with a locked door. Again, it starts by trying to turn the key with pressure 1. However, when this approach turns out not to work, this time the agent shows adapted behaviour. It does not try to increase the pressure, but immediately switches to the alternative action instead.

6 Non-local Dynamic Properties

This section presents dynamic properties for larger parts of the process, i.e., at a nonlocal level. Within these properties, γ is a variable that stands for an arbitrary trace.

GP1 (door eventually unlocked)
Global property GP1 expresses that eventually the door will be unlocked.

∀t: state(γ, t, EW) ⊨ arriving_at_door ⇒
     ∃t'≥t: state(γ, t', EW) ⊨ door_unlocked

GP2 (learning occurs)
Global property GP2 expresses that if the maximal resistance of the door is bigger than the maximal rotation force that the agent can exert, then at some point in time learning will occur.

∀t: state(γ, t, EW) ⊨ d(mr) ∧
     ∀t: state(γ, t, internal) ⊨ max_p(mp) ∧ mr > mp ⇒
          ∃t' state(γ, t', internal) ⊨ c

GP3 (mr > mp ⇒ door eventually unlocked)
Global property GP3 expresses that if the maximal resistance of the door is bigger than the maximal rotation force that the agent can exert, then at some point in time the door will be unlocked.

∀t: state(γ, t, EW) ⊨ d(mr) ∧
     ∀t: state(γ, t, internal) ⊨ max_p(mp) ∧ mr > mp ⇒
          ∃t' state(γ, t', EW) ⊨ door_unlocked

GP4 (mr ≤ mp ⇒ door eventually unlocked)
Global property GP4 expresses that if the maximal resistance of the door is less than or equal to the maximal rotation force that the agent can exert, then at some point in time the door will be unlocked.

∀t: state(γ, t, EW) ⊨ d(mr) ∧
     ∀t: state(γ, t, internal) ⊨ max_p(mp) ∧ mr ≤ mp ⇒
          ∃t' state(γ, t', EW) ⊨ door_unlocked

GP3 and GP4 are formulated separately because their proofs differ. Next a number of intermediate properties are formulated that form a kind of milestones in the process of opening a door and learning.

M1 (at door ⇒ preparation to turn key)
Intermediate property M1 expresses that after the agent stands at the door the agent will prepare for turning the key.

∀t: state(γ, t, EW) ⊨ arriving_at_door ⇒
   ∃t' > t: state(γ, t', internal) ⊨ p1(1)

M2 (lock reaction represented)

Intermediate property M2 expresses that a lock reaction will be represented internally.

∀t: state(γ, t, EW) ⊨ lock_reaction(r) ⇒
   ∃t' > t: state(γ, t', internal) ⊨ s2(r)

M3 (alternative action)

M3 expresses that if lock resistance is internally represented and the agent has learned, then at some later point in time the agent will perform the action a2.

∀t: state(γ, t, internal) ⊨ c ∧ state(γ, t, internal) ⊨ s2(r) ⇒
   ∃t' > t: state(γ, t, ouput) ⊨ a2

M4 (increasing rotation pressure)

M4 expresses that under the condition that agent has not learned c yet, the rotation pressure that the agent exerts on the key will always reach the minimum of the maximal resistance of the door and the maximal force that the agent can exert.

∀t, ∀mp, ∀mr, ∀sl
   not state(γ, t, internal) ⊨ c ∧ state(γ, t, EW) ⊨ d(mr) ∧
   state(γ, t, internal) ⊨ max_p(mp) ∧ sl = minimum(mr, mp) ∧
   state(γ, t, EW) ⊨ arriving_at_door ⇒
      ∃t' > t: state(γ, t', internal) ⊨ p1(sl) ∧ ∃t" > t': state(γ, t", output) ⊨ a1(sl)

Finally, a number of additional properties are needed in order to prove the relations between the properties.

A1 (maximal force)

Additional property A1 expresses that the maximal rotation force that the agent can exert on the key is constant.

∃mp ∀t: state(γ, t, internal) ⊨ max_p(mp)

A2 (maximal resistance)

Additional property A2 expresses that the maximal resistance that the door can offer is constant.

∃mr ∀t: state(γ, t, EW) ⊨ d(mr)

A3 (Closed World Assumption)

The second order property that is commonly known as the Closed World Assumption expresses that at any point in time a state property that is not implied by a specification to be true is false. Let Th be the set of all local properties LP1-LP14.

∀P∈ At(ONT) ∀t: not Th |-- state(γ, t) ⊨ P ⇒ state(γ, t) ⊨ not P

7   Interlevel Relations

This section outlines the interlevel connections between dynamic properties at different levels, varying from dynamic properties at the local level of basic parts of the process to dynamic properties at the global level of the overall process. The following interlevel relations between local dynamic properties and non-local dynamic properties can be identified.

GP3 & GP4	$\Rightarrow$ GP1
M2 & M4 & LP7 & LP12	$\Rightarrow$ GP2
M2 & M3 & M4 & LP7 & LP14	$\Rightarrow$ GP3
M4 & LP13	$\Rightarrow$ GP4
LP1 & LP3 & LP5	$\Rightarrow$ M1
LP2 & LP4	$\Rightarrow$ M2
LP8 & LP9 & LP11	$\Rightarrow$ M3
M1 & M2 & LP6 & LP10 & LP12 & A1 & A2 & A3	$\Rightarrow$ M4

The proofs of M1, M2, M3, and GP1 are rather straightforward and left out. A proof sketch of the other properties is provided.

Property M4 can be proved by induction. The induction step is

$\forall t$: state(γ, t, output) $\models$ a1(p) $\wedge$ p < sl $\Rightarrow$
$\quad \exists t1 > t, \exists t2 > t1$:
$\qquad$ state(γ, t1, internal) $\models$ p1(p+1) $\wedge$ state(γ, t2, output) $\models$ a1(p+1)

The induction base is given by properties M1 and LP10, providing p1(1), and a1(1). The induction step is proved along the following lines.

- "not a2" holds at all times during which "not c" holds.

This is proved on the basis of "not c" and A3. A3 states that if a2 cannot be derived from the specification at a certain point in time, then "not a2" holds at that time. So pick any point in time at which "not c" holds and try to prove a2 from all local properties and the additional assumptions A1, A2, and A3. If a2 can be proven, it is due to LP11. The condition of LP11 is p2. The only way to prove p2 is through LP9. The conditions of LP9 are c and s2(r). The condition c is in direct contradiction with "not c". In the above the temporal elements of the proof were not mentioned. To complete this proof these elements do play a role, for example, c cannot change its truth more than once. It starts out false and remains false until (by application of LP7) it becomes true. Once c is true, it remains true by application of LP8. Therefore, as long as "not c" holds, "not a2" also holds (and even a bit longer).

- a1(p) holds

In proving the induction step, the condition is assumed. Thus a1(p) holds.

- d(mr) holds

Direct from A2.

- p < mr

This is true, since p < sl and sl is the minimum of mp and mr.

- lock_reaction(p) holds.

All conditions of LP12 hold (i.e., a1(p), not a2, d(mr), p < mr), thus LP12 can be applied, which makes sure that lock_reaction(p) holds some time later.

- s2(p) holds

Based on lock_reaction(p), M2 can be applied, thus some time later s2(p) will hold.

- p1(p+1) holds at some time point t1 later than the chosen time t.

By application of LP6 some time later (call this time point t1) p1(p+1) will hold . Note that the conditions of LP6 are met: p < mp holds, since p < sl, and sl the minimum of mp and mr.

- a1(p+1) holds at some time t2 later than t1.

This is proved by applying LP10 with p+1. This proves that the induction step holds.

Now assuming that the antecedent of M4 holds, implies that subsequently (over time) LP1, LP3, LP5 and LP10 can be applied. In that manner, from arriving at the door, an observation of that fact is derived, leading to an internal representation thereof (s1), leading to an internal state in which p1(1) holds, leading to an output state in which a1(1) holds. Therefore, all circumstances hold for the induction step to be applicable. Application of the induction step leads to the conclusion that at some point in time p1(sl) holds in the internal state and some time later again a1(sl) holds in the output state. Thus proving the conclusion of M4 under the assumption that the antecedent of M4 holds. This concludes the proof by induction of M4.

Property GP2 can be proved as follows. Since mr > mp, sl = mp. Applying M4 gives us ∃t': state(γ, t', output) ⊨ a1(mp). By application of LP12, we get some time later lock_reaction(mp), application of M2 gives us, some time later again, s2(mp). Finally, application of LP7 provides us with the learned c.

The proof of Property GP3 follows the following subsequent time points of interest: application of M4 gives a time point t1 such that p1(mp) holds, application of M2 give a time t2 such that s2(mp) holds, application of LP7 gives a time t3 such that c holds, application of M3 gives a time t4 such that a2 holds, application of LP14 gives a time t5 such that door_unlocked holds.

The proof of property GP4 is rather short, by application of M4 at a certain time t1 a1(mr) will hold, by application of LP13 a later time t2 exist at which door_unlocked holds. All proofs can be worked out in more details by using the timing parameters of the local properties involved.

8   Representational Content

In the literature on Philosophy of Mind different types of approaches to representational content of an internal state property have been put forward, for example the correlational, interactivist, relational specification and second-order representation approach; cf. [8], pp. 191-193, 200-202, [1]. These approaches have in common that the occurrence of the internal state property at a specific point in time is related to the occurrence of other state properties, at the same or at different time points. The "other state properties" can be of three types:

- A. *external world state properties*, independent of the agent
- B. the agent's sensor state and effector state properties, i.e., the agent's *interaction state properties* (interactivist approach)
- C. *internal state properties* of the agent (higher-order representation)

Furthermore, the type of relationships can be of (1) purely functional *one-to-one correspondences*, (e.g., the correlational approach), or (2) they can involve more *complex relationships* with a number of states at different points in time in the past or future, (e.g., the interactivist approach). So, six types of approaches to representational content are distinguished, that can be indicated by codings such as A1, A2, and so on. Below, examples are given.

8.1 Correlational Approach

According to the Correlational approach, the representational content of a certain internal state is given by a one-to-one correlation to another (in principle external) state property: type A1. Such an external state property may exist backward as well as forward in time. Hence, for the current example, the representational content for internal state property s1 can be defined as world state property arriving_at_door, by looking <u>backward</u> in time. Intuitively, this is a correct definition, since for all possible situations where the agent has s1, it was indeed physically present at the door, and conversely. Likewise, the representational content for internal state property p2 can be defined as action property a2, by looking <u>forward</u> in time, or, rather, as world state property door_unlocked. However, for many other internal state properties the representational content cannot be defined adequately according to the correlational approach. In these cases, reference should not be made to one single state in the past or in the future, but to a temporal sequence of inputs or output state properties, which is not considered to adequately fit in the correlational approach. An overview for the content of all internal state properties according to the correlational approach (if any), is given in Table 1. These relationships can easily be specified in the language TTL.

Table 1. Correlational approach

Internal state property	Content (backward)	Content (forward)
s1	arriving_at_door	lock_reaction(1)
s2(r)	lock_reaction(r)	*impossible*
p1(1)	arriving_at_door	lock_reaction(1)
p1(2)	*impossible*	lock_reaction(2)
p2	*impossible*	door_unlocked
c	*impossible*	*impossible*

8.2 Temporal-Interactivist Approach

The temporal-interactivist approach [1; 5] relates the occurrence of internal state properties to sets of past and future interaction traces: type B. This can be done in the form of functional one-to-one correspondences (type B1), or by involving more complex relationships over time (type B2). In this paper the focus is on the more advanced case, i.e., the B2 type. As an example, consider the internal state property c. The representational content of c is defined in a semantic manner by the pair of sets of past interaction traces and future interaction traces (here InteractionOnt denotes the input and output state ontology and IntOnt the internal state ontology; $\gamma_{\leq t}^{\text{InteractionOnt}}$ denotes the trace γ up to t, with states restricted to the interaction states):

$$\text{PITRACES(c)} = \{ \gamma_{\leq t}^{\text{InteractionOnt}} \mid t \in T, \text{state}(\gamma, t, \text{IntOnt}) \models c\}$$
$$\text{FITRACES(c)} = \{ \gamma_{\geq t}^{\text{InteractionOnt}} \mid t \in T, \text{state}(\gamma, t, \text{IntOnt}) \models c \}$$

Here the first set, PITRACES(c), contains all past interaction traces for which sequence of time points exists such that at these time points first o1 occurs, next a1(1), next o2(1), next a1(2), next o2(2), next a1(3), and next o2(3). For this example, a learning phase of 3 trials has been chosen. The second set, FITRACES(c), contains all future interaction traces for which no o2(r) occurs, or o2(r) occurs and after this a2 occurs.

An overview for the representational content of all internal state properties according to the temporal-interactivist approach is given, in an informal notation, in Table 2.

Table 2. Temporal-interactivist approach (semantic description)

I.s.p.	Content (backward)	Content (forward)
s1	o1	a1(1)
s2(r)	o2(r)	if c (defined by o1, ..., o2(3)), then a2
p1(1)	o1	a1(1)
p1(2)	o1, a1(1), o2(1)	a1(2)
p1(3)	o1, a1(1), o2(1), a1(2), o2(2)	a1(3)
p2	o1, a1(1), o2(1), a1(2), o2(2), a1(3), o2(3)	a2
c	o1, a1(1), o2(1), a1(2), o2(2), a1(3), o2(3)	if o2(r), then a2

Table 3. Temporal-interactivist approach (syntactic description, backward)

I.s.p.	Content (backward)
s1	is_followed_by(γ, o1, input, s1, internal) & is_preceded_by(γ, s1, internal, o1, input)
s2(r)	is_followed_by(γ, o2(r), input, s2(r), internal) & is_preceded by(γ, s2(r), internal, o2(r), input)
p1(1)	is_followed_by(γ, o1, input, p1(1), internal) & is_preceded by(γ, p1(1), internal, o1, input)
p1(2)	$\forall$t1,t2,t3 [t1$\leq$t2$\leq$t3 & state(γ, t1, input) $\models$ o1 & interplay_up_to(γ, t2, t3,1) & not [$\exists$t11,t12,t17 [t11$\leq$t12$\leq$t17$\leq$t3 & state(γ, t11, input) $\models$ o1 & interplay_up_to(γ, t12, t17,3)]] $\Rightarrow$ $\exists$t4 $\geq$ t3 state(γ, t4, internal) $\models$ p1(2)] & $\forall$t4 [state(γ, t4, internal) $\models$ p1(2) $\Rightarrow$ $\exists$t1,t2,t3 t1$\leq$t2$\leq$t3$\leq$t4 & state(γ, t1, input) $\models$ o1 & interplay_up_to(γ, t2, t3,1)]
p1(3)	$\forall$t1,t2,t5 [t1$\leq$t2$\leq$t5 & state(γ, t1, input) $\models$ o1 & interplay_up_to(γ, t2, t5, 2) $\Rightarrow$ $\exists$t6 $\geq$ t5 state(γ, t6, internal) $\models$ p1(3)] & $\forall$t6 [state(γ, t6, internal) $\models$ p1(3) $\Rightarrow$ $\exists$t1,t2,t5 t1$\leq$t2$\leq$t5$\leq$t6 & state(γ, t1, input) $\models$ o1 & interplay_up_to(γ, t2, t5,2)]
p2	$\forall$t1,t2,t7 [t1$\leq$t2$\leq$t7 & state(γ, t1, input) $\models$ o1 & interplay_up_to(γ, t2, t7,3) $\Rightarrow$ $\exists$t8 $\geq$ t7 state(γ, t8, internal) $\models$ p2] & $\forall$t8 [state(γ, t8, internal) $\models$== p2 $\Rightarrow$ $\exists$t1,t2,t7 t1$\leq$t2$\leq$t7$\leq$t8 & state(γ, t1, input) $\models$ o1 & interplay_up_to(γ, t2, t7,3)]
c	$\forall$t1,t2,t7 [t1$\leq$t2$\leq$t7 & state(γ, t1, input) $\models$ o1 & interplay_up_to(γ, t2, t7,3) $\Rightarrow$ $\exists$t8 $\geq$ t7 state(γ, t8, internal) $\models$ c] & $\forall$t8 [state(γ, t8, internal) $\models$ c $\Rightarrow$ $\exists$t1,t2,t7 t1$\leq$t2$\leq$t7$\leq$t8 & state(γ, t1, input) $\models$ o1 & interplay_up_to(γ, t2, t7,3)]

Note that these relationships are defined at a semantic level, and are thus of type B2a. Different interaction state properties, separated by commas, should be read as the temporal sequence of these states. Again, a learning phase of 3 trials has been chosen. In order to obtain a description at a syntactic level, the relationships given in Table 2 are characterised by formulae in a specific language, TTL in our case. Thus, the representational content of a certain internal state is then defined by specifying a formal temporal relation of the internal state property to sensor and action states in the past and future. A number of such formal temporal relations are given in Table 3. Because of space limitations, only the backward content is shown.

Within Table 3, the following abstractions are used:

is_followed_by(γ, X, I1, Y, I2) $\equiv$

$\quad \forall t1: state(\gamma, t1, I1) \models X \Rightarrow \exists t2 \geq t1: state(\gamma, t2, I2) \models Y$

This expresses that X is always followed by Y.

is_preceded by(γ, Y, I1, X, I2) $\equiv$

$\quad \forall t1: state(\gamma, t2, I1) \models Y \Rightarrow \exists t1 \leq t2: state(\gamma, t1, I2) \models X$

This expresses that Y is always preceded by X. These abstractions can be used like is_preceded_by(γ, s1, internal, o1, input), is_followed_by(γ, o2(1), input, s2(1), internal), et cetera. The next abstraction describes that the interplay between agent and environment in which the agent increases pressure and the environment increases resistance is performed up to a certain level of pressure.

interplay_up_to(γ, t1, t2, 1) $\equiv$ t1$\leq$ t2 &

$\quad$ state(γ, t1, output) $\models$ a1(1) & state(γ, t2, input) $\models$ o2(1)

interplay_up_to(γ, t1, t4, 2) $\equiv$ $\exists$t2, t3 [t1 $\leq$ t2 $\leq$ t3 $\leq$ t4]

$\quad$ interplay_up_to(γ, t1, t2, 1) &

$\quad$ state(γ, t3, output) $\models$ a1(2) & state(γ, t4, input) $\models$ o2(2)

interplay_up_to(γ, t1, t6, 3) $\equiv$ $\exists$t4, t5 [t1 $\leq$ t4 $\leq$ t5 $\leq$ t6]

$\quad$ interplay_up_to(γ, t1, t4, 2) &

$\quad$ state(γ, t5, output) $\models$ a1(3) & state(γ, t6, input) $\models$ o2(3)

8.3 Second-Order Representation

In approaches to representational content of type C, internal state properties are related to other internal state properties. For example, in Sun's dual approach to cognition [12; 13], conceptual level state properties are related to subconceptual level state properties:

On this view, high-level conceptual, symbolic representation is rooted, or grounded, in low-level behavior (comportment) from which it obtains its meanings and for which it provides support and explanations. The rootedness/groundedness is guaranteed by the way high-level representation is produced: It is, in the main, extracted out of low-level behavioral structures. (Sun, 2000).

Two possibilities arise: either the other internal state properties are not considered to be representational (this seems to be Sun's position), or they are themselves considered representations of something else. In the latter case, which is explored here, the conceptual level state properties become second-order representations: representations of representations. In the main example of this paper, the internal state property c can be considered to be at the conceptual level, whereas the other, s and p properties are considered subconceptual. Then, in the spirit of [12], the representational content of c can be defined in terms of the other internal state properties as shown below. However, keep in mind that this approach only makes sense if the low-level internal state properties are considered to be representational already.

Backward: c will occur if in the past once s1 occurred, then p1(1), then s2(1), then p1(2), then s2(2), then p1(3), then s2(3), and conversely. Formally:

$\forall t1,t2,t3,t4,t5,t6,t7$ [$t1{\leq}t2{\leq}t3{\leq}t4{\leq}t5{\leq}t6{\leq}t7$
   & state(γ, t1, internal) $\models$ s1
   & state(γ, t2, internal) $\models$ p1(1) & state(γ, t3, internal) $\models$ s2(1)
   & state(γ, t4, internal) $\models$ p1(2) & state(γ, t5, internal) $\models$ s2(2)
   & state(γ, t6, internal) $\models$ p1(3) & state(γ, t7, internal) $\models$ s2(3)
      $\Rightarrow \exists t8 \geq t7$ state(γ, t8, internal) $\models$ c] &
$\forall t8$ [state(γ, t8, internal) $\models$ c $\Rightarrow$
$\exists t1,t2,t3,t4,t5,t6,t7$ $t1{\leq}t2{\leq}t3{\leq}t4{\leq}t5{\leq}t6{\leq}t7{\leq}t8$
   & state(γ, t1, internal) $\models$ s1
   & state(γ, t2, internal) $\models$ p1(1) & state(γ, t3, internal) $\models$ s2(1)
   & state(γ, t4, internal) $\models$ p1(2) & state(γ, t5, internal) $\models$ s2(2)
   & state(γ, t6, internal) $\models$ p1(3) & state(γ, t7, internal) $\models$ s2(3)]

Forward: if c occurs, then in the future, if s2(r) occurs, then p2 will occur. Formally:

$\forall t1$ [state(γ, t1, internal) $\models$ c $\Rightarrow$
    $\forall t2 \geq t1$ [state(γ, t2, internal) $\models$ s2(r) $\Rightarrow$
       $\exists t3 \geq t2$ state(γ, t3, internal) $\models$ p2]]

9 Validation

A large variety of techniques exist for (automated) verification of relevant properties of complex systems, for examples see [9; 14; 16] and the references in these papers. In the current research, the specifications of representational content have been validated in two ways: (1) by relating them to the local dynamic properties by mathematical proof, and (2) by automatically checking them for the simulated traces.

    An example of the former is as follows. Consider the formula that presents the backward representational content for internal state property c in Table 3. Consider first the direction from observations to c. Given o1, o2(1), o2(2), and o2(3) at the different subsequent time points the proof obligation is c. Given o1, by applying (in this order) LP3, LP5 we obtain p1(1) which we need to derive from the given o2(1) using LP4, s2(1) and by application of LP6 on p1(1) and s2(1) we obtain p1(2). Given o2(2), by application of LP4 we obtain s2(2) and on the basis of p1(2) LP6 is again applicable resolving into p1(3). Given o2(3), apply LP4 to obtain s2(3), and using p1(3) LP7 is applicable and c is obtained. These dependencies are graphically represented in Figure 3. The reverse direction again depends on property A3 and all local properties.

In addition to the software described in Section 5, other software has been developed that takes traces and formally specified properties as input and checks whether a property holds for a trace. Using automatic checks of this kind, many of the properties presented in this paper have been checked against a number of generated traces as depicted in Figure 2. In particular, the global properties GP1, GP2, GP3, and GP4, and the intermediate properties M1, M2, M3, and M4 have been checked, and all turned out to hold for the given traces. Furthermore, all properties for representational content denoted in Table 3 have been checked. The duration of these checks varied from one second to a couple of minutes, depending on the complexity of the formula (in particular, the amount of time points). Success of these checks would validate our choice for the representational content (according to the temporal-interactivist approach) of the internal state properties s1, s2(r), p1(1), p1(2), p1(3), p2, and c. However, note that these checks are only an empirical validation, they are no exhaustive proof as, e.g., model checking is. Currently, the possibilities are explored to combine TTL with existing model checking techniques.

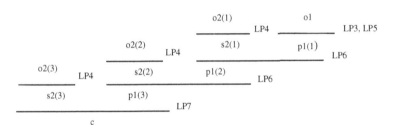

Fig. 3. Proof Tree

Although they are not exhaustive, even the empirical checks mentioned above have already proved their value. Initially, one of these checks did not succeed. It turned out that the backward representational content defined for p1(2) was not correctly chosen. At that time, it was defined as follows:

∀t1,t2,t3 [t1≤t2≤t3 & state(γ, t1, input) ⊨ o1 &
interplay_up_to(γ, t2, t3, 1)
  ⇒ ∃t4 ≥ t3 state(γ, t4, internal) ⊨ p1(2)]
& ∀t4 [state(γ, t4, internal) ⊨ p1(2) ⇒ ∃t1,t2,t3 t1≤t2≤t3≤t4 &
state(γ, t1, input) ⊨ o1 & interplay_up_to(γ, t2, t3, 1)]

According to the above notation, the sequential occurrence of the state properties o1, a1(1), and o2(1) always implies that state property p1(2) will occur. However, a close examination of Figure 2 reveals that this is not always the case. Whenever the agent has learned, it will not increase its pressure on the key anymore. As a result, the extra condition not c had to be added to the representational content. All the other checks concerning the properties of Table 3 did succeed immediately.

10 Discussion

The classical correlational approach to representational content requires a one-to-one correspondence between an internal state property of an agent and one external world state property. For embodied agents that have an extensive reciprocal interaction with their environment, this classical correlational approach does not suffice. In particular, an internal state in such an agent does not depend on just one state property of the external world, but is affected both by external aspects of the world and by internal aspects of the agent itself and the way in which these aspects are interwoven during the (ongoing) interaction process.

Given this problem, it is under debate among several authors whether adequate alternative notions of representational content exist for such an embodied agent's internal states. Some authors claim that for at least part of the internal states it makes no sense to consider them as conceptual or as having representational content; e.g., [2; 7; 11]. Other authors claim that some notions of representational content can be defined, but these strongly deviate from the classical correlational approach; e.g., [1; 5; 8].

Given the above considerations, the case of an intensive agent-environment interaction is a challenge for declarative approaches in the sense that internal states depending on such an interaction have no simple-to-define representational content. The formally defined and validated representation relations presented in this paper show how it is still possible to obtain a declarative perspective also for such a case. It is shown how formal methods allow to address the temporal structure entailed by suitable representation relations in these cases in a manageable declarative form.

More specifically, in this paper, for some notions of representational content it was explored in a case study how they work out, and, especially, how the temporal structure can be handled by formalisation. The processes of the case study have been formalised by identifying executable local dynamic properties for the basic dynamics. On the basis of these local properties a simulation model has been made. The formalised specifications of the representational content of the internal state properties have been validated by automatically checking them on the traces generated by the simulation model. Moreover, by mathematical proof it was shown how these specifications are entailed by the basic local properties. This shows that the internal state properties indeed fulfil the representational content specification.

The use of the temporal trace language TTL has a number of practical advantages. In the first place, it offers a welldefined language to formulate relevant dynamic relations in practical domains, with first order logic expressivity and semantics. Furthermore, it has the possibility of explicit reference to *time points* and *time durations* that enables modelling of the dynamics of continuous real-time phenomena, such as sensory and neural activity patterns in relation to mental properties. These features go beyond the expressive power available in standard linear or branching time temporal logics, such as LTL and CTL.

Moreover, the possibility to quantify over traces allows for specification of *more complex adaptive behaviours*. As within most temporal logics, reactiveness and proactiveness properties are specified. In addition, in TTL also properties expressing different types of adaptive behaviour can be expressed. For example a property such as "exercise improves skill", which is a relative property in the sense that it involves the comparison of two alternatives for the history. Another property of this type is trust monotony: "the better the experiences with something or someone, the higher the trust". This type of relative property can be expressed in our language, whereas in standard forms of temporal logic different alternative histories cannot be compared. For an excellent review of standard temporal logics, see [15].

Note that, in addition to simulated traces, the TTL checking software is also able to take other (e.g., empirical) traces as input, enabling the validation of the representational content of internal states in real-world situations.

References

1. Bickhard, M.H., Representational Content in Humans and Machines. *Journal of Experimental and Theoretical Artificial Intelligence*, 5, 1993, pp. 285-333.
2. Clark, A., *Being There: Putting Brain, Body and World Together Again*. MIT Press, 1997.
3. Jonker, C.M., Snoep, J.L., Treur, J., Westerhoff, H.V., and Wijngaards, W.C.A., BDI-Modelling of Intracellular Dynamics. In: A.B. Williams and K. Decker (eds.), *Proc. of the First International Workshop on Bioinformatics and Multi-Agent Systems, BIXMAS'02*, 2002, pp. 15-23.
4. Jonker, C.M. and Treur, J., Compositional Verification of Multi-Agent Systems: a Formal Analysis of Pro-activeness and Reactiveness. *International Journal of Cooperative Information Systems*, vol. 11, 2002, pp. 51-92.
5. Jonker, C.M., and Treur, J., A Temporal-Interactivist Perspective on the Dynamics of Mental States. *Cognitive Systems Research Journal*, vol.4, 2003, pp.137-155.
6. Jonker, C.M., Treur, J., and Wijngaards, W.C.A., A Temporal Modelling Environment for Internally Grounded Beliefs, Desires and Intentions. *Cognitive Systems Research Journal*, vol. 4(3), 2003, pp. 191-210.
7. Keijzer, F., Representation in Dynamical and Embodied Cognition. *Cognitive Systems Research Journal*, vol. 3, 2002, pp. 275-288.
8. Kim, J., *Philosophy of Mind*. Westview Press, 1996.
9. Pokorny, L.R. and Ramakrishnan, C.R., Modeling and Verification of Distributed Autonomous Agents using Logic Programming. *Proc. of the Second International Workshop on Declarative Agent Languages and Technologies, DALT'04*. Lecture Notes in Artificial Intelligence, Springer Verlag, 2005 (this volume).
10. Pozos Parra, P., Nayak, A., Demolombe, R., Theories of Intentions in the Framework of Situation Calculus. *Proc. of the Second International Workshop on Declarative Agent Languages and Technologies, DALT'04*. Lecture Notes in Artificial Intelligence, Springer Verlag, 2005 (this volume).
11. Reiter, R., *Knowledge in Action: Logical Foundations for Specifying and Implementing Dynamical Systems*. MIT Press, 2001.
12. Sun, R., Symbol grounding: a new look at an old idea. *Philosophical Psychology*, Vol.13, No.2, 2000, pp.149-172.
13. Sun, R., *Duality of the Mind*. Lawrence Erlbaum Associates, 2002.

14. Vasconcelos, W.W., Norm Verification and Analysis of Electronic Institutions. *Proc. of the Second International Workshop on Declarative Agent Languages and Technologies, DALT'04*. Lecture Notes in Artificial Intelligence, Springer Verlag, 2005 (this volume).
15. Vardi, M.Y., Branching vs. Linear Time: Final Showdown. *Proceedings of TACAS 2001 - Tools and Algorithms for the Construction and Analysis of Systems*. Genova, Italy, April 2-6, 2001. Lecture Notes in Computer Science, Volume 2031. New York, NY: Springer-Verlag, 2001, pp. 1-22.
16. Walton, C., Model Checking Agent Dialogues. *Proc. of the Second International Workshop on Declarative Agent Languages and Technologies, DALT'04*. Lecture Notes in Artificial Intelligence, Springer Verlag, 2005 (this volume).

Author Index

Lecture Notes in Artificial Intelligence (LNAI)